Lucy Winchester

Christmas Carol Kauffman

Cover Artist

David W. Miller

Christian Light Publications, Inc.
Harrisonburg, Virginia 22801

LUCY WINCHESTER
Published by Christian Light Publications, Inc., 1992
by arrangement with Herald Press, Scottdale, Pa. 15683.
Copyright ©1969 Herald Press
All rights reserved.
Printed in the United States of America

10 09 08 07 06 05 04 03 02 01   8 7 6 5 4

Cover by David Miller

ISBN: 0-87813-549-9

Dedicated
to the memory of
the late J. D. Mininger
pastor, missionary, evangelist, author
whose profound yet simple, Spirit-filled words
played a great part
in helping Lucy Winchester
make the most important decision
of her life.

Preface

This is a true story about real people. It is surprising to learn there are those who think that labeling a story true makes every word of conversation, every detail of each incident as it actually happened. For a writer to reach this level of accuracy would be humanly impossible. Lucy concluded that this story is 90 percent fact.

It was after knowing and closely observing Lucy for several years that I first approached her for her story. "Lucy," I began with a good deal of hesitancy, "would you consider telling me your life story, and allow me to write it for a youth magazine?" She neither smiled nor frowned. Instead, she looked me full in the face a prolonged thoughtful minute. "If," she answered quietly, "just one young or older person would profit by all the mistakes I've made, I'm willing to share it. Never would I tell it to bring glory or attention to myself. I want none of that."

It was over a year before I could find time to start working. The first thirteen chapters were written in a hospital bed after the birth of our fourth child. Because the doctor detected a heart murmur, he kept me in bed two weeks. The moment I was given permission to sit up, I asked for a bed table.

As soon as Lucy learned her story was accepted for publication, she insisted on giving me a notarized statement certifying the entire story is founded on fact, is true, correct, told to me by herself, written by her permission, that she gave me the right to add or deduct what I deemed wise, and that she gave consent to the book publication. It was signed May 12, 1945.

To be sure, Lucy never told me she was a beautiful young woman. Her brother showed me photographs which unquestionably proved it. Never did she intimate she had a sweet, loving personality. Those who knew her best told me that, and much more.

It was Lucy's wish that all names used be fictitious except two, Gussie Jenkins and Norvena Sellers, both deceased before the story was written. Too, all names of towns and places she preferred fictitious. I complied.

When she first held the book in her hands her eyes glistened with tears. Her lips quivered as she said, "Now my greatest wish is that God will let me live to learn of one soul influenced to accept Jesus Christ because I told my story. Then I'll know I didn't go through all this in vain."

CHAPTER 1

THE DAY from early morning had been depressingly humid. Every human and animal craved cool water which few could find. Motionless air, like sticky steam, came up from the Mississippi, then hung over entire Crawford County, four miles inland from Harper Landing. The late afternoon sky was running its colors together, huge spoonfuls of hot reds and much-too-warm blues. No rain was predicted.

In a clearing stood the screenless, two-story, six-room frame house. It was paint hungry, markedly battered, and too small for the nine Winchesters.

Lucy added wood to the three-footed block-leveled cookstove, then wiped her forehead with her forearm, one as wet as the other.

"Mom," she exclaimed. "How can you take it? Aren't you almost as hot as this stove?"

The frail, gray-haired woman looked at Lucy and blew her breath in the opposite direction. Giving the yellow cornmeal mush in the iron kettle one more stir with the long-handled wooden spoon, she stepped back and wiped the perspiration from her face and neck with the corner of her faded green gingham apron. "Just about," came her breathy reply. "But I guess every woman in these parts makin' supper is as hot as I am. Or you. There's nothin' I know of we can do about it, or we'd do it."

Mrs. Winchester dropped on a chair by the open window and smoothed back her damp hair. "I'll let it cook a while." She drew several long hot breaths, then tried fanning herself with her apron bottom.

"Mom."

"Yes."

"Will this be enough since we're having mush?" Lucy carried the brown earthen crock of peeled potatoes from the table to her mother.

"Is it more'n half full?" The woman lowered her face close to the crock.

"Just about," answered Lucy staring at her mother with a concerned expression.

She shook her head as she carried the crock back to the table, trying to stifle the groan she felt in her throat. "Just to make sure it'll be enough, shall I peel two more big ones?"

"Might be best, Lucy," she answered returning to the stove once more to stir the hot, bubbling mush on the hot, hot stove. "Why not light the lamp? Is it gatherin' up a storm you think?"

"No, Mom. Why, no!" A startled expression crossed Lucy's young face.

"It's gettin' dark early tonight," insisted Mrs. Winchester.

"Why, Mom!" Lucy's voice revealed more than astonishment. In it was a tinge of pathos mingled with dread. Gently, very gently she added, "The sun's above the barn, Mom. It'll be weeks before the days start getting shorter. Don't you remember Father had me read it to him in the almanac last week?"

"Sure. I remember now." And she rubbed the back of

her neck.

While Lucy sliced the potatoes for frying, she watched her mother. She herself was as tall, as strong or stronger, and weighed a little more. Of this she was confident without stepping on scales. She glanced at her own strong arms, then her mother's thinning ones. Hers had kneaded many a loaf of bread, ironed bushels of garments for the family from Father down to little Corkie. Lucy Winchester was twelve.

"It's—" Lucy hesitated, debating in her young mind whether the truth might hurt her mother's feelings. Then she ventured with added tenderness, "It's your eyes, Mom."

Mrs. Winchester nodded knowingly.

For months Lucy had been noticing her mother's eyesight slowly fading. "Oh, Mom, I do wish so you could get glasses."

"Maybe I can someday when—" Her mother's sentence hung unfinished, but each knew how far in the future that day might be.

"Someday," Lucy muttered under her breath. She felt like shouting that evasive word. She had heard her father say it repeatedly for the past two years. *Someday as soon as we can, Mom'll get them glasses.*

She had needed a visit to an oculist when Lucy was ten. Vividly now Lucy recalled the morning when her mother couldn't thread a large-eyed needle, and she had done it for her. Since that day Lucy had been sewing on all the buttons, all the patches, darning all the socks, needling up all the tears, snags, and slits, to help save Mom's eyes until Father could see his way clear to take her along to town for those glasses.

3

Someday, again sighed Lucy under her breath. It was always floating around too high, too far beyond her mother's reach. Every time her father went to town with a load of wood, or ties, there was flour to bring home—and sugar, coffee, baking powder, salt, sorghum, plus stockings (few stockings), shoes to be repaired, matches, oil, and tobacco; those real necessities that don't grow on big or small farms, or flourish wild on bushes for free picking. So Mom's glasses were still on the list of needs.

Flossie and Loretta were both old enough to wash dishes, make beds, sweep floors, bring in water, or pull weeds in the garden. Kenneth was big and smart enough to feed the chickens. But somehow all three had a way of dodging work for play and pulling the wool over Mom's eyes. So Lucy baked the bread, the biscuits, the pies, the cookies. It was Lucy who told Mom to sit down to dry the black-handled knives and forks and the spoons. "You can do that without looking. Here, put them in this clean bread pan." So it was Lucy who got dishpan hands. Strong, healthy Lucy washed and hung and took down the big washings, ironed what had to be ironed. It was Lucy who cleaned, dusted, swept, and cooked. It was Lucy who missed school more than she attended. It was Lucy who learned from her father how to cut Kenneth's, Floyd's, and little Corkie's hair, so it would get cut when necessary; for Father was in the timber from dawn till dark and was too weary to run a home barber shop.

"What are you looking for, Mom?" Lucy turned the potatoes. They sputtered in the hot grease, filling the kitchen with a savory, salty, raw-potatoey goodness.

"I thought I had a handkerchief here in my apron bib. Must have dropped it someplace."

4

"Here it is." Lucy picked up the hand-hemmed flour-sack handkerchief and tucked it in her mother's apron bib, adding a pat on one shoulder. "There you are." She turned the potatoes again. They were already a delicious brown. "Say, Mom, do you know what Aunt Polly told me yesterday when I took the buttermilk over?" With swiftly moving hands Lucy started setting the table.

"No. What?"

"You couldn't guess?"

"I've not got the slightest idea. What, Lucy? Tell me."

"Well." Lucy held a plate in both hands. Her cheeks matched the pinkest part of her dress which wasn't faded as much as the back. "She said there's going to be a preacher from someplace far off, I don't know where from, but he's coming to the Black Bend Schoolhouse to preach every night for a week."

"I see. No, I didn't hear about it."

"And it starts tonight." Lucy all but skipped to her mother's nearness. "Can I go, Mom?"

"Is Aunt Polly going?"

"Well, she didn't say for positive. But I'd think she would. She wouldn't have far to go." Lucy spoke with increasing excitement and anticipation. "I'm almost sure Emma Davis is going. I could meet her at the Knob. Oh, Mom, say I can go. Please say yes, Mom." Lucy was close enough to kiss her mother. "You will, won't you?" She was tall enough to look over her mother's shoulder. She could smell her damp hair. It wasn't offensive. It was just the way Mother's damp hair smelled.

"But how about coming back home, Lucy? It's— Well, let me think about it for a while. After all, your father will have the last say about it."

"I could walk with Emma and Joe to the Knob and run on home from there. I wouldn't be afraid. It's full moon, Mom. I want to go so much. Won't you please ask Father for me?"

"Want to go where?"

Lucy jumped.

John Winchester hung his frayed straw hat on a nail behind the kitchen door, looking at Lucy instead of the nail. His black eyes flashed. Lucy tried desperately not to let her father know her legs and arms were trembling when she laid the knives and forks.

"Where'd you say?" he repeated with a stern tone demanding an answer.

"To the schoolhouse, Father." Lucy scarcely looked up. She dropped a fork but found it quickly.

"And what's agoin' on there?" John Winchester poured water from the wooden bucket into the gray granite basin on the woodbox beside the door and proceeded to wash his tawny hands, water splashing in every direction.

"It's a meeting, Father."

"What sort of a meetin'?"

"Well, it's to be—"

"Well, say it. Out with it. Is it some more of that religious stuff you're always wantin' to traipse after? Huh?" He ran his watery hands over his sweaty face.

"There's going to be a preacher from another state, Father," she explained with effort to remain calm.

"Eh?"

"Aunt Polly's going, I think."

"She is, is she?"

"At least I'd suppose so. She's the one who told me about it. I'm—I'm sure it's going to be good, Father." Lucy

6

put the few chairs up to the table. Kenneth, Flossie, Loretta, and Floyd sat on the long wooden bench her father had made. The color in Lucy's cheeks deepened.

"Well, I wish your Aunt Polly would tell you once to stay at home." John Winchester walked over to Lucy and stood very straight, towering above her like a huge column. "That's where young ladies your age belong, 'stead of gally-flounderin' 'round to schoolhouses an' the like to listen to some preacher or some man who pretends to be a preacher gettin' women an' girls all worked up over things they never done or stuffin' their heads with tomfoolery."

John Winchester seemed thoroughly pleased over his speech. He hurried on. Lucy's deep blue eyes were riveted now on his face. Her flushed cheeks were burning. A strand of blond hair fell down over her left eyebrow. "Lucy," his voice softened a bit, "your place is right here, right here," he pointed to his wife Maggie, "helpin' your mother. Understand?"

"Well, John," began Mrs. Winchester with caution, for only on rare occasions had she ever ventured even a slight disagreement. He spoke with authority. There was finality in his decisions. He looked at his wife with mingled surprise and sudden interest. "Lucy's been awful good help around here, John. Just awful good help," she repeated. "You've never seen her get out of doin' her share an' more'n her share."

To her surprise John was listening, shifting his glances from her to Lucy several times. "I don't put much stock in them there meetin's myself," she went on, "but she's had to miss a lot more school than most girls her age on 'count of me. An' she's never once complained about it either,

John. I feel she deserves to get out once in a while. Them meetin's can't do her no harm. Now can they?" It was Mrs. Winchester's turn now to be surprised at her own speech.

Suddenly John Winchester sat down, unlaced one shoe, and kicked it off. "Now, Maggie," he began, "listen to me. It's all a lot of foolishness. You'll agree I'm right on that. What's more, I get so sick an' tired hearin' her repeat that Bible jibber-jabber she drags along home. You know how it goes around here every time she hikes them four miles to that Sunday school on Sundays." Off came the second shoe. "Fer the past two years now, ever since that Sunny Creek thing started, every time she enters this house—" John raised his voice. "Every time," he glanced over at Lucy to make sure she was hearing, "I have to hear that girl tellin' Corkie an' Peggy an' Floyd those religious fairy tales. An' they don't know any better than to jes drink it all in an' believe it. An' she tells it to 'im for the truth. Yes, she does. An' then she takes to singin' those crazy songs. Walkin' all over God's heaven in golden slippers an' the like I never heard. I'm fed up an' tired of it."

"But really, John," suggested his wife, now a little frightened, "you're not in the house much. How then does it bother you so?"

John Winchester stood up again thrusting his hands deep into his overall pockets. "An' now she wants to go nights. Days isn't 'nough. I say, young lady—"

"Go where, Father?" Kenneth, Flossie, and Loretta seemed to come through the door en masse. Mom had already put the dish of hot mush on the table.

"Pour the water, Flossie," said her father.

"Hey, Lucy. Are you going someplace tonight?" inquired

Kenneth.

Had she tried, Lucy couldn't have answered for the lump in her throat. She dished the potatoes.

"The milk," reminded Mrs. Winchester. "Is it on, Lucy?"

It wasn't, and Lucy ran to the springhouse to get it.

"Where's Lucy going, Mom? Loretta put her arm lovingly around her mother's shoulder. "Tell me."

"There's a meetin' at Black Bend. But—"

"Is she goin', Mom?" broke in Flossie.

"No," shouted Mr. Winchester. "She's not." He sealed his verdict by taking his place at the head of the table and tapping his knife handle twice on the red-and-white oilclothed tabletop.

"Oh, goodie-goodie," chanted Kenneth when Lucy returned with the milk. "You can't—"

"Kenneth!" When John Winchester spoke in that tone, and his heavy eyebrows all but met, every other Winchester knew it was time to swallow their words. He had authority over his children and, when necessary, used that authority in no uncertain methods.

Lucy was more than a little astonished. She looked at her father's lips slightly parted. His eyes met hers. She saw no trace of harshness. She was baffled.

CHAPTER 2

THE SUPPER was eaten in silence until Corkie burned his tongue with a spoonful of hot mush. That was taken care of with soothing words and kisses from both Mom and Lucy. But Corkie wouldn't try the mush again until Lucy stirred, salted, blew, and tasted it first. As soon as the potato dish was scraped of the last tiny speck and the mush bowl wiped clean with a moist bread crust, the meal was called finished. Not always did the Winchesters enjoy a dessert. Seldom did the cats or dog get leftovers worth mentioning.

John Winchester usually went straight to the barn after supper, but this evening he sat on the woodbox working on his shoe with a pocketknife.

Lucy stacked the dishes and sudsed the dishwater with the homemade lye soap. Mom went over the bare wooden floor with the side-worn broom. The cracks were just wide enough that it wasn't always necessary to use a dustpan. The chickens had discovered a place where they could slip in under the kitchen and pick up the few bread crumbs which fell through. As usual after supper the six children under twelve were outside playing hide-and-seek.

Out of the corner of one eye Mr. Winchester watched Lucy at the dishpan. Her strong arms worked swiftly. Once he thought he saw a tear fall into the sudsy water. It could have been perspiration. He continued fiddling with his shoe until the dishes were nearly all washed. Lucy didn't trust herself to look up, but she knew her father was there. She could hear his heavy, steady breathing.

Suddenly he sprang to his feet and went to the door. "Flossie."

A faint answer came from behind the lilac bush.

"Flossie Winchester," he repeated with more volume.

Flossie came running. "Yes, Father. Did you call me?"

"I most certainly did, young lady. Now you get in here and wipe them dishes fer Lucy."

"Oh, sure I will," she darted past him but got a sound rap on her shoulder.

"Shame on you. You're plenty big enough to help 'thout bein' told each an' every time." He put on his shoe.

"Well, I was just ready to come in, Father," whined Flossie peevishly.

"Repeat that if you expect me to believe it. Now take the dish towel and begin working."

John tied the laces.

He went to the barn. For some time he stood in the open door facing west. He puffed his pipe and gazed out at the distant hills. The clouds and the colorful sunset were at their splendid best, as if dressed for one of nature's beauty contests. The moon was waiting her turn.

It was all true, John thought to himself. He couldn't argue with his own thoughts on that matter. Lucy had been a good worker in spite of her silly notions on religion. How she did remind him again tonight of his only sister, Mabel. Every day she grew to look more like her. John kicked loose a clod of dirt. *Same long blond hair, same creamy fair complexion, same rosy cheeks, same gentle eyes—soft and blue—same strong build.* He kicked at another clod. *Lucy twelve. Twelve already? She'd easily pass for fifteen.*

John shifted his pipe and cleared his throat. Mabel was seventeen when pneumonia took her. Mabel Winchester, the prettiest girl in Dunken County. Everyone said so. Everyone liked her. She never had an enemy. Three fellows had tried to win her hand. And now—closer than his sister, his own daughter Lucy was looking so much, so terribly much like—

"Stand over, Duff." John Winchester slapped his horse on one hip. "Go." In a few minutes they were at the yard gate. "Lucy," he shouted. "Hey, Lucy."

"Yes, Father." She stepped outside the door.

"Get your dress changed an' come on out."

Lucy's one hand grabbed the porch post and for a moment she stood as half frozen, dazed.

"Go on—get ready."

What could Father mean? Oh! He couldn't. Trembling all over, Lucy ran up the stairs two at a time. In a few minutes she was at the yard gate tying her belt as she ran.

Maggie Winchester reached the door just in time to hear John say, "Jump up here in front of me. I'll take you myself this once. You're not trampin' over no roads or knobs after night with Emma an' Joe Davis."

"Well, I'll be," is all she said.

Lucy felt like turning around and flinging her arms around her father's neck and kissing him. What ever had come over him? She couldn't recall one time having an urge to hug her father before now. Not one. He was a man to be honored, feared, and obeyed without question.

Mrs. Winchester sat in deep thought. Had she heard right? What had come over John? She would wait until the children came in to ask questions. Better yet, ask Lucy herself. She'd sit barefoot on the porch and try to cool off before bedtime.

Lucy's heart and thoughts were in a tumult as Duff galloped along the dusty road. Who could explain this sudden turn in her father? She pinched both arms to make sure she was alive and that this was real. She wanted to laugh out loud. And cry. Her thick blond hair, slightly wavy, blew across her father's face.

That was a sensation John Winchester had never before experienced. Blond hair across his face. His own beautiful daughter's hair. Hair exactly like Mabel's. He made no effort to brush it away. Duff knew the road.

The schoolhouse was lit up with several hanging oil lamps. About two dozen people had already gathered inside, and more were coming afoot. A few horses were tied at the hitching posts.

"Now listen, Lucy," spoke her father in deliberate undertones. "I'm goin' on down to Sunny Creek Tavern an' I'll be back here at 'xactly nine o'clock. See?"

"Yes."

"There's a clock in the schoolhouse, isn't there?" He helped her off.

"I think so."

"Well, now, you're to be right there on them steps on the outside when I come back."

"Yes, Father. I'll be there."

"Whether the meetin's over or not. Understand?"

"I understand. I won't make you wait on me. I promise. Oh, you've been so kind to bring me, Father. How can I tell you how glad I am?"

John Winchester was off, leaving a cloud of dust.

Shyly Lucy stepped inside. She scanned the schoolroom but saw no Aunt Polly. She tried to hide her keen disappointment. She had wanted to go home and tell everyone she had sat beside Aunt Polly. A lady sitting close to the front turned around. Mrs. Fetherstone. Lucy knew her, one of their nice neighbors who called on them several times a year. Once when Lucy was about five, Mrs. Fetherstone brought her a tiny china cup and saucer. Lucy still had the cup but the saucer had been broken.

Mrs. Fetherstone motioned for Lucy to come and sit beside her. She moved over. "It's so nice to see you, Lucy. My, my, child, I had to look twice to be sure it was you. You've grown up, Lucy. What a lovely young lady you're going to be soon! Did you come alone?"

"No. Father brought me."

"Your father?" exclaimed Mrs. Fetherstone, eyes widening with astonishment.

"On his horse," added Lucy smiling and blushing.

"Well, I—"

"Good evening, young lady." The man held out his hand and shook Lucy's firmly. "I've already met this lady here beside you, Mrs. Fetherstone, and what's your name?"

"Lucy Winchester." Lucy smoothed her dress folds over her knees while looking up at the man.

"Lucy?"

She nodded.

"Well, I'm Brother Bustleton, your evangelist for a week." He smiled down on her with such a sincere, open-faced, pleasant manner. Lucy was quite taken aback. "Lucy Winchester," he remarked. "Well, to my way of thinking you've got the most beautiful name in all the world because Lucy's my wife's name."

"It is?" Blushing, she returned his smile. All at once she felt light. Lighter than she could remember ever feeling; a happy lightness, not giddy, not frivolous. So he thought Lucy was a beautiful name. No one had ever told her that before. Sometimes she had imagined how it would be if she could change it to one that was really beautiful, like Lenora or Vlonda or Elizabeth Ann.

"I see more folks coming in. I must shake hands with everyone. Excuse me, please."

"Mrs. Fetherstone," whispered Lucy leaning close to her, "do you think he really meant what he said to me?"

"Of course he did, child. Do you think an evangelist would go around flattering folks just so they'd like him and come back? He's not that kind of preacher, Lucy. I'll stake my life on it. Now don't you wonder another minute. He really must think the world and all of his Lucy."

As the preacher passed her at the aisle on the way to the platform he stopped long enough to say, "There's not many here tonight your age, Lucy. But you just keep coming anyhow every night."

"I hope I can come." She pushed back a stray blond lock which insisted on brushing her forehead.

Lucy was almost too shy and too happy to help sing. She sat motionless, scarcely taking her eyes from Brother Bustleton's radiant face. He himself led the singing. Then he prayed. His sermon was presented in a sincere, honest, convincing way. He read frequently from his Bible with such dramatic but simple clarity that even a twelve-year-old Lucy could understand. At least much of it.

"Now," he continued, "I'll read to you what Isaiah, the

Old Testament prophet, wrote. 'He [that means Jesus Christ] is despised [that means furiously hated] and rejected of men [men wouldn't recognize Him; they turned Him down like a no-good man]; a man of sorrows, and acquainted with grief [much, much grief, all kinds of heartaches—He was familiar with every kind]: and we [men, women, boys and girls who are old enough to know right from wrong] hid as it were our faces from him [we just covered our eyes and refused to look at His sinless face]; he was despised, and we esteemed him not [we put no value at all on the love and mercy He gave us] . Surely he hath borne our griefs, and carried our sorrows: yet [in spite of all this] we did esteem him stricken [as though He had some horrible contagious disease], smitten of God, and afflicted.' "

Brother Bustleton lifted his eyes and looked straight at Lucy and continued, " 'But he was wounded for our transgressions [He was scourged because we went places we had no right to go], he was bruised for our iniquities [for all our crookedness]: the chastisement of our peace was upon him; and with his stripes we are healed. All we like sheep have gone astray.' I'll go over this once more and make it plainer if I can. I want everyone here from the youngest—"

Lucy's head turned. She held her breath. Her hands clutched her belt. Up she got as though she had been struck. Brother Bustleton stopped short. Every head turned as Lucy hurried to the door.

The evangelist was puzzled. What had he said to cause such a sudden departure? He had thought the girl was listening to his preaching.

"Just about time, young lady, or I'd a come in an'

fetched you out." John Winchester's voice was too loud, too stern. It slashed Lucy's heart like a sharp whip. Oh, did the people inside hear him?

"Sorry, Father," she faltered feebly, "but there wasn't a clock after all that I could see."

"It's past nine." He helped her on Duff.

"But, Father, have you been waiting long?" Already her happiness was turned to fear.

Her father made no answer. They were off on a trot.

"I came out as soon as I heard the horse, Father. Believe me. I got right up and came right out."

After clearing his throat twice he said dryly, "All right then. All right. But listen. This is the first time an' the last time you're comin' down to Black Bend when there's meetin's on. How late does that man run on?"

"I don't know, Father. But I think he was near the end. Really, I do." She was glad he couldn't see two tears trickling down her cheeks.

"Lots of folks there?"

"Yes." She tried to control her unsteady voice.

"Well," John Winchester gave Duff a crack on the rump with his whip, "you're not comin' back to find out how long he runs either. A girl your age orter be in bed by nine. The fellers in Sunny Creek may give that preacher a good chasin' yet if he ain't careful what he says, comin' in here tellin' all them sob stories an' like I said, gettin' women an' children all tore up till they don't know who or what to believe about God or themselves or their families."

Lucy wiped her face with the palm of her one hand. "There were men there tonight, Father. They weren't all women and children." After she made the statement she was frightened, for she remembered she was only twelve.

"Makes no matter, Lucy. You're not agoin' back." There was nothing but finality in that statement and Lucy knew it.

She could feel her father's hot breath on the back of her neck. Oh! Had he been drinking? Never had she known him to be guilty of that. Often he had gone to the tavern to play cards (so he claimed to Mom), but to Lucy's knowledge he had never come home drunk. She feared now to speak. Her own breath came in spasmodic intervals and her heart was thumping until she felt it in her neck and ears.

Never again? Not permitted to go back one more time to hear Brother Bustleton! Oh! What had changed Father's mind in the first place? And now already the pendulum had swung in the opposite direction. Why? Why? What a gigantic disappointment!

Her own father she would probably never understand. Many times on a Sunday afternoon several men of the neighborhood would sit with John Winchester around a table under the cherry tree beside the house, or in the kitchen on cold or rainy days, to play cards by the hour. Not, however, for money. Every Winchester from Mom to little Corkie knew when Sunday afternoon rolled around, it was time to clear out and stay out, far enough out not to be heard. Any child who interfered with John Winchester's favorite sport was severely flogged. And there wasn't one Winchester who needed a second flogging for the same offense. Father ruled his house. This Lucy knew well. She'd never ask or even hint to anyone she'd like to go back to Black Bend. Not even to Mom.

"Thanks, Father, for taking me tonight." Her voice was scarcely above a whisper and a little unsteady.

She ran into the house and went straight to her room upstairs.

There was no need to light the small oil lamp to undress, for the light of the moon coming in the east window was doing a magnificent job. With a double and a single bed in a twelve by twelve room there wasn't much chance for privacy. Lucy was thankful for one thing: Loretta and Flossie both slept soundly.

How glad she was she didn't need to face anyone now or answer questions. Quietly she slipped into her ragged gown, a queer creation from one of Mom's old cast-off dresses. Tiptoeing to the window in her bare feet she knelt in silent bewilderment. The moon and the tiny faraway star diamonds held her gaze until she felt numb.

God, she breathed, *O God, I do so want to know more about You. You must be wonderful to understand. If only I had a Bible. I might learn a little more what You're like. I need You so badly. I know Father won't change his mind and let me go back—but I wish I could, oh, so much, God. I wish You could change Father's mind. But it's no use for me to try. If I beg, he won't let me go to Sunny Creek Sunday school either. He was wounded—and bruised— and hated—God, it's so sad about Your Son, Jesus.*

Suddenly without warning tears filled Lucy's eyes. They fell from her chin onto the windowsill. She didn't try to stop them. She couldn't have if she had tried. No one saw. No one cared. No one. Unless—unless God did. She wasn't sure.

It was almost morning when Lucy fell into a troubled sleep. She dreamed she was holding a wounded lamb in her arms and the blood from the wound was making a big red blotch on her dress front, growing bigger every second. Then suddenly Kenneth snatched the poor lamb away from her, trampled it with his heavy shoe, and in spite of Lucy's screams no one stopped him—not Flossie, nor Floyd—not even Father who stood there and laughed at it all.

Lucy woke with a start. She sat up in bed. Loretta and Flossie were still sound asleep but she could hear someone, perhaps Father, filling the woodbox, and she knew it was time to get up and hurry downstairs.

CHAPTER 3

L UCY WORKED diligently all day in spite of her
short and disturbed night. She had little to say to
anyone. She worked the yeast bread and formed
the loaves, then ironed with the two flatirons heated on
the cookstove. Mom churned butter (she could do that in
spite of her poor eyes) and Lucy patched Corkie's pants.
To be sure, Flossie, Floyd, Kenneth, and Loretta all cast
wondering, inquisitive glances her way, but Lucy pre-
tended she didn't notice. Her quiet independence tormented them.

"Lucy," remarked her mother, stopping momentarily to
rest on the churn handle, "I figure there's not many girls
your age who can cook and mend and patch and sew like
you can."

"I'm glad you taught me how, Mom," came Lucy's
reply. "I'm glad you started me on real simple things
before your eyes got bad. I'm glad I can sew for you, even
if it's not as neat as you did it."

Flossie and Loretta on the other side of the room had
their heads together whispering and making eyes at Lucy.

Near suppertime Flossie met Lucy, not by accident,
coming from the garden with a head of cabbage.

"Smarty, smarty," she glared tormentingly.

"What do you mean by that, Floss?"

"You think you're so smart because you got your way

last night. Don't you now? You think because you over-powered Father, you've got the whole world by the tail."

"I didn't overpower Father."

"Oh? Well, who did then? I'm sure it wasn't Mom. She'd know better than to try that. Tell me, what went on down there anyhow that you're so still about it? Isn't it fit to tell? If I went to something so great, I'd tell everybody all about it. I sure would." Flossie picked up a small stick and gave Lucy a crack on one ankle.

"Flossie," she said trying hard to suppress her feeling, "Mom told me if I found you out here, to tell you to come in and peel the potatoes

"She never. I don't believe it."

"She did so." Lucy's voice was positive, emphatic. "Do you think I'd lie to you? Go in and ask her if I lied. If I did, I'll eat everything I've got on."

"Huh." A small hummingbird would have had little difficulty perching on Flossie's lower lip.

In spite of her disappointment over Father's decision, Lucy had one thing to be glad about and that was that her mother evidently was going to continue Father's example and insist that a normal ten-year-old girl was old enough to help with small duties about the house. By all appearances Flossie was normal both mentally and physically. Lucy caught herself humming softly, very softly. At the garden fence she put the cabbage down long enough to pick a purple aster and stick it in the top buttonhole of her dress. Its soft, dainty petals made her washed-out dress look even more washed-out. The fact never occurred to her. Not yet. She wasn't one to spend long sessions in front of a mirror in an effort to discern what one color did for another.

Lucy was a very attractive girl. Today, because it was unusually warm, she had pinned her long, blond braids up around her head.

Involuntarily as John Winchester observed Lucy across the table that evening, the same uncontrollable emotions went through him as the night before. He struggled to stifle them. It made him feel queer and unfamiliar. He tried to avoid looking at Lucy, but something insupportable brought his eyes back to her. She talked only to Corkie and then with subdued, endearing words. How fresh, how beautiful, how mature she looked! It nearly frightened him and he hated being frightened, especially by a woman, a child, a woman child of his own. What bright, eager eyes she had! And that expression on her face after the way he had talked to her less than twenty-four hours ago. What was behind that expression? No wonder Corkie loved her. John sipped coffee and tried apple butter on freshly baked bread. That silky blond hair. Like Mabel's. Why did she put it up like that?

John was the first to leave the table. He lit his pipe and walked slowly toward the barn. "No—no sir," he declared puffing on his pipe, "I'm not, I'm not changin' my mind tonight. She's not goin' back. That's what I told her an' that settles it. I've got to keep an eye on that girl an' that's 'xactly what I mean to do. Some fool of a man'll be wantin' to step out with her all too soon. Twelve," he puffed faster, "she looks an' acts like a girl fifteen already."

Not until Lucy and her mother were in the kitchen alone the next day did Mother come right out and ask Lucy questions.

"Well, tell me now," began her mother, "what was the meetin' like? Who all was there? And Aunt Polly, was she there? Didn't you like it at all?"

"Like it, Mom? Oh, it was wonderful! Just wonderful. I loved every minute of it."

"Well, you've been so mum about it all, I jes' wondered. You scarcely talked all day yesterday, and that's not like you."

"Well, Mom, I guess I was just thinking. Really I could have stayed all night and listened. That preacher is so nice, Mom. He explains things so good. You just can't believe how he can make verses in the Bible seem so real and interesting." Her countenance changed abruptly. "But, Mom," she bit her lip until she feared it would bleed, "Father told me on the way home I can't go back."

"He did?"

"Not one more time. And he told me the men at the tavern might chase that preacher, Brother Bustleton, out of the county and never let him come back."

"Why, Lucy. What kind of man is he? Maybe he's—"

"Oh, no, Mom," she shook her head. "He's not what I think you were about to say. No, no. I don't know why anyone would want to chase him away. All I know is Father told me the men at the tavern said he gets folks all tore up. But that's not at all what he's here for. Don't you see—I mean, can't those men see he's here to help people so they won't get tore up or— Well, I don't know how to say it, Mom, but he wants people to be good and do right so they won't want to make trouble and be mean." Lucy came close to her mother and lowered her voice. "He's absolutely wonderful, that Brother Bustleton is, and if I never get to go back, I know I won't forget the things he told me and the things he preached about. He was so nice and friendly to me like we were acquainted. He told me his wife's name is Lucy too."

"Really? How nice." Mom looked up and smiled faintly, searching her daughter's face.

"He invited me to come back every night. I was about the only girl my age there. There may have been others but I didn't look back. I don't know if Emma was there or not. I just sat and looked and listened. If Father really meant what he said last night—" Lucy put one arm across her mother's shoulder and their faces almost touched. "Oh, Mom, I know I'll never get to go back. I'm so hurt. Oh, I want to so bad, Mom. But one thing he said I'll never forget. Tell me, did you think Lucy was a beautiful name when you named me that?"

"Of course I did—we both did. Your father helped pick it out."

"Oh, Mom, I just wish—"

"Wish what, Lucy?" Mrs. Winchester folded her thin arms across her apron bib.

"Oh, if I only had a Bible of my own."

The silence lasted several seconds. "That's something I never had either, Lucy. If I would-a had one, I wouldn't-a been able to read it nohow. I never got to finish the fifth grade like you did. If I could'a read it, I wouldn't-a been able to understand it. Nobody does but the preachers an' I reckon lots o' them don't really either."

"But, Mom," put in Lucy, "Brother Bustleton says a child can understand what's necessary. He said if he could understand everything, he'd be like God. Why, I understood what he said. I think I did. Listen, if I remember he read something like this. 'He was despised—'"

"Despised? Who is despised?" The back door closed with a bang.

Lucy jumped. She had neither seen nor heard her father coming.

"Were you talking about me, young lady?" he demanded, scowling, eyes snapping with condemning accusation.

Lucy drew back with a shudder. "No. No, Father, Why?"

John Winchester came so close to Lucy she could feel his hot breath on her face. She drew back.

She winced. "Honestly, Father, I was not talking about you. I was only telling Mom about—"

"Telling her what that preacher put in your head the other night. That's it. Huh? I just thought so."

"But, Father—" exclaimed Lucy, "let me explain to you."

He ignored her statement. "Instead," he panted, "of doin' your work, now you spend your time standin' 'round relatin' all that junk to yer mother. That preacher over there is teachin' children like you to despise their fathers. Now isn't he?"

"No!" cried Lucy almost frantically. Her eyes were swimming in tears.

"That's it I'll bet. Teachin' girls like you to despise their hardworking fathers who cut wood all day to feed an' clothe 'em an——an' send 'em to—" Short of breath, he cut his stammering sentence short. He pounded his fist on the table until the lid on the sugar bowl rattled.

Lucy was shaking now from head to foot. "No, Father," she pleaded. "Truly not. He told us all to love and honor our parents. He did. Please, please don't think such things of Brother Bustleton." Lucy could hardly keep from sobbing out loud. She felt like running down the road screaming at the top of her voice.

"Brother Bustleton!" shouted her father with indignation. "Brother? Now don't you ever let me hear you call that sneaky vagabond your brother again."

"He's not my brother, Father," panted Lucy. "He's everybody's b—" she caught herself in time.

"And you're never goin' down there to Black Bend Schoolhouse one more time as long as you live under my roof, do you hear?"

"Yes, Father," answered Lucy tearfully. "I hear."

She sank on a chair and buried her face in one arm on the table.

"Really, John." Mrs. Winchester rubbed her hands nervously. She stepped closer to her husband. "John," she began.

"And what have you got to say now?" He put his arms akimbo. "Sticking up for that girl again against me? She was talking to you, Maggie, my wife, yes, and about me, wasn't she?"

"Absolutely not, John. And I don't think she heard anything so bad that would—"

He cut her off abruptly. "Yes, it would. It would ruin her. She'd most likely turn out to be a lazy good-fer-nothin' Sunday school teacher like that Miss Basin. Or worse yet, some good-fer-nothin' preacher's—" Now he cut himself off. That was certainly one word he didn't intend to slip out now. "And," he continued, his eyebrows knitted together, "if I catch her one more time foolin' her time away tellin' our youngsters those silly Bible tales an' singin' them stupid, senseless songs in my hearin', I'll keep her from goin' to Sunny Creek every Sunday too. Wish I'd never took her that first night. I jes' lost my head an' I don't know why." John Winchester left the house as

27

abruptly as he had entered, banging the door behind him.

The weeks made a month. School started. John Winchester decided Lucy was needed at home to help her mother and the school wouldn't break up if she didn't go. As John Winchester decided, so things would be. Lucy stayed at home and got up early enough to pack four lunch pails five days a week, while she was preparing breakfast for nine. How she worked. Mom's eyesight was failing fast. There was less and less she was able to do to help. Lucy pushed her gently away from the stove many a time.

"Mom, please come over here and sit down. You might catch your sleeve on fire over the stove like that. It's dangerous. Now please. I'll do it."

"I've got to help, Lucy," she insisted.

"But, Mom dear, please listen to me. It's for your own good. We don't want you to get burned and have to go way off to a hospital, do we?"

"No. "

"Then be a good little mother, Mom, and let me do the work around the stove."

Lucy pitied her mother with all her heart. And Lucy dearly loved her mother. Never had she gotten a scolding or harsh word from her except when she was little and got into things. How thankful Lucy was she herself was strong. There were apples now to be canned and dried, barrels of kraut to be made, onions to be pulled and strung up for the winter. There were outing flannel petticoats to sew up by hand for Peggy, and little pants for Corkie. This would be the hardest job to undertake, for they would have to come out of what was still wearable in Kenneth's frayed ones. How Lucy did work! And without grumbling.

CHAPTER 4

SPRING CAME. Lucy had been inside the schoolhouse only twice, once because of a drenching rain to deliver Floyd's buckle rubber boots and to hear the short Christmas program the children stumbled and giggled through. But not one day as a pupil. Her desire to get an eighth-grade education was as great as ever. But Lucy's hopes were steadily thwarted each new day. Mom's eyes grew worse. It seemed to her it didn't trouble Father as it should have and as it did her. Glasses were mentioned occasionally, but it always brought Father's eyebrows together and made him reach invariably for his pipe. Perhaps he thought a trip to the doctor would be a waste of money. Once Mrs. Winchester stuck several fingers into a can of hot grease mistaking it for water.

"Mother dear! Mom! I warned you to stay away from the stove. Oh, you'll get blisters. Look at your poor fingers. Shall I wrap them?"

"Not yet."

As a result of the painful burn Lucy had more work to shoulder. But Mom's praises for her good work boosted her spirits a great deal and even helped relieve her tiredness.

The following day two-year-old Corkie fell down the cellar steps, escaping with no bones broken. Only painful bruises. He begged Lucy (no one else could do it as she could) to carry him wherever he wanted to be carried.

29

Often he wanted Lucy to sit and hold him on her lap, while she softly hummed snatches of songs she had learned at Sunny Creek Sunday school. She always held him facing the kitchen door, and when she heard the latch click, her humming quickly ran into, "Now don't you feel better, Corkie dear?"

It was eight months since that memorable night at Black Bend; and two hundred and forty days since her father had warned her and set down the penalty, if she was once caught singing a religious song, or retelling the children some tale from Sunny Creek. She had taken special precautions. Yes, extra special. Secretly John Winchester was gratified. So Lucy was allowed to continue her four-mile pilgrimage each Sunday to hear Miss Basie's religious teachings and learn new songs and relearn old ones. Just why her father let down the bars on this matter puzzled Lucy more each Sunday, unless it was because he was more relaxed at the card games with her four miles away.

Much too often when John met Lucy's eyes across the table, he had a feeling they were rebuking him. Sometimes they were pleading. He hated being tormented by a thirteen-year-old daughter who was growing each week into the living image of Mabel. Her aunt. Yes, Mabel was her aunt. The fact had never occurred to him so vividly. He thought of Mabel always and only as his sister.

One day Corkie fell when he tripped on a stick of wood Kenneth had dropped before he reached the woodbox. Just bruised again, they all decided. John did not take him to a doctor. Lucy knew how to soothe bruised bodies and a little boy's broken spirits and make tears go away. She tried.

Weeks passed. School closed. Summer came and still Corkie was constantly begging Lucy to hold him and carry him around. She even stirred mush with one hand and held him on her left knee. She could if she put her left foot on a chair rung. Corkie cried or whimpered most of the time when Lucy wasn't holding him. She got tired. Her strong arms and back felt the strain of all the carrying plus cooking, cleaning, washing, ironing. Lucy got very tired. Sometimes she moaned in her sleep much of the night. Several times she dreamed she had dropped Corkie and he had cried all the more. More than once she dreamed she was carrying huge buckets of water up a steep hill and would fall under her load and there was no one to come to her assistance. Sometimes she woke herself in the middle of a dream, screaming for help with the weight of her burden. Her sisters evidently never heard her screams or they actually weren't as loud as they were in her dreams. No one knew how many times Lucy cried during the night because she was too tired to sleep. No one knew of the prayers she prayed.

Fall came with its colorful leafy grandeur and cool, crisp mornings—the season Lucy loved best. But Corkie still cried. No one but Lucy could get near him or he'd scream in fright.

"Aren't you spoiling him rotten, Lucy?" reprimanded her father one evening.

"I hope not, Father." She was stroking his hair very gently. Corkie found the place under Lucy's neck on her left shoulder. The place just made to fit a little head. After Father left the house, she carried him to the farthest corner of the kitchen and held him.

"Couldn't I take him into the sitting room, Mom? It's

quieter in there. Just for a few minutes?"

"All right.

"Oh, you poor dear little lamb," she began softly. "Lucy's poor little lamb."

Corkie opened his eyes and turned his head in time to see tears in her eyes.

"Corkie." Her voice was soft and full of compassion. "You're Lucy's little lamb wounded so bad it hurts me too, Corkie dear. Lucy loves her little lamb and so does Jesus."

Corkie fell asleep in her arms. Gently she carried him to his bed in her parents' room. She put him down carefully. For some time she stood watching him. She noticed his breathing was unusually fast. She pulled back the thin blanket.

Lucy tiptoed to the door. "Mom," she whispered. "Mom." Mrs. Winchester was shelling lima beans, one thing she could do well by touch. "Come. I need you right away."

Lucy led her mother to Corkie's bed. She stood horrified. "Mom."

"What is it?"

"You can't see it? It's a lump! Corkie's been hurt worse than we knew. Oh, Mom, can't you see it?"

Her mother shook her head. "Where, Lucy?"

"On his back. Right there." Lucy pointed. "That's why he's been crying so. No wonder, Mom. Who wouldn't? And he's only two. He's not been growing one bit of late. The last couple of days I thought he weighed less, but I never mentioned it. Won't Father call a doctor out? Oh, he's got to." Sadly her mother shook her head and wrung her hands.

"Poor dear little Corkie." And Lucy stepped out on the back porch to think and cry.

The next day was Sunday. Lucy did not go to Sunny Creek. Instead, she sat by Corkie's bed or held him most of the time. Flossie and Loretta did help Mom fix the dinner.

Lucy was all but crushed when her father responded with no outward alarm or pity when he saw the lump. If Mom suggested seeing or calling a doctor, it was not done in Lucy's hearing. While John Winchester and his gang played cards all Sunday afternoon in the kitchen, Lucy kept Corkie upstairs with the door securely closed.

She told Corkie stories she'd heard Miss Basie tell in Sunday school, about the wee baby in a basket, about Jacob's dream of seeing angels going up and down a great ladder which reached from earth to heaven, about Daniel the lions couldn't eat because God locked their big mouths. She told about a baby lamb who was lost and had a broken leg and was found by Jesus and carried in His arms *just like I carry you, my little lamb, Corkie.*

She stroked his forehead, his thin arms, and counted his fingers. She sang to him about how little tiny grains of sand make a big, big hill someday and little drops of water make a big ocean someday. She sang to him how Jesus loves everybody in the world: the rich and poor, the well, the sick, the fathers and mothers, and little two-year-old boys. He whimpered a little now and then when she shifted her position, but he listened quietly. No one downstairs imagined what was going on up in Lucy's room. And somehow before the afternoon was over, she wouldn't have cared if someone or all of them knew everything. Corkie was her first charge. Corkie needed everything she could do or give to help ease his pain. She was going to do it if it killed her. Corkie loved her as nobody living ever had. Her stories and songs he enjoyed. Why should she care or fear who knew how she entertained and comforted him?

How utterly mistaken John Winchester was when he remarked to Maggie one Sunday morning, "Well, it looks like Lucy's had her fill of trampin' the road to that Sunday school, doesn't it?"

Maggie made no answer.

"She'd rather go upstairs an' sleep, wouldn't she?"

"I don't know as she'd rather, John. She stays home to take care of Corkie. He won't let me or Flossie touch him or even give him a drink anymore."

"Huh. Well, that's the strangest thing I ever. Well, anyhow, I figured when Lucy reached her teens an' got a little common sense in her, she'd leave off that stuff she's been goin' after."

Again Maggie Winchester made no reply.

Upstairs that very afternoon Lucy was holding Corkie on her lap. "Honey lamb," she began lovingly. "Do you really like to hear me sing to you about Jesus? Do you, honey?"

She felt his head answering yes. She kissed his head. She bent her head low and kissed his nose. She lifted one hand and stroked her own cheek with it. It felt unusually hot. She hugged him close. Corkie winced.

"Oh, forgive me, honey. I forgot and squeezed too hard. It hurts your back?"

Again she felt his head answer yes.

"Hurts bad, doesn't it? Well, Lucy'll be more careful. Jesus loves little boys. Jesus loves them even more than I know how to. Now I'll sing and you try to take a nap. You dear little lamb."

CHAPTER 5

SUNDAY AFTER Sunday Lucy took Corkie upstairs where they could be alone. Flossie and Loretta never interfered. Corkie wouldn't let them try to hold him, and furthermore they liked playing boys' favorite games with the boys.

The lump on Corkie's back was getting larger, darker, and more painful. He refused to eat even for Lucy. John did go on Duff beyond Black Bend one morning to Doctor Price's home office and asked him to drive over and take a look at Corkie. The doctor promised to come right after dinner.

"Lucy," began John, "you uncover him and tell the doctor what happened and how he's been acting."

She had it told in five minutes. John shifted uneasily.

"What is it, Doctor?" he asked.

"Never saw anything like it in my thirty years of practice, John."

"What can you do for him?" This Mrs. Winchester asked, nervously rubbing her arms.

"Well, I've never even heard of such a thing. I'll have to go back and look through my medical books. In the meantime just keep him as quiet as possible. You might try laying him across a rolled up pillow on his stomach. Get a pillow and I'll show you."

But Corkie screamed the moment the doctor touched him.

"Well," concluded Doctor Price after a long breath, "I see you've got a real sick little boy here and a real problem on your hands. I wouldn't try rubbing anything on it, and whatever you do, don't try opening or messing with it. He has a pretty high fever. I can tell that without taking his temperature." He left six pain pills to be taken one each evening with a little milk or cocoa. "They're to help him sleep," he explained.

Before Thanksgiving not even Lucy could move Corkie except with the greatest of care. Mrs. Winchester tried to hide her feelings and keep back her tears to help brace up Lucy. Her anxiety about Corkie now far outweighed her concern about her own handicap. How she longed to help more with the work and how she longed to do something to relieve Corkie who seemed to be wasting away hour by hour.

The day came when Corkie no longer cried. His occasional whines were weak and pitiful. If someone touched his bed, he nearly went into convulsions.

One Saturday about twelve forty-five someone knocked on the kitchen door. The family was finishing dinner. John Winchester answered the knock.

"Mr. Winchester?" The cheery voice came from a young lady he judged to be in her middle twenties.

"Yes, ma'am." He too sounded rather pleasant.

"I'm Miss Basie, Mr. Winchester." The young lady's smile exposed one deep dimple.

"Miss—who?" This time John Winchester's voice definitely was not pleasant.

The young lady did not let it baffle her.

Lucy had heard. She knew. She was suddenly covered with goose pimples. The bite of bread in her mouth would not go down. Her spoon fell to the table.

"Miss Basie, Mr. Winchester. I'm the teacher at the Sunny Creek Sunday school." She saw the man scowl as he came outside to talk. "I came by to find out why Lucy's not been coming anymore. She's missed so many Sundays that I feared she must be ill or something."

John stepped to the edge of the porch and spit. "Well," he said at length, "Lucy's in there at the table. She can come out an' answer for herself. Come here, Lucy."

She was trembling from head to toe as she made her way to the door.

"I feared you might be sick, Lucy, but you don't look sick to me," Miss Basie remarked pleasantly. "You're looking fine. And so much taller than when I last saw you. Where have you been all these Sundays? We've all been missing you."

Lucy wanted to dash out and throw both arms around Miss Basie's neck and tell her how sorry, how truly sorry she was to have to miss. Oh, she wanted to tell Miss Basie how she loved her, admired her, believed in her teachings, and above all how she longed and prayed she could come back. But her father was right behind her now. If only just Miss Basie and she could walk down the road together and talk.

"Well, Miss Basie," began Lucy choosing her words carefully, "you probably didn't know Corkie, my littlest brother, has been very sick for a long time."

"Oh, no, I didn't know that, Lucy. I'm sorry to hear about it. Isn't he better?"

"No, Miss Basie. Not at all better. Only worse and because I'm the oldest, I miss school and Sunday school to help take care of him because Mom—you know how I told you once about her eyes, you know."

"Yes, I remember."

"Well, I can't leave Corkie or Mom unless things get better."

"It's not that you've lost interest in Sunday school, is it?" Miss Basie's countenance brightened.

An awkward silence followed. Lucy picked at her fingernail. "Oh, no, Miss Basie," she answered. "Don't think that."

John Winchester coughed.

"I'm so glad to hear that, Lucy. I've wondered about you so long I just had to come and see. I borrowed the neighbor's horse. I had hopes for you. You always took such an interest in the lesson discussions and seemed to understand more than the others your age. I could see you growing steadily over the three years you've attended. I'd been praying that you'd accept Christ as your personal Saviour while you were young. So many promising young people put it off until their lives are wasted. You know the world is a great attraction and I want to see you spared. I have a keen interest in you, dear."

John Winchester cleared his throat with forced vehemence. Lucy reddened and bit her tongue. Miss Basie continued. "You remember I promised a Bible to everyone who would come regularly for five years. I mean a nice good Bible and I was so hoping—"

John Winchester would not tolerate more. With one hand he pushed Lucy back beside the door frame and towered above the young lady, eyes snapping.

"Now look here, Miss Basin—"

"Miss Basie," she corrected politely.

"Well, Miss, I was about to call you—no matter—Basie

then it is. I want you to understand my Lucy's not comin' back to your Sunny Creek Sunday school one more time. Understand?"

"Is she attending some other Sunday school? I only came to inquire, you know."

"No, she's not attendin' Sunday school anywhere 'cause I'm not lettin' her. I never did approve of that silly church an' I know now more'n ever I never will. I only let her go them three years 'cause she was workin' plenty hard helpin' the missus an' had to miss a lot o' school an' all; so I let her have Sunday afternoons off jes' fer a change an' so's she could get outdoors a while. But I never," here he came down on the palm of his left hand with his right fist, "never thought you'd be tryin' to plow things in her young head like what you said 'bout acceptin', whatever that means."

"Why, Mr. Winchester, I—"

He cut her off without mercy. "It's true we do have a little sick boy here. An' it's true she couldn't go on account o' him. But I want you to know," he pointed his finger at her, "I don't believe in your teachin's one single speck an' I don't want any o' my children hooked up with that sorta stuff."

"But, Mr. Winchester," she took one step closer to him. There was only truth and complete composure etched on Miss Basie's face. "I'm thoroughly convinced it's what Lucy has learned in our Sunday school that makes her so sweet—so beautiful, so unusually lovely. Everyone can see it on her face."

"Sweet?" he shouted. "Beautiful and lovely you call her?"

"Haven't you noticed it, Mr. Winchester?"

John Winchester got white around the mouth. He tried to moisten his dry lips.

Miss Basie straightened her shoulders. "Mr. Winchester," she said, "Lucy has an outstanding beauty, an unspoiled beauty only God brings out on a person from within. And she's probably so close to you you don't notice it."

"Well, well," panted Mr. Winchester. "What a speech-maker you are. I do declare, Miss Basie. You're all wrong about what I know and see in my daughter. Yes, she is beautiful and her own father knows it without anyone comin' 'round tellin' me. And I don't want her life ruined with no trash—an' that's 'xactly what I think teachers like you an' preachers have to hand out."

"Trash?" Now Miss Basie's knees shook. This remark she was not prepared for. But why let this man make her shake when she knew she was right? To herself she went over it. *No weapon that is formed against thee shall prosper.* She took a step closer and looked him straight in the eyes without blinking. He was not going to scare or humiliate her. She wouldn't let him. "I hope you will change your mind about me and my teaching, Mr. Winchester. I stick to the Bible and that's the infallible Word of God. That's all I ever teach my pupils. I never argue with God's Word because it's the truth that will stand till the end of time. Why, if the leaves on all these trees in your sight were devils, all agreeing with you, the truth would never change. Other men have torn it to shreds, ignored it, burned and buried it, and hundreds of people have been burned to death at the stake and thrown into pits for lions to devour only because they believed God and His Word. The Bible never will be destroyed. It's useless to try. It may be trash to you, Mr. Winchester, but right this minute there are enough men living who've memorized portions of it, and if they got together, they could compile and complete it correctly in a short while. You can keep Lucy away from Sunday school, but I dare say you can't reach in and take out of her memory all she's learned. You don't even need to try. You can't. And what's more, I'm going to pray that every song and every verse and every Bible story she ever heard at Sunny Creek will stay with her as long as she lives. And I hope you'll live to change your mind, Mr. Winchester."

"I'm not about to change it," he retorted with indignation. "Go back in the house, Lucy. All this won't help you none."

Lucy obeyed but not without a sorrowful glance at Miss Basie.

"Tell Lucy good-bye then for me, Mr. Winchester. I'm glad I've learned why Lucy hasn't been with us. I'd write to her, but I have my doubts if you'd let her have my letters."

"Your thinkin' is correct on that." His answer was so dry it crackled.

She took two steps and turned around. "I love that girl. I want her to know it." Miss Basie's voice was unsteady now. "I want you to know it too, Mr. Winchester. In fact, I wish all the folks in ten counties could know it and help me pray for her. Good-bye."

John went straight to the barn. He knew he could not face Lucy for several hours at least. No one had ever heard of John Winchester being afraid of anyone, or anything. He determined he wasn't going to be ashamed either. Once more he stood at the barn door. It was some time before he thought of lighting his pipe. Over and over the things Miss Basie had said, and Lucy's own confession, waded deep in his foggy, muddled mind. He forgot what he went to the barn to do. His shoulders sagged. His two hands, rough from work, cultivated his hair and plowed his scalp. He took out his red bandanna and blew his nose. That he did the second time. And the third.

I'm thoroughly convinced that it's what Lucy has learned—she's beautiful—haven't you noticed? Oh, no, no, Miss Basie—how wrong can a father be? How far off the truth track had he gone? Then Lucy hadn't had her fill? She actually wished she could go back?

The long tormenting monologue of his thoughts would drive him insane unless he could get hold of himself. Right now. But he stood there rubbing his hands.

Lucy did not return to the table. Loretta and Flossie had already stacked the dishes and washed them. Lucy slipped into the bedroom to see Corkie.

His wasted body hung over the pillow, face turned slightly to one side so that he could breathe better, just as she had fixed him before dinner. Both tiny hands stretched above his head. He was fast asleep. For once he wasn't whining. Lucy knelt on one knee to take a closer look at his white face. Oh, how she wanted to take him in her arms! It would lift the heavy feeling in her heart if she could just tell Corkie what she wanted to tell Miss Basie but couldn't. "You poor dear little lamb." She stopped breathing for a moment. Her hand shook as she brushed the hair back from his forehead.

"Corkie," she whispered. "Corkie!" She touched his cheek. She touched his foot. She shook him gently.

"Corkie!" she screamed.

She stumbled, blinded with tears, into the kitchen. "Come to the bedroom, Mom. Oh, Corkie's dead! I just know he is."

"Oh, Lucy," gasped Loretta, all but dropping the plate she was wiping. "Are you sure?"

"Come and see for yourself. You too, Flossie. Let Mom in first. Oh, one of you go call Father! I hope he didn't leave. Hurry."

Lucy gathered her limp, lifeless little brother up in her arms and held him tight against her breast. Over and over she kissed his face, drenching it with her hot tears. "Oh, he's gone. And when? Oh, Corkie, dear."

Mom and Flossie both cried softly. Lucy sobbed uncontrollably. She didn't care who heard. No one loved him as she did. No one would ever love her as he did. Of this she was more than certain.

"Don' t take it so hard, Lucy, dear," begged her mother. "Let me hold him a while. Take me to the rocker and hand him to me." Lucy obeyed. Then she dropped on her knees beside her mother and stroked Corkie's arms and legs.

"Oh, Mom, I can't help taking it hard. I was sure he couldn't live. We could all see it coming. I did. Oh, he got so pitifully thin. But I'll miss him so. I know he'll be better off," she sobbed as though her heart would break. "But, Mom, he's the only one who understood me anymore."

"How can you say that, Lucy?" asked her mother between sobs.

"Because it's true. I could tell him anything and he liked to listen to me."

Peggy came running, followed by Loretta, Floyd, and

Kenneth, then Father. Lucy got up and leaned hard against the wall and cried. Peggy was frightened and clung to her mother's dress when Flossie led them to the bedroom. Gently, slowly, Mrs. Winchester laid her little son on the bed where she and John slept.

John Winchester was not expecting this tonight. Certainly he knew it couldn't be far off, but tonight of all nights. But he told himself lots of people had buried a child, some more than one, and the rest of the family went on living and working and made the best of it. They could too. They'd have to. So why go to pieces? But he was not ready yet to face Lucy.

"Oh, John," cried Mrs. Winchester before he reached the bedroom. "Corkie's gone. We never heard a sound from him. Lucy came in just before Miss Basie left and found him dead."

John spoke not one word. He simply stood and stared at the little body on the bed. He didn't go close to him.

"Lucy's takin' it awful, awful hard, John," whispered Mrs. Winchester wiping her eyes.

"I suppose," he said in a parched voice. "Where is she?"

"I saw her go upstairs," Kenneth said.

John hesitated at the stair door. He opened it. Slowly, his feet like lead, he climbed the stairs. It had been so long since he'd been upstairs he wasn't sure which room the girls used. His chest rose and fell with heavy breathing. "Lucy," he said huskily, "are you—is that you in there?"

He heard no answer but he heard her sobbing. He opened the door. He stepped closer to her prostrate body on the bed. Hesitating like a timid boy beside a mature crying woman, he just stood there. With three fingers he touched her blond hair until he felt her ear. "Don't take it so hard." His voice was throaty, thick, unreal. But Lucy cried all the harder. She buried her face in the pillow. He touched her shoulder with a very gentle touch. "Don't cry like that," he said huskily. "You'll make yourself sick."

"There was only a tinge of kindness in his voice. "I've got to get on Duff an' go to town now. Come on down an' help the girls get the house straightened up 'fore anyone comes. I don't know how soon the undertaker'll get here, but I'll drop by to tell Aunt Polly an' Mrs. Fetherstone. They'd want to know, don't you s'pose?"

Lucy sat up on the edge of the bed and looked at her father through her tears. Oh, why couldn't he always be a little kind and gentle and understanding? How did he ever get to be so stern and set in his ways and hate God and religion and good people like Miss Basie? Lucy could not put together the puzzle pieces of her father's actions. Nothing fit.

"Yes," she answered. "They should both know it."

In the kitchen below Lucy heard her father say, "Now, Flossie, an' you too, Loretta, you help Lucy get things in place. You know full well your mother's in no condition, an' this long ordeal with takin' care of Corkie has about wore her an' Lucy out. Lucy's 'bout to cry herself sick. So you get busy while I'm gone."

"Where you goin'?" asked Floyd.

"Ask Lucy or your mother. I've got to hurry."

Both Aunt Polly and Mrs. Fetherstone got there before dark. They sat up all night. It was their way of expressing sympathy. For the first time she could remember, Lucy was told to sit down and let someone else do the work. Mrs. Fetherstone's gentle and kind words were like oil on her broken heart. She even invited Lucy to come over and spend a whole day with her after Corkie was laid to rest. How she would love to do that! But she knew better than to be overjoyed with the prospect, for she was certain her father would never hear to it. She was sure he would suspect they'd talk about the meetings at Black Bend and the evangelist, Brother Bustleton.

The boys and Peggy went to bed at their usual time. Loretta and Flossie and Mrs. Winchester, Aunt Polly, and Lucy sat in the meagerly furnished sitting room.

"I see," remarked Aunt Polly, "you still have John's grandmother's big latch-lid Bible." She pointed to it on the small high-legged stand.

"For some reason he prizes it highly," answered Mrs. Winchester. "He never lets anyone open it. Just has me dust it a couple times a year or so."

"Why won't he allow anyone to touch it?" inquired Mrs. Fetherstone.

"I really never found out," answered Mrs. Winchester. "Sometimes I've wondered myself if he's got money or something valuable inside. He's given the children strict orders to leave it latched. He says the back is weak and loose an' will come off. You know what I mean, that stiff cover on it."

"I suppose then," suggested Aunt Polly, "he never reads it?"

"Never, Polly. Never."

"Then what good is it to him or the family?"

"Polly, you are askin' me things I can't answer," replied Mrs. Winchester.

Aunt Polly turned to Lucy. "By the way, Lucy, Mrs. Fetherstone was telling me you got to go to hear Brother

Bustleton only once and that was the first night. Didn't you like his preaching or what? I didn't get there but twice but I enjoyed those two nights immensely."

Lucy's face turned a hot pink. She tried to put her finger over her lips, and Mrs. Fetherstone caught the sign and immediately changed the subject.

For over an hour Lucy sat with a wistful, wondering, hungry gaze fixed on the latched book on the table in the dimly lighted room. She did not cry outright, but silent tears rolled down the front of her dress. She excused herself and went upstairs.

CHAPTER 6

ITT WAS four days after Corkie had been buried quietly
that John Winchester came into the house quite unexpectedly to get some money out of his strongbox in the
bedroom. He told Maggie he had a chance to ride along to
town with a neighbor taking a load of corn in to be ground.
Lucy had just finished a big ironing and Mom told her to
rest a bit. Lucy had forgotten to close the door between the
bedroom and sitting room. Her back was toward the open
door and so intently was she looking at the object before
her, she did not hear her father's footsteps.

"Lucy Winchester!"

Lucy's heart all but stopped.

Her father sprang across the room, grabbed her by the
arm, and shouted. "Why are you—you of all people on
earth, you the sweet beautiful Sunday school girl, disobeying me like this? Answer me, Lucy. You know you've
been given orders never to open my grandmother's book.
Why are you deliberately goin' against my orders? Answer
me. Don't jes' stand there like a dead fence post."

She tried, but Lucy could not answer. Her tongue froze
in her mouth.

"What were you doin' in here anyhow? We never open
this room 'cept on special occasions. An' that book is a keepsake, not a toy to be played with. Don't you remember I said
none of my children were to touch this book?" He rapped his

48

fingers on the edge of the table. "Don't you remember?"

"Yes, Father, I remember now."

"Now? Well, when did you forget about it? And how many other times have you been sneakin' in here snoopin' in my grandmother's Bible? Huh?"

"This is the first time. Honest it is, Father." Her entire body was shaking like a leaf. He pushed her back against the wall and held her there, his angry eyes matching the fury in his voice.

Mrs. Winchester in the kitchen was clutching at her throat, fear making her weak and helpless. She too was trembling.

"Now you tell me the truth, Lucy Winchester. Remember, even if you are thirteen, I am well able to give you a flogging. You the oldest. Why did you deliberately disobey me?"

"I—I was just hunting for something."

"Huntin' fer something like what? Fer money?"

She shook her head. Her eyes were ready to release a stream of tears. John saw it. He floundered. He cleared his throat. He paced the room.

"Well, look here, Lucy," his voice lowered as he faced her, "if you think I got money hid in there, you're mistaken. I never had as much as one penny in that book. My mother never 'llowed me to play with this keepsake an' neither can any of my children. Are you ready now to tell me what it was you were huntin' fer? Speak up, Lucy." He held one hand high above her.

"Oh—oh, Father," cried Lucy. "I was hunting for that— that—" she was shaking now with sobs.

"That what? I warn you once more now, out with it or you'll get it."

"That Scripture Br—Brother," she was afraid to say it, but she knew she must and receive the consequences, "Bustleton read that night when—"

"Brother Bustleton!" he roared with fury now. "Didn't I tell you to never let me hear you mention his name in this house once more?"

"Yes." The tears were coming fast now. "Yes," she repeated feebly, "but how can I tell you—what I wanted—to find—if I can't tell you—the truth?"

John Winchester nearly danced with rage. He turned completely around several times shaking both arms.

"Lucy, why do you cause me so much trouble? You get on my nerves. An' too often. I just don't understand you at all." The cords in his neck and the veins at his temples stood out in bold outlines. "You're not too big to flog. I could take you out to the barn and do it if I wanted to and maybe I'd orter. But I'll punish you another way. I'm goin' to send you upstairs to your room an' don't you dare show your face until I call you down. Understand?"

"Yes."

"Look. You broke the back loose. Fer that you'll stay up there twice as long as I was agoin' to make you."

In his anger he lifted the Bible up and a picture about four by seven inches fell to the floor. He grabbed it up fiercely. "An' did you find this?" he demanded in a disappointed and smitten voice.

"I never saw it, Father. Who is it?"

John gazed at it for some time. "It's my sister, Mabel." He held it up so she could see it. "I want to keep it. The only sister I ever had."

"She's—real—pretty, isn't she?" Lucy remarked feebly. "May I—see it—closer?"

"I was about to tell you to go upstairs now. I mean now. But I'll let you see it this once."

She wiped her teary eyes. "Why, Father," she gasped brokenly, "you never told us about her."

"Who does she favor?"

"Not you. Why—didn't I ever see—it—before?"

Her father crossed the room with uneven steps.

"I never knew who she favored." He stuck the picture in the Bible. "Go on now an' do as I said. You've upset me so, Lucy. I don't know what to think anymore."

"I don't know—what—to think—of myself either—Father," cried Lucy. "I'm just—so all mixed up—I—I— And now Corkie's gone!" She climbed the steps with aching legs, sobbing all the way up.

"John." Mrs. Winchester was in the bedroom waiting. She took him by the sleeve. "John—" Her hands were shaking.

"Now, Maggie, I don't want you to go pity that girl. She's got a few things to learn." The sternness of his voice cut her.

"But, John, listen. I know she disobeyed but—"

"Did you let her in that room?"

"Well, I just told her to sit and rest a while. She did an enormous stack of ironin' and never fussed about it once. I just can't believe she meant to do wrong or break that back loose."

"Well, I tell you, that Lucy can act so good, then turn around and behind my back do some of the sneakin'est things you ever heard of."

"Oh, John," she pleaded. "I believe Lucy wants to be good. I doubt if she even realizes she's being sneaky. Lucy's a good girl."

"Now, Maggie, cut that out. You just pamper her."

"She's so good and kind to me, John."

He led her to a chair in the kitchen. "You sit down an' calm yourself an' I'm aleavin' word by you now to see to it Flossie and Loretta fix the supper an' Floyd's to feed the chickens an' Kenneth's to fetch in the wood and I mean enough for tonight an' tomorrow mornin'. Lucy's not to come down."

After John had gone with the neighbor, Mrs. Winchester found her way to the stand in the sitting room. She felt the Bible to make sure the stiff back was on right, the latch securely latched, and the precious keepsake was in its exact position. There it had been for fifteen years. John had placed it so the day after they were married and moved into the house. Her head ached—ached all over. Why was John so unreasonable with Lucy? Maybe if his mother had allowed him to look into it an' read it, maybe things might be different today for everyone.

Just exactly what she was hunting for, Lucy herself wasn't sure. If she could only have a talk with Miss Basie. Could there be any truth at all to what she had told Father, that it was what she had learned in Sunday school that made her sweet and beautiful? If Miss Basie saw her now, she certainly wouldn't think she had learned anything to make her sweet or beautiful. She felt anything but beautiful. She felt like telling Father a good many things he wouldn't call sweet to listen to. Oh, if she could only tell him to sell that old keepsake and put the money toward glasses for Mom. Oh, she wished she could give him a piece of her mind a mile long.

Downstairs Maggie Winchester was wishing she could help Lucy find what it was she was looking for. She had a good notion to go in there and get that book and carry it upstairs and let Lucy look to her heart's content. It would be all of three hours until John returned. Would she dare do it? What if one of the children found out and reported to John? At least seven times Mrs. Winchester stood at the open stair door below and listened with her hand behind her ear. Should she go up? She could feel her way even though she couldn't see. The coming down would be harder and Lucy wouldn't dare help her down. Twice she was sure she heard Lucy crying.

Little did John Winchester suspect that his punishment was the kindest thing he could have done for Lucy. She loved being alone and seldom had the opportunity. By the time she reached her room, she was so weak she thought she would faint. Weary and brokenhearted she dropped on the wooden box by the east window. All the prayers, tears, dreams, and crushed hopes she had experienced at that window went on parade before her. She cried until she could cry no longer. Then as though out of nowhere like a sweet voice from heaven she heard Miss Basie telling Father, *Tell Lucy I'll be praying for her. I love that girl.* A stronger voice she heard in rich full tones, sincere and confident, *He was wounded—He was despised—He was a man of many sorrows—He bore your griefs—He carried our sorrows. He was wounded like a lamb.* Was that what he read, the man with the voice of God? Christ, a wounded, bleeding lamb? Oh, if she could only talk to Miss Basie and Brother Bustleton. But she would never own a Bible of her own. Never. She knew it now.

Then she recalled that awful dream, the lamb—the blood on her dress—Kenneth trampling it—Father laughing. Blinding hot tears overcame her again. There she sat until a strange calm came over her. A new unexplainable lifting of sorrow. Peace like a soft cloud hung over her and seemed to fill the entire room. What was this thing, this new calm that made her heart light—when minutes before it had been so heavy? It was covering her completely. Her heart was beating slower. She drew a long, thankful breath.

A knock on the door. Before Lucy could get to her feet the knob turned.

"Lucy, I brought this."

"Mom, did you come up here alone?"

"Take it quick before Father gets back." She handed Lucy two molasses cookies and a slice of her own snowy bread, spread with apple butter.

"Mom, you shouldn't have."

"I'd have brought you milk too, but I had to feel with one hand, you know."

"Oh, Mom, you're too good to me. Thanks, thanks," and Lucy flung her arms around her mother's neck and kissed her twice. "I'm really not hungry yet, but I'll eat it for your sake."

"Please do, Lucy. This—is," her voice broke, "is just killin' me."

"I should help you down. Oh, Mom, what if you'd miss a step and fall. Then Father would know you came up here and he'd think I called you."

"I'll be real careful, Lucy."

Lucy could hear her mother crying as she went down. She didn't close her door until she was sure she had reached the bottom step safely. "Mom."

"Yes. I'm down now."

"You make Flossie and Loretta help real good till I can come down."

"They will, Lucy. Now rest. I'm not tellin' any of 'em why you're up there but that you need a rest."

It was late the next morning when John Winchester called for Lucy to come down. He waited until no one was in the house but Maggie.

He was completely taken aback. He had a long speech all prepared to give Lucy, but when he saw the glow of peace on her face, his tongue would not form the words. He could not believe his eyes. He scrutinized her with what he intended to be a devastating accuracy. And now—now he felt helplessly unprepared and inadequate to say anything. Surely he expected her to look angry and hurt. Better yet, ashamed. He could find no trace of any of these feelings. Her eyes weren't even red. Nor swollen. Lucy's face was serene, almost angelic when she smiled at him. Smiled? He didn't intend to smile in return. She was making fun of him. Tormenting him with her faked righteousness. Some of Miss Basie's sleight-of-hand methods to precede more trickery.

Her hair was neatly combed, her blond braids around her head. Her cameo face was like Mabel's. He drew back. It was more than he could take. This daughter of his standing there so tall, so strong, so fresh and beautiful. A daughter any father should be proud of. Proud? Yes, in his inmost soul he had to admit, hard as it was, that he was proud of Lucy. But she'd never find it out. Never. Never. Just because she was a beauty of a girl, he did not intend to let her get by with anything.

"You can fix yourself some breakfast, Lucy," is all he said and left the house.

"Thank you, Father."

He did not look back or answer.

CHAPTER 7

FOUR MORE years and Mrs. Winchester was near total blindness. With the growing needs of his fast-growing children John never could lay aside enough for a special fund to take his wife to an eye doctor.

"I'd have to most likely take you clear to Chicago or Cincinnati or some such big city, Maggie. We'd have to go by train and put up in some hotel. We jes' can't afford it."

Lucy wanted to tell her father if he'd gone without his tobacco from the time he first knew Mom's eyes were failing, he might have had a nice nest egg years ago. To be sure, she could never bring her regretful thinking to words. He took Mom's blindness as one of those inevitables that might come to anyone's family. John Winchester never lost any sleep over it.

Peggy was at the head of her class in the second grade. Both Flossie and Loretta saw no purpose in going beyond the seventh grade, and their father heartily agreed they'd had enough education. "So now, girls, I give you strict orders. You're both good-sized an' healthy an' I expect you to help Lucy with all the work. Understand? Not just what you like to do."

"Yes, Father," they chimed in minor duet.

To them, work was absolute drudgery. Both complained when Father wasn't about. Lucy wanted the house cleaned when it wasn't even necessary. Lucy insisted the yard needed a raking when that wasn't at all necessary. Lucy saw weeds in the garden nobody else saw. To Flossie and Loretta it seemed Lucy could invent work to be done.

"Maybe we'd have better stayed in school after all," voiced Flossie, each word tinted with regret.

"Well, don't you want to get ready to be a good housekeeper?" asked Lucy one day when Loretta fussed and fumed about polishing the stove.

"Well, I hate housework," pouted Loretta. "I can't help it I'm put together this way. I'd rather work in the field or out in the orchard or just sit on a hillside and graze the cows or do things like that. In here it's the same old thing over and over and there's no end to it."

"Me too," added Flossie. "I just detest all kinds of housework. I'd rather work outside and have a little freedom."

"Then you never expect to have a home of your own?" asked Lucy.

Flossie shrugged her shoulders. "It hasn't bothered me any yet. I might meet a rich guy someday and he can hire a maid to do the work. I wish we weren't so poor. Why are we? I wish I had twenty dresses instead of three. There's so many things I wish I had I couldn't write them all down in a week."

"Then I'd suggest you learn to sew, sister Floss," remarked Lucy. "If you'd learn to make your own dresses, who knows, someday maybe you could get a job in a big city helping a fine seamstress who might have a rich son."

"Dreamer girl. That's what you are, Lucy. My, what big ideas you must have in that head of yours. I wish I did like to sew, but I don't. And that's that. I'm glad you take a fancy to it."

Four years had only added more charm and natural

beauty to Lucy. John Winchester couldn't avoid watching her. "My sister all over," he said to himself. "And Mabel was the prettiest Winchester in seven counties."

Often when Lucy had a chance to be alone with her mother, she'd take one wrinkled hand in hers and caress it, or sit beside her with one arm around her shoulder. She talked to her in tender, affectionate tones about Sunny Creek Sunday school and the Bible stories Miss Basie read to them. Mom listened intently, never interrupting her storyteller.

"I hope you like to hear these stories, Mom, because it does something for me since Corkie's gone."

"Well, yes, I do. It's interesting. But I dunno whether to believe it or not."

"It's in the Bible, Mom. So it's got to be true."

"Yes, but how do you know it's true? Jes' 'cause Miss Basie said so? I get all confused. Maybe if I could-a learned them things when I was a child, it would all be different."

"But you're not too old to learn, Mom. I guess no one is too old to believe if they can think."

"But, Lucy," whispered her mother, "you know what Father would say if he found out all these things you're tellin' me. Yet you do it. I can tell you enjoy tellin' it all to someone an' I'm the only one who'll listen. So if it makes you happy—all right then. I won't tell him."

Lucy sat in deep thought.

"I know just about what Father would say, but my heart gets so full sometimes, Mom, I just got to spill out to someone. Nobody can ever keep me from believing in my heart. Nobody can look inside my mind and know what I'm thinking. Miss Basie said once if you tell someone you love God, then you love Him all the more."

To Lucy's utter astonishment her father told her one morning to get ready and go along to town with him.

"What for, Father?"

"You need slippers. You're too big now to wear those clumsy-lookin' ones you got on."

"Oh." Lucy glanced at her feet. She couldn't believe he meant what he said. What had happened? Up to this moment Lucy as well as all the other Winchesters wore what their father brought home for them. If the shoes were too large, they wore them anyway. Lots of shoe toes had been stuffed with cotton or old rags. If the shoes were too small, they were handed down a child or held in waiting. John Winchester never could admit he had made a mistake. The mark on the paper Lucy had given him was faulty or the clerk in the store made the mistake. It was impossible for him to say, "I was wrong," even in a card game. His friends knew and overlooked his selfish trait.

On the way to town in the spring wagon Lucy talked pleasantly about the fresh spring air, the wild flowers in bloom, the birds chirping, the early lettuce and onions shooting up in the gardens they passed. She had never talked this much to her father in one day. Never. He hadn't much to say, but he didn't cut her off either. Mrs. Fetherstone was hanging out wash when they passed. They waved to each other. Mrs. Fetherstone dropped the two clothespins she had between her teeth to exclaim, "Well, what's happened to the Winchesters!" She watched until the wagon turned the corner.

John's tobacco and the groceries were purchased first. Then the slippers. The shoe department was at the rear of the general store, back of the men's and boys' work clothes. John Winchester sat beside Lucy with a pleasant expression which was the closest to a smile Lucy had ever seen on her father's face. He watched the clerk try on several different styles.

The clerk was ready to bend over backward to please his customer. "You have a nice foot to fit, Miss Winchester. They all look becoming on you. Don't you think so? Which do you like best?"

Lucy looked at her father. "You choose," she said. "I'll be satisfied. More than satisfied with any of these."

"Which feels the best, Lucy? It's your foot what's got to wear 'em. I like those black shiny ones."

"These patent leather ones, Mr. Winchester? They are beautiful, and beautiful on her."

John nodded. "We'll take 'em. Put 'em on her to wear home."

Aside from the fact that the patent leather cost a little more than John had intended to pay, he seemed pleased.

"Thank you, Father," whispered Lucy and she gave his hand a quick squeeze.

He felt his heart skip a beat. Just why he did not know. All he did know was that it gave him a real sense of satisfaction to see Lucy walking out of the store with so graceful a stride and such a grateful attitude.

"Now, Lucy," he said, "I have to take Duff over to the blacksmith shop to be shod. That's no fit place for a young lady to be hangin' 'round nohow. I don't think it'll take long. You remember we came past a small park in the center of the square, don't you?"

"Yes."

"There's a concrete seat around that spring. You walk over there an' wait on me. I'll be along an' pick you up.

See?"

"Yes."

"You'll be all right?"

"Sure, Father. Of course I will. I've never sat in a town square but I'll like it."

"You take care now an' don't get your slippers scuffed up."

Lucy found the fountain and the seat around it just as her father had described. What a pleasant fresh morning it was! Sitting there in her new slippers, watching the gentle bubbling of the spring and the birds hopping about unafraid, waiting their turn to bill a fresh drink, was a new and exhilarating experience for Lucy. She felt like talking to them. She felt like laughing at the bubbling spring water. She reached over and let the wet coolness run over her hand. The bright sun on the moving water made it sparkle with a thousand prisms.

"Good morning."

Lucy jumped. She looked up in surprise.

"Did I scare you? I really didn't mean to." Beside Lucy stood a tall young man in clean blue overalls and blue shirt. He held his hat in one hand. Lucy was too surprised to answer. She looked up at him with large, startled eyes.

"Aren't you Lucy Winchester?" He smiled down into her astonished face.

"Yes." There was a tinge of uncertainty in her answer. She tried to hide her uneasiness.

"I'm Thomas Hammon. We've never met, I know, but I've been wanting to meet you for a long time."

"Me?" asked Lucy shyly. She was not used to talking to men. When had she? Not since the night at Black Bend. Her mounting color only enhanced her natural beauty.

"No one but you, Lucy." His eyes smiled as well as his lips.

Now she was getting embarrassed. The young man saw it and hastened to explain. "You see, I've been hearing about you through my uncle."

"Your uncle? I don't understand. Who is your uncle?" Lucy moved an inch or two away from him.

"Charlie Morehouse. He goes over to your house every Sunday afternoon to play cards."

"Well, I don't quite—" Lucy's neck got almost as pink as her cheeks.

"I know you don't understand, Lucy, but I'm about to tell you. My uncle has been telling me for several years now what an attractive daughter John Winchester has and that I ought to meet her. He told me you're the prettiest girl this side the Mississippi."

Lucy hung her head. She was afraid now to look up. This was a greater surprise than coming to town to get slippers. Her entire body quivered.

"I see now my uncle was right. Lucy, you are an attractive young lady."

She looked up a moment, then down with real apprehension.

"May I sit here beside you?"

Lucy was at a loss to know what to answer.

"You haven't said no; so I take it I may." He sat down beside her. The gentle breeze played over the soft waves of her hair, sending loose wavy strands around her lovely oval face. Her blue and white gingham dress hung in graceful folds around her slender legs. He noticed her pretty slippers.

"Talk to me a little, Lucy," said the young man with

twinkles in both eyes. "I want to hear your voice. If it's as sweet as the rest of you, good. I'm sure it is."

"What do you want me to talk about?" She looked up smiling faintly. She folded her hands in her lap.

"Well, start by telling me all about yourself. Anything would interest me. Just anything at all to get acquainted. You see, Uncle Charlie has been telling me what a perfect young lady you are and—"

"But he doesn't know me," interrupted Lucy. "When did he ever see me? I never stand around on Sundays and watch the men playing cards. I don't even know the names of all the men who come to our house."

"I believe you. But somehow, I don't know just how, he seems to have the impression you're one girl in ten thousand. And I'd like to come and call on you some evening. You just tell me when and we'll go for a ride."

Lucy was shocked, stunned. She opened her mouth but could not speak.

"You're holding me off," he laughed pleasantly. "Did I hear you say I may come, Miss Lucy?" He bent close to her and looked with eagerness into her lovely face.

"Why—" she began. "Why—I—hardly know what to say, Mr. Hammon."

"Just call me Tom, Lucy."

"Well," she began, "it's like this, Tom." She spoke his name with hesitancy. "My—my father is a very—"

"Strict?"

She nodded. "And I'm sure—absolutely sure he—" Lucy turned and looked in the direction her father had gone with Duff a little while ago. Oh, how long was it now? What would he think—what would he say if he returned and found her with a man—a perfect stranger, sitting beside her? Of course she'd try her best to explain what happened, but would he believe her? Would he accept any of her explanation? What should she do? Run to find him? No. He said the blacksmith shop was no fit place for young girls. He ordered her to stay on the concrete bench and she promised she would. Lucy stood up. She looked frightened. Thomas Hammon laughed out loud.

He caught her one hand in his. "Please don't be scared of me, Lucy. You look like a beautiful rabbit scared to death. Don't run away from me. I wouldn't hurt you for anything in the world." His voice was kind, tender, and sincere. "Please sit down beside me. I saw your father driving toward the blacksmith shop. I happened to be with my Uncle Charlie. He asked your father if he came into town alone and he said he brought you along and you were at the spring in the park waiting for him. Then Uncle Charlie suggested I come over here and meet you. He said he'd talk to your father and try to hold him up a while so that I would have a chance to meet you. Now don't you see how perfectly wonderful this all worked out for both of us? It's almost like a fairy tale, isn't it? Isn't it, Lucy?"

Lucy sat beside Tom and gave him a faint smile. She felt as though she were waking from some pleasant dream but had no right to feel pleasant about it.

"You're beautiful, Lucy. Absolutely charming. I've waited a long, long time for this moment; so please don't disappoint me."

Lucy glanced in the direction of the blacksmith shop again. How did she know this stranger was telling her the truth? She felt a little skeptical and Thomas Hammon could read it in plain letters on her face.

"You mean to say your father would object to my coming to see you?"

"I'm sure he would."

"But why? He must not have a very good opinion of me. And that disappoints me a great deal. Or do you have a boyfriend?"

"Oh, no—no—it's not that. But it's my age. I'm only seventeen and—and—" She blushed a deeper pink. She fumbled with the edge of her sleeve. "I've never been away much. You don't know my father, Mr. Hammon."

"Please call me Tom, Lucy."

Lucy hardly knew how to say it but say it she must. She hated to put her father down to anyone. She did not want to say one unkind word about him. Especially after showing this unexpected kindness to her. After all, in spite of all his harshness she knew she loved him. She simply couldn't discuss it. Not now.

"I'll have to help you I see, Lucy," Tom ventured with a note of impatience in his voice. "Your father is evidently very strict with you. Isn't he?"

She nodded.

"Well, Lucy, that's all right with me. Some fathers aren't strict enough. But it seems to me when a girl reaches seventeen and is as lovely and sensible and mature as you are, she ought to be able to decide some things for herself. At least begin to. You must decide who you'd like to date. Don't you agree with me?"

That was a new thought to Lucy. She hadn't realized she was mature or unusually ladylike. To be sure, she did not realize she had personal charm. Most of the time she had entertained a deep sense of frustration and inferiority. What was this Thomas Hammon telling her?

"Don't you think I'm right, Lucy? Please answer me."

"Maybe so," came her soft answer. She wanted to smile but feared to.

"Oh. Then," he smiled and touched her arm, "we'll have a ride. I hope you give me a date soon. Tell me when I may come for you. You set the evening and the time and I, Tom Hammon, will be there."

Lucy was lost. For a moment she forgot where she was. Her heart skipped several beats and music like angels playing on harps seemed to be carrying her off, up, up into a cloud of sheer joy. It was the strangest happiness she had ever experienced. What was it? Something so new, unheard of, undreamed of. Not the same kind of happiness she felt when Miss Basie said she loved her.

Thomas Hammon could easily read Lucy's face. He could see she was being carried away in the first awakening of young love. It pleased him, delighted him, encouraged him. He wished he could have a picture of her sitting there delighted with the wonder and expectation of first love.

Lucy came to earth!

"Oh, really, Mr. Hammon," she sighed. "I will have to ask my father first. There is absolutely no other way for me to do it."

"Well," his voice was saturated now with fresh disappointment. "How soon can you let me know?"

"Oh," Lucy jumped up. "Go. Please. There comes my father now."

When Thomas Hammon saw the genuine terror on Lucy's face, he left without being told twice.

"Come, Lucy," Father called cheerfully. "It took me longer than I thought it would."

Was he apologizing for being late? For making her wait? He hadn't seen then? He wasn't going to be furious with her?

Lucy drew a long breath of relief as she climbed up into the spring wagon.

"Get tired waitin' ?"

"No. It was very pleasant sitting there."

"Charlie Morehouse came by an' was atalkin' to me 'bout buyin' our place."

"Oh." Lucy looked at her father in surprise. "Are you going to sell it?"

"No. Course not. Whatever put sech an idea in his head I'll never know. An' what's he got anyhow to buy with? He's jes' a man who likes to talk."

Little was said the rest of the way home. Lucy's thoughts were in one constant whirl. She was certain now her father had not seen the young man. Perhaps she should tell him all about it now. Take him into her confidence and tell him everything. Every detail. And how she answered the young man. Surely he'd commend her for not giving Tom an answer without consulting him. But her father was so unpredictable. He might be furious and take her pretty new slippers away from her. Oh, no. Would he do that? Or give them to Flossie? But when they reached home, Lucy had not been able to bring herself to confiding in him.

In her prayer that night she added a sentence she had never prayed before—in fact, never thought of praying. "Lord, if it's Your will, help Father to say yes when I ask him. Please, Lord."

Two weeks went by and Lucy had not mustered up the courage to ask her father the question which was on her mind day in, day out.

One evening in June Lucy was busy working in the flower bed in the front yard along the fence. It was growing dark and she wanted to finish the job before she'd be forced to quit. A man on horseback stopped just outside the fence where she was on one knee.

"Good evening, Lucy."

Lucy stood up. "Mr. Hammon," she gasped.

"I surprised you, didn't I?"

"Yes." Her face grew radiant. "You certainly did."

"Did you ask him yet?"

"Not yet." Lucy looked toward the woodpile where she thought her father was working. "You see, I—I—" She couldn't select the right words.

"When are you going to, Lucy?" There was real disappointment in each word.

"I—really can't say. I—" Lucy kept looking toward the woodpile.

"Shall I ask him myself?"

"Well, that might be best—I—I think. But really—I'm—not sure, Tom." She felt an unnerving weakening flutter all through her body.

"Lucy, you look so frightened again. I don't understand why you need to be afraid. Don't you remember what I told you about deciding things for yourself? Listen." He jumped off the horse and stood as close as he could to the fence. "Come here to me." He touched her chin and made her look up at him. He smiled down on her lovingly, tenderly, and with a manly graciousness. "Maybe you didn't know I've been going past your house several times a week now. Did you?"

"No." Her eyes widened.

"Well, I have. Ever since I met you in town. I've gone by just to get a glimpse of you. That's how much I care. You have no idea, Lucy. And this is the first time I've had a chance to speak to you. I'm not about to let you run away from me either. If your father sees me here, I'll just explain what I'm after. I'm not afraid or ashamed to talk to him."

It would have been a miracle if none of the Winchester children would have seen a man with a horse by the fence talking to Lucy. One did see. Soon all of the children saw. It was no miracle. John Winchester also saw, dropped his ax, and hurried over to the fence and stood close to Lucy.

"Good evening, Mr. Winchester." Thomas Hammon held out his hand. Awkwardly John Winchester shook it.

"Warm evening, isn't it?"

"Pretty warm," agreed Mr. Winchester.

"I'm Charlie Morehouse's nephew, Mr. Winchester."

"Yes?"

"You know me then?"

"Guess I do a little."

"I met—" he saw Lucy's mouth open, then he added quickly, "I've seen your daughter, Lucy, several times as I was passing by, but tonight's the first time I got to speak to her; so I thought I'd just stop and say hello."

John Winchester looked long at Lucy, then at the young man. He said not a word.

"My name's Thomas Hammon, Mr. Winchester. I wondered if you'd let me come and see Lucy some evening soon?"

"What fer?" snapped Mr. Winchester.

Thomas Hammon wanted an answer, not a question. He tried to act calm.

"Well, sir," he said running one hand around the brim of his hat, "I guess for the same reason you once went to see Mrs. Winchester. It's what makes the world go on, you know. I want to help it go on. I'm not exactly a kid anymore."

It was Lucy's father who was baffled now. He felt like flying into a rage. This, the very thing he had been fearing for years. He pulled out his red bandanna and wiped his face, all the while looking over Lucy from head to foot.

"Well, I tell you, young man," he began at last, "Lucy's a little too young yet to be steppin' out. What's more, she's got a mother that's nearly blind to care fer an' her place is right here in the home fer a while." He stopped to get his breath and gather together the loose ends of his scattered thoughts. "No—I can't let her go out yet. She's too young. She's got plenty o' time to think of men later on."

Thomas Hammon understood perfectly there was no use to talk or argue or discuss the question any longer. So he tipped his hat and said good night.

"Now, Lucy," began her father in that stern voice she so much dreaded, "did you ever meet that fellow before?"

"Once."

"When?"

"The day you took me to town."

"What? Where?" he demanded.

"Where you told me to wait for you."

"By the spring? In the park?"

"Yes."

"Did you arrange this behind my back, Lucy Winchester?"

"No, indeed not. He just walked by and stopped and spoke. I never saw him before."

"I see. Well. So you let him stop right there an' make love to you? The first time you met? Lucy Winchester, what kind of girl are you?"

"But, Father. Listen. He just introduced himself to me. He said Charlie Morehouse, his uncle, was one of your good friends who comes here to play cards with you every Sunday. He just asked if he could come to see me sometime and get better acquainted."

"Indeed. Well. And what did you tell him?"

"I told him I'd have to ask you first."

John Winchester studied his daughter until his breathing slowed down. "Lucy." And once more Lucy witnessed her father's attitude change abruptly. He placed one strong hand on her shoulder so gently it surprised her beyond words. "Lucy—Lucy," he repeated, "that's the thing to do. Don't you never, never go out with no man till I say you can."

Lucy tried to swallow the lump in her throat. She did not answer him. When she looked up into his face, she wondered when or if that day would ever come. She doubted it very much.

John was wondering something quite the opposite. What would he have said had he been the young man on the other side of the fence? Lucy was beautiful even in the gathering night. No one could contradict that.

He slept very little that night. Something made John restless and uneasy. Lucy couldn't leave. She dare not. Yet John Winchester knew the day surely would come in spite of everything. If she lived—if she lived! Tonight she had reminded him of Mabel more than ever before. And Mabel was seventeen.

Maggie sat up in bed and shook him. "What's wrong,

John?"

"What's wrong?"

"You've been tossin' an' groanin', John. Are you sick?"

"Oh. I'm all right, Maggie. Lie back and go to sleep."

Long into the night Lucy sat on the wooden box by the east window. After she was sure Flossie and Loretta were fast asleep, she crawled out of bed. She determined she was not going to allow their many questions to upset her. They would tease her, no doubt. So would Kenneth and Floyd, but not in Father's hearing. She was confident now he would not allow that. She touched her shoulder where he had placed his hand, that loving pressure of his tawny, hardworking hand.

"Dear God," she prayed, "help Father say yes before too many months or years." Then she fell into a peaceful sleep.

One evening when Lucy and her mother were sitting alone on the back porch, she asked, "Do you suppose Father would let me go back to Sunny Creek again?"

"I have my doubts. Do you really want to?"

"I would so love to have a Bible. If I could work out for someone, I could soon save up enough to buy one myself. The girls could do the work. They're big enough, Mom. Would Father let me work out?"

"Oh, Lucy." Mrs. Winchester found Lucy's arm and squeezed it in both her hands. "How could I ever get along without you? You know the girls don't go ahead like you do."

Lucy couldn't bear to see the tears in her mother's blind eyes. "There—there, Mom," she said. "I won't mention it again ever."

CHAPTER 8

SCHOOL STARTED at Black Bend the first of September. Pupils were dismissed early the first day. When the teacher asked for volunteers to stay and help her clean blackboards, Floyd was the first to raise his hand. Kenneth and Peggy went on home.

Forty-five minutes later the teacher thanked Floyd for his splendid help and dismissed him with a cookie and two wintergreen candies to munch on his way home.

"Sonny." Floyd was greeted by a young man wearing a broad smile and a plaid bill cap. They met at the Bend a quarter of a mile from the schoolhouse. "Aren't you one of the Winchester boys?"

"Yes."

"Listen to me then. Your sister, Lucy, she is your sister, isn't she?"

"Yes."

"Will you do me a favor if I give you a dime?"

"A dime?" Floyd's eyes danced. He had never had a dime all his own in all his nine years. His smile reached from ear to ear. "You mean to keep?"

"Of course to keep. I wouldn't give it to you, then ask for it back, would I?"

Floyd twisted his head and raised both eyebrows.

"Now this is what I want you to do for me. What's your name, sonny?"

"Floyd."

"Are you ten?"

"No. Nine."

"You're old enough to deliver a letter then, aren't you?"

"I guess so."

"All right then." From his shirt pocket the man pulled out a sealed envelope folded once and held with a rubber band. "I'm Thomas Hammon."

"I know."

"How do you know who I am?"

" 'Cause I remember. You stopped by the fence on your horse one night."

"That's right. I did. But now, Floyd, my boy, I want you to keep this a secret. See? I don't want you to tell one soul on earth about this. Can you keep a secret?"

"Sure." Floyd was still smiling with eagerness.

"Then you take this letter and slip it to Lucy the first chance you get while nobody's looking." He handed Floyd the letter and patted him on the head. "Remember, sonny, don't let anyone know about this. Don't even tell your dog."

"No." Floyd beamed on the shiny dime in the palm of his hand. He was elated.

"And you know," cautioned Thomas Hammon, "I'll know whether or not you delivered this letter for me."

"How?"

"That's my secret. Be on your way now, good boy." Floyd went toward home whistling and trotting up dust.

He soon located Lucy in the hen house. "Lucy," he whispered.

"Yes. What's on your mind, Floyd?"

"Is anyone else in here?" he looked around.

"No. Why?"

"Here then. Take it, Lucy, quick so nobody sees." He handed her the folded letter somewhat crumpled now and damp with perspiration.

"What is it?"

"A letter," he whispered standing on his tiptoes to reach her ear, "from that guy on a horse Father went over and talked to that night. I knew him, but I can't remember his name now. You know, don't you?"

Lucy's face grew crimson. She stuck the letter inside her dress with an unsteady hand. She looked out the one dusty hen house window toward the house, then her eyes shifted to the yard fence.

"You act surprised, Lucy."

"Surprised? Of course I am. Floyd, who else knows about this?"

"No one but me and you, Lucy. I promised not to tell a soul, not even Fido. And you're not to tell either. He made me promise."

Speechless now and wide-eyed, Lucy hurried to the house with the pan of fresh eggs. What could this be? Where could she go to read it? The house was too small. Oh, if she only had a room all her own. She couldn't risk opening it anywhere at this time of day.

Once at the supper table Lucy heard the paper crack when she passed the soup bowl. She paled and held her breath. Evidently no one else heard it. And no one at the table seemed to notice that every now and then Floyd cast quick glances in Lucy's direction. He was wondering too where he could hide his precious prize money.

Not until Lucy was positive her sisters were sound asleep, did she carefully get out of bed. Taking the small oil lamp in one hand, a match between her teeth, and the letter in the other hand she went slowly to the small clothes closet, carefully closing the door. How thankful she was it didn't squeak like most of the doors in the house. The lamp lit, she placed it on a narrow shelf between the studding. Carefully, holding her breath, she unfolded the one-page letter.

Dear Lucy,

I have passed your house many times in the past two months and several times had the pleasure of catching a glimpse of you through the window. I knew it was you because of your blond hair. You didn't see me, did you? I can't forget you, Lucy. I think of you all the time. I have never forgotten how beautiful you were on that park seat that morning. I love you, Lucy. [The paper in her hands shook.] *I want to be the first man to tell you that.*

When is your birthday? You'll soon be eighteen, won't you? How soon do you think your Father will let me come to see you? I have it all figured out how you can send me a letter. I found a nice flat stone about the size of a large meat platter and I put it in a clump of tall grass just outside the garden fence close to the plum tree. You won't have any trouble finding it. Please, Lucy dear, write me a letter and put it under the stone when no one is looking. This is our secret. Your brother Floyd is not to know a thing about this. I'll be by on Saturday night after dark and look for your letter. Lucy, please don't disappoint me.

In love,
Thomas Hammon

Lucy stood breathless. She could feel a quivering sensation through her entire body. She was frightened, bewildered, numb with wonder, yet strangely pleased. Her life seemed to be cut in two, half glorious, expectant, and miraculously lifted on fluttering wings, yet half chained to drab, fruitless, unromantic wistful thinking. Was she completely falling apart? She read the letter again, puffed out the light, and put it back where it belonged.

For a long hour she pressed the letter against her heart under her nightgown. She hadn't held anything this close to her since that afternoon when Corkie didn't cry anymore or flinch. She was holding then something very dear to her she would have to part with forever. Now she was holding something given to her and her alone to keep. No one would take this from her and bury it in the cold, damp ground. It was past midnight when she tucked the letter under the mattress at her head and closed her eyes.

Saturday night, Lucy, as well as Thomas Hammon, was glad it wasn't full moon. Lucy had been living in a dream world for five days. Tom waited until he saw the last light go out in the Winchester house. He tied his horse a quarter of a mile down the road and walked to the plum tree. He felt around with his foot. The flat stone. Yes. Anxiously, almost feverishly, he lifted it. It was there.

He all but ran back to his horse. By the light of a lantern he tore the red string tied securely around two uniform sheets of brown wrapping paper.

Dear Thomas,

Floyd gave me your letter and no one else knows about it. Twice I saw you pass our house. I'm sure now it was you. I was upstairs in my room by the east window. I don't know yet when my father will let you come to see me. I haven't asked him yet. I will be eighteen on the third of November. You are the first man who has ever told me he loved me or anything like that. How old are you? And when is your birthday?

With love,
Lucy Winchester

Thomas Hammon folded the letter without reading it twice. He was more than a little disappointed. He couldn't tell whether his letter had pleased her or not. She did not ask him to write again. But at least she answered his questions, and he went to bed a trifle more encouraged than when he lifted the secret stone mailbox.

It was a full month before Tom met Floyd alone on his way home from school. The letter in his pocket was two weeks old.

"Hey there, sonny." He was coming out of the timber on horseback. "Where's your brother and sister?"

"Kenny stayed home today with a toothache. Peggy's over the Knob already. I stayed to clean erasers and sharpen pencils for the teacher."

"Fine. How about earning another dime?"

"I'd like to." Floyd grinned. "I didn't have a chance to spend the first one yet but I'll put another one with it. It's in a safe place where nobody will find it."

"All right. Here's another letter for Lucy. And a dime for you. Remember now, it's our secret."

"Sure. I know."

Floyd found Lucy in the hen house again. It worked perfectly once. It worked twice. Lucy tucked the letter inside her dress and read it by the oil lamp in the clothes closet.

Dear Lucy,

I was very glad for your letter. It was short but I love you for it. I love you more than ever, Lucy. I can hardly wait until we can be together and talk and get to know each other better. I want to get you a present for your birthday November 3. You'll be eighteen. Think of it, Lucy. I want to get you something you'd like. Won't you give me some suggestions? I never bought a gift for a girl before and I want to please you. It should be something I can hide in the tall grass while it's still standing and before the snow and ice come to flatten it. Or if you'd rather, I could send it with Floyd. I am twenty-two. My birthday is in January. Please put another letter under the stone. Please tell me you love me a little. I believe you do but are afraid to tell me. I'll be by every night until I find a letter. Bye for now. Don't make me wait too long, Lucy dear.

I love you,
Tom

It was several days before Lucy could find paper to write on. So few letters ever went out from the Winchester home that writing paper, stamps, and envelopes were never on the list of needs. She wouldn't dare ask Kenneth for a sheet out of his school tablet or he'd wonder what for. If she asked Floyd, he'd wonder how she delivered the letter.

While Lucy was dusting the pantry shelf, she found a small roll of wallpaper yellowed and brittle. She remembered now, there had been a half yard left when they papered the sitting room. She waited until Flossie and Loretta were outside taking down the dry wash before she cut off a piece from the cleanest end. Running upstairs she formulated her plan. The paper wanted to curl. She cut two pieces almost alike and put them inside a folded apron and then under the mattress for pressing. Before the girls came in, she was downstairs and had carefully burned every scrap in the cookstove.

Tom found the letter Saturday night. Again it was tied securely with red string.

Dear Tom,

I'm thankful my letter made you glad. I think I love you a little. I'm glad you love me. But this is all so new to me. I can't explain how it makes me feel. What I would love to have for my birthday more than anything else is a Bible. I've been wanting one ever since I was twelve. I went to the Sunny Creek Sunday school for three years and if I could have gone two more years I would have gotten one as a reward. My father made me stop going. He has no use for religion. But I must not tell you anything unkind about my father. A Bible is the only thing I can think of that I really want more than anything else.

With love,
Lucy

A Bible? Why a Bible? It would have been the last thing he would have guessed a girl would want from her lover.

Tom lay awake for a long time thinking. She enjoyed going to Sunday school? So Lucy was that kind of girl? Surprise, wonder, and conflicting ideas clamored with his respect and adoration. Yes, he did without question or reservation love that girl. Could it be that opposites attract each other? In the morning he reread the letter. It struck him now like a message from a foreign country, yet written in perfectly plain English. Disbelief struggled with anxiety. Admiration with doubt. Madness of love with irritation. He wouldn't rush to town to find a Bible; he'd weigh, consider, and ponder his declared love at least another day.

After Lucy had secretly slipped out in the night to put Tom's letter under the stone, she returned to her room with a queer disquieting feeling. Was she wrong in doing this behind her parents' backs? If Father knew, he'd be so angry. What would he do to her? She shivered. But had she promised him she'd never write letters? No. Then she wasn't disobeying. *O God,* she prayed, *if I've done wrong, please forgive me.*

Lucy slept very little that night.

CHAPTER 9

LUCY WAS sitting by the window. Everyone else in the house was fast asleep. It was ten o'clock, the last day of October. The pale moon revealed the form of a man in the road below. Lucy knew it was Tom. He stopped for a minute by the plum tree, bent low, then disappeared. Her heart thumping, she descended the stairs slowly, cautiously on tiptoe, her old shoes in her left hand. She heard her father snoring in sound sleep. Once outside, she put on her shoes and ran to the stone. Safely upstairs again she went to the closet with the oil lamp.

Dear Lucy,

Your letter caused me to do a lot of thinking. You said you loved me a little. I was hoping you'd say very much. I love you more than a little. Lucy, I love you with all my heart. I am certain now you must be my very own soon. [Lucy caught her breath.] *In three days you will be eighteen. Any girl at that age is free to do as she pleases. A girl eighteen does not have to be held down by her father or anyone.* [Lucy almost coughed. She swallowed the strange annoying sensation in her throat.] *I have a plan I am sure will bring you happiness, the like of which you have never known. I found a Bible in Black Bend but it is not nice enough. So I want to take you with me to*

Crawford and together we'll buy the very best Bible in town. Then we'll get married. [Lucy's hands trembled so much she could scarcely hold the paper.] *Uncle Charlie told me your mother was only eighteen when she married your father. Lucy, my dear, you've stayed at home and worked hard long enough. You wouldn't be leaving your blind mother without help.*

Please, darling Lucy, come and live with me and be my wife. No one else could ever make me happy but you. And I'll make you happy. You can go to church and Sunday school all you want to and no one will prevent you from going. I know where we can get a little farm only six miles west of your home and the house is by a beautiful stream. You would be thrilled. Lucy, dear, I cannot wait much longer. I love you so deeply. It seems like years since the day I first met you. I think of you all day and dream of you at night. In three days you will be a beautiful grown lady of eighteen. After everyone is sound asleep, slip down and come out to see me. I'll be waiting for you. I'll have my horse down the road. We'll reach Crawford by daylight. [Lucy felt faint.] *You'll make me the happiest man in the world, Lucy. No one will ever, ever love you as I do. Your folks will all get over your being gone. Lots of other girls have left home and many more will. It's the best thing to do, Lucy, my darling. Your dear heart will have whatever it longs for. Remember, dear, on your birthday, November 3, when everyone is asleep, I'll be waiting for you.*

> *Loving you forever,*
> *Tom*

Lucy all but fell with the lamp. She was actually weak. It was much too cool to sit by the window to pray; so she crawled into bed. She was facing the greatest struggle of her life now. She covered her face, for suddenly she was shaking with sobs and hardly knew why. Uncertainties plagued her, yet her heart swelled with overflowing love and joy. But why was she crying? Where in all the world would she ever meet another like Tom? But he could never realize how she loved her dear blind mother. With fists both tightly clenched she tried to hold on to this new love with one, and fearful duty with the other. Mom only eighteen when she and Father were married? Why hadn't she known that? Why Mom was only forty-five now and seemed so old. Why? Why had her life been such a heavy strain?

Tom. Dear loving Tom. A Bible to call her own. To open it up in her own home anytime and read it unafraid? And go to church anytime and as often as she liked? No one to stop her? A little home by a stream? A husband, tall and handsome and kind? A Tom who really, truly loved her and no one else! Lucy wiped her tears on the quilt.

True. Flossie and Loretta were big and strong enough to take over all the house and garden work. They depended too much on her. Lucy was thankful again Mom had taught her to bake, churn, wash, iron, clean house, and sew.

Lucy rolled over, tucked the letter under the mattress, and fell asleep.

The next two days she lived in a continual dream. But there was a constant duel, leaving her troubled and weary. She lost her appetite. She wasn't herself at all. Once she poured coffee in the dishwater and then cut twice as much bread as the family usually ate.

"Lucy," asked her father, "what's on your mind? Are you sick?"

"No.

"Are you sure?" He was thinking of Mabel as well as of Lucy.

"Really, I'm not sick. Why? Do I look sick?"

"You're sorta pale. You're not eating much, I've noticed."

Lucy looked away. At once she took the dishpan off the nail behind the stove and determined to prove to everyone she was not sick. Wistfully she looked out the window and watched her father walking toward the woodpile. He too was growing old and gray.

Tomorrow—tomorrow she would be eighteen. She spent a sleepless night, trying one side of her single bed, then the other. How could God be displeased with her if marrying Tom meant she'd have a Bible all her own? How could her decision be out of God's will if it meant she could go to church and worship Him every Sunday? This *must* be His way of answering her prayer. Then why fret? Why question? Yes, why? Oh, what a glorious thought. Her heart wanted to shout with great relief.

Three times during the night Lucy got out of bed, tiptoed to the stairway, and stood there. She must go down and have a confidential talk with Mom. Her father was a sound sleeper whenever he snored. He was snoring. Maybe she could help Mother get out of bed without waking him. They could put coats on and go out on the porch and talk. That's what she'd do. She put one foot on the first step. She waited, listening, trembling, weighing her decision. Something was gluing her to the step. She could descend no farther.

"You must decide some things for yourself. A girl eighteen is free—free."

All at once Lucy wished she had never met Thomas Hammon. What was he doing to her? Why was she torn so between fear and anticipation, between her own happiness and hurting another? Every nerve in her body twitched and tightened. Would things ever get unraveled? She was getting cold; her teeth chattered. Every minute now was crucial, demanding, priceless. She went back to bed. Lots of girls had done it, and many more would, and the world went on. It will again.

Somehow Lucy lived through the next day. It had never been the custom to make any great celebrations for birthdays in the Winchester home but it was an evening for eating popcorn. Flossie did the popping and Loretta salted it. Peggy filled the dishes and passed them around.

"Well, Lucy," said her mother, "it's good, isn't it?"

"Very good. Very good."

"So you're eighteen already. My, when I think back I can hardly believe I was married at your age."

John Winchester tapped his shoe heel on the floor. "Sh, Maggie. Don't put any ideas like that in Lucy's head."

Lucy choked on three grains of popcorn. She excused herself and stepped outside to get her breath.

Everyone laughed at her when she returned. "Looks like you had to cough until you cried," remarked Kenneth teasingly. "I'm going to see how many grains I can put in my mouth now. Start counting, Lucy. Here I go."

As usual Lucy straightened up the kitchen before going to bed. Every bit of fallen popcorn had been swept together and thrown in the stove to crackle and burn.

What a nice smell to go to bed on! It had been a pleasant evening together. But Mom looked much too old for forty-five and Father looked extra tired. But he had worked hard all day getting wood ready to take to town. He hadn't been stern or grouchy about anything. Wonder of wonders.

At ten-fifteen Lucy was up and dressed. She put on her blue-and-white gingham dress (the best she had) and her light, well-worn brown coat. She carried her patent leather slippers. Slowly, carefully, she made her way to the bottom step. Across the kitchen she inched in stocking feet scarcely breathing. It seemed to take her fifteen minutes to open and close the door. On the porch she hesitated. The night was much cooler than she had expected. Her heart pounded. She shivered. She put on her slippers and walked to the road.

She thought she saw him waiting under the plum tree by the fence several rods from her. She took several steps and waited. Then she knew it was Tom and he ran to meet her, caught her in his arms, and nearly lifted her off her feet.

"Oh, you dear blessed girl," he whispered. "You did come, didn't you? I've been waiting an hour. I knew you would. You'll never know how happy this makes me." He was leading her down the road, his arm around her. "You're gorgeous tonight, darling. You're beautiful, Lucy. At last we're together. I have the horse and wagon down there. It's not far, darling."

Lucy stopped short. "But, Tom," she began pulling herself away from him. "I—I came to tell you—I feel we should wait a little while yet." She was nearly out of breath.

"Wait!" he exclaimed with alarm. "You say wait? Why? Oh, no, Lucy my love. You can't possibly mean it. No! Think how long I've waited for you. You're eighteen, Lucy."

"Yes, Tom," she faltered touching his arm. "I know. But really I—I—"

"No, Lucy. There's no buts. You can't disappoint me now. I just can't take it. Look at me, dear." He pulled her close to him and ran his one hand over her blond hair. "Just look how perfectly this has worked out for both of us." He was leading her along with him again. "We're almost to the wagon now. We're going to Crawford. Together, Lucy, dear. We're getting you that Bible you want more than anything." He tightened his arm. "And think of it, darling, I've spoken for that little place I told you about. Just see how perfectly everything has worked out for us. We can move in right away tomorrow."

They were at the wagon now. Lucy was shivering. She was fighting desperately to keep back tears.

"Are you cold, darling?"

"I had no idea it would be this chilly. Tom. Oh, please listen to me."

"Here." Tom took off his coat and folded it around her with extreme tenderness. "I can spare it. I can't let you catch cold now. Let me help you up."

Lucy drew back. "Please, Tom," she cried. "I know you can't understand me. I can't understand myself. I'm so— oh, Tom, how can I explain to you how I feel when I hardly know myself? It's not that I don't love you. I know I do. I want to go with you and be your wife—really I do. I want to have a Bible and go to church and live in a little house all our own. But we're eloping, Tom."

"What of it, Lucy? Big high-up folks have eloped. What's wrong with eloping?"

"Well," she fumbled with the top button on her coat. "I thought only people who wanted to be naughty or had a fight or something at home ran off and got married secretly."

"You're wrong about that, darling. And what's more, your folks will be relieved to learn they didn't have to make a big wedding for their daughter. I'm quite sure your father couldn't afford to buy you a fancy white wedding dress and give a reception for relatives and friends. Could he?"

"No, Tom. You're right. I hadn't thought of it in that way. No, my father is far from well-to-do."

"He'll have one less to feed and clothe. So he'll be ahead financially."

Lucy stood in deep thought. She wiped her unbidden tears. "If Father could only save enough to take—" The sentence dangled unfinished.

"Up we go now." And Lucy was on the wagon seat before she could say another word and Tom was beside her. "We're on our way to Crawford now, my love." And they were off.

Lucy's head was still in a whirl. The night was not only cold but dark and the uncertain landscape ahead seemed so solitary, immense, and lonely. Was she big enough, woman enough, strong enough to face it? All in a few minutes something real and strangely important was behind her, gone, gone forever, never to return. She fastened her gaze straight ahead. In her head ran the mad refrain, *Don't do it, don't do it. I'm doing it, I'm doing it, do it, do it.*

"Oh, Lucy." Tom drew her close to him. "Think how wonderful it's going to be. First we'll get your Bible. Then I'm going to get you a new coat and at least three new dresses."

"Oh, Tom." She looked up at him in sheer wonder. "Do you—"

"Of course I have the money, dear. I've been working and saving for a long time for this day. I've never squandered my money. I've dreamed of a pretty wife and a cozy home for years. We're going to eat in a nice restaurant, too."

"Oh, Tom. Really?" Lucy clasped her hands and tried to smile. Her lashes were still wet. "I've never been inside a restaurant."

"Well, you'll be having quite a few first experiences before the day is over, my beloved. You'll see." He patted her clasped hands affectionately and kissed her on the cheek.

"If I could only forget how hurt my mother will be, Tom." Tears came that she could not hold back.

"I won't ask you to forget your mother, Lucy. But just for a little while now so we can enjoy each other. I'll take you back home to see her any time or as often as you want to go. Look up at me, darling. Let me hear you say you trust me and love me."

"I do, Tom. Truly I love you."

"And you trust me too, don't you?"

After three sleepless nights Lucy was tired, very tired. It was hard to think or reason.

"Tell me you trust me, Lucy."

Her head fell on his shoulder. She closed her teary eyes. "You do. I know it now. The rest of your life you just put your pretty blond head on Tom Hammon's shoulder. I am your provider, your lover, your protector right now, and soon I'll be your husband. As long as I have my strength you'll never go in want, Lucy dear."

On and on they drove through the long dark night, sometimes fast, sometimes slow, a few times very fast. Before they reached Crawford, Tom had convinced Lucy they were doing the right thing, that eloping was what the two people involved made of it and for them it meant the door to endless happiness.

This was the first time Lucy had been in a city of any size. Crawford, the county seat, looked enormous to her. Tom took the horse to the livery stable and they walked three blocks to a clean, well-lighted restaurant. Daybreak was well on the way.

CHAPTER 10

WHEN THE thermometer on the back porch dropped below forty, John Winchester started the fire in the kitchen stove before washing his face. The mercury was deliberating between thirty-seven and thirty-eight. Maggie was soon seated on her cushioned chair beside the stove ready to help Lucy plan breakfast. Fried mush, coffee, sorghum, biscuits, and canned blackberries would taste very good on a frosty morning. No one could make biscuits as fast and as light as Lucy.

"John," remarked his wife looking in the direction of splashing water, "I can't help but remember those first biscuits I made the next mornin' after we got married. I remember I gave what was left to the dog and he got most of them."

"I remember," answered John.

"Just think what all Lucy can do well at eighteen. My sakes, at her age I knew practically everything about farm work but little about cookin'. My older sister helped Mama in the house."

Without another word John Winchester was off to the barn to start the chores.

Of course Loretta and Flossie were not surprised when Lucy wasn't in the room when they woke up. She never was. Lucy would be in the kitchen mixing pancake batter, frying mush, cooking oatmeal, or rolling out biscuit dough.

"Where's Lucy?" asked Flossie.

"Where's Lucy?" echoed Loretta looking around the kitchen.

"Isn't she upstairs?" asked Mrs. Winchester.

"No. I supposed she was down here. Hasn't she started breakfast, Mom?"

"Are you sure she's not upstairs, girls? She's got to be," insisted Mrs. Winchester.

"But she's not," answered Flossie. "Where could she be up there? Under her bed?"

Mrs. Winchester got to her feet. She grabbed the back of the chair. "Go back and see, Flossie. Loretta, step outside. Maybe she went to the garden to see what got frosted an' I just didn't hear her go out."

Both girls returned. "Mom, Lucy's not upstairs. I knew she couldn't be."

"And she's not in the garden or hen house."

"Then where is she?"

When John Winchester came in for breakfast, the table wasn't set, nothing was cooking on the stove, and all five children were clustered around their mother talking in frantic excitement.

"What's going on in here? What's wrong with you all?"

"Where's Lucy?" everyone asked in unison.

"Lucy?" John's arms dropped limp. He let his cap fall to the floor. Mrs. Winchester was wringing her hands and Peggy was crying and clinging to her mother's arm.

"Is—is she gone?" John's startled look matched his voice.

"We've looked everywhere," said Loretta.

"I looked in the hen house twice," put in Floyd.

"And in the garden," said Loretta.

"I went to the cellar," added Kenneth.

"We don't know where else to look," cried Peggy.

"Well!" John grabbed the table for support. His knees wobbled. "Well, I'll be!" His chest rose and fell with dismay. Then fear.

"Do any of you," he asked harshly, "have any idea what might have happened to her?"

Five heads shook in mute dismay.

John paced the kitchen like a lion in a cage. Would Lucy play a trick like this? Would she now? Sudden fresh terror struck him. Could she have been kidnapped? Who—who but—

He picked up his cap and started for the door. "I'm goin' to town at once." He slammed the door and ran to the barn.

The five children stood on the porch in fearful silence and watched their father gallop down the road on Duff. He went straight to the Charlie Morehouse place. He stopped at the gate and called with a loud insistent voice, followed by a shrill whistle through his fingers.

Charlie opened the door, his mouth full of breakfast. "Yes."

"Can you tell me anythin' about your nephew, Thomas Hammon?"

"What you mean, anythin'?"

"I mean, do you know where he is?"

"No, I don't, John." Charlie slowly scratched his head behind one ear nonchalantly.

"Do you know where he's been the past twenty-four hours?"

"Well—" he drawled, "he was helpin' me in the timber all day yesterday." Charlie made no effort to leave the porch. The expression on his unshaven face was absolutely expressionless.

John drew his lips in a straight tight line over his teeth and swallowed hard. "Listen, Charlie, do you know any more you haven't told me about that young man?"

Charlie Morehouse read fire in John's eyes.

"Well," he mused, rubbing his whiskery chin with his left hand. "I tell you, John, I recall now he said somethin' 'bout goin' over to see 'bout rentin' the Haffer place. Yeh, seems he did."

"What?" exploded John, gritting his teeth. "You—you mean— What fer was he goin' to ask 'bout the Haffer place?"

"Well, now," began Charlie with calm deliberation, "I guess he figured when a pretty gal gets to be as old as her mother was when she got married—well—"

"You mean—" choked John. He was angry enough now to cry. Instead, he swore and was off down the road.

The telephone office was a half-room affair in the front of Mrs. Sharon's home in Black Bend.

"Good morning, Mr. Winchester." Her voice was saturated with both questions and sympathy, for such an early call could mean only sickness or death.

John was panting as he lunged through the door. "Is something wrong, Mr. Winchester?"

"Yes. I—I want you to—put a call, a long-distance call in fer me to—"

"Where? Mr. Winchester. Oh, I'm so sorry."

"To the courthouse at Crawford."

"The courthouse?"

"Yes," he panted, almost out of breath. "An' hurry. I—I want to talk to the man who grants marriage licenses." John felt as though he might explode any second. He rubbed his hands.

"I believe it's a woman who grants those, Mr. Winchester. I'll put your call in."

"Hurry," he frowned. He felt hot now. "You know, the justice of the peace or whoever—"

"All right, Mr. Winchester." Mrs. Sharon took the pencil from behind her left ear and started to ring. "Just a minute. Do you care to say who's involved in this?"

"That's what I don't know," he groaned. "I want to make sure."

While Mrs. Sharon was putting in the call, John paced the floor, clearing his throat, muttering constantly.

"Here you are, Mr. Winchester."

He took the receiver. His voice was so husky he spoke with considerable difficulty. "This is John Winchester. Yes. I'm here in Black Bend. Yes. I want to tell you that if anybody comes in—with a young lady—with blond hair—named Lucy Winchester, she's my daughter. Yes. If she comes in fer a marriage license, you're not to grant it. Lucy Winchester. She's my daughter. This is her—What? What? You say they've already been there? She was with a Hammon? What? Fifteen minutes ago?" John Winchester's right hand clumsily clutched the top of the wall telephone. "You say they're already married? You're tellin' me the truth?" he groaned with anger and agony he had never before experienced. "Yes—No," he panted. "That's all."

"Your Lucy is married?" asked Mrs. Sharon half apologetically, eyes widening.

John only sighed heavily, shook his head in painful, fearful unbelief, and left, forgetting to pay for the call.

When Mrs. Sharon saw how crushed he was, she shook her head also but asked no more questions. She knew in time she'd learn the whole story and someday remind him he owed her ten cents.

At home once more John Winchester dropped on a chair as though he had been running for miles and was completely exhausted. "She's married."

"Married?" Mrs. Winchester covered her mouth to stifle a scream. She swayed and Loretta caught her and begged her to sit down. "Who to, John? Are you sure?" Her face turned ashen.

"It's true," mumbled John. "To that Thomas Hammon. The rascal. Who else? Flossie, pour me a cup of coffee. I feel sick."

"Yes, Father. Don't you want something else?"

He shook his head as though he were too tired to talk. Flossie and Loretta were crying and the younger children clustered around their mother wide-eyed and frightened, expecting the worst. But to their amazement Father held his peace. He simply shook his head to their questions. They had never seen him like this. He refused to discuss the matter with anyone, even Maggie. His extreme quietness alarmed her. After John left the house, she asked Loretta to take her upstairs.

"What for, Mom?"

"I want to know what's missin'."

Upstairs they found very little missing.

"She left everything but her blue-and-white gingham dress, Mom. She can't be married. If she was, why didn't she take everything with her?"

"Maybe she's coming back to get them. Oh, Lucy," cried her mother. "Loretta, let me feel one of her dresses." She buried her face in it and sobbed. "Oh, Lucy, would you do a thing like this to me? How could you? How could you when you know I need you so?"

"Don't cry like that, Mom," begged Loretta. "I'm here. You're not alone."

"I know. I know," sobbed Mrs. Winchester, "but Lucy's been such a comfort to me. Take me down. It's cold up here. Oh, Loretta, wherever she is, she can't be warm in that old brown coat of hers. Look and see if it's gone."

"It's not here, Mom."

"Then I guess she took it."

CHAPTER 11

TOM KEPT his promise. After the marriage vows were pronounced by the justice of the peace in the courthouse, they went immediately to a book and stationery store and Lucy selected her Bible.

"Does it make you happy, my dear?"

"I'm simply thrilled, Tom. It's beautiful. Oh, how can I thank you enough?"

"Your happy smile is thanks enough for me, Lucy. Now we're going to a department store."

"It looks too grand, Tom. I've never been in a place like this." She hesitated.

"There's a first time for everything, Lucy. Come." He took her by the hand. Nor did he stop until she had two new house dresses, a beautiful silk one, material for a warm winter dress, and a navy coat which was a perfect fit.

"I'm so proud of you, Lucy," beamed Tom. "There's not a man in Crawford with a wife half as beautiful as you. No one would ever guess what you're carrying in that fancy pink paper." He squeezed her arm. "Would they?"

"My Bible, my priceless birthday present."

"I kept my word, didn't I? And I will again. Now, we're going to a furniture store. Let's try that one across the street."

Tom let Lucy make the final decision on a stove, a table

with four chairs, a bed complete, a dresser, and a cupboard. Nor did they stop shopping until they had purchased bedding, towels, dishes, cooking utensils, lamps, a washtub full of groceries, and items too many to list.

Lucy felt like Alice in Wonderland. "Can we get it all in the wagon, Tom?"

"We've got to, darling."

They had been shopping all day. Lucy was so tired she could scarcely walk.

"We'll eat another good warm meal in a restaurant, my love, then strike for home. It's getting dark early and might get pretty cold for us."

"How far do we have to go?"

"Nine miles. Nine miles to talk and be happy and get better acquainted, darling, and love each other."

"Will we go straight to the Haffer place?"

"No. No, dear. It would get too late to unload and set things up tonight. Don't you worry about one little thing, Lucy dear. Your husband has everything planned." He kissed her affectionately. "We'll stay with Uncle Charlie's tonight. He and Aunt Susie will be waiting for us with open arms."

"But they don't even know me, Tom."

"Makes no difference, my love. I've been telling them all about you, what a sweet lovely young lady you are, and they won't be disappointed."

"You mean—they knew you were going to come and get me and take me off to get married?"

"Of course, Lucy. They seem like my real parents. I was left an orphan at eleven and they took me in. They've been wonderful to me. As soon as I was of age, Uncle Charlie started giving me wages. He taught me how to work and save and how to stretch a dollar."

"Oh, Tom." There was a special radiance on Lucy's face when she looked up at him. She grabbed his arm and held it. "You're just wonderful. I had no idea. I feel better knowing that you told them. Really I should have told mine too. Yes, Tom," she suddenly sobered. "I should have. Will they receive us with open arms? My parents? Oh, I wonder, Tom. I am afraid my father—"

"Don't fret about him, darling. What will be, will be. Remember, we're living our own life together now and we are not going to let anyone interfere."

They did receive Lucy with open arms. Uncle Charlie and Aunt Susie both kissed Lucy and congratulated Tom, and beaming all over, told him what a beautiful wife he had and how very fortunate he was. It was bedtime, but Aunt Susie served hot chocolate and fresh sweet rolls.

"You're just too good to us," exclaimed Lucy. "Shall I call you Aunt Susie too?"

"To be sure. Nothing would please me more. You are our new daughter-in-law."

What fun it was to fix up a little house and have dishes and a teakettle and a sugar bowl to call her own! What girl wouldn't be happy to be Mrs. Thomas Hammon? Lucy repeated it over and over countless times. And her very own beautiful Bible. No need to hide it. More than once when Tom came in he found Lucy reading.

"Happy girl?"

"Yes."

"Been happy all day, darling?"

"What would have made me unhappy?"

"I hope nothing, my dear." Tom wasn't certain, but one evening he thought he noticed a distant yearning in her soft blue eyes.

"I hope you won't get too lonesome here alone while I'm working in the timber."

"I do get a little lonesome, Tom." Lucy smiled and he planted a kiss on her cheek.

Lucy had visited Sunny Creek Sunday school one Sunday out of four. When Sunday afternoon came Tom said he was tired and would rather rest. "You go on, Lucy, if you want to. I'd like you to stay here. But if you really want to go, go ahead."

"I wish we could go together," she remarked wistfully.

"The roof would fall in if I stepped inside."

"Why?"

"Because I've never been there. Uncle Charlie never went to church or Sunday school. He rested on Sundays."

"Rested playing cards?"

"Well, he didn't play cards all day, Lucy. That was rest from timber work."

"You'd enjoy going to Sunny Creek if you'd try it once, Tom."

"I would?"

"I'm sure you would."

"I'm sure I wouldn't, Lucy. You go on."

"But you said you'd rather I'd stay home with you."

"That's what I said. But you do as you want to, Lucy."

Lucy stayed at home.

One evening in late December when Tom came in with an armful of wood, he found Lucy reading her Bible and he could tell at once she had been crying.

"What's the matter, Lucy?"

"Nothing." She closed the Bible and started taking the prepared supper out of the warmer.

"But you've been crying, Lucy. Tell me what's wrong."

"It's nothing, Tom."

"But you're keeping something from me. I can't have that. We're to confide in each other about everything."

"Supper's ready. Come, let's eat."

"I will eat," answered Tom, "after you've told me what's troubling you. I don't like to come in and find my wife with red eyes."

"Well, then, Tom—it's like this. I love my Bible. I wanted it more than anything else in all the world. I love you dearly for getting it for me. But—"

"But what, Lucy? You are aggravating me."

"Every time I open it, it tells me how bad and mean I've been."

"Lucy," shouted Tom in disgust. "Stop reading it then. What's in that book that makes you feel what you know perfectly well you aren't? I won't have that book turning you into a depressed, sad, red-eyed wife. Come now. Let's eat. I'm hungry."

She handed him the potato dish.

"When did this queer reaction start, Lucy?" he asked eyeing her closely. "You mean each and every time you read that Bible you feel sad and bad and mean and all that?"

"No, Tom. I just found it today. I've been hunting and hunting."

"Hunting for something to make you feel mean? Lucy Hammon." He struck the table with the palm of one hand.

Lucy drew a long, deep breath. "Tom," she began, "let me tell you. The time I went to Black Bend one evening to hear that evangelist, Brother Bustleton, he read a verse I've never forgotten; but I couldn't remember exactly how it went. It says—I found it today—it says, *All we like sheep have gone astray; we have turned every one to his own way. . . ."*

"Lucy." Tom's voice was reprimanding and almost curt. "Now listen to me. I'm four years older than you are and you can take a little advice from me. You are acting very foolish about this. You are allowing yourself to be upset and unhappy over nothing. You put that Bible away someplace and forget it. Understand?"

Lucy bit her lip and looked down.

"Come, come," he insisted. "Start to eat. Come, I said. Take a bite."

"I will—I will, Tom. Just let me try to gather myself together. I feel a little squeamish in my stomach. I really did run off like a bad sheep. I can't forget Mom. I wonder so how she is."

"All right, all right, Lucy. Let's drive over there right after supper and find out how your mother is."

A new idea came to her. Would Tom let her invite them all over for a meal? He said he'd do anything to make her happy. They had plenty in the house to eat. She turned the idea over in her mind.

"Tom," she ventured, looking him full in the face, "may I invite my folks over for supper some evening?"

"When?" He looked up in surprise.

"Whenever you say, Tom."

"Do you think they'd come? Come here and eat with the man they refused to allow to date their daughter?"

"I don't know, Tom," remarked Lucy thoughtfully. "You said we could drive over to see them right after supper. I could ask them then."

"Did you think I meant that, Lucy?" His voice startled

her. It was almost icy.

"You mean you didn't?"

"Seriously now, Lucy. Did you think I actually meant what I said?" He laughed.

"Why, Tom," cried Lucy. Her voice was hurt, wounded. "I thought you always meant everything you ever told me." She was fighting tears. "Everything, Tom. Oh, I did. I did."

Chapter 12

LUCY WAS pleasantly surprised one afternoon when Mrs. Fetherstone called on her.

"Have you seen your mother lately, Lucy?"

"I'm terribly sorry to tell you I haven't seen Mom since—" Lucy's cheeks warmed. She could feel the color creeping to the surface.

Did Mrs. Fetherstone know?

"Since when, dear?"

"I hate to say this, Mrs. Fetherstone," she answered with apparent difficulty and looking momentarily at the floor, "but it's true." She pressed two fingers over her lips. "I'm guilty of leaving home without saying good-bye. I—I slipped out at night. You haven't heard?" When Lucy looked up, her eyes were sad, speaking all her regrets.

"I heard something about it, Lucy, but one never knows if the story is straight, coming from this one and that one. Now I didn't come here to press you into telling me anything you don't care to of your own free will."

"Tom persuaded me, Mrs. Fetherstone," began Lucy studying the pattern on the wallpaper. "He was twenty-two. I was eighteen. But even so," she drew a long breath and leaned back in her chair, "I would feel better in my heart if I had told Mom." Lucy tried desperately to control her emotions. "I keep wondering about her. She's almost constantly on my mind. It bothers me more than I want anyone to know. Have you seen her lately?"

"Yes, dear. I stopped by last Thursday. I don't want to frighten you but she looks bad."

"Oh, Mrs. Fetherstone, how?" Lucy clutched at her throat.

"She looks so tired. So thin. And she had such a look of despair on her face. Maybe I shouldn't be telling you this, Lucy, but I thought you ought to know."

"It's—it's because of me, I fear." Lucy's tears had to come. They were uncontrollable.

"I didn't come to make you feel that bad, Lucy. Don't cry, please. Really I've been wanting to call on you just to keep in touch. And to tell you your mother would love to see you."

"Did she ask about me? Did she say she wanted to see me? Did she tell you I could come home?" Lucy said all this in one unbroken breath.

"She definitely wants to see you, Lucy." Mrs. Fetherstone shifted on her chair and twisted the chain on her pocketbook around her one finger. "I'm sure she loves you dearly, Lucy."

"Oh, I know she does," agreed Lucy through her tears. "We were very close to each other. But Father, what about him? Did Mom say?"

"I can't answer about him, Lucy. It might be best to slip home sometime when he's not there. You know him better than I do."

Lucy bent forward and covered her face in both hands, then stepped to the bedroom and returned with a handkerchief. "Mrs. Fetherstone, why is my father so hard to understand? I just don't understand him. If—he—could—always be like he was a few times—but—" Lucy shook her head.

"Listen, Lucy. You've shed enough tears. I came to tell you something else too. You remember Brother Bustleton?"

"Of course."

"Well, he's coming back to Black Bend to hold another week of special meetings in the schoolhouse."

"Really? Excuse me just a minute. I've got to wash my face. Tom doesn't like to come in and find me with red or teary eyes." She was soon back from the kitchen. "When is he coming?"

"He starts tomorrow night. I wondered if you knew about it."

"I hadn't heard. It's wonderful news. I'd love to go."

"Then I'll stop by for you. We'll go together. You know that man never stopped asking about you after you got up the way you did and went out that night. My dear child, everybody was startled."

"I had to meet Father, Mrs. Fetherstone. I didn't dare make him wait."

"I figured that. But as I was saying, you remember Brother Bustleton told you his wife's name is Lucy."

"I remember."

"I wonder if he'll know you this time. You've grown so tall and you're so womanly. My, my, Lucy, what wonders six or more years can do to a girl! Well, I shouldn't stay long. I'll stop by tomorrow night. As for me, I'm going to drop everything and go every night. He's a wonderful evangelist and is so sincere and—well, how shall I say it—just good about making the Scriptures plain. They simply come alive when he preaches. So long now. You'll be ready at seven fifteen. I'll try to be prompt unless the roads get too bad."

"You know," Lucy followed Mrs. Fetherstone to the door, "I hardly know what Tom will say about me going."

"You mean he might object?"

"I'm not sure. He might."

"Well, tell him he's invited too. Tell him I'm giving him a special invitation. You mean he might have to be coaxed?"

"He might, Mrs. Fetherstone. Or I might have to coax him to let me go."

"Well, I'll tell you, Lucy. I missed going to church for fifteen years on account of Mack objecting. The best fifteen years of my married life. But one day I came to this conclusion, that I couldn't afford to miss heaven on account of my husband. It was hard at first to spunk up and go by myself, but I got so hungry to be with God's people, and I got so anxious to know the truth about my soul's destination I had to strike out alone. I finally found what I needed for my peace of heart and mind. This is an individual matter. It's a personal thing, Lucy. Nobody can find God for me or for you. I have to answer to Him for my own deeds, not Mack's. So now I go every chance I get. I marked the verse in my Bible where it says *unless we are willing to leave all, father or mother, son or daughter, to follow Him we are not even worthy to be called His followers.* I noticed you have a Bible there on the table."

"Oh, yes. Isn't it lovely? Tom got it for me on my birthday."

"Then surely he wouldn't object if you'd go to the meetings, would he? Bless your heart, Lucy. Tom must be a good husband."

"Oh, he is, Mrs. Fetherstone. He's a wonderful provider and a real worker too. We love each other very much."

Lucy got ready. Tom objected at first but finally said she could go.

"Tom." Lucy threw her arms around his neck. "Thanks for saying I may go. You remember what you promised me, don't you? I'll come straight home when the meeting closes. Bye, Tom." She kissed him.

He returned her smile with a slight tinge of guilt.

Lucy ran out to meet Mrs. Fetherstone.

For some time Tom stood at the kitchen window looking at the long gray shadows slowly turning black. How sweet, how young and radiant, how fresh and beautiful Lucy looked when she threw her arms around him. But why was she so anxious to go to listen to some preacher he didn't know? What kind of character was this man that women were so eager to go hear? Why had he made such foolish promises and so hastily? Jealous? But who wouldn't be with a wife as beautiful, as charming, as sweet-natured as Lucy?

She could talk of nothing else at the breakfast table.

"I've just got to go again tonight, Tom. It was wonderful helping all those people sing. And then the sermon. Tom, I wish you would have been there with me."

"Really?" he sipped coffee with disinterest.

"Yes, really. Won't you go along tonight?"

"No."

"Tomorrow night?"

"No."

"It doesn't last so late."

"But when I come in, I like to sit down and enjoy my home. We have it cozy and comfortable; so why not stay here and appreciate it? Together?"

"Would you object if I went tonight with Mrs.

Fetherstone?"

Tom picked at the meat on his plate. Slowly he spread a slice of bread.

"You're not answering me. Please, may I go?"

"If you go, Lucy," he said almost peevishly, "it will be without my consent. Uncle Charlie never brought me up on such stuff."

Tom did not finish his supper. Lucy got ready, but when she left, Tom would not tell her good-bye. She went with a heavy heart.

The next night Lucy walked to Black Bend Schoolhouse, in spite of Tom's objecting.

"Lucy," he remarked tersely the fifth night as he watched her put on her pretty navy coat, "I did not know I was marrying a gadabout."

"I wouldn't leave you for any other reason but to go to church, Tom. I've got to settle this one night before those meetings close."

"Settle what?" demanded Tom angrily.

"I mean, make a choice."

"A choice?" he snapped. "Between me and that lousy preacher over there who has you hypnotized?"

"No! No, Tom. You got me all wrong. I must choose between myself and you and God."

"Me and God! Lucy!" he panted. "Are you going out of your mind?"

"I might if I don't settle this, Tom. I can't go on like this any longer. It's eating my heart out."

"What's eating your heart out? Talk sense to me, Lucy."

"This condemnation, Tom," cried Lucy. "This burden of sin I've been carrying around."

"What sin?"

"My own sins, Tom. Not yours or anyone else's. I love you, Tom. You've been a wonderful husband to me. I love you more than any human being on earth. But I love God more."

"More than me, you say?" Tom's eyes looked bloodshot. He sniffed. He ran one hand nervously through his hair.

"I love you with all my heart, soul, and mind, Tom. But—"

"It sure looks like it, running off night after night and leaving me here alone." The palm of his hand went down on the table increasing his seething temper. "Don't you think I get lonesome with no one to talk to?"

"I asked you to go along with me."

"But I don't want to go into that crowd. You know I don't care for crowds."

"It's a delightful place to go, Tom. The people are all friendly and listen very well. It's wonderful."

"Must be," he snapped sarcastically. "Sure must be. But it makes me jealous, you going off night after night to hear that great, wonderful hypnotist preacher. Well, I want you to know I'm jealous. And I have a perfect right to be." He was shaking now. He picked up his cap and threw it across the kitchen. It almost landed on the stove.

"God's been jealous of me for a long time, Tom." Lucy was trying to remain calm. "He demands my first love. My complete devotion and obedience. I plan to make my decision tonight."

"After all I've done for you," he yelled. "Now you turn against me for no reason at all."

"No. Never, Tom. I'll never love you less or turn against you. This will make me a better wife than I have been."

"It's not true, Lucy," shouted Tom unbuttoning his shirt

collar. "You are turning against me. I never, never, never supposed you'd treat me like this."

"I'll prove to you, Tom, that I'm not turning against you. The meetings will soon be over and you'll see how much I love you. You promised the day we got married I could go to church all I pleased and I went only one time to Sunny Creek because you wanted me to stay home. This is different."

"Yes, it's different. You said it! It's worse because you leave me at night—and night after night after night. I don't think you really love me, Lucy, or you'd stay at home like a good wife should."

"Oh, Tom, dear." Lucy flung her arms around his neck and looked pleadingly up into his drawn face. "I do love you. Truly I do."

He pushed her away. "I can't believe you mean what you say."

"Lucy," called Mrs. Fetherstone.

She opened the door. "I'll be right out."

When Lucy got home she found the house dark. She called. No answer. She lit the oil lamp and carried it to the bedroom. Tom was not in bed. She went to the living room, put the lamp on the table beside her Bible, and sat down to think.

Perhaps after all she should have stayed at home. Tom had never abused her in any way. She had vexed him. Never had she seen him so worked up. So hurt. Surely he cared for her very much. The only disagreement they had ever had was on the subject of religion. Oh, where was Tom?

An hour passed. Lucy was beginning to feel sick. What if he'd never come back? Repeatedly she looked out the west window, then the back door. "Oh, Tom, Tom," she cried out loud.

"Be not deceived; God is not mocked: for whatsoever a man soweth, that shall he also reap." The passage Brother Bustleton had used for his sermon two hours ago was repeated over and over in her mind. Was she going through this soul agony about Tom now because she ran off and hurt her own dear mother?

Oh! No! God, it couldn't be. I didn't leave Mom all alone. She had Flossie, Loretta, Kenneth, Floyd, Peggy, and Father. O God! This would be far worse if Tom didn't come back.

O God, bring him back so I can tell him I'm sorry I hurt him. But if I hadn't gone tonight, I wouldn't have made my decision. O God, I was so happy when I went forward and took Brother Bustleton's hand and took You into my heart as my own personal Saviour. You gave me such peace. Don't let me lose it now.

Another hour passed. Another long fear-filled hour of struggling and praying, until at last Lucy felt the presence of the Lord surrounding her like a soft, warm blanket. She sat exhausted—but calm, waiting, waiting.

The door opened.

"Oh, Tom!" cried Lucy running to him with outstretched arms. "I'm so glad you're back. Oh, so glad, Tom."

"Oh, you are, are you?"

Lucy smelled something very peculiar on Tom's breath.

"Where have you been, Tom?" She took hold of his coat lapels and searched his face. His eyes were bleary and his eyelids droopy.

"What does it matter to you where I've been?"

"It matters a great deal, Tom."

His strange cracked laugh frightened her.

"Let me help you take your coat off. Come, sit down, Tom. Let's talk." She led him to a chair in the living room.

"So you're ready to talk? Well." His head wobbled. "Talk then. But not about that wonderful meeting and that wonderful preacher. None of that."

Lucy moved her chair close and sat beside him. She held his one hand in both of hers. "Did you go to town, Tom?"

"Yes. Where else could I go when you left me alone?"

"Have you been drinking?" She put her face close to his. No answer.

"Tom," she touched his one cheek.

He drew back. "It's all your fault, Lucy. I never touched drink until tonight. You—"

"Oh, Tom," she shuddered. "How is it my fault?"

"You drove me to it." His lower jaw twitched. "Yes, you did, Lucy. I'm not drunk. I'm not. I know what I'm saying. And I'm not sick—but—I'm hurt—and I want to go to bed."

"I'll help you, dear." Lucy's heart was pounding violently and the cords in her neck tightened. She helped him undress and get into bed. Sinking on her knees beside him she stroked his forehead with tenderness.

"Forgive me for hurting you, Tom," she whispered. "Really, truly, I love you with all my heart. I'll be true to you as long as I live. You've been good to me and I'll tell everybody that. I want to make you happy, Tom. But I had to go tonight to make my decision."

Tom turned his face toward the wall. "I said not to talk about that junk."

"All right, Tom. I won't. But will you take me over home

115

someday to see my mother?"

"What for?"

"I just want to tell her I'm sorry—"

"Sorry you married me?" His voice was thick, sullen. He pulled the blanket over his mouth.

"No. No, Tom. Sorry I went off like I did."

"Indeed you won't tell her that." He lifted his head on one elbow and stared at her angrily. "That would be the same as saying you're sorry you married me."

"Oh, no, Tom. You take me wrong. I mean, I'm sorry I didn't ask her first or tell her about you when all the while I knew she'd be hurt. Mrs. Fetherstone told me she's grieving and—and looks so old and thin and sad. Don't you see what I mean, Tom?"

"Like a blind bat, Lucy." He dropped his head. "I'd still be waiting for you if you had to ask them first. They're unreasonable, selfish, and—and—oh, Lucy, my head hurts. Get a cold rag and let me sleep."

She kissed him on the forehead, then on the lips. "I'll do it, dear. I'll prove to you I love you."

"If you don't love me more than you do your folks," his breath came in huge bunches, "and that preacher and—and that Bible of yours—you'll never prove it to me."

Lucy lay awake all night.

Mrs. Fetherstone stopped for Lucy the next evening.

"I can't go tonight," called Lucy from the back door.

"You can't?"

"No, Mrs. Fetherstone. Tom's not feeling well and I'm staying at home with him."

"That's too bad, Lucy. Hope you can go along tomorrow night."

"I'll see. Thanks for stopping."

CHAPTER 13

ONE AFTERNOON while Tom was in the timber Lucy decided to walk through the snow to Black Bend Schoolhouse. The pleasant-faced teacher answered her knock.

"Good afternoon. I suppose you're the mother of one of my pupils. Come in."

Lucy stepped in the vestibule. "I'm Mrs. Hammon. I'm Peggy Winchester's sister. Is she here today?"

"Yes. Shall I call her out or do you want to step in?"

"Will you please call her out?"

"Certainly."

"Peggy." Before she had a chance to see who it was, Lucy was hugging her and showering her with kisses. "How are you, Peggy?"

"Why, Lucy. Where did you come from?"

"Home. We're living on the Haffer place. Oh, I just had to come and see you. How's Mom?"

"She's not so good."

"How do you mean?"

"Well, I don't know how to tell you, but she sits and cries a lot."

"Why? Can you tell me, Peggy? Oh, I'm so sorry to hear this. Why does she cry?"

"I'm not sure about everything she cries about but I think it's mostly because Father won't take her to see you.

She begs him almost every day."

"Oh, Peggy," cried Lucy half sobbing. "What else can you tell me?"

"What about?"

"About Mom. Are her eyes worse?"

"They're as worse as they can get, I think."

"Oh, my. Poor soul. Do you know when Father's going to take a load of wood or ties to town?"

"No. He never tells us when he's going. Mom wants someone to send you word to come home to see us all, but—" Peggy shrugged and shook her head.

"Father won't have it?"

"Guess that's it. Father's real peeved at you, the way you went off in secret. He wouldn't even talk to any of us for about a week."

"Listen. Tell me, are Loretta and Flossie good to Mom?"

Peggy shrugged her shoulders.

"Do they do up the work all right?"

'Well, not the way you did it. The house isn't very straightened up sometimes, but Mom can't see it. Father fusses sometimes about their cooking, but we get along all right—I mean pretty good."

"But the girls aren't real kind to Mom?"

"Well," Peggy twisted her belt and frowned, "not as kind as you were."

"Is that what makes her cry?"

"I guess it's part of it."

"What else?"

"I don't know exactly. Seems she wants to talk to you about something. Because whenever Father tells her to quit crying so much, she always says, 'Well, if I could only have a good talk with Lucy, maybe I could.' "

"Oh, Peggy." And Lucy folded her sister once more in her arms. "When you get home tonight, tell Mom when no one else is around; whisper to her, Peggy, and tell her I'd write her a letter if she could only read it."

"I could read it to her."

"Well, I didn't bring any along. But tell her you saw me and I asked about her and tell her I love her like I always did and tell her I'm real sorry I couldn't tell her good-bye when I left. Oh, Peggy, I can't stay any longer or I'll cry. Wipe your eyes. Don't let the children in there know you had tears or they'll wonder. Are Kenneth and Floyd in school today?"

"Just Floyd. Kenneth quit to help Father with the wood."

"Oh, my. That's a shame. He was too young to quit school."

"But Father's arms hurt. I guess he's got rheumatism or something. He groans a lot."

"Well, listen, honey, don't tell Floyd what all I've told you. Will you? And all you've told me. Will you?"

"Not if you tell me not to."

"Good girl. Just tell him I asked about the family. Go back in now and maybe someday, if my prayers are answered, I can have you over to spend a week with me."

"Oh, Lucy," smiled Peggy. "I'd like that." And she reached up and kissed Lucy on the lips.

"Tell Mom I'm praying for her too. I know how, Peggy, because I'm a Christian now."

"A what?"

"I accepted Christ one night right in this very schoolhouse. When Brother Bustleton was here holding meetings."

"Oh." Peggy's mouth hung open with blank incomprehension.

Before Lucy left, she peeked through the crack of the swinging door into the schoolroom and caught a glimpse of Floyd. "Tell Floyd hello for me."

"I will. 'Bye, Lucy. I'm so glad you came."

"So am I, dear."

Later at home Lucy answered a knock at the door. She invited Brother Bustleton to come in, but she wouldn't invite him to sit down. His stay might last too long and Tom would soon be coming in from the timber and she should be starting supper.

"Brother Bustleton, I know you're here to find out why I've missed coming."

"You haven't given up then?"

"Oh, no, Brother Bustleton. Indeed not. My experience means more to me than that. My husband hasn't been feeling well."

"Tomorrow is our last night, you know."

"So soon?"

"I have an urgent invitation to begin meetings in Ashville; so I must be leaving. I came to find out if you wouldn't like to be baptized tomorrow night. Several others have requested baptism before I leave."

Lucy hesitated. "I'd like to be."

"You understand what baptism is, don't you? It's not for salvation but for an outward sign of your inward cleansing."

"I know."

"Then you'll be there with the others?"

"If I can, Brother Bustleton, I'll be there. I'm not sure my husband will agree to my leaving. I'll have to consult with him."

"I see. Well, Lucy, maybe if I could talk to him, I could convince him how important this is to you."

"Oh, no, Brother Bustleton." Lucy's face showed her alarm. "Please don't try to talk to him here. If you should meet him on the road by accident, it would be different. But not here. I can't take time to explain any more now." He noticed Lucy glancing frequently toward the road. "If I'm not there tomorrow night, it won't be that I've turned back or didn't want to come."

"I see. Well, I'll be on my way then. Remember what the Bible says, 'He that believeth and is baptized shall be saved.' You do believe and the obeying follows with the baptism. You see, they go hand in hand. You'll miss a real blessing and an essential act of obedience if you put off your baptism."

"I know, Brother Bustleton."

" 'To him that knoweth to do good, and doeth it not, to him it is sin.' I'll go now. And hope to see you tomorrow night."

Tom opened the door and closed it with a bang.

"So you had company, didn't you, Lucy?" His lip twitched with anger.

Lucy was at the stove frying potatoes. "Who do you mean?"

"You know very well who I mean. I met that contemptible preacher down the road. Where was he if he wasn't here?"

"Did he tell you he was here?"

"I didn't ask him. But I'll bet he was. Confess, Lucy. He was, wasn't he?"

"Yes, Tom, he was. But only for a few minutes. He didn't even sit down because I didn't ask him to."

"Well, what did he want? Answer me, Lucy." Tom grabbed her by one arm until his fingernails dug into her flesh. She flinched a little.

"Please, Tom, don't be angry with me. I didn't know he was coming. He stopped to tell me tomorrow night will be the last service and—"

"He wanted to know why you missed a couple of his precious sermons. Am I right?"

"Well—yes."

"That's none of his business."

"Well, according to his calling he thinks it is." It was next to impossible for Lucy to keep from acting excited.

"I'm mad, Lucy," Tom shouted. "I wouldn't want to slap you but I am mad. That man had no business calling on my wife when I'm not here. How often has this happened and I never knew it?"

"This was the first time, Tom. I tell you the truth."

Tom looked Lucy straight in the eyes. "Are you telling me the truth?"

"I have never told you an untruth, have I?"

Slowly his grip on her arm loosened. "Not that I know of." He stepped to the opposite side of the kitchen and looked at her searchingly. There was a new flushed radiance in her sincere open face, more appealing than he had ever noticed before, and he hadn't come in and found her crying for days.

"And, Tom." She looked at him with the face of a healthy, happy child who had never known anything but trusting love, security, and peace. He held his breath. He had never seen her more beautiful. Some blessed illumination he could not describe seemed to envelop her. "Tom, dear," she said, "you'll believe me now when I tell you

God's truth, that Brother Bustleton is interested in nothing more than my soul. I have a soul, Tom, that will never die. It will live on and on and on forever—for all eternity and Brother Bustleton's only one of God's messengers to help people like me get ready to die and go to be with the Lord someday. Oh, Tom, you'll believe me, won't you?"

He stood speechless.

"Well," he said at long length, "when you tell me like that and look at me the way you do—I guess I'll have to believe you. But," he started to wash his hands, "I'm still jealous and I can't help it."

The next evening Mrs. Fetherstone stopped once more for Lucy.

"No," decided Lucy, "I'm not going tonight." She closed the door.

Tom smiled a smile of triumph.

But the next minute Mrs. Fetherstone opened the door and stepped inside.

"Well, Tom," she exclaimed beaming on him, "I see you're up. Feeling better tonight?"

Tom looked embarrassed. He was embarrassed.

"You haven't had your supper yet? Well, I was hoping you'd go with me for the last night, Lucy. I'll wait till you've eaten. We might miss the song service but I'll wait. You know the last night's going to be the best. There's going to be a number baptized and that's always such an impressive service. It's not so cold tonight. You two surely have a nice little home here. Tom, you're blessed with a good wife. I'll step in the next room and wait for you, Lucy. Don't let me spoil your supper, Tom. You're looking real well. I hope you feel as good as you look."

Lucy took a few bites, all the while searching Tom's

bewildered, annoyed expression. There was no question that he was more than embarrassed. He looked as though he wanted to explode.

"What do you say, Tom?" asked Lucy hesitatingly and very softly.

Mrs. Fetherstone called from the next room. "She's waiting for you to tell her to hurry and get ready, isn't she, Tom?" She followed her question with a short laugh. "You aren't going to object, are you, Tom? Tonight's the last service."

Tom swallowed hard. With extreme difficulty he swallowed his pride, his fury, his jealousy, his indignation, and said in a yeasty tone, "Go on, Lucy. Get ready."

It was Lucy now who was embarrassed. She knew Tom did not want her to go. She watched him stare at his half-filled plate. He hadn't eaten a bite. He looked as though he wanted to cry but was too angry. His eyelids twitched and he pressed two fingers hard against his one temple.

Mrs. Fetherstone stepped into the kitchen and punctured the silence. "We'd best be going, Lucy. I tell you, Tom, Lucy's young only once. I missed out when I was her age and I regret it to this day. Meetings such as we've been having are the source of all my joy."

He watched Lucy leave with Mrs. Fetherstone. He saw her turn around and look at him before she closed the door. Why did he allow that woman to come into his house and overpower him? She too must possess some hypnotic influence. Why did he listen to her and just sit there like a crazy fool and watch Lucy leave? He despised himself for it. His penetrating thoughts tore his body with explosive force. His head ached. His eyes became swirling pools of green hideous misery. Revenge got him to his feet, pulled on his overcoat, smashed his cap over his ears, blew out the light, and sent him to the barn muttering words not fit for publication.

At the schoolhouse Brother Bustleton shook Lucy's hand and blessed her for coming. That evening three women, a man, and a young boy were baptized with Lucy.

"And now, Lucy," said Brother Bustleton, "I'll say good-bye. God bless you and make His face shine upon you and give you peace. And remember, pray for me that I'll help other souls find peace in Christ Jesus; and I'll pray for you. Be sure to read your Bible every day and remain steadfast no matter what comes. You'll have trials, but Christ was tempted in every way possible to man and He understands each of us. Remember, it's the last mile of the way that counts. Many start out and give up, but be true, Lucy."

"That's what I want to be, Brother Bustleton."

CHAPTER 14

A S LUCY feared, she found the house dark again. She was determined not to let herself be overcome this time with frantic imaginations. Hadn't she left the baptismal service with that miraculous sense of being united with Christ? Didn't she come home with full assurance all her sins were forgiven, blotted out forever, leaving her with a deep settled peace? She would not be upset. She would not wring her hands or make countless trips to the window and the door. She would not submit to tears but wait calmly and count her blessings.

She put wood in the stove and started a pot of fresh coffee. Tom would be cold and hungry when he returned. If she smelled liquor, she determined not to scold him, or say one word to irritate him or hurt his sensitive feelings. She would make every effort to prove her love and fidelity. She cleared the table, swept the floor, and set down two clean cups and saucers.

From her Bible she took out the tracts Brother Bustleton distributed to everyone who had been to the last service. She pulled her chair closer to the stove and read the blue printed sheet.

Humility is perpetual quietness of heart. It is to have no trouble. It is never to be fretted or vexed or irritated, never disappointed. It is to expect nothing done against me. It is to be at rest when nobody praises me, and when I am blamed or despised. It is to have a blessed home in myself where I can go in and shut the door and kneel to my Father in secret and be at rest and peace, as in a deep sea of calmness when all around and above me is trouble.

Lucy read the blue sheet once more and sat in deep meditation. "Dear Lord," she breathed, "help me have this humility when my dear Tom comes home."

She hurried to the window. She was certain she heard men's voices. She dashed to the kitchen door and looked out. A new light snow was falling. Two men, each on a horse, were nearing the house. One jumped off and ran up the steps. Lucy opened before he knocked.

"Are you Mrs. Hammon, ma'am? The man's voice was throaty. He removed his snowy cap and leaned heavily on the door casing with one hand.

"Yes." A chill made Lucy grab at her heart. Sudden fear took hold of her.

"Well, ma'am—your husband's had a bad accident."

"What?" gasped Lucy. Her lips lost their color. "Where?"

"At Black Bend Tavern, ma'am."

"When?" Lucy swayed but caught herself.

"A while ago, Mrs. Hammon. I hated to come to tell you but I knew someone had to."

"Tell me," cried Lucy, "what happened?"

"Well, it was like this, ma'am." The man kept rolling his cap around his one hand. He acted extremely nervous and had to cough phlegm from his throat repeatedly. "We were all havin' a good time playin' around an' drinkin' an' Lew Sailor jes' got too full. He didn't know right what he was doin' an' first thing we knew"—at this point the man on the second horse came up to the door—"well, he an' Joe Black got into a fight. All over nothin', ma'am. Your Tom

127

saw how Joe was alayin' it on to Lew pretty hard an' Tom—he stepped in to help Lew. Then is when your husband got hit."

"Tell me. Is he hurt real bad?" Lucy was nearly breathless.

"Pretty bad, Mrs. Hammon," put in the second man. "Lew's a big man an' orful strong when he's drunk. He thought Tom got up to help Joe. 'Twasn't that way 'tall."

"When that Lew Sailor is full," remarked the first man still rolling his cap, "he's as strong as a lion. Loses all his senses. He up an' gave Tom a blow with his fist right on the back of his neck, then he picked up a bottle off the bar an' hit him one on the head."

"Oh, no!" cried Lucy. "How is he? Tell me!"

"Sorry, ma'am, but we're afraid your Tom is dead."

"Oh!" screamed Lucy. "No! No! It can't be my Tom is dead. Are you sure he's dead?"

"Sorry, ma'am. We worked over him till we saw 'twas no use. He was knocked right out. Never knew what happened. He—he didn't suffer none, ma'am."

Lucy would have fallen but some unseen hand held her. "Take me to him," she cried. "Please take me."

The first man on the porch shifted on his snowy shoes and glanced at the second who shook his head. "It's pretty cold, ma'am. You'd better stay here. We are on horseback. The tavern's no fit place for you nohow. Can't we go get someone to come over an' stay here with you till the coroner—you know? Ain't you got folks nearby who'd come if we went an' told 'em?"

"Do you"—Lucy was shaking now until her teeth chattered—"you—know where the Morehouse place is?"

"Yes."

"If Mrs. Morehouse could come—I'd appreciate it. Or my Aunt Polly, Mrs. Jake Bechtold."

"I know where they live too. An' your folks? How 'bout them?"

Lucy shook her head. "Mother is blind and Father's not too well."

In a daze Lucy staggered from room to room, crying softly. *Why, oh, why did she leave Tom tonight? If she'd stayed at home, this never would have happened. She wanted to scream. Was this her punishment for going against his wishes? Oh, would God forever hold this against her?*

She was responsible for Tom getting killed. Killed! By the blow of a drunk man! Tom had never taken a drink until she aggravated him. What was this malicious intent crushing the very life out of her? And who would come to her assistance? Who could? Who would ever faintly understand her situation?

She sank like a rag on the chair by the stove. The fire was almost out and she hadn't noticed. Corkie. Poor dear Corkie. Her first experience with death. Her sweet little lamb she had called him. Oh, how it hurt when he was taken from her. The only person who understood her longing child heart. And now she was a woman, a married woman so short a while. What monster, what liquor-filled monster did the fates allow to snatch her own dear Tom from her! She was completely falling apart.

The tract. The thin blue printed sheet. Lucy took it from her Bible and wiping her eyes, read it once more.

Before Uncle Charlie and Aunt Susie arrived, Lucy had found a measure of peace from the tract. She recalled several Scripture passages Brother Bustleton had given from memory. *I will never leave thee, nor forsake thee. The Lord is my shepherd. Let not your heart be troubled.* She must face this terrible blow, this unspeakable grief, knowing God allowed it. She must trust Him. She would trust Him. But it hurt. Oh, how it hurt! Fresh hot tears streamed down her swollen face. Her limp body must be a bottomless well of tears. If she could only run to Mom and cry. Maybe Father will be glad when he hears this. She groaned. Where was that calm? Why couldn't she hold on to it? It was slipping through her fingers.

The little home. So cozy and clean and comfortable. The pretty new stove, the dishes, the table where they faced each other to eat. The colorful throw rugs, the warm covers on the bed, the chickens. O God! It was all turning to cold dead ashes before her eyes. Who wants a cozy house which isn't shared? No husband! No love!

"Oh, Lucy, my dear." Aunt Susie took Lucy in her arms. "We just can't believe it's true. You poor dear girl."

"I'm going to see to it that that Lew Sailor gets his just dues, so I am, Lucy."

"No, Uncle Charlie. Please don't try it. I'm sure the man didn't realize what he was doing. And it wouldn't bring Tom back. When he comes to himself, I'm sure he'll be ashamed and sorry."

"You mean we're to just let a man like that go unpunished?"

"Uncle Charlie," said Lucy sadly, "his own guilty conscience may be all the punishment he needs."

"We came to stay all night with you, dear," said Aunt Susie patting Lucy gently on the shoulder. "You look so tired and worn. Can I get you a glass of warm sweetened milk or something?"

"No, Aunt Susie. I'm not at all hungry. On the stove is a fresh pot of coffee. You and Uncle Charlie have some. I fixed it especially for Tom. I knew he'd be cold when he came home." Lucy shook with sobs.

"Why did he go to Black Bend anyhow?" asked Aunt Susie.

"Oh, Aunt Susie," Lucy looked too exhausted to talk. "I don't know what to tell you. I'm so, so tired. If you don't mind, I'll lie down a while."

"You just do that, my dear. We'll be right here if you want anything at all."

Lucy closed her eyes, talking to God. She turned her heart wrong side out. *Take it, Lord, sweep it, wash it, mend it, and put it back where it belongs. Oh, I'm so terribly tired.*

She had just fallen asleep when there was a knock at the door. She dressed and stepped into the kitchen. Uncle Charlie, Aunt Susie, and Jake Bechtold were talking furiously in undertones. "Lucy," Uncle Jake took her in his arms. "This is awful. Simply awful! Here's a letter from Aunt Polly."

Dear Lucy,

You poor dear child. Can it be true? I've been wanting to come to see you but I've been down on my back for four months now with rheumatism. It's very painful. Please come along home with Uncle Jake and stay here with us. Lock up your house and come. We need someone to work for us and there's no one we'd rather have around. You can decide later what to do with your things and all. Uncle Jake will help you. Please, dear, I know how

hard it must be for you, but try to brace up.
Remember the Lord's hand is not short to help you
in a time like this. And He never lets anything come
upon us but what we are able to bear by His help.
Do come.

> *With much love,*
> *Aunt Polly*

"What say, Lucy?"

"Help yourself to coffee, Uncle Jake. I'll gather my things together and go back with you."

"Tonight?" asked Aunt Susie with surprise.

"I think I should. Yes, tonight. I'd better be there with Aunt Polly while Uncle Jake takes charge of things for me. You two might as well go on home before the roads get drifted shut. I do so thank you for coming. I won't be long in getting ready, Uncle Jake."

"That's all right, Lucy. Don't hurry yourself. I came in the wagon and brought two warm blankets along. I brought them inside to warm up."

It was almost four o'clock when Lucy walked into Aunt Polly's bedroom.

"Oh, bless you, my dear girl. God bless you and comfort your dear heart."

Lucy knelt beside the bed and her head was on Aunt Polly's shoulder.

"He will, Aunt Polly. He has already. Oh, I'll never really understand why this had to happen but—oh, Aunt Polly, somehow I just must trust Him anyhow. There's no other thing to do or I'll lose my mind. Why is it you know the Lord, Aunt Polly, and Mom takes so little interest in spiritual things?"

"Well, you see, I was the youngest. For some reason our father never saw to it any of us got to church and he rested the horses on Sundays. When Father died, I was seven and your mother was about eighteen, already married. We moved half a mile from a little church in Landon Valley. A neighbor girl asked me to go along with her one Sunday and I liked it. My sisters never went but I kept on going. From the start I had a longing to know more about God. I just took to spiritual things. I see myself all over in you, Lucy. I'm the only one in our family who ever became a Christian, sorry to say."

"Aunt Polly, did you know Mabel? I saw a picture once; Father showed it to me. He said she was his only sister. Did you know her?"

"Only saw her once, Lucy. You favor her a great deal, I believe. As I recall, she had very pretty blond hair like yours. She died young—still in her teens, didn't she?"

"Father seems to think an awful lot of her picture. I can't understand him, Aunt Polly. I long to go home to see Mom, but I doubt if Father would let me in. Oh, why is he so hardhearted?"

"You know, Lucy, the last time I was over there, your mother actually told me she wished she could believe like I and you do."

"Oh, Aunt Polly, did she really? You know, I was baptized tonight at Black Bend."

"Not tonight, dear. You mean last night. We've started a new day. It's going to be morning soon. Please take off your shoes and lie down here beside me and rest. You dear precious girl, you look so weary."

"Oh, I am, Aunt Polly. I'm so tired I could almost die."

Lucy buried her face in her hands and shook with sobs.

"I want so much to go see Mom. Ever since the night I ran off and got married."

"Ran off?"

"You mean you never heard how I left?"

"No, child, no. I haven't been out of the house for months and months. No one's been here to tell us anything. Rest a while now, dear. We'll talk more later."

Uncle Jake looked after all the funeral arrangements. It was a great relief to Lucy. They decided since Aunt Polly was laid up, the service would be held in the Bechtold home. It was a cold blustery day, with winds piercing the heaviest overcoats. A dozen or more friends and a few strangers came. Among them were Mr. and Mrs. Fetherstone and Miss Basie, whose words of sympathy and comfort meant more to Lucy than all the expressions from the other people together.

Lucy had partially prepared herself for the great disappointment. Not one of her family came. But she was overwhelmed by grief when Uncle Jake told her he had seen her father in town that very morning and urged him—begged him to come and bring the family.

"I couldn't budge him, Lucy," he told her. "I said all I dared. But you just keep your chin up. Your father will have to pay for the way he's been acting. It'll all come out in the wash, you just see."

If Miss Basie hadn't sat by Lucy and held her hand and whispered words of comfort from the Bible, she would have collapsed completely at the funeral. Two things cut her like a double-edged sword: the absence of her parents and the fact that Tom was not prepared for death.

The night was still. The storm had blown itself out. The fields were white with a heavy mantle of snow sparkling like trillions of highly polished diamonds. Lucy stood at the window of her bedroom next to Aunt Polly's looking out over the stillness and took a long sober look at her tragedy. Tom—so young, so strong and handsome, good, kind, loving to her—buried in that cold, snow-covered ground.

In her hands she clasped the beautiful Bible—her birthday, her wedding, her most precious gift. It would always remind her of him and how happy he was to be able to please her with it. Yet it was the very thing—the only thing that became a wedge between them. How strange, how very strange life was. Without her Bible the tomorrows would be unbearable.

CHAPTER 15

IT WOULD be far from the truth to say Lucy lived in constant victory over her crushing blow. Repeatedly she read the blue printed essay on humility until she had it almost memorized. But invariably she admitted to God that she was falling short of perpetual quietness of heart, never to be disappointed, or never to wonder at what was done to her. She tried desperately to conceal the penetrating memories of that last week with Tom and the fears of a lonely future. Every night she told God she was resigned and at peace in her heart if this was God's will for her. But the ifs and the tears, the whys, the loneliness, the longings, and the sense of guilt became so enmeshed they sent Lucy to her knees beside her bed several times a day. No one but God would be allowed to step into her soul and know the naked truth about her sufferings. Uncle Jake and Aunt Polly need not know, should not know, must not know. So before she left her room, Lucy prayed, waited, and brushed away the mask of grief before she faced them. It was not easy.

Lucy proved to be a splendid nurse and housekeeper. Aunt Polly was more than gratified. She was delighted and told Lucy so many times. Before a month passed, Aunt Polly was able to be led to the table to eat. Lucy's cooking and baking whetted her appetite and energized her entire body. But Aunt Polly wasn't as blind to Lucy's silent grief as Lucy thought.

"Jake," she remarked one day, "haven't you noticed how sad and melancholy Lucy looks sometimes? Not often, but at times."

"Sure I have. But I marvel she doesn't look sad more often. I think it's nothing less than a miracle she's bracing up like she does. How many girls could be half as sweet and cheerful as she's been and step in here and take hold of the work like she's been doing? I think Lucy's a wonder."

"I believe her secret is right there in that bedroom where she is this minute. I think she knows it when her feelings come to the surface and she slips in there. Every time she comes out, she's had a lift. I can see it."

"Maybe you don't talk enough to her about it. Poor girl, maybe that's what she needs."

"Well, Jake, Lucy knows she can open up to me about anything on her mind anytime and I'll give a listening, sympathetic ear. We've discussed lots of things—lots of things, Jake, you know nothing about. Lucy's a brave, brave girl. I believe she's helped me more than I have her. She's told me a lot about her desires to live right and know God better and her struggles before she left home. She's shared with me her childhood dreams and frustrations over her father's attitudes and her longings to finish school and her concern for her mother. We've talked a lot."

"But she doesn't discuss Tom?"

"Seldom. I think she avoids mentioning his name because she doesn't want to break down. And you can depend on it, I'm not bringing him up to make it hard for her. Not me."

One warming winter forenoon Uncle Jake drove Lucy

over to her house in the spring wagon. He had asked Mrs. Fetherstone to meet them there to make it easier for Lucy and help them load her things.

"Will we get all her furniture and everything in your wagon?" asked Mrs. Fetherstone when Jake called on her.

"All Lucy has over there we'll easily get in my wagon if we load it right. You see Charlie Morehouse went over before the funeral and got Tom's horse and took Lucy's chickens over to his place. He's settling with her for that. They were very fond of Lucy from the start, you know. I'm not sure they were real happy about her going off to hear that preacher the way she did but they like Lucy."

"It's partly my doings Lucy went that last night," Mrs. Fetherstone admitted, "but I still believe I did the right thing. Our loyalty to God has to come first. He won't take second or third place. This might have happened to Tom if she'd never gone."

"Well," answered Jake Bechtold, his voice peppered with skepticism, "I'm not making no judgments or conclusions about nobody. We can't change that night nor what happened, but we can do what we can for Lucy now. She's done wonders for her Aunt Polly and the least I can do for her, I mean the best I can do for her, won't be good enough, if you get what I mean."

"I'll meet you at her place, Mr. Bechtold, and Mr. Fetherstone will be there too."

"Good. We can use him."

"Where's she taking her things?"

"Over to our place for the time being. She's got to vacate. The place has been rented."

"You know, Uncle Jake," said Lucy when the two men were ready to unload the kitchen stove, "it would make me very happy if you'd drive over home and give the stove and rocking chair to my mother."

"What!" he exclaimed squinting and lifting the bill of his cap.

"I mean it, Uncle Jake. Mom needs a new stove badly even if she can't see it or shouldn't be working around it. She could feel it before it gets hot. And the rocker. She needs it lots worse than I do. Please, Uncle Jake, could you—would you take them over before dark?"

"What if someone's there who won't allow me to unload them? Is there such a possibility?"

Lucy glanced lovingly at her pretty new stove and comfortable rocking chair and slowly shook her head. A pensive expression like a newly spun web veiled her face. "Then I don't know what you can do but bring them back here. It would make me so happy to give them to Mom."

"Just as you say, Lucy," answered Uncle Jake with a blank, dubious expression. "You're going along?"

"No, I'll stay here with Aunt Polly and start the supper."

"Then you'll go along, won't you, Fetherstone?"

"Guess I'd better." And after Lucy and his wife went into the house he remarked, "I tell you, Jake, that Lucy Hammon is one of the queerest mortals I've ever heard tell of. After all she's taken off that father of hers an' he refusin' to come to Tom's funeral an' all. My wife's been tellin' me things off and on. Now she up an' treats 'em like this, givin' a brand-new stove an' a nice rocker like that. Beats all. She's got some funny ideas if ever anyone did."

"Well, she and her mother always got along well. She's givin' this to her, you understand."

"Yes, I understand. But the whole family will benefit from the stove. I think it's a crazy idea."

"Well, it's like this," answered Jake with a degree of hesitancy, "it's got something to do with her religion, I think. She and my wife are pretty much two of a kind. They believe in returning good for evil whether it makes sense or not. And, after all, you know Maggie Winchester is my wife's older sister and Polly feels right sorry for her. Maggie never had an easy life. She's never had much to do with and now gone blind. If John would have taken proper care of her when this first started, they might have saved her eyes. Now mind you, I don't know that, but I'm saying they might have. Same with little Corkie. Polly said all along John should have been more concerned over him. But that's just how he is and I doubt anything will ever change John Winchester."

"He's a hard worker, John is," stated Mr. Fetherstone.

"That he is. No. John Winchester's not a lazy man."

Lucy could scarcely wait until Uncle Jake got back. As soon as she heard them coming in the lane, she ran out onto the porch. The wagon was empty.

"Delivered safe and sound," Uncle Jake announced opening the door about an inch. Then he swept the wet snow off his heavy shoes before coming inside.

"What did Father say?" Lucy was wide-eyed and nearly breathless with excitement.

"He wasn't there. We put the stove on the porch. They'll have to let the other one cool off first, you know."

"Yes, of course. And the rocker?"

"We took that inside. Left your mother sitting in it."

"But it was cold, wasn't it?"

"She sat in it anyhow, Lucy."

"What did she say?"

"What did she say? You mean what didn't she say. She

asked about fifty questions."

"About me?"

"Certainly about you." He took off his plaid jacket and hung it up.

"Oh, Uncle Jake. What all did she ask? What all did you tell her? And did—did she cry?"

"Some. Yes, she did. Yes. But not all the time. Sometimes she smiled. I know we left her smiling. Now, Lucy, don't forget you've got something boiling there on the stove."

"Oh, that's right." She dashed to the stove and lifted the lid. "What else can you tell me?"

"Well, she seems to be satisfied you're here with us."

"Were the girls there? Flossie and Loretta?"

"Yes."

"What did they say?"

"Well, now, I don't remember hearing them say much of anything. They just stood there surprised or dumb-founded you'd do such a thing. Now set the table for Mr. and Mrs. Fetherstone too, Lucy."

"No, no, Jake," objected Mr. Fetherstone. "We've got to be goin' right now. I got my chores to do."

"Well, thanks to both of you," exclaimed Lucy. "I'll always be grateful for your help."

"It was a pleasure, my dear," said Mrs. Fetherstone and she planted a kiss on Lucy's flushed cheek.

Lucy was very thoughtful and serious during supper.

"Uncle Jake?"

"Yes."

"I know I've been hounding you with questions, but did Mom send any kind of—a—message for me? I mean— well, did she tell you anything special—just for me?" Her question was filled with anxiety.

"Well, now," began Uncle Jake slowly, "she didn't have much chance to tell me anything special or privately that is, if that's what you mean. There stood your sisters, eyes, ears, and mouths open, and Mr. Fetherstone too, but she did take hold of my coat sleeve and sorta pull me down to her an'—"

"Did she really?"

"I'm about to tell you, Lucy, that she whispered to me she'd like to have a talk with you."

"She did? What else?"

Jake Bechtold shifted on his chair and gulped coffee which was hotter than he expected. He blinked and blew and blinked again before he answered. He looked somewhat embarrassed.

"Do you recall, Jake?" suggested Aunt Polly with a tiny thread of admonition. Then turning to Lucy, she added with graciousness, "Your Uncle Jake isn't a first-class memory expert, Lucy."

Lucy was quivering now with excitement. How could Uncle Jake forget so soon? Didn't he realize any word, just one single word, from her mother was of utmost importance to her?

Uncle Jake pulled out his blue bandanna and had a lingering coughing spell. His forehead got damp. He pushed his cup of coffee over and while aimlessly stirring it, said, "Well, seems to me she said something about praying for her. Lucy, it's slipped my mind. I was so intent on getting home and getting things put away and done up I just can't remember. I'll have to go to the barn now and finish the chores."

Lucy looked at Aunt Polly, and Aunt Polly looked at Lucy. Neither spoke out loud but their understanding eyes exchanged volumes. Lucy nodded. Aunt Polly nodded.

CHAPTER 16

L UCY WAS losing weight.

She enjoyed helping Aunt Polly, but her too frequently sleepless nights were adding up to fatigue
and loss of emotional control. Time was not bottling up
her tears. In fact, the months ahead were becoming more
frightening every day. And where was that deep quiet
calm, that sweet settled peace, that sense of security in
God, and genuine humility which knows no fretting? If all
the days were nights, she might become a mental invalid.
If all the nights were days, she would never be able to
hide her feelings at all. What was happening to her? She
prayed every night. But too often she wasn't sure her
prayers were properly worded. Did God accept her heart-
torn, heart-emptying supplications? Did they even reach
His footstool? Did they go beyond the treetops?

One morning Lucy was sweeping a light snow off the
board walk from the porch to the front gate. It was the
last week in March. An icy, compelling wind made her
shiver. Her gloveless hands were red and numb.

A boy with a lunch pail came running and called before
he reached the gate.

"Lucy." He was panting for breath.

"Floyd. Is something wrong?"

"Lucy. Mom is sick," he gasped.

"Oh! Real sick?"

"I think so." He was so short of breath he could scarcely talk. "She—she wants Father to—come and get you an'—"

"He won't do it?"

Floyd shook his head. "Mom begged him last night. And this morning too. Peggy told me to—run up here—before I go to school—and tell you. We don't—know what to do—Lucy. Mom was crying when—we left. I got to hurry or I'll be late."

"Where's Peggy?"

"She went on. I don't know if I can—catch up—or not. I'll try."

"Wait a minute. What did Father say when Mom asked him to come get me?"

"He said you ran away without asking and you can run back without asking."

"Is that what he said, Floyd?"

"Yes."

"Is that all he said?"

Floyd nodded. "I got to hurry."

"Thanks for telling me, Floyd," she called as he ran away. "Wait. Floyd, come back."

He came. "You're tired, aren't you?"

"Sure. From running. But I got to, Lucy."

"Come in the house with me and warm up. Come on. I'll ask Uncle Jake if I can borrow the pony. I'll leave right away and you can ride with me to the corner. Then you won't be late."

In ten minutes they were on their way down the road. Floyd jumped off at the corner and Lucy took the road to the right.

A year's drama rolled before her, leaving her on the verge of panic. With mounting emotion she pulled on the reins to turn the pony in the lane. The smolderings in her breast were almost greater than she could contain.

Her legs wobbled ridiculously as she tied the pony to the gate. Should she knock? She did, trembling. She heard footsteps.

Loretta opened the door.

"Loretta." Lucy's voice was hardly above a whisper. "I— I came to see Mom. Where is she?"

Loretta was too astonished to answer. She pointed toward the bedroom.

"May I go in and see her?"

Loretta nodded and motioned for her to come in.

At the foot of the bed stood Flossie. Her eyes widened and her mouth dropped open when she looked up. Lucy tiptoed to the bed and bending low took one slender hand in hers and held it to her cold cheek. "It's Lucy, Mom."

"What's that?"

"It's Lucy."

"What? Lucy?" Her sightless eyes searched for Lucy's face.

"Yes, Mom. I came to see you." She stroked her mother's warm forehead and planted a kiss on her fever-ish lips. "Are you real sick, Mom?"

A faint moan was her answer.

Flossie and Loretta stood speechless.

"What can I do for you? Tell me, Mom. I came to help you if I can."

Her mother drew a long weary breath and whispered so faintly Lucy scarcely heard. "Pray."

"You say, pray? I will, Mom. I've been praying for you every day. For a long time. Tell me, is there something special?" Lucy got down on her knees.

"Something special you want me to pray about?"

"I—I want to—believe."

"You mean in—in God, Mom?"

"In—your—Jesus."

"Oh, Mom," cried Lucy, tears rolling down her cheeks. "You mean after the way I ran away without telling you—you want to believe in—my Jesus?"

"Yes," she whispered.

"Oh, Mom! How glad I am I came! I'll pray right now."

Loretta and Flossie left the room and stood whispering in the corner of the kitchen. Lucy prayed with her mother, then took off her coat and scarf and hung them on a nail behind the bedroom door. "Girls," she said stepping into the kitchen, "if I can do anything at all to help you, let me know. Will you?"

Neither answered. They simply stared at her. Lucy went back into the bedroom, pulled up a chair, and sat close beside her mother holding one hand and kissing it repeatedly.

"Are you resting better, Mom?"

A sweet smile seemed to lift the distressed expression on her thin, wasted face. Lucy watched her eyelids flutter and her lips twitch. For ten minutes or twelve she studied her mother's face. With each slowing breath it looked more peaceful, more serene. Then almost angelic.

Lucy held her breath. She stood up. She let her mother's hand rest on the quilt. It was limp.

"Mom," cried Lucy. "Mom! Girls! Come here. Look! Look!"

"What is it?" whispered Flossie.

"She's happy. Look at that smile on her face."

Lucy bent over the silent body and kissed the damp

forehead once more. "God bless you, darling. You couldn't go till I got here, could you? O God," she cried, "thank You for sending Floyd to tell me." And Lucy leaned on the head of the bed and cried glad tears very softly.

She recognized the heavy footsteps on the porch. Her whole body trembled. She might have fainted, but she caught hold of the bed.

Lucy lifted her head and took one step to meet him. She held out her right hand. Her father stepped back speechless. His chest rose and fell. He looked Lucy full in the face, breathing as though he had been chopping wood very hard and fast.

"Father," whispered Lucy.

He had never seen her more beautiful. He tried to clear his throat, then gave it up. His shoulders sagged.

"Father," she repeated, looking up into his face with a sad but sweet expression. Her eyes were swimming in tears. "Will you forgive me—and let me come back home?"

For a second he stood mute.

"Come—back?" he panted. "Lucy!" And clasping her in his arms he held her close while tears, real tears John Winchester never knew he had, welled up and fell on Lucy's beautiful blond hair.

It was a most unexpected but precious baptism. She was strangely thrilled and completely amazed.

CHAPTER 17

EVEN THOUGH John Winchester had been very angry at Lucy for many months, in fact, so furiously angry that he told himself repeatedly he'd die before he'd invite her to come back, secretly he was anxious to see her. His house was not a place to play hide-and-seek. If Lucy deliberately and with premeditation left his house, he most certainly was not about to hoist a flag of welcome for her return. Nor did Maggie's pleadings alter his decision. He was unmovable.

But this was totally unexpected. There she stood, Lucy as real as life; taller, thinner, looking at him out of those pleading blue eyes, holding out her hand asking forgiveness. The unexpected impossible. His mask fell off before his pride could catch it. What could he do but respond to those glistening grief-filled eyes? What could he do but take her in his arms? Should he tell her he would gladly forgive her? He had never told anyone such a thing. Absurd. No, he couldn't, even with that thief Tom six feet under the sod. The scoundrel. There stood Flossie and Loretta, mouths gaping. John Winchester's neck grew hot. He dropped both arms and made for the washbasin.

Lucy was not altogether disappointed when her father didn't say he'd forgive her. After all, she was glad he didn't order her out of the house. She didn't expect him to kill a fattened calf or bring out a gold ring. The way he took her in his arms, the sweet wet drops on her head were far more than she had ever dreamed could possibly happen. The unexpected. The unexplainable.

"Father," Lucy followed him to the washstand, "you don't know yet what happened before you came in."

"What?"

"Come into the bedroom and see."

He moaned. He stood motionless and rubbed and rubbed the back of his neck.

"Is—is she gone, Lucy?"

"Can't you tell, Father?"

He stepped closer, almost fearfully close. He stood fixed, rigid, scarcely breathing, staring at the breathless one, then at long last gave two heavy sighs. The kitchen clock was ticking much too loud. It punctured the awful stillness with rude, uncaring ticks.

"Doesn't she look happy?" asked Lucy softly, touching his arm.

John Winchester kept his answer inside. Right now he didn't trust himself to answer. He was not a man of emotion, and since Lucy wasn't sobbing her heart out, he could control himself, take hold of himself, master himself. He was greatly relieved Flossie and Loretta weren't crying hysterically.

Without a word he returned to the washstand and started to wash. He put on his cap and opened the door. He hesitated. He walked slowly back into the bedroom and looked once more to make sure all signs of life were gone.

"I've got to go to town," he said to Lucy. "Loretta, go out to the woodpile behind the barn an' tell Kenneth to take Duff an' go to school and get Peggy an' Floyd. I'll take

Doc. Don't wait on me for dinner. I'll get back soon's I can."

His hand trembled ridiculously when he knocked on the undertaker's door. A small, middle-aged woman in a long, white bib apron opened the door.

"I'm John Winchester." His voice didn't sound natural. He knew it. He was startled and embarrassed at himself. Is this what the ordeal of the death of a companion could do to a woodcutter? Something dreadful and fearsome, something all out of proportion dangled over and ahead of him. He wanted to seize it but couldn't. He looked at his feet.

"Yes, Mr. Winchester. Come inside." The woman pointed to a high-back armchair in front of an open fireplace. "Be seated, please."

"No," he answered shaking his head. "I've got to be goin' back. You tell Mr. Kieffer"—he tried to clear his throaty voice; his voice still wasn't natural—"my wife passed away."

"I see. When, Mr. Winchester?"

"Oh, I suppose an hour or so ago. I—I wasn't in the house when it happened. You tell Mr. Kieffer to come out. We live—"

"Yes, Mr. Winchester, Mr. Kieffer knows where you live. He'll be right out. He took the horses to get them shod."

"Yes—an'—" John was breathing heavily, much too heavily. He was ashamed of himself.

"Shall I get you some brandy, Mr. Winchester?"

"No. No. You tell him there's to be no funeral service, no singin' an' no ado of any kind. I'm not one of them that's up to that." He was completely out of breath now. He took out his handkerchief and wiped his face twice.

"Well, I'll tell him what you said, Mr. Winchester. But someone always reads a short prayer, you know, at the grave, Mr. Winchester. It's the custom, you know." The woman's voice was low and almost musical. She spoke in an appropriate, sympathetic manner.

John ran his one hand back and forth across the bill of his cap and started toward the door. "Does a person have to go by the custom in these parts?" he asked.

"Well—I don't know what to tell you, Mr. Winchester. I'll have to ask Mr. Kieffer about that." Her smile was mingled with pity and surprise.

" 'Twon't be at all necessary as far as I'm concerned," stated John. "We're not church people an' I can't afford to pay a man to read a prayer."

"I see. Well, Mr. Kieffer can read some few words from a little book an' there'll be no extra charge, Mr. Winchester, I'm quite sure."

Chapter 18

SPRING CAME. How Lucy did plunge into the work! She washed windows inside and out, aired bedding, scrubbed floors, polished everything polishable, planted early garden, gathered fresh tender dandelion greens, and arranged pussy willows for a house bouquet. She tried every new recipe she had learned from Aunt Polly and baked and cooked on her own beautiful stove. She put forth every effort to drown her own sorrow by working and cooking to please her brothers and sisters and father.

He didn't lavish praises on her, but she could tell he appreciated her work and enjoyed her meals. Lucy herself ate with a better appetite than she had for months.

But home without Mom wasn't home. After looking at that empty rocking chair for a month Lucy experienced such a loneliness it was almost more than she could bear. And she missed Aunt Polly tremendously. Flossie had matured into quite a stunning young lady and was fully aware of it. She resented Lucy's motherly advice and wasn't about to take orders from her about anything even if Father did say Lucy should take Mom's place. It was all right for the first couple of weeks when everyone and everything was new and strange with Mom gone, but the newness got old and dull and frayed Flossie's nerves. Why should runaway Lucy, Mom's pet, come back and act so important? Even if Peggy and Loretta were stupid and placid enough to submit to Lucy's whims and every suggestion, she wasn't about to. It was disgusting the way Loretta and Peggy and even Kenneth ran to Lucy with their troubles and secrets and only God knew what all. Lucy could but whistle and Floyd would dance to her tune. And whatever Lucy cooked, fried, baked, or concocted the boys ate as though it was fit for a king. They had not reacted like that to all her hard kitchen work over the long hard months.

"Poo-poo," snapped Flossie to Loretta one afternoon in the garden, "if Lucy thinks she's going to boss me around all the time, she's got another guess coming."

"Why, I haven't heard her trying to boss you or any of us around. What do you mean?"

"She's been doing it. Every day. You're just too dull to notice it. Just because she happened to be born first, she thinks she's got every right to take the lead over all of us."

"Well, someone's got to take the lead, Floss. How would we ever get things done if she didn't? You know how the wash always piled up before she came. You know how we never got the ironing done before she came back. You know half the time we didn't get our beds made all day and supper was hardly ever ready when Father came in. I'm glad Lucy's here. And I don't think you have a right to feel the way you do."

"Well, that's a pretty speech you made, now isn't it? And to your older sister. Well, you ought to be ashamed of yourself. I was good enough to take the lead after she ran off. You know I was. Maybe we didn't always get everything done on the minute, but I'm not going to be a slave and kill myself and ruin my health before I get married.

Not on your life. But you've got to admit I did pretty good all the while Lucy was gone. And now she steps in and plans all the meals just like I don't know how to boil water."

"Why, Flossie Winchester. That's absolutely not true. I heard her this very morning asking you which you'd rather have for dinner, rice pudding or rhubarb sauce."

"Well, she knows I detest both. She did it just to see if I'd make a face."

"Oh, Flossie, what on earth ails you, anyhow? I think you got out of the wrong side of the bed again this morning. What's eating on you?"

"Well," retorted Flossie with a toss of her head, "you just see, whenever you or I get a boyfriend, she'll try to put a broomstick in the wheel just because it didn't turn out so sweet and grand for her."

"Why would she do that?"

"Because she's jealous, stupid. Lucy's so jealous it's sticking out all over."

"I think you got your wires crossed, Floss. I don't think Lucy's jealous or bossy one bit. She's been washing the dishes so you can save your pretty hands you think so much of. She's the one who's been fixing the school lunches because you said you hated to. And didn't she offer to make you that pretty new dress the minute she heard you say you hated to sew? Now didn't she?"

Flossie made a face and ran into the house. She ran through the kitchen and upstairs, almost knocking over a pitcher of milk on the corner of the table. She flopped on the bed and let her imaginations run wild. Lucy *was* Mom's pet. There was no disputing that. And she *did* have some uncanny influence on Father way back there when she was only twelve. And he did take her to Black Bend himself on Duff. She, the second born, had never been able to bend Father to her whims or fancies. When had he taken her to town to get her black patent leather slippers? When had he eaten five of her pancakes for breakfast? When had he ever told Lucy to ask her what ought to be done? And why did Lucy have to be the one to favor Father's one and only beautiful sister, Mabel, he just about worshiped?

She saw it under Lucy's pillow. She picked it up. Holy Bible. She brushed her one hand over the soft black leather cover. She opened it. "To Lucy from Tom on their wedding day, November 3." Flossie broke out in goose pimples. In the center of the book was a dainty handkerchief neatly folded. Several lines on the printed page were underlined in pencil. *He is despised—he was wounded—he was oppressed—he was taken from prison—* Flossie turned page after page reading short phrases underlined. *Fear not: for I am with thee—no weapon that is formed against thee shall prosper—every tongue that shall rise against thee in judgment thou shalt condemn—*

Flossie jumped. Footsteps on the stairs. Quickly she tucked the Bible under the pillow and began taking down her hair.

Lucy was humming softly when she entered. It was some strange, lonesome, made-up tune she had never heard or hummed before. "Well, Flossie," Lucy asked, aproning herself, "what are you hungry for?"

"Nothing in particular."

"Well, help me decide what to have for supper."

"Makes no difference to me what we have. You fix it and we eat it, don't we?"

"Can't you name just one thing you'd like, Flossie? I'm sorta tired planning the meals."

"What's wrong with you?"

"Oh, I don't know," answered Lucy. "I've just been sorta tired all day. Maybe spring fever." She tried to laugh.

"You're inferring I'm not doing enough to help you."

"Oh, no, Flossie. Not at all. Don't take me wrong. It's just myself, I guess. I—I miss Mom. And Corkie. I wouldn't wish them back for anything, but oh, I don't know, I've just been sorta draggy all day thinking about them."

"And Tom," Flossie added with an intended sneer.

"Yes," admitted Lucy feebly. "I miss him a lot. I sorta dread this time of day when it's getting dusk. I can't explain why, but it's easier when it's daylight or dark."

"I don't understand that," snapped Flossie. "I like this time of day. In fact, the best."

"I wouldn't expect you to understand," answered Lucy sadly. "You just have to go through it to be able to understand and I hope to God you won't ever, ever have to."

The look Flossie gave Lucy was cruel and devastating. Lucy went downstairs with a heavy heart, regretting fervently she had admitted what she did to her sister. Would she ever be able to understand Flossie any better than she did Father? She wondered.

CHAPTER 19

LUCY TRIED her best to be pleasant and natural, especially when her sisters were in the same room. An occasional glance in the small wood-framed mirror convinced her she must gather up the fragments of her uneasy heart and brush away that absorbing look of preoccupation. She reminded herself scores of times that this heartbreaking experience was a personal thing and she must suffer it in privacy. She dare not display her feelings anymore nor expect any degree of sympathy from anyone.

June was just around the corner. Lucy begged God to help her shake off the unnerving weakening she felt. She decided to go outside and fill her lungs with the fragrant summer air and let the warm sun bathe her entire body. Strolling through the garden she examined the potato leaves, the carrots, the beets, the beans. Her heart felt a little lighter, her spirits a trifle brighter. She went into the house and opened the seed box.

"What you going to do, Lucy?" asked Loretta.

"I think I'll plant some lima beans where we had the early lettuce. It's such a lovely morning to work outside, and for some reason I just like the feel of garden ground in my hands."

"Do you want me to help you?"

"You really don't need to," answered Lucy. "Unless you

would like to take out two pails of water for me."

"Sure."

"Just set them down there at the edge of the garden."

"What else do you want me to do?"

"Well, let's see. I tell you what. Why don't you go down there across the road and see if those wild raspberries are ripe yet? If they are, we could have a cobbler for dinner."

"All right, I'll go. I hope they're ripe."

Lucy was busy dropping lima beans when a horse and wagon stopped at the gate. She looked up in glad surprise, and dropping her hoe, hurried to greet Uncle Jake and Aunt Polly.

"Morning, Lucy," called Uncle Jake, and before Lucy could answer, he was helping Aunt Polly, practically lifting her down from the wagon seat. "Can I leave the missus here with you while I go to town?"

"Can you!' exclaimed Lucy almost in ecstasy. She threw her arms around Aunt Polly's neck and kissed her. "What would make me happier? Aunt Polly, it's been so long since I've seen you. I've been lonesome for you."

"Child, I've been lonesome for you too. I've been wanting to come over every week but just wasn't quite able. But now since it's warmer, I feel much better."

"You're looking good, Aunt Polly. Do you feel as well as you look?"

"Well, I don't know how well I look. I was in bed for three weeks after your mother passed away."

"My, my, Aunt Polly." Lucy was holding Aunt Polly by the arm and leading her slowly toward the porch steps. "Do you mean you took it that hard?"

"It was a very— What shall I say?" She stopped long enough to draw a deep breath. "Well, a personal and touching loss for me for some reason, Lucy. I suppose because I felt for you. I thought of how you'd miss her and I guess my sympathy got the best of me. Listen, dear, I noticed you were working in the garden."

"But that can wait. We want to visit. Let me bring the rocker outside so you won't need to climb the steps. We can enjoy the warm sunshine together. I'll sit here on the steps."

"Where's everyone else?" asked Aunt Polly, seated in the rocking chair.

"Well, Father went to town with a load of wood. I don't know where Kenneth is if he didn't go with Father. He seldom does. Of course Floyd and Peggy are in school. It closes Friday. Flossie went with Loretta to try to find some wild raspberries down the road."

"Then it's just you and me. Well, tell me, how are things going?"

Lucy folded her arms and took a long deep breath. "How do you mean?"

"Is your father good to you?"

"He hasn't spoken one harsh word to me since I came home."

"He's surely asked you about the night you left, hasn't he?"

"Never once mentioned it, Aunt Polly."

"Then he's forgiven you, don't you think?"

"I really don't know. I know Mom did." Lucy's lashes brushed her flushed cheeks.

"Does he ever talk about Tom?"

Lucy shook her head. "He's never spoken his name in my hearing."

"Your father is a very strange man, Lucy. I often wondered how or why he fell in love with your mother. By the way, did that Mr. Proctor ever stop here to see you?"

"Who?"

"The man who gave the prayer at your mother's grave."

"I remember a man giving a short prayer, but why would he call on me? I never knew who the man was or who told him to pray. I was surprised."

"I asked him to, Lucy. That was all my doings. I've known Mr. Proctor for years. He's a fine Christian and one of our closest neighbors. I thought I couldn't see your dear mother put away without a little touch of God in it. I was afraid your father wouldn't have it, so I slipped a note to the undertaker to let the man give a prayer."

"It was a beautiful prayer, and I did appreciate it if no one else did."

"Your father never mentioned anything about it?"

"No. Never a word."

"I offered to pay Mr. Proctor for his trouble. He never knew your mother and he left his work to drive clear over, but he wouldn't take a cent. I told him you were the only Christian in the family and if he ever went by this way to drop in and give you a word of encouragement."

"Well, Aunt Polly, I'll tell you, if he'd stop here to see me and Father would be at home I don't know what might happen."

"Maybe I shouldn't have suggested it. I surely wouldn't want you to get into a row with your father. Have you been to church or Sunday school since you came home?"

Lucy picked up the corner of her apron string and pressed the hem between two fingers. Her expression sobered abruptly. A shadow of disappointment, frustration, and near gloom swept over her. "No, I haven't been anyplace, Aunt Polly. I just never felt like walking those four miles alone to Sunny Creek. And I don't even know if they have services there anymore. I haven't seen Miss Basie since the day of Tom's funeral. She told me then she was getting married and might move to Alabama. Sundays are always such long, lonely days for me. I spend most of the day up in my room. But," Lucy's eyes filled with tears, "up there my thoughts and memories go almost wild. Seems I just can't rise above it all. I have my Bible and I read some every night before I go to bed and on Sundays but, Aunt Polly, there's so much I can't understand at all. It just makes me more confused all the time. If I only could have finished the eighth grade. I feel so dumb."

"Now, now, child," chided Aunt Polly, gently leaning over and patting Lucy's one hand. "You are not dumb. Why, my dear, there are doctors and lawyers and statesmen who can't understand much of the Bible. At least they claim they can't. I think they feel it's smart to say it contradicts itself. I'd sooner be in your shoes and believe enough to know how to be saved and keep saved than just throw up my hands and cast the Bible aside and refuse to believe any of it because I couldn't understand all of it."

"Keep saved, you say?" Lucy looked up sharply.

"I guess that's what I said, didn't I? Well, when you're saved and you know it, you'll want to obey and please God in everything. And you won't grow cold or turn back. I guess you'd call that keeping saved."

Lucy looked off in the distance at nothing but her own tangled thoughts. She drew another long breath and slowly shook her head.

Aunt Polly took her by the arm. "Look at me, dear. You

seem so sad."

Lucy made no reply. Her head dropped and a lone tear dropped onto her lap.

"Do you care to share something with me, dear?"

"No one knows, Aunt Polly."

"Knows what, child?"

All at once Lucy gave way to her pent-up feelings and she shook with sobs. She had stayed a prisoner in the dungeon of her own thoughts long enough.

"Why, Lucy," cried Aunt Polly. "What is it? You must not bear this alone whatever it is. Tell me. I'll understand. Has your father mistreated you?"

Lucy shook her head.

"Do the girls help you with the work?"

"Pretty good. Yes. Loretta and Peggy are very good to help me."

"Has someone hurt your feelings?"

Lucy did not answer.

"You're brooding over Tom?"

No answer.

"Because he wasn't ready?"

No answer.

"I thought you had the victory over that, Lucy. You mustn't go on blaming yourself. Just take it as a part of your life, dear child. Oh, I hate to see you so sad, Lucy. You've been so brave. What can I do for you? Please tell me."

Lucy lost all control of herself. Tears came faster and faster. There was no stopping.

"You poor dear girl," cried Aunt Polly helplessly. "Thank God I stopped by, but I'm not helping you one bit. Isn't there something, just one thing, I can do for you?"

"Oh, yes," cried Lucy. "If you can't help me, nobody in all the world can. Oh, Aunt Polly, I'm—"

"Why, hello, Aunt Polly," called Loretta.

Lucy was shocked. Embarrassed and stunned to be found crying. There came Flossie and Loretta with berry-stained hands and a pail half filled. She quickly wiped her face with her apron but it was too late. Her sisters had no uncertainties about what she had been doing.

"We got enough for a cobbler," Loretta said to Lucy almost apologetically.

Lucy nodded without looking at the pail.

"Come on, Loretta," said Flossie, "let's go sit on the pump bed to stem them. How long you been here, Aunt Polly?"

"Oh, about forty-five minutes or so. I stopped to chat and rest while Uncle Jake's gone to town. Let's walk out to the garden, Lucy. Show me what you were doing."

"You're sure you feel able?"

"I think so with your help. I want to see your garden."

"What d'you s'pose is wrong with Lucy?" whispered Loretta seating herself on the pump bed.

Flossie shrugged her shoulders and raised both eyebrows. She colored.

"She's been looking sad at times all week. Haven't you noticed?"

"Well, did you go tell her what I said?" snapped Flossie. "No, I never."

"Well, I'll bet somebody's been telling her things." Flossie's neck got red in spots and she stemmed berries furiously.

"Things like what?"

"Be still. Here they come."

Chapter 20

I T WASN'T impossible to stem berries and at the same time cast glances out of the corner of her eye to the two walking confidentially in the garden. Flossie's imaginations soared and spiraled. They were both distressing and hounding. Her hands shook. She watched Lucy and Aunt Polly go into the house which only added to her suspicions.

"Come on, Loretta, let's go in too."

Flossie tried to act natural and even pleasant. But there sat Aunt Polly on the rocking chair almost in the center of the kitchen; so she had to walk in front of her to set the table. What was taking Uncle Jake so long in town? "Shall I set places for you and Uncle, Aunt Polly?" she asked, forcing a smile.

"No, Flossie. Surely he'll come any minute. It's four-thirty already. And here come Floyd and Peggy. Well, well, children," she exclaimed, "how nice to see you again! You didn't expect to find me here, did you? Come here, Peggy. Give Aunt Polly a kiss. You are a fine-looking girl and so big, and you can do lots of things to help Lucy, can't you?"

"Well, I do whatever she asks me to," smiled Peggy.

"That's a good girl."

Lucy had washed her face and was mixing the dough for the cobbler.

"I'll tell you what you can do now, Peggy," she said. "Go gather the eggs and feed the chickens. Loretta's going to help Floyd milk tonight because Flossie cut her thumb this morning. You'd better change your dress first, don't you think?"

"All right."

Aunt Polly talked on and on about her rheumatism, her poor neglected garden which was too much for Uncle Jake to take care of properly, her much delayed spring cleaning, and finally how glad she was it was warm at last.

"And, Flossie," she remarked bending forward in the rocker and patting her on the arm as she passed, "you certainly are blossoming out. I guess that's one way to say it," she chuckled. "You look like a real young lady with your hair up like that."

Flossie all but shuddered. What was she going to blurt out next? Was Aunt Polly making light of her? She tried to smile even though she didn't feel like smiling. "What shall I do now, Lucy?" she asked with purposeful eagerness.

"Well, let's see. Did you fill the sugar bowl?"

"I will."

"I think it's wonderful how you girls work together," remarked Aunt Polly beaming and snapping her velvet handbag. "When I was your age, I couldn't make a pie fit—That's Uncle Jake whistling. Well, it's been nice to see you all. I'm coming," she called out the door. "I'll try to get over oftener, girls, since it's warmer. You come to see me if ever you can. I do wish we could keep in touch more often now since your mother's gone. And, Lucy," she said turning and waving one hand, "tell your father I'll be back to have a— Come outside with me a minute, Lucy." And

Lucy helped Aunt Polly to the wagon.

Flossie met Lucy on the porch. Her face was red and her lips tightly drawn. "Now you tell me what Aunt Polly told you," she snapped.

"What do you mean?"

"You know what I mean, Lucy. She told you something about me. Didn't she?"

"I haven't the slightest idea what you're talking about. She didn't tell me anything about you. What could it have been?"

"Lucy," and Flossie gripped Lucy by the arm, "you make me mad. Yes, plain mad. Aunt Polly was talking about me when you two were in the garden. I could tell you were."

"Did you hear her mention your name?"

"No, but something tells me she was. And you were crying when we came back with the berries. And you both stopped talking because you didn't want me to hear what you were saying. And Aunt Polly blushed."

"Blushed? I didn't see her blush."

"Well, she did. And I'm going to insist you repeat what she told you. Every bit of it."

"Well, Flossie," answered Lucy pulling herself loose and going up the steps, "not one thing Aunt Polly told me would interest you in the least. Come on, now, and put away your foolish imaginations. I just don't know what's eating on you, but something is."

"There's nothing eating on me," retorted Flossie.

"You're troubled or worried about something, Floss, or you wouldn't be acting like this. I'm surprised at you."

"There's nothing troubling me," declared Flossie. "But just because things went the way they did for you—you and Aunt Polly needn't try to meddle into my affairs."

"Your affairs?" exclaimed Lucy. "What affairs?"

"Never mind," snapped Flossie with resentment.

"Well, if you'd share this mystery with me now since you've said this much, perhaps I could help you."

"Never mind," glared Flossie. Her voice cracked. "I don't need your help." Flossie dashed up the steps ahead of Lucy. She turned abruptly and facing her with eyes half closed said, "What's Aunt Polly coming back to talk to Father about?" Her forefinger was pressed hard against Lucy's chest.

Lucy drew back. "Well, I'll tell you sometime, Flossie, if you calm down. But not now."

"Why not now?" Flossie followed Lucy across the kitchen.

"Because I'm not ready yet and you don't need to insist."

"Jake," began Aunt Polly when they were on their way, "we've just got to do something for Lucy." She unsnapped and snapped her black velvet handbag several times.

"Well," answered Jake, sending tobacco juice out over the left front wagon wheel, "what you got in mind? I thought we have been doing our level best."

"But I've never seen her as blue as she was today. She cried to me as though her heart was breaking."

"I just knew it was coming. Once she found out."

"What do you mean, found out? What do you know I don't know?"

Jake looked at Polly with a quick jerk of his head. "I don't know what you're talking about. I mean about Flossie. What else?"

"Oh, that. Well, I never told her."

"Never told her? I thought that was one reason you wanted me to let you off. You mean you never mentioned it to Lucy?"

"I meant to. I had it on the end of my tongue several times, but when I found her so low in spirits, I just couldn't bring myself to telling her. She never gets out. Just spends most of Sundays up in her room, and she says it's when she's up there things press in on her."

"Like what?"

"Well, we went to the garden to talk and she told me how she hid Tom's letters under the mattress and read them at night in the clothes closet, and when she sits at the window, she imagines she sees him standing under the plum tree waiting for her and things like that."

"You mean she thinks she sees his spirit?"

"Oh, of course not, Jake. Not really. But she's nervous, Jake. And she's worried about herself and her— Jake, listen, I want you to take me back over there again after school's out and she has the summer work all lined up and I want to have a talk with John."

"What about?"

"I want to convince him he ought to let Lucy come back and stay with us."

"You convince John Winchester he ought to do something?" Jake laughed out loud and tilted his hat on the back of his head. "Something he doesn't want to do? Who do you think you are, Polly Bechtold?"

"I know it sounds ridiculous but I'm going to try it. He won't turn me down because I won't let him." And Aunt Polly reseated herself with assurance.

"Well!"

"Lucy needs to get away from there. And Flossie and

Loretta are old enough to go ahead like they did before she went back. Lucy didn't say so, but I have a hunch the girls, especially Flossie, shove work on her. She looks sorta sick, Jake. Now really."

"But if Flossie's got it in her head now to—"

"I know. I know she might go off and leave Loretta with the work."

"You should have told Lucy. I just wonder what John would do if he knew what was going on. I know what I'd do."

"No, you don't, Jake. You can talk because we never had any children. Flossie's got a turn all of her own. She's quite a young lady and you can't deny she's real attractive. And once she discovers it herself, and I believe she has, her father might as well try to stop Niagara Falls."

"Guess who was here today, Father?" said Lucy dishing up the supper.

"No idea. Who?"

"Aunt Polly."

"Oh, and what brought her over?"

Flossie gave one quick glance at Lucy, then at her father. She poured water, trying to hum as she poured. Some went on the table. She quickly grabbed a towel and wiped it up.

"Nothing special," answered Lucy. "She just rested here and visited while Uncle Jake went on to town."

As soon as the dishes were wiped and put away, Flossie went upstairs. Lucy helped Peggy with her final arithmetic problems and the boys finished spading the garden.

Flossie was in bed, her face to the wall, when Lucy entered. Quietly she lit the lamp and read a chapter in her Bible. She knelt beside her bed and buried her face in both hands.

O God, she prayed. *I'm not a bit humble anymore. I fret about my future and I'm letting my troubles pull me down. I feel so weak. And, dear God, whatever is troubling Flossie, help me know how to treat her, for in my heart I have no ill will toward her that I know of.*

Lucy was still on her knees when Loretta came upstairs. "Has Father gone to bed yet, Loretta?"

"He was dozing on the rocker when I came up."

"Father." Lucy tiptoed across the kitchen and touched him lightly on the arm.

John Winchester looked up, startled.

"Father," she said, "excuse me, but will you do me a favor?"

"A favor?" He couldn't remember Lucy ever coming to him like this. How sweet and girlish she looked with her blond braids hanging nearly to her waist. He rubbed his eyes. "What favor?"

"You know that plum tree down there by the fence?"

"Yes."

"It doesn't bear fruit anymore, does it?"

"Never did amount to a hill of beans. Why?"

"Well, Father—" Lucy twisted one hand over the other. Her voice got husky and red spots appeared on each cheek. "I wish you'd—you'd cut it down."

"Cut it down?" John Winchester put both hands behind his head.

"Yes."

He stood up. A puzzled expression crossed his face. "Cut it down. What fer?"

"It would make it—a lot easier for me if it was down. I think."

"Easier? What are you talking about, Lucy?"

"Well, you see—" She leaned on the edge of the table for support. Her voice trembled a little and she bit her lip to keep back the tears. "He—met me there—the night I left. And I just wish I would never—have to look at it again."

At last it was out, out of her self-imposed isolation. John Winchester had never seen anyone with such a pleading look and such sorrowful eyes. He took one long, deep breath. "Lucy," he said running his hands deep into his overall pockets, "I'll do anything in my power to help you forget the man that came sneakin' around here an'—"

"Oh, please, Father," Lucy's one hand went to her throat. "He's gone and—"

"An' a good thing he is, Lucy." And she saw fire in her father's eyes. She shivered.

His fury lasted but a moment. He stepped close to Lucy and put one hand on her shoulder. "I'll go do it right now. Right now."

"I didn't mean tonight, Father. It's dark."

"The sooner, the better." And without another word her father lit the lantern and went straight to the barn for his ax.

With a desolate, lonely heart Lucy sank on the wooden box beside the window and watched the flickering lantern moving along the road. It stopped several feet before the plum tree.

Lucy's heart nearly stopped. She grabbed her arms and held them tight against her. She was confident she saw a man the size of Tom disappear very suddenly in the darkness beyond the plum tree.

CHAPTER 21

LUCY GAVE a stifled gasp. Her neck throbbed. She pressed her tightly clasped fists against her cheeks and bit her tongue. Flossie stirred in bed.

The ax struck one mighty blow after another. Chips flew. Lucy could see them like little white-breasted birds flying in front of the lantern. She could see her father's strong, sure arms wielding the ax.

Flossie sat up in bed.

Lucy's heart was pounding and racing so violently it thundered in her ears. She strained every nerve to watch. Now. Now. She heard a cracking, a snapping of wood, then one dull thud and the plum tree lay on the ground. She gave a deep sigh of relief.

Carefully crawling over Loretta, Flossie put one bare foot on the floor, then another, and made her way to the window, trembling like a leaf. Her teeth almost chattered.

Lucy jumped. "Flossie!"

"What's going on down there?" she demanded. Her voice, panicky, was more than a whisper.

"Father just chopped down the old plum tree," whispered Lucy. "Sh."

"The plum tree?" Flossie's tone this time was almost a scream. She clutched at the neck of her nightgown with both hands. She was shaking convulsively.

Lucy sensed more than consternation in Flossie's voice.

There was utter dismay. Fear. Even horror. "It's quite all right, Flossie," she whispered. "I asked him to do it."

"You?" panted Flossie, giving Lucy a push which almost sent her off the wooden box. "You mean to tell me you told Father to cut down that tree?"

"Why, yes. I did. What's so terrible about that? It bothered me. You don't understand why, but it did. Why does it matter to you? I don't understand."

"Oh, Lucy," stormed Flossie stamping the floor with indignation. "You just think you're doing something real smart, don't you?"

"Sh. You're waking Loretta."

"Well, what of it? I'm so upset I—"

"Flossie," said Lucy trying to be calm, "why are you so worked up? What difference does it make to you about the tree? It didn't bear fruit anymore. I thought if it was gone I—I wouldn't be seeing things anymore. I just had—"

"Seeing things?" interrupted Flossie with a strange wild expression on her paling face. "Listen to me, Lucy Hammon." And she shook one finger in Lucy's face. "I know now you and Aunt Polly were talking about me. And you lied to me. And I know now you're jealous of me. I told Loretta you'd try to boss my affairs and you've started now by asking Father to cut down that tree. Well, I tell you once and for all, Lucy," she stood uncomfortably close, blowing vexation in Lucy's face, "you are not going to succeed in your scheme and you'd better not try it either."

Lucy was dumbfounded. Speechless. She shivered. Was she going to faint? She felt woefully clumsy and strange.

"I'm going to get dressed," snapped Flossie turning on her heels, "and I'm going down. Just you stay there in bed, Loretta. This doesn't concern you anyhow. Go on back to sleep. I'm going to tell Father," she continued turning to Lucy again, "what's what. Right now. Tonight. I might as well face him now. I'd rather do it this way and have it out with him than beg to come back years, I mean months, later, like you did."

Lucy slumped. She was smitten. The blow put fresh, unexpected fears and bewilderment in her troubled heart. What was this sudden malice in Flossie? These cruel insinuations from her younger sister who must be caught in the spinning, whirling, dizzying, magnetic power of some secret romance. What else could Flossie possibly mean?

Lucy got up, swayed a moment, then caught Flossie by the arm. "Listen," she cried, "you will never know how sorry I've been for the thing I did. The way I did it. You'll never know how I've grieved over my conduct. Nobody but God knows what I've gone through because of what I did." Lucy's face was drenched in tears.

Flossie jerked herself loose. "That's not saying it would go that way for me," she snapped.

"That's quite true." Lucy felt so tactless and weak. "And I hope it never will," she added. "I have no idea what you mean, Flossie—I mean I know nothing of your private affairs; but whatever it is, I think it's best you tell Father right away. Whatever you do, don't ever run off secretly like I did."

"Get your dress on and go down with me." Flossie's words were direct and commanding.

"I didn't undress," answered Lucy.

"Well, I know you didn't. I knew it all the time," answered Flossie irritably. "I heard you ask Loretta if Father went to bed. Oh, yes, I did. I wasn't asleep. I heard you go downstairs."

"And did you hear me ask Father to chop down the tree?"

"No. But I sure did wonder what you wanted with him."

Puffing and panting, Flossie stepped into her dress. Her hands shook so much she could scarcely get the buttons in the holes. "Come on," she ordered, "you're going to hear it all and answer some questions too."

Lucy rubbed her face. Was this a bad dream?

Lucy braced herself against the wall. A tumult of frantic, incredulous grief tormented her out of all proportion. One second she was cold like marble and without feeling; the next, burning with feverish shame. She had set a bad example not only for Flossie but for Loretta and Peggy. And Floyd and Kenneth. She saw it now bigger than life. She was the one Father should reprimand soundly. She was the one Father ought to flog. Not Flossie. She would step up and plead for Flossie. She'd beg Father to be easy on Flossie for this, whatever it was she was about to expose. She'd ask him to lay down the penalty on her. It couldn't hurt any more than the remorse she had already suffered. Then Flossie would surely believe she loved her and hadn't lied. Oh, what was wrong with Flossie?

They were in the kitchen when Father entered, lantern still burning. He looked up in surprise. He saw Lucy's tearstained face.

"What's wrong with you? Didn't I do it right?"

Before Lucy had time to answer, Flossie stepped up to her father and held out one hand. "Give it to me," she said bluntly, trying desperately to be as bold as she had intended.

John Winchester dropped the lantern on the floor.

"Give you what?"

"The note."

"What?"

"That note you've got." She reddened. The irregular lines of her mouth were tightly compressed. She batted her eyes.

"What note?" John Winchester's eyebrows met. "Have you gone crazy?"

"The note you found in that tree you cut down." Flossie's face suddenly turned a sickly, gray, ashen color. Her hands and her voice trembled with a growing apprehension she despised.

John Winchester's arms sagged as though he'd been shot. Then his big frame stiffened. "Have both of you girls gone crazy?"

Lucy got white. "Oh, Father," she cried throwing her arms around his neck. "Please don't be hard on Flossie. I'm the one who set a bad example."

"What on earth?" He held Lucy out at arm's length and glared at her. "What under heaven is this all about?"

"I don't know what it's all about, Father," answered Lucy feebly, "only I know it'll hurt me very much if you punish Flossie. I didn't know she'd care if I asked you to cut down the plum tree. I never dreamed she had a note in the crotch of that tree."

"A note?" he shouted. "Indeed. Now what is this?" John Winchester turned to Flossie. "What's goin' on here anyhow? I didn't see no note in that tree, but after this maybe I'd better be on the lookout. Go ahead now. Let's hear what this is all about." He towered above her, standing much too close for comfort.

Flossie felt as though she were crumbling. She opened

her mouth but not a word could she speak. Her frightened, downcast eyes glanced toward Lucy.

"Well, speak," yelled her father impatiently. "You say you put a note in the crotch of that there plum tree?"

Flossie's tongue was paralyzed.

"Well, if you can't or won't talk, then who was it for? Can't you say somethin'?"

"It was for me," muttered Flossie feebly.

"Oh, how stupid," snorted her father. "You put a note in the tree for yourself?" His face twitched with disgust plus growing anger.

Flossie swallowed several times. She was going to be very brave and now her nerves were ready to snap. Baffling fears were blasting every intent. Father looked so huge, so strong, so stern, and fierce. She stepped back.

"For yourself?" he repeated.

"Well," she confessed, "Clem Linsdale said he was going to come by and—and put—"

"Clem Linsdale?" asked her father raising both eyebrows. He almost staggered to the nearest chair and sank into it. The stern look on his face slowly softened. He put one big palm down on the table.

Silence filled the kitchen. Each one heard only his own breathing.

He looked up. "Clem Linsdale, you say?"

Flossie was too shocked now to answer. Father was not going to fly into a rage? He wasn't going to be angry? Not try to slap her?

She watched him run one hand back through his hair twice. "Well," he said at length, "if Clem Linsdale wants to give a message to one of my daughters, he needn't hide no notes in plum trees. He can come to the door like a gentleman to say what he's got to say to her face."

Flossie gasped. "Really, Father? You—you wouldn't let Tom come to see—"

"Let the past alone. Never mention that scoundrel's name in this house. Do you hear? How long's this been goin' on between you an' Clem?"

"Not long."

"Well, you both go on up to bed now. I'm tired an' it's gettin' late."

"All right, Father," answered Flossie, "but I want to know something first. If Lucy didn't know Clem was going to put a note in that tree for me, then why did she ask you to cut it down?"

"She can answer that fer herself."

"All right then, Lucy," demanded Flossie, turning and facing her with haughty superiority. "Why?"

"Well," began Lucy looking very tired and sick, "several times—I saw a man, or I thought I did—and I—well, I suppose now it was Clem."

"Oh, I see," snapped Flossie, "so you mean you've got a man who's been putting notes in that tree for you too?"

"No. No, Flossie," cried Lucy. "Believe me. I tell you the truth. I'll explain when we get upstairs."

"But tell me the truth right here in this kitchen where Father can hear it. Didn't Aunt Polly tell you when Uncle Jake was out hunting mushrooms he saw Clem and me together down the road there the other Sunday?"

"No, she did not, Flossie."

"I'm telling you girls again now," remarked their father, "go on to bed. But," he added with no uncertainty in his voice, "if any more of my daughters go out with men behind my back I'm goin' to lay them right over my knee and give 'em a good flouncin' they won't soon forget."

And with that he went to his bedroom and closed the door.

He forgot to blow out the lantern. Flossie crossed the room, picked it up, and started to unlatch the door.

"What are you going to do, Flossie?" asked Lucy.

"I'm going down there and find that note. I'm not waiting till morning."

"Don't you want me to go along? It's dark."

Flossie nodded.

Neither spoke a word. Lucy was so weak she stumbled and nearly fell several times.

The tree lay parallel with the road. Lucy took the lantern and held it while Flossie looked all around and under every branch. She put the lantern on the ground and together they turned the tree completely over. No note.

"Lucy," fretted Flossie, "do you suppose Father actually has it?"

"No. I can't believe he'd deceive you like that."

"Well, then where is it? I know Clem put one here for me. He said he would."

Through the darkness came a low whistle.

Flossie heard it. So did Lucy. They looked at each other. Neither spoke.

"Flossie," came a loud whisper and out of the shadows stepped a man.

"Clem," cried Flossie. "I can't find it."

He came closer. His face showed his perplexity.

"Mr. Linsdale," exclaimed Lucy, "I know you're wondering why our father chopped down the tree a while ago. Well, it's all my fault. I didn't know you and Flossie were using it or I wouldn't have asked him to do it—but I thought several times I was seeing Tom—and it—bothered me awful. I—I had no idea it was you. I'm sorry. I apologize. Truly I didn't mean to be a hindrance to Flossie."

Lucy could say no more. She was choking. She turned and hurried back to the house.

CHAPTER 22

FOR WELL over an hour John Winchester lay wide awake searching the blank ceiling for answers. Stark, absorbing, conflicting thoughts dammed back the natural river of sleep. Deceived again. Why? How could this possibly have happened after he had made it so emphatic to his entire family that Lucy's stunt had infuriated him? Now Flossie. Whom was she taking for her pattern? Flossie. When did she grow up to such daring conduct? Pretty? Yes. With something distinctive and undefinable about her. Tall, snappy-eyed, chic. So utterly different from Lucy. Lucy.

John Winchester folded his hands behind his head and drew in a long, labored breath. How young, how sweet, how hauntingly sad, wistful, and strangely innocent she had come to him with her shocking request. Why—why couldn't she have gotten involved with someone as important and popular and well fixed as Clem Linsdale? John stretched. Down! Yes, down forever that poor excuse of a tree which never bore what it was guaranteed to. He sincerely hoped Lucy could now forget that thief Tom. He squirmed.

Clem. John smiled in the direction of the door. The Linsdales were one of the most prosperous farmers in Dunken County. Clem's father was a first-rate card player. If his son was interested in one of his daughters, it would be to his credit in more ways than one. Nor would he consciously do anything to hinder a budding romance. If this should lead to marriage, it would recompense at least in part for the humiliation Lucy had brought on the Winchesters' humble home. Even though he was often uncomfortably aware of the fact that he could neither read well nor write a finely worded letter, that was no reason why his daughters shouldn't strive to marry well. Undoubtedly Clem would have the wherewithal to buy Flossie the fancy, frilly, extravagant things he was certain she'd be hankering for. He smiled again at his speeding thoughts.

Suddenly John Winchester got out of bed. He picked up his overalls. He'd go down there and try to find that note and ask Lucy to read it to him in secret. He had a perfect right as a father and head of his house to know what was going on. But before his hand touched the doorknob, he changed his mind. That might spoil the whole thing. If he found it, Flossie would be furious. She'd tell Clem and he'd be furious. No, he'd relax and go to sleep. He didn't want to do anything to fan the ill will of any Linsdale.

Clem had often stopped at the Winchester place to return a borrowed tool or trade a load of feed for wood. He had seen Flossie on several occasions but had taken no personal interest in her until they met unexpectedly on a certain Sunday afternoon when she was hunting violets along the road. She was standing under a bloom-covered dogwood tree, one hand holding her blue bouquet, the other tucking back a lock of hazel brown hair, when Clem passed on horseback. He pulled on the reins and turned his horse around. More than once he had agreed with other young men in the community that Tom Hammon had married the prettiest girl in the county. This was the first time Lucy's sister struck him as being particularly attractive. He was quite taken aback. In fact, standing there in her red-and-white checked jumper and snowy white blouse (one of Lucy's creations) Flossie was more than merely attractive.

"Flossie," Clem said, tipping his hat, "has the card game started yet?"

"I really don't know," she answered, smiling her sweetest shy smile. "Your father hadn't come yet when I left the house. I guess they were waiting for him."

"Well, he sent me over to tell your father he can't come today. A horse kicked him in the face last night. You stay here till I hurry up to the house. I want to tell you something."

Flossie waited with fluttering emotions. There was a special radiance about her when Clem returned. Her sparkling eyes met his as he jumped off the horse and stood tall and erect before her, his hat in one hand.

"You know what Tom Hammon told me one day in town?"

"When?"

"Soon after he and your sister were married."

"No. I've no idea. What was it?"

"He said he put a big flat stone close to a plum tree down there on your place and he and Lucy hid love letters under it."

"What?" Flossie's eyes widened with astonishment.

"You never knew anything about it?"

"No. Well, of all things. Is it still there?"

"Let's go find out."

Clem led his horse and together they walked down the

road to the plum tree. The stone was still there. Clem turned it over. Flossie watched with silent curiosity.

"You're a pretty girl, Flossie," Clem remarked, glancing down on her with a smile that lit up his entire face. She blushed a beautiful peach. "Do you have a boyfriend?" He tapped the stone with the toe of his shoe. Flossie shook her head teasingly. "Then why can't I be?" he asked musingly. "You've grown up suddenly or something's happened to you, Flossie. I—I had no idea. Look," he said, "look right here." He put three fingers deep in the crotch of the plum tree. "Why can't we do one better?"

"What do you mean?" Flossie's eyes were fairly dancing now. She quivered with happy excitement, completely new and startling.

"If you promise me you'll come and get it," he ventured with sudden boldness, "I'll hide you a note down in here."

"You—you will?" smiled Flossie. "When?"

"Let's make it Thursday night."

Flossie tingled with sheer delight. "All right, Clem," she agreed, radiant as a newly formed star in a blue heaven.

Then the unexpected. Uncle Jake passed, stopped his horse, spoke a few words, and drove on. But he turned around (Flossie saw him) and gave them a prolonged, questioning look.

From that moment Flossie entertained uneasy feelings. Of course he'd go straight home and report to Aunt Polly. Why wouldn't she have apprehensions when Aunt Polly had a private, confidential conversation with Lucy, and then say she'd be back to have a talk with Father? Everything, yes, everything pointed to that needle of suspicion that hung over her and pointed her out as the guilty one.

Less than fifteen minutes after Lucy went upstairs, Flossie tiptoed in. She sat on the edge of Lucy's bed. "Lucy," she whispered, "I believe you now."

"I'm glad. I wouldn't lie to you, Flossie. Did you find the note?"

"I have it here but I haven't read it yet. Clem did put it in the tree. But just as he was walking back to his horse, he noticed someone with a lantern and watched. He saw Father chop down the tree, and after he came back to the house, Clem ran over and got it. I'm sure glad you explained to him, Lucy."

"So am I."

"I hope you can sleep now."

"I'll try. I hope you can too."

From that night Flossie showed a much better attitude toward Lucy. She helped her plant the rest of the garden. She grumbled less about helping with the monotonous repetition of never-ending household duties. Her interest in Clem wasn't something she had to keep secret and she mentioned his name unhesitatingly and frequently to Lucy.

A week after the plum tree episode Flossie faced her father at the barn door. "Say," she said raising her eyebrows and smiling, "couldn't I go along to town with you the next time you go?"

"What fer?"

"I'd like to select material for a couple new dresses. I haven't got anything fit to wear."

"I see." John leaned heavily on his pitchfork handle. "I guess you mean fit to wear on a date with Clem Linsdale."

"Well, yes. I'm sure you don't want me to go out with

185

him looking shabby, do you?"

"No." He gave her a sweeping first glance, then a lingering one of consideration. He was suddenly confronted with the consciousness that his second daughter was no longer a high-strung, unpredictable adolescent but a high-spirited, sensitive, proud, unpredictable young lady. Her demands might become deplorable. Flossie wasn't another Lucy. She'd never be satisfied with dress material. She'd want slippers, jackets, purses, gloves, hats, perfume, and God only knew what all. He shook his head. "I don't think I should take you to town with a load of wood," he reasoned, "but," he scratched his head, "I'll get you enough for two dresses."

"You'll get something gay and pretty, won't you? Something I'd like?"

"I'll try to."

"Nothing drab or old-fashioned looking, Father. You know, none of that funny figured calico like you used to bring home for Mom."

"I know. I know," he answered.

John Winchester drew marks on the ground with the fork prongs. True as truth he never could scrape together enough money to get Maggie glasses; so how could he possibly manage to supply this flowering, love-captured miss with her extravagances? But he would do his best if he had to go without socks and a shirt on his own back. It would give him the height of personal satisfaction if the neighbors learned that the son of Howard Linsdale was calling on his daughter, Flossie.

And when John brought the package home, Flossie was more than satisfied. "Why, Father," she exclaimed, "I'm delighted." She draped the soft cream-colored lawn with bright orange flowers over her left shoulder and rubbed it against her cheek. "It's beautiful. So is this piece of voile. Look, Lucy, isn't it pretty? You call this peacock blue, don't you?"

"It's very lovely," agreed Lucy. "I guess it's peacock. It'll look nice on you."

Lucy made both dresses. Flossie had a good form to fit and when they were finished, she admired herself.

"Flossie," remarked Lucy thoughtfully while finishing the hem, "Clem is very handsome, isn't he?"

"You think so? Well, so do I. He's the handsomest fellow in the world, I'd say."

Lucy cut the thread. "I was just thinking," she said, expressing her inmost thoughts, "how wonderful it would be if you were both Christians."

Flossie looked up sharply. She cleared her throat and wrinkled up her nose. "Now, don't start on something like that," she remarked in biting disgust.

Clem came to see Flossie every Sunday afternoon. Usually they took a long walk. On one occasion he brought along a second beautiful sorrel and the two rode away together glowing and laughing.

Lucy stood at the door and watched until they were out of sight. How supremely happy Flossie looked. How stunning in her new voile dress and hazel brown hair. What a handsome gentleman Clem was. A great lump was rapidly growing in Lucy's throat. Her eyes shimmered with blinding tears. She hurried upstairs and sank onto the box by the east window.

Oh, why hadn't she waited and gone with someone Father approved of? Oh, how cruel, how short and unexpected could life be? Did God have favorites? Oh, Tom—

Tom, oh, why did Father hate him so? He never even tried to learn to know him. He never gave Tom a thread of a chance. Oh, why couldn't he have let Tom call for her at the door as he wanted to? Tom was every bit as handsome as Clem Linsdale. Every ounce as much a gentleman. Why, why does Father still despise the very ground that covers Tom's dear body? How could she go on much longer living under this roof and watch Flossie enjoy to the full the life she had had snatched from her? How could she carry this deep sorrow another day and sleep in the same room with one reveling in such divine happiness? No, she was not jealous of Flossie. She was glad for her. The tract. *Humility is perpetual—never to be fretted—wonder at nothing—O God.* Her head dropped onto the hard windowsill.

Lucy cried until her sobbing shook her entire body, the room, the house, the world, her entire past, her entire lonely, tilting, disconnected future, her black-draped eternity.

Clem came to see Flossie every Wednesday evening also. It was nobody's guess that he was headlong in love with Flossie Winchester and wasn't having any trouble winning her affection.

One evening when the two were speaking in sweet nearness in the sitting room, Lucy decided to prove to herself she wasn't jealous. She'd surprise them with freshly popped corn.

"Want something to nibble on?" she asked smiling sweetly.

"How nice," exclaimed Clem jumping to his feet and bowing thanks. He took the two dishes of hot, buttery corn. "Thank you very much, Lucy." Then turning to

Flossie he said, "Say, that sister of yours is mighty pretty."

A hurt expression like a dark streak cut across Flossie's face. She ate popcorn nervously.

Moments later Lucy heard someone call from the porch.

"Hi, Lucy."

Lucy looked up in surprise.

"Aunt Polly," she cried. "Come in. Did you come alone?"

"No, Jake's out there with your father. I just had a talk with him."

"You did? Where?"

"Out there where he was fixing fence. And it was a good talk. Let's sit down a bit and I'll tell you about it."

CHAPTER 23

"**W**ELL," SMILED Aunt Polly as she and Jake started home that warm summer night, "you're going to have to admit I won."

"You mean we won."

"Well, I was right proud of you tonight, Jake. You sure put in a few good words at the right places, I must admit."

"John was in unusually good spirits for some reason. Just never will be able to figure that man out."

"Clem Linsdale was in the house seeing Flossie."

"In the house?" shouted Jake Bechtold.

"I said in the house, didn't I?"

"Was that his horse tied to the post?"

"Lucy said it was. And said also her father approves of it."

Jake looked at his wife, then spit tobacco juice. "Huh. He's a man hard to figure out. Must have a crisscross mind in him. I'm glad Lucy's leaving. But he's goin' to miss her."

"Well, he ought to," mumbled Aunt Polly. "I won't feel one bit sorry for him either."

"He thinks a lot of Lucy, Polly."

"He ought to."

"Well, he admitted it to me. After you went into the house, he let go of himself a little. He's real concerned about Lucy."

"Did he say he was?"

"Not in so many words, but he had quite a time keepin' control. Just between you and me I believe down in his heart he thinks the sun rises and sets on her. I said on Lucy, Polly, not what she did. I could have just punched him in the nose. I could have."

"Jake. What are you saying?"

"Well, I felt like it. He thinks so much of her but he's too stubborn to admit he's mistreated her about Tom."

They drove on in silence.

"Polly."

"Yes."

"When did you tell her we'd be over to get her?"

"I said likely Saturday or Sunday toward evening."

"We'd better go Saturday. You know John has those men there every Sunday. We don't want to make a show of it, do we?"

"Of course not. The first thing we've got to do is make that girl some new dresses."

Saturday Lucy had all her things packed. All her things were easily tucked in one large packing box. She carried her coat. She kissed Loretta and Peggy good-bye. Peggy clung to her arm and cried all the way to the wagon. She stepped up to kiss Flossie but Flossie stiffened and said with a pout, "I just don't think it's one bit nice of you to go off like this when I was going to ask you to make my wedding dress."

"Why, Flossie," answered Lucy, "you didn't tell me you were engaged."

"Well, you might have guessed that."

"I should have I suppose, but I was waiting for you to tell me, Flossie. I'll be glad to make your wedding dress if you'll bring the material over to Aunt Polly's. I'll cut it out and put it all together for you whenever you say. Just find a pattern or show me how you want it made."

John Winchester standing close by was trying desperately to control his emotions. He worked the toe of his right shoe into the dusty ground and his fingers fumbled with bolts and screws and bits of twine in his overall pockets. Lucy's face was flushed damp with fresh perspiration. The hollow place in the front of her neck was throbbing. He tried to swallow the unwelcomed obstruction in his throat. He glanced off in the distance. "Don't bother Lucy with a dress, Flossie," he said dryly. "I might sell a calf and buy you one."

Lucy held out her one hand. He caught it. She lifted her face and kissed her father on the cheek. Her wet lashes left a tiny wet spot. He helped her up onto the seat beside Aunt Polly. "Too crowded fer you?" he asked.

She shook her head.

"You'll—come back. Won't you?"

If she heard, Lucy did not answer.

He sighed.

They were off.

John Winchester was smitten with a loneliness completely unknown. He leaned bodily on the gate and watched the wagon until it was out of sight. Two leaving home almost at once. Yes, he could honestly say he was glad and proud Flossie would soon be married to Clem Linsdale. And Clem could handle Flossie if any man could. And she might need some handling—vain, quick-tempered, dashing Flossie. The wood dollars would reach farther with both girls gone. That was one comforting thought. Loretta was thirteen and a real worker. Another comforting thought. Kenneth was fifteen and not many lazy bones in him for a fast-growing boy. Peggy was more like Lucy in disposition than any of the girls and she was surprisingly obedient. She may be different with Lucy gone. A loneliness John Winchester would not admit to himself enveloped him. He felt dismally old. He shook himself. He filled his pipe and walked slowly toward the barn.

The chores could wait. He must quit this ridiculous pondering and take command of himself. He'd miss Lucy, her breakfasts, her bread, her cobblers, her tempting biscuits, but most of all herself. Why hadn't she confided in him? Why did she have Aunt Polly come and tell him? If she had the courage to come and tell him to cut down the plum tree, then why couldn't she have told him everything? He was ready to consent to her going over to Jake's once he knew. What else could he have done? He wasn't going to be unreasonable even if it was hard to see her leave. He placed two rough fingers on the spot on his cheek where she had kissed him.

He recalled now that Lucy had been looking worn and pale at times. Too often. Nor had he heard her even attempt to sing for weeks. Would she sing over at Jake's? Would she be happy there, happy enough to sing? Those silly, ridiculous Jesus songs? Would she ever sing again? Or laugh? Or, oh, no! Lucy couldn't die! He'd smoke that horrible thought out of his mind.

Aunt Polly had taken great pains to make a cozy room for Lucy. She trimmed snowy white curtains with blue and put a beautiful new blue-and-white quilt on the bed. More than that, she finished two multicolored braided round rugs she had started before she got down with rheumatism. Lucy was thrilled.

"It's just too lovely, Aunt Polly."

"Now you hush. Too lovely, nothing. You just come in here and relax and do as you please. It's all yours."

"Aunt Polly?"

"Yes?"

"You wouldn't mind if I talk about Tom sometimes?"

"If you want to talk about Tom, you just feel free to talk about him all you want to, my dear. And why not? He's the father of your baby, isn't he? And you'll be telling him who his father is, won't you?"

"Oh, Aunt Polly," and Lucy threw her arms around Aunt Polly's neck and hugged her, "you're so good to me. Oh, just think," she raised both arms and held them high above her head, "I can talk about Tom over here and I'm going to do it right now. I'm dying to talk about him. And I'm not ever, ever going to let my child think his father was anything but a good, kind, decent, hard-working, handsome father who loved me, loved me, and loved us both very, very much. And he didn't die a murderer or a thief, or a scoundrel. He died trying to save another man from being murdered." Lucy was nearly out of breath.

"You're absolutely right, Lucy," said Aunt Polly. "My child. I didn't know you had it in you to express yourself like this. Go ahead and say what you want to if it makes you feel better."

"Oh, Aunt Polly, I've been penned up for so long I feel like getting up on the housetop and shouting to the whole world that I had a husband, a dear husband who was true to me. Maybe he really came from a very remarkable family. He couldn't help it he was left an orphan. He—he knew how to love. He was a gentleman, but Father wouldn't— Oh, well, no use saying all that again. I wouldn't shout that from a rooftop but I'd like everyone to know I will give honorable birth to our child. I fear the future without Tom. Yes, I do. More than anyone knows. But by God's help I'll work to give my baby everything I longed for and couldn't have. I will, Aunt Polly. I will."

"I'm sure you mean it all very well, Lucy dear. Now after you've unpacked your box—I emptied the dresser drawers—you may come out to the kitchen if you want to. Is there anything you're hungry for?"

"Aunt Polly, this may sound crazy but I'm hungry for the funniest things."

"Like what?"

"Some of that hot, wilted, sweet-sour cabbage and cottage cheese all black with lots of pepper."

"Well, now I don't think either of those things will be impossible to fix. I'll see."

One morning while the two were cutting cabbage for the winter's supply of kraut, Aunt Polly asked, "Lucy, wouldn't it be something if Brother Bustleton would come back to Black Bend again?"

Lucy gave a big sigh. "I'd like to see him again sometime, but not now. I'm sure he'd be very disappointed in me."

"Why?"

"Why? Because I'm not what I was the night I was baptized, the last time he saw me."

"But look what all you've been through. You still believe what you did that night, don't you?"

"I still believe in God, of course I do; but Aunt Polly, I haven't been living in perpetual victory, far from it. Sometimes I've felt sorta hard toward God for taking Tom from me. Maybe since I've confessed it now to you, I can get rid of it. I really want to."

"You pray every day, don't you?"

"Of course."

"Well, Lucy, if you ask God every day to keep His hand over you, He'll do it. And don't you ever doubt it."

CHAPTER 24

ONE BRIGHT morning in late August Mrs. Fetherstone arrived in time to bathe the tiny newborn.

"You have a very sweet little boy, Lucy," she cooed, smiling sincerely into the pink blanket.

"Thank you," answered Lucy. "I think too he's pretty nice."

"Who wouldn't?" added Mrs. Fetherstone as she continued. "He came on my birthday. Did you know that?"

"Really?"

"That's right. I feel quite honored. August the twenty-eighth. We'll have to keep in touch and celebrate together, won't we, you precious little cherub? You know he looks a lot like Tom."

"That's what Aunt Polly said too," Lucy commented wearily. She closed her eyes.

"I'm going to get him a gift the very first time I go to town. Have you picked out a name?"

Lucy opened her eyes. "John Eldon."

"John Eldon," repeated Mrs. Fetherstone finding the rocking chair in the corner of Lucy's room. She cradled the infant in her left arm and patted him gently.

"I thought," explained Lucy taking a deep breath and running one hand across her forehead, "perhaps it might please my father if I'd name my son John. But I'm going to call him Eldon. That I know."

Mrs. Fetherstone saw a tear trickle over Lucy's temple and she also saw Lucy try to hide it in her pillow. "Polly," she called to the kitchen, "when you have that tea fixed for Lucy, you come in here and take over. I don't want to spoil this little boy by holding him too long. You come on in and sit down and let me do that ironing for you. I told my husband he wouldn't need to stop for me until about noon. So I'm here to help work, not sit around. Lucy dear, does your father know you have your baby?"

"Uncle Jake went over on horseback after early breakfast."

"Do you look for him to come over soon?"

"I just don't know," came Lucy's hesitant answer. She covered her eyes with one hand.

"Here's your tea, Lucy." Aunt Polly served it in her highly prized, hand-painted china cup and saucer. "Say," she looked out the window, "there comes your father now. You go to the door, Mrs. Fetherstone."

"Good morning, Mr. Winchester. Come in."

"Mornin'." His Adam's apple went up and down. "I came to see Lucy." He stated his purpose with serious impulsiveness while removing his straw hat.

"Of course. Of course," blinked Mrs. Fetherstone. "Come with me. Right in there."

"Hello, Father," Lucy smiled up at him.

"How are you, Lucy?" The concern in his tone was not veneer. His voice was husky, even tense.

"I'm all right. How are you, Father?"

"I'm all right," he blinked twice. "Are—are you tired?"

"Do I look tired?"

"To me you do. Yes." He shifted uneasily on his feet.

"Don't you want to see my baby?"

"Oh, yes. Sure."

"Aunt Polly fixed me that basket there on those two chairs. He's in there."

John Winchester turned, took two steps, and looked down at the tiny pink face, eyes closed in sleep. He cleared his throat, all the while holding his hands behind him.

"Who do you think he looks like?" asked Mrs. Fetherstone stepping to the bedroom door and looking in.

"Well," disappointment was in every word, "not—like —his mother—"

"But isn't he sweet, Mr. Winchester, Grandpa Winchester?" dimpled Mrs. Fetherstone. "Isn't he just the dearest little bundle from heaven? Wouldn't you say?"

John Winchester's forehead beaded with August perspiration. "Yes," he agreed without nodding. What else could he say? It was a sweet baby. How could Lucy have anything but a sweet baby? But the image of Tom.

"Have you named him yet?" he turned and faced Lucy, forcing a lagging smile. He wiped his forehead.

"John Eldon."

John Winchester looked surprised.

"I've decided I'll call him Eldon. Is that all right with you?"

"Why, yes, of course. Of course." He ran one hand deep in his overall pocket. "Here's a little somethin' to help you get what you might be needin'." And he handed Lucy a silver dollar.

"Thank you, Father. But you need it, don't you?"

"I've been savin' it fer you."

"Thank you, Father. Charlie Morehouse paid me for

199

the chickens and—and the horse and Aunt Polly bought my red rug so I could get some things and pay the doctor."

"I see," her father ran one hand around his hat brim twice. He looked sober, tired, and much too old. "I must—go." He seemed to be scrambling for the right words to say. "Take care of yourself, Lucy, an'—you know what I said—when you left."

He waited.

He shifted nervously.

He waited.

The silence was embarrassing and nerve-fraying. His tongue felt stiff.

"Good-bye, Father," said Lucy picking at the sheet. "I wish the girls," she was fighting to control her emotions now, "could come over and see me and the baby too."

John left without a word.

Mrs. Fetherstone hurried to the door. "Just a minute, Mr. Winchester," she called. "Lucy wants me to ask you if Flossie is married yet."

"Yes. She got married the week after Lucy came over here."

"Lucy said the next time you see them to tell them she wishes they'd come over and see her and her baby."

"All right." He seemed to be anxious to leave.

"Just one more thing, Mr. Winchester. Lucy wants to know where they're living."

"As far as I know they're still at Clem's folks. They couldn't find a place to suit them."

"All right," called Mrs. Fetherstone, "that's all."

"Lucy," began Aunt Polly standing at the foot of her bed, "what was it your father was referring to?"

"Well, when we left, didn't you hear him say, 'You will

come back, won't you?' "

"I see. I thought he said something like that but I wasn't sure. I noticed you didn't answer him."

"I couldn't, Aunt Polly. I just got all choked up inside. I—I didn't want to cry—but if my baby looks like Tom, and I'm sure he thinks he does, and if I couldn't mention Tom's name over there or talk about him," Lucy moaned, "how could I endure it? I will talk to my son about his father all I want to if I have to go live in a cave." Lucy's tears broke.

"Don't cry, Lucy dear," begged Aunt Polly sympathetically. "You shouldn't let yourself get so unnerved now. You need your strength."

"I know it, Aunt Polly," cried Lucy, "but since my baby looks like Tom—"

"He may change and come to look exactly like you."

"But if he always favors Tom and my father despises him so, he'd likely mistreat my little son. No. I won't give him a chance. If little Eldon looks like Tom, God did it and I'm glad of it."

"Of course God did, Lucy. I'm glad you feel that way about it. Tom would be so proud of him. He's such a perfectly formed baby as the doctor told you. Now, you just rest and don't fret or worry about a thing in the world. You don't need to think about going back home. You have a home right here with us."

"Oh, but, Aunt Polly," said Lucy firmly, "as soon as I'm able, I must go out and find me a—"

"What?" interrupted Aunt Polly. "You weren't going to say find a job, were you?"

"Why not?"

"But you have a home right here as long as you care to

stay. Why, Uncle Jake is as proud of your baby as if it was his very own."

"Well," answered Lucy feebly, "we'll see."

Mrs. Fetherstone finished the ironing before her husband arrived.

"I'll just take one more peek at little Eldon," she said musingly as she tiptoed to the basket. "Bless his little heart. God bless you both, Lucy. I'll be going now. And you come and spend a week or two with me anytime, just anytime you want to."

"Thank you. I'll remember that."

"Good."

Lucy loved her little son. With every passing day he looked more like Tom. With every passing moment Lucy loved him more. She'd work, she'd slave if need be, she'd live to her utmost, she'd even die for Tom's child.

Peggy and Floyd walked over to Uncle Jake's one evening after school. Floyd just smiled and smiled and kept on smiling, first at Lucy, then at the baby. Peggy asked if she could hold him.

"Sure you can, Peggy. Here."

She carried him through the house, smiling constantly. "He's so tiny, Lucy. And so cute. Why don't you come back real soon? I could help you take care of him."

Lucy made no answer.

"Please, Lucy."

"How are you girls getting along with the work since Flossie's gone?"

"Well," Peggy rocked on one foot, "we're doing the best we can, I guess. But Father keeps telling Loretta you make better coffee than she does and that makes her feel bad. And he tells her her pancakes are too thin and that makes her feel bad."

"Poor Loretta," said Lucy.

"And he tells her her patches don't hold on tight like yours did."

"And that makes her feel bad too, doesn't it?" asked Lucy.

Peggy nodded. "Lucy."

"Yes."

"Why don't you have Uncle Jake bring you and your baby home tonight and surprise Father? He'd really be glad."

"He would?"

"I sure do think he would be."

Lucy put one arm around Peggy's shoulder and drew her close against herself. "Guess we'll put little Eldon back in his basket now, Peggy dear. I'm so glad you and Floyd came. When you get home, tell Loretta to come over the first chance she has."

"Shall I tell— Please, Lucy, shall I tell Father to come and get you?"

"No, dear," Lucy shook her head. "Please don't tell him that."

Peggy's eyes filled with glistening tears. She ran to the road and Floyd after her.

CHAPTER 25

B
Y THE time John Eldon was two months old no one who had ever seen Tom Hammon could question whom he favored. Same eyes, same forehead, same nose, mouth—in fact, he was all Tom. Some people even suggested that Lucy call him Tommy.

Lucy had been thinking her situation through and through and every time came to the same conclusion. She shared her thoughts with no one but her son. The time had come. "You sleep well tonight, little lamb," she whispered, "for this will be your last night in this basket, in this room. Tomorrow, yes, tomorrow we're going on a trip. Just you and your mother."

Lucy broke the news at the breakfast table when Uncle Jake passed the omelet. "I guess," she began, surprising herself with her bravery—she had practiced her speech repeatedly while dressing—"this will be my last meal with you for a while."

"What?" exclaimed Uncle Jake dropping his fork against the edge of his plate.

"It's like this," explained Lucy, selecting her words with care, "you two have been good to me long enough. You've been wonderful. Like real parents. I want you both," she glanced at Aunt Polly, "to know I appreciate your kindness more than I can ever tell you."

"But, Lucy, what we've done we've done gladly out of

love. Not because we felt obligated to you."

"I'm sure of it, Aunt Polly. But I feel very sure the time has come for me to get a job. Eldon will soon be needing clothes and I need things. I can't expect you folks to clothe and feed us when I'm able to work."

"But where will you go, child?" fretted Aunt Polly. She hadn't taken a bite yet.

"I don't know. But I've prayed about it for two months now and I believe God will help me find work somewhere. I just have the confidence He will."

"And the baby?" Aunt Polly bent forward and looked searchingly in Lucy's face.

"Oh, I'll take him with me. Of course."

"How can you hold a job with a baby, Lucy?" This Uncle Jake asked.

"All I can say is, time will tell. I want to start out as soon as I've helped you with the dishes, Aunt Polly."

"Oh, Lucy," and Aunt Polly was fighting tears, "we'll miss you both something awful."

"We'll miss you too, Aunt Polly. But I'm sure I shouldn't wait another day. I've got to start out before cold weather sets in. I've considered this from every angle."

"Then you're not going back home?" asked Uncle Jake rather grimly.

"I am not going back home," stated Lucy with finality.

Lucy had packed all of Eldon's things, her own, and her Bible the night before in a forty-eight-pound flour sack. Some of her clothes were so badly worn she left them for Aunt Polly to use as mop rags. The bag was scarcely more than half full and she could easily carry it over her shoulder with a small rope and carry Eldon in her arms. He weighed less than nine pounds.

She was coming out of the bedroom when Aunt Polly called, "Lucy, your father is here."

"What? My father?"

He entered without knocking. "Well," he said, "I see you're ready."

"Ready?" Lucy's arms suddenly felt limp.

Her legs shook.

"I came to get you. Peggy said you were ready to come home now."

"Peggy told you that?" Lucy thought his voice almost had a thrill in it.

"She's all excited."

"But, Father," faltered Lucy—her face got very warm, but her hands felt cold—"I didn't tell Peggy you should come for me."

"Well, were you having Uncle Jake bring you over?"

"No."

"You were going to walk over?" he frowned.

"Well, it's a nice morning and I was going to start out and—" Her knees wobbled. She felt her own voice quiver.

To Lucy's surprise her father reached out his tawny hands and took the baby out of her arms. She saw him smile when John Eldon looked up into his face. "Shall we go?" he said inching to the door. "Peggy hasn't talked 'bout another thing but this baby since she was over here."

Lucy was shaken. She began to struggle frantically with a series of baffling ideas. When had she ever seen her father smile like that? Would he be kind to Eldon after all? She tried to smile at Aunt Polly as she said good-bye, but she could hardly speak for the lump in her throat. In a daze, she followed her father to the wagon. He all but lifted her up on the seat. Aunt Polly went to the gate and waving said, "Good luck, Lucy. We'll miss you."

Before they reached the big oak tree, Lucy felt she had pulled herself together. It wasn't easy. She was glad she had her baby in her arms so that her father couldn't see her arms trembling.

"I would like to get off at the corner," she began.

"Get off?" exclaimed her father. "Get off; what fer?"

"I'm starting out to look for work." She looked down the road. She could hear him gulp. She heard him gasp for breath.

"Fer work?" he panted. "What do you mean? Won't there be enough work to suit you over home?" The muscle under his right eye quivered.

"But I've got to work for wages, Father." She waited one breathless moment, then continued. "I've got my baby to support. I need clothes badly and so does he." She talked rapidly now so that her father couldn't interrupt her. She had to make her point clear, and immediately. She was confident of the rightness of her decision. She would not change it. "I can't expect you to supply our needs. You're getting old—I mean older every day and I absolutely couldn't feel right coming back home, two of us now, and be a burden on you." She did not glance over to see his bleak look of surprise merging into dismay. "My baby might get sick sometime like babies do and I'd need a doctor and I couldn't expect you to pay for that. Uncle Jake helped me out when I needed some things for him and I mean to pay him back as soon as I can. I appreciate it that Peggy wants me to come home, but I've made up

207

my mind to strike out on my own and make it alone."

She saw the reins in her father's tightly clenched hands trembling. She did not trust herself to look at him. He was breathing like one in disbelief or distress or both. "I'm almost twenty-one and I'm a mother and I've got this child to think about first. God gave me a strong body and I mean to use it to give my son an education. It's going to be hard without a husband and without a father for my son." She looked straight ahead and straightened her shoulders. "If Tom had lived," she said with shameless boldness, "he would be a good provider. And I'm sure he would have let drink alone and been a real good father to this baby of ours. And, Father, I want to tell you this, if you would have given Tom a chance and gotten acquainted with him, if you'd been half as nice to him as you've been to Clem Linsdale, everything today might be altogether different. Who knows, maybe Tom's real father was a rich man, a lawyer or a doctor or a professor." Lucy was almost out of breath.

John Winchester got hot around his collar. He unbuttoned it. He forgot what he was going to say. He picked up the whip. The horses heard it and quickened their steps before he touched them.

They were nearing the corner where Lucy wanted to get off. He gathered up her sack.

He drew on the reins and the wagon stopped. John Winchester jumped off and Lucy heard him groan when his feet hit the ground. He reached up, took the baby, and stood aside. He made no effort to help Lucy down. He stood with silent remonstrance engraved on every inch of his sullen face.

Lucy held out both arms. He gave her the bundled

treasure. "Thanks for the lift, Father," she said softly. She had never seen his strength shrivel as at that moment. And she knew she was responsible. Her words had snuffed his flame of hope. "I'll tell you where I am when I find work. I'll always love you, Father." She was unsuccessful in holding back her tears. "I'm sorry to disappoint you—and Peggy, but I'm absolutely sure I'm doing the right thing. I can't afford to disappoint my son. And—I'm sure this is what Tom would want me to do for his son." Two tears splashed on the baby's blue blanket. "I loved Tom. I loved Tom," she repeated, "and nobody on earth will ever again tell me I can't speak his name."

It seemed to Lucy that years passed while her father stood there wiping his face with his red bandanna. Would she ever understand him? Did her mother understand him? "Well," he said without looking at her, "if you can't find a job—you can come home." He cleared his throat. "If you want to," he added.

He was finished.

He did not shake her hand.

He turned and stepped up into the wagon.

Lucy watched him drive away, and a fountain of tears void of spite or rebellion or retaliation streamed down her face.

She hadn't gone far until she had to unbutton her coat. She was wearing the pretty navy one Tom had bought for her on their wedding day. The October sun was bright and the two bundles she was carrying were heavier than she had imagined. By the time she had walked a mile, she had to sit down and rest. Several children headed for Black Bend School passed her and looked wonderingly at the strange sight, a young woman with a baby and a flour sack bundle. They ran on like young deer.

The first house she passed was the Morehouse place. She hadn't seen Mrs. Morehouse since the day of Tom's funeral. She was outside hanging tea towels on the wash line.

"Is that you, Lucy?" she called.

"Yes."

"Is that your baby?"

"Yes."

"Wait. I want to see him. I heard you had a little boy. Oh, isn't he sweet! For all the world Tom. The image of Tom, Lucy."

"That's what everyone says."

"Where are you going?"

"I'm out hunting for a job."

"A job?"

"Yes. Do you know anyone who needs a hired girl?"

"No, I don't, Lucy. Most folks around here have girls of their own big enough to help. I'm sure the Blackshaws could use a hired girl, but they say they couldn't pay more than fifty cents a week."

"Well, I certainly hope I can do better than that," answered Lucy.

"Then you'll have to go on into Black Bend, my dear. So your sister Flossie is married too."

"Yes."

"Sure is too bad they can't get along better. I always thought a lot of Clem Linsdale."

"Can't get along?" gasped Lucy.

"You mean you haven't heard? Where have you been?"

"I've been with Aunt Polly and Uncle Jake. The Bechtolds. I just left there a while ago. No, I didn't know

Flossie and Clem weren't getting along."

"Well, maybe it's hearsay. I hope so."

"I saw my father this morning and he never told me a word about it."

"He didn't? Well, it's a shame if it's true. I always feel bad when newlyweds can't agree. Maybe it's all patched up by now if the report had any truth to it at all. You know how rumors get started sometimes."

"Well, I've got to hurry on my way, Mrs. Morehouse. I'm glad I got to see you."

"Well, I'm even more glad I got to see you, my dear. And good luck. But as I told you, you may have to go into Black Bend to find a job that pays anything."

CHAPTER 26

HALF A mile beyond the bridge Lucy stopped at a house behind two large lilac bushes. A phonograph was spinning off a lusty band number. She hesitated, then knocked. A woman with biscuit dough on both hands, some in her hair, and flour on her long green apron came to the door

"No," she said in a pleasant, friendly manner, "I couldn't use a hired girl. I have three boys and I've taught them how to help me. You've got a right nice baby there and I do hope you find what you're looking for. It might be tough. You look tired, miss. Won't you step in and have a cup of coffee?"

"Thank you kindly," answered Lucy, "but I should be on my way. What time is it?"

"Our clock says ten-forty-five. I'm not sure it's correct."

By noon she reached the crossroad. Hesitating, Lucy looked to the right, then to the left. Her shoulder was getting sore from the rope. She decided to sit on the ridge along the road and rest long enough to feed Eldon. She wished now she had taken the coffee the lady offered her. *O God,* she breathed, *please keep Your hand over me. Today, Lord. Today.*

A sudden chilly wind made her shiver. She drew the blanket up over the baby's face. A heavy cloud loomed in the northwest. "Darling," she said getting up, "I hope it won't rain on you. You've been so patient, you dear little lamb. Now we're going to go on again. Oh, I wish you could pray with me. 'When two of you shall agree on anything'—it's in the Bible, darling—'it shall be done for you.'"

A man on horseback came galloping up. He gave Lucy a curious glance and hurried on. But he hadn't gone a quarter of a mile when he turned around and came back. "Lady," he said tipping his hat, "I know this is none of my business, but something told me to come back and ask you if—well, I'll put it this way: Are you going somewhere?"

"I'm going somewhere," answered Lucy, "but I'm not sure just where."

"Are you lost?"

"Not that, sir. I'm out hunting for work."

"Sure enough? What kind of work?"

"Really, housework is the only thing I know much about."

"Well, I've got a sick wife at home and we need someone badly. I mean right away. Could you—would you want to try it?"

Lucy's heart almost leaped. "Where do you live?"

"Down the road two and a half miles."

Lucy's freshened spirits suddenly wilted once more.

"We live on the Haffer place. Would you by any chance know where I mean?"

The Haffer place! Oh, how could she? Of all places on earth she hadn't thought of going there to work. Instantly her entire span of days with Tom flashed before her. Her face must have turned pale, for the man on horseback said apologetically, "I hope I didn't scare you, lady."

"Oh, no," she answered feebly. "I—I—yes, I know the place."

"I work on the railroad. I moved the family out here in the country because it's better for the children. And we have more garden space."

"You have children?" inquired Lucy, shifting the rope.

"Seven. And with their mother down in bed—well, we need help, lady. I'll give you two dollars a week if you'll come. The four oldest go to school. And the baby walks. Is that your baby?"

"Yes."

"Separated?"

"Oh, no, sir. I lost my husband before my baby was born. Oh, no, sir, if Tom had lived, I wouldn't be out hunting for work, believe me."

"I see. How old is your little one?"

"He's two months."

"Well, you'd really have your hands full, I can see that. Can't your mother keep your baby and you take the job until I can find someone else?"

"I have no mother. No, I have to keep my baby with me. We wouldn't consider being separated."

"Well." The man seemed to be weighing the question. "Do you know of anyone else I could get?"

"No, sir, I don't."

"Well, I tell you. We're desperate for help at once. I kept Annie home from school today, but it's more than she can handle and I don't like to have her miss more than's absolutely necessary. I've got to go back to work in the morning or I could help. It's tough with seven children and their mother down, you know. There's a storm coming up, lady. Will you come?"

"I'd like to," answered Lucy slowly, pushing her fears aside with great effort. "I'd try my best if I come. I do need work."

"Let me take your sack bundle." She handed it to him. "I'll go on and tell Mrs. Ashbury—yes, Ashbury's the name. I'll tell her you're on your way. I call this plain luck, lady."

Lucy shivered. The Haffer place. The cozy house where she and Tom lived, loved, slept, laughed, ate, and disagreed. Oh, how could she go back? He noticed her sober expression. "Isn't two dollars enough? I just couldn't pay more even if you deserved more and you probably will. You look like the substantial, dependable type."

"I know how to work," answered Lucy.

"Then you'd better come right on without delay. Looks and feels like rain any minute. I'd let you go on my horse and I'd walk, but he's much too frisky with strangers."

"I'll walk."

Lucy was in sight of the house when it started to sprinkle. She held Eldon tight against her shoulder and hurried as fast as her legs would take her. Just as she reached the yard, it began to pour.

Mr. Ashbury opened the door. "Good. You made it. I should have asked you your name. Please pardon me."

"Lucy Hammon."

With a glance she saw the house was very modestly furnished. Nothing looked quite natural, yet hauntingly, tantalizingly familiar. It was like a walking dream. A gray granite teakettle was steaming on the cookstove exactly where her own beautiful new stove had stood eight long months before. Eight eternities before. She felt faint. Two small girls with dirty faces and dirty dresses were playing on the floor in the living room.

On the large kitchen table was a dish with a few cold

beans in it, a platter holding three cold biscuits, a bowl of sorghum, and a green glass pitcher with a little milk in it.

"Mrs. Hammon, now we want you to feel at home here," said Mr. Ashbury. "So first take off your coat. And here, I put a pillow in this box for your baby. Best I could do. Have you had your dinner?"

"No, I haven't."

"You must be hungry then."

"Yes, truthfully I am, Mr. Ashbury."

"Annie," he said, "you put those beans in a pan and warm them up for the lady. Don't let them burn now. Shall we call you Mrs. Hammon or Lucy?"

"I'd much rather you'd call me Lucy."

"All right. And, Annie, you run to the cave—no, I'll go. It's raining too hard. I'll go get a jar of fruit. But first let me take you in to meet my wife. She'll be telling you what to do first and second and so on. I'll have to go to town rain or no rain and get her some medicine and a few groceries."

Mrs. Ashbury was a dark-eyed, plump, pleasant-faced woman nearing forty. She gave Lucy the impression she had never been happier to see anyone and she asked her a dozen questions about herself, her family, her baby, her husband and what he died of. The woman didn't seem to be seriously ill; at least, the only hindrance to her fluent speaking was an occasional deep coughing spell. By the time Annie had the beans warmed, Lucy had given Mrs. Ashbury a brief history of her life.

"And you say you and your Tom slept in this room?"

"Yes," answered Lucy looking toward the door.

"You won't let it bother you, will you, Lucy?"

"This little chat with you will help, Mrs. Ashbury,"

answered Lucy. "It's helped me already."

"Good. Now go eat your dinner and rest a while and see to it that your baby is comfortable. I told Joe to fix the box for him. I hope it'll be all right. It's what we used for Jimmy before he got too big for it. He's asleep there on the sofa, Lucy. He's sixteen months now; so you won't have to lift him much. Annie, now you do the dishes and show Lucy where we keep the pans and kettles and everything. Show her how the draft works on the cookstove. Then you get the house straightened up before Papa gets back from town and see if you can find clean dresses [cough] for Ruby and Kathleen. And wash their faces, Annie. I don't see how they got so dirty."

The warmed-over beans, cold biscuits dipped in sorghum, and blackberries were decidedly refreshing and actually quite palatable. Lucy wiped the dishes Annie didn't rinse, because they had to save water. She swept the kitchen and shook the foot rug at the back door.

"Come here, Ruby and Kathleen," whispered Lucy, "let me wash your faces while Annie gets clean dresses."

Annie faced Lucy smiling from ear to ear, chin to hair line. "These are the only two I could find," she said. "Mama couldn't wash this week. Everything else is dirty."

Annie was very sure she was going to like this Lucy Papa had found to come and cook the meals, bake light bread and biscuits, sweep and clean and wash dishes so that she could go back to school. She liked the gentle way Lucy moved the soapy rag over her sisters' faces and the friendly way she talked to them while she buttoned their clean dresses.

At Mrs. Ashbury's suggestion Lucy gathered up two bushel baskets of dirty clothes and put them in a large galvanized tub to soak until morning. "The washing will be the most important job for tomorrow" she said, "but you can leave the towels and bedding for the next day. It's piled up so it would be too much to do it all in one day. I don't want to kill you. You likely have diapers and things to wash for your baby too. Yes, and there's Joe's work clothes. I nearly forgot about them. You decide when you'd rather do them. For supper make corn bread if you know how."

"I do."

"The children love it and so does Joe; so I try to always have it once when he's home. You see, he's gone for two or three days at a time, not often four. He's brakeman on the I.C. That's why we need someone to pack the lunch pails and help them get off in time."

"Well, Mrs. Ashbury, you try to relax while I'm here. I've packed many a lunch box for my brothers and sisters; so I'm sure we'll make out. You just tell me what to fix and how much. While I'm here, I know it'll be best for me if I'm kept busy. It's time to feed Eldon now."

"Sure, Lucy. Annie, you can peel the potatoes. Lucy, you can cut them up for the soup. Better see if there's plenty of milk. And you help yourself to the milk any time you want it."

By the time Lucy had the corn bread ready for the oven, the door burst open and in bounded Oliver, Elizabeth, and Paul, all three soaking wet and their feet plastered with oozy, gluey mud. They grinned bashfully at the strange lady and proceeded to the bedroom to ask Mama who she was.

"Say," exclaimed Mrs. Ashbury in exasperation. "You get back out there and take off those muddy shoes. You ought to know better than to come in here with all that mess. The lady in the kitchen is Lucy. Now, you cooperate with her. She's come to help us out and I don't want any of you making her more work than's necessary."

Long before the supper dishes were washed and put away, Lucy was ready to drop, but she kept her feelings concealed as much as possible. With seven children, where would she sleep? She knew a room to herself was an impossibility.

Mrs. Ashbury called her to the bedroom and told her what to make for breakfast, what to put in the lunch pails, and informed her that Joe had to have his breakfast at four-thirty so that he could reach Branton on time. "You know, he can't be late and hold his job, Lucy. I'm sorry you'll have a short night your first night here. And I'm sorry we can't provide you with a good bed. I guess you'll have to use the couch over there. You'll find covers in that big chest. Annie, show Lucy how to open the folding cot. Ruby and Kathleen use that. The boys have the little bedroom and Annie and Elizabeth will make a bed on the floor at the foot of our bed."

"Then I'm crowding someone off the couch." Lucy's voice was despondent and fatigued. It all but snapped in two.

"It can't be helped, Lucy," answered Mrs. Ashbury. "We're crowded but we'll make out the best we can. I must have Joe bring home some more blankets the next time he gets his pay even if we have to skimp on something else."

Lucy got Eldon ready for the night and put the box bed on two chairs placed securely beside the well-worn prickly green couch. She untied her flour sack and took out her Bible. For a few moments she held it in her hands, then put it back in the sack. She dropped on one knee.

Dear Lord, she breathed, *I'm too tired to read one word tonight. Please keep Your hand over me and my baby. You understand.*

Without any effort Lucy was soon in sound sleep between the two worn covers.

CHAPTER 27

L UCY TRIED to recall the day in her childhood when she didn't help her mother in the house or garden. It seemed to her she was born to work. But it had never been like the Ashbury home.

There were jobs staring her in the face from every angle, and she wasn't going to be guilty of shrinking from any of them. She would earn her board (which was good) and couch bed and the two dollars a week Mr. Ashbury had agreed to pay her. Although she thought her mother had taught her how to make the best light bread anyone ever ate, she readily made bread the Ashbury method. She determined to do everything the way plump, friendly Mrs. Ashbury did it and without comment or question.

Very soon her attitude created a pleasant atmosphere in the home and the seven children loved her. Not only did Mrs. Ashbury relax but so did Lucy. To her glad surprise she could be herself, free from pressures and the fears she had dreaded. She pushed back the haunting memories of once living in the house with Tom and caught herself singing and laughing and talking about Tom whenever she felt like it. Mrs. Ashbury thoroughly enjoyed listening to Lucy relate her experiences and asked her to set up the ironing board outside the bedroom door so that she could watch and listen better. She had a way of drawing Lucy out, and almost before she realized it, Lucy had shared with Mrs. Ashbury most of her child-hood, her trips to Sunny Creek, her hunger to know God, her love for Corkie, her mother's failing eyesight, her encounter with Brother Bustleton, her baptism, and most of what happened to her since that awful night when the two men called to inform her of Tom s tragic accident.

"It's like a storybook, Lucy." Mrs. Ashbury brushed away a tear. "I could listen to you all day."

Not once did Mrs. Ashbury criticize Lucy's work. "After you leave our home," she said, "I'll give you a good recom-mendation and you shouldn't have to look long for a job. And I hope you get a place where you can have a room to yourself and not have to work as hard as you do here. More than that, Lucy, I hope you get twice what we give you. I know it's not enough. And I'm glad you take time out to play with your baby when he needs attention. He certainly is a good-natured little fellow."

There was only one thing that kept Lucy from being completely at ease in the Ashbury home. There was no place where she could be alone to read her Bible and pray.

Seven normal children couldn't possibly act normal inside a four-room house on cold evenings and weekends and refrain from making noisy noise. Lucy got accus-tomed to it. As a rule it was fun noise with much laugh-ter. But until Lucy had made an early fire in the kitchen stove (so that she could have breakfast on time), packed four school lunches, served breakfast to seven, fixed some-thing special for Mrs. Ashbury, bathed and fed Eldon, washed dishes and kettles and pans, scrubbed floors, baked bread and cookies, churned butter twice a week, made beds, washed and ironed twice a week, washed dia-pers every day, patched, darned, combed hair, washed hands and faces for three many times a day, mopped up spilled things, greased Mrs. Ashbury's chest, and heated flannel rags morning, noon, and evening, and finally seen to it that the children were all settled for the night, the lamps puffed out, little Eldon was properly cared for, fed, and fixed for the night, Lucy had no strength left to pray.

The first night she told God what He already knew, that she was too tired to read one word in her Bible. The second night she was completely exhausted. *God,* she explained as soon as her head touched the pillow, *You know how it is—from morning till now—all these children—just keep Your—"* and every night Lucy fell asleep telling God the same line. In the morning she remembered what she had tried to tell God, then went blank. She really did feel bad because she was neglecting to read the Bible Tom had given her, but all day she was much too busy to spend more than moments dwelling on the fact. *Dear Lord, I won't always be here. I'll have more time someday. You understand.*

One day when Mr. Ashbury came home, he handed Lucy a letter.

"For me?" Her eyes widened with surprise.

"It's from Herman Sellers' wife."

"Herman Sellers' wife? Who's she?"

"All I can tell you is that I work with Herman occasionally and I told him you were here helping us out."

Dear Lucy,

I know you will be surprised to hear from me. Herman told me you were working for Ashburys who live out from Black Bend a mile or so. The last I heard about you was when you lost your husband.

*Joe told Herman you have a baby boy. Herman and
I have been married six months. I have a good husband and we've rented and fixed up a nice cozy
little place. If you ever get over to Branton, please
stop in to see me. We live upstairs above the
Flangenweiler Harness Shop on Third Street. It's
easy to find. I haven't seen you since you sat in front
of me in the old Black Bend Schoolhouse over ten
years ago. Remember the fun we had at recess and
over the noon hour? When Herman came home with
news you were at Ashburys, I decided to send you a
letter. If Herman forgets to give it to Mr. Ashbury,
I'll pull his ear. If Mr. Ashbury forgets to give it to
you, I'll tell Herman to pull both his ears. Men are
forgetful sometimes. Write to me, Lucy, won't you?
But better yet, come to see me. We'd have lots to talk
about if we'd cover ten years. Best wishes.*

Your old school chum,
Norvena Black Sellers

"Mr. Ashbury," smiled Lucy looking up, "I hope you
didn't mind I read it first."

"Not at all."

"I have the supper all ready to put on the table." She
hurried to the living room and tucked the letter inside her
Bible on the mantelshelf.

With Lucy's excellent care, Mrs. Ashbury was out of bed
before Thanksgiving. But the day after the big dinner of
two stuffed roasted chickens, Paul, the first grader, had a
high fever and blotches of red all over his stomach, neck,
and face.

"Dear me," exclaimed Mrs. Ashbury. "I believe you've

got the measles, Paul."

Lucy was struck with sudden fear. "What if John Eldon gets them?"

"He could, Lucy. I don't want to frighten you but there's a possibility anyone who's never had them could, you know."

"Even me?" cried Lucy in fresh horror.

"You've never had the measles?"

"Not that I know of."

"Well, there's more than one kind, you know. I don't know positively this is measles but it certainly looks like what Annie had."

"When?"

"She was a baby, Lucy. You're really worried, aren't you?"

"Do grown women, mothers, get measles?" asked Lucy, her one hand over her mouth. She picked up her baby and felt his forehead. She put the palm of his little hand against her cheek.

"My mother got measles after she nursed her eight children through the long ordeal. I well remember. She was a very sick woman and Father was terribly worried about her."

"Oh, Mrs. Ashbury!" gasped Lucy. Her voice was tense with dread.

"We'll have to get this boy back in bed at once. Crawl in, Paul. Lucy, make two large glass fruit jars full of hot water. It'll help him break out faster, I hope. We can't let these go in on him. That could be serious."

Oliver came home from school that evening with a fever. "Go straight to bed," said his mother. "You're getting the measles too. You've probably picked these up in school."

"Oh, why?" pouted Oliver. "I don't want to go to bed, but the teacher said that's what Marty Woods has got."

Mrs. Ashbury cast a sweeping woeful glance at her brood of children and sighed wearily. "Then we're in for it."

"I want to leave," stated Lucy. There was certainty in her voice.

"Well, really I can't blame you, my dear," said Mrs. Ashbury. "I hate to give you up now, but if I were in your place, I'd feel as you do. I'll just have to keep Annie out of school to help me if you leave."

"When do you expect Mr. Ashbury home?"

"I sorta expect him tonight," answered Mrs. Ashbury looking at the calendar.

But he didn't come until the following evening. "Mr. Ashbury," began Lucy as soon as he was inside the door, "I think it's best I leave here at once."

"Joe, we've got a mess of measles," put in his wife. "Paul and Oliver are in bed and Lucy's plenty anxious about her baby."

"For this week's wages," suggested Lucy, "will you drive us over to Branton in the morning?"

"To Branton, you say?"

"Is that asking too much?"

"No. Not at all. I supposed you'd want to go back to your Aunt Polly. But if you want to go to Branton, I'll take you. Gracious, Lucy, after all you've done for Mrs. Ashbury and our big family, why would I charge you for driving you to Branton? It's only six miles. How early do you want to start out?"

"How about right after breakfast?"

"Whatever you say, Lucy. I have the day off; so the sooner we leave, the sooner I can get back and get the wash started. No indeed, Mrs. Ashbury, you're not doing that yet. I don't want you to get a backset. I'm going to see to it that you take care of yourself."

The road from Black Bend ran right into Third Street. The only time Lucy had been in a town of any size was the day she married Tom. She sat rigid, holding Eldon snugly against her.

"Now here we are," announced Mr. Ashbury bringing the horse to a sudden halt. "Flangenweiler's Harness Shop. And you say your friend Mrs. Sellers lives upstairs? You see the stairway? All right and here's your two dollars, Lucy." He helped her down and handed her the flour sack bundle. "And again many thanks for your great kindness to us all. You were a godsend if ever a person was. And I wish you everything well."

"And I thank you, Mr. Ashbury, for giving me, a perfect stranger, a job. I hope none of the other children get the measles."

Lucy's heart was thumping, almost hammering when she finally reached the top of the stairs. She felt dizzy and a moment of nausea overwhelmed her. She hesitated. Bewildered as in a foggy dream, she knocked three times with caution.

She thought she heard padded footsteps. She tried to take command of herself.

CHAPTER 28

NORVENA OPENED the door. "Lucy! It's got to be Lucy Winchester." And she placed a hand on each shoulder.

"Yes, Norvena. Lucy Hammon now."

"To be sure. Come in. Let me take your baby. He's beautiful, Lucy. Take off your wraps and we can talk. You look like your sweet old self, Lucy—yet you're— Well, we've both changed. Ten years. My. How are you? Take a chair."

"Well," began Lucy sinking into the chair, "to tell you the truth, Norvena, I haven't felt quite like myself all day. I did have to work pretty hard at Ashburys but I'll soon be all right, I'm sure. Then, too," she tried to smile, "I guess I got sorta excited about coming here to see you. You know, the trip with my baby."

"Excited? Well, I'm the one who's excited." And Norvena squeezed little Eldon and cooed over him.

"Well, you see," went on Lucy, "this is a milestone in my life because I've never been in Branton before. Actually I was never beyond Black Bend until the night I married Tom. We went to Crawford. You know," she laughed, "I'm just a country girl and, believe it or not, it' s quite a thing for me to come to a city like this. It was very nice of you to invite me to come to see you. And while I'm here, I want to do some shopping. There are so many things I need."

Lucy looked down at her shabby, ill-shaped slippers and blushed. "I hope you'll go with me."

"I'll be glad to. We have some real nice stores here in Branton. Lucy, your baby's a dear. How old is he?"

"Three months. I'll take him, Norvena. If you were busy, don't let me keep you from your work." Lucy almost staggered toward Norvena.

"Are you sick, Lucy?" Norvena caught her by one arm. "Sit down and take it easy. We can put your baby here on the sofa. There now. He'll be all right, won't he?"

"I'm—ashamed, Norvena." Lucy looked up with a troubled expression in her eyes, blurred with dreadful uncertainty.

"Ashamed of what?"

"To be acting like this as soon as I arrive. I—I just don't understand what's the matter with me. I'm sorta dizzy."

"You needn't be ashamed, Lucy. Can't I get you something? A cup of coffee?"

Lucy shook her head.

"Tea? Soda? Cordial?"

"Will you drink a cup of tea with me?"

"Of course," answered Norvena, and she hurried to the kitchen to make it. "I'll be there in a minute, Lucy. I have hot water on the stove."

"Tea never tasted better, Norvena. I'm sure I'll be all right after a good night's rest. You see, over at Ashburys they were terribly crowded, nine in the family and only two bedrooms. I slept on a couch in the living room with two children on a folding bed in the room and my baby in a box on two chairs."

"Well, Lucy, I'd be more than half sick! If I miss one good night's rest, I'm way off balance the next day. You're going to stay here tonight if I have my say."

"May I?"

"You're going to and that settles it. You and—What's his name?"

"John Eldon."

"You and John Eldon will have a room to yourselves, and the bed has a good mattress on it if I do say so myself. And you can sleep as late as you like."

"Thank you so much, Norvena. Then we'll go shopping, and then I must get out and hunt for a job. Would you know anyone who'd give a young widow with a baby a job?"

"You mean housework?"

"Yes."

"I wouldn't know of anyone offhand. We might see if there's anything listed in the paper. But don't be in a hurry. You'd better rest here several days before you go out and hunt for work."

Lucy didn't realize how exhausted she was until she began to relax. Her arms and legs got limp, almost numb, and her eyelids felt as thick as heavy drapes. She could scarcely hold her eyes open. She felt as ill-shaped and shabby as her slippers.

"Are you warm enough, Lucy? I'll put more wood in the stove if you're not."

"I've been cold all morning."

"Here, then, let me pull the rocker closer to the stove. How's that?"

"Fine, Norvena."

The remainder of the forenoon was spent rehearsing bygone days. Lucy strained every nerve in her body and mind to act cheerful and alert. Little did Norvena guess the special effort she had to make to answer correctly the many questions. At intervals Lucy felt as though she were suspended on a swinging wire and it left her light-headed and trembling. Then she was running in a mad race with time, with no hope of winning. What was happening to her? She pinched her arms and bit her tongue.

Somehow she managed to eat a little of Norvena's dinner but nothing tasted good.

"I know it's been hard on you to tell me all this," said Norvena holding Eldon on her lap. She stroked his head and kissed one dimpled hand. "It's ruined your appetite. I'm so sorry. Maybe I asked you too many questions."

"No," answered Lucy. "No, you didn't. I'm just tuckered out."

"It's all so sad. If I had gone through all you have, I'm sure I'd be in my grave."

"You can't die because you feel like it, Norvena. Lots of times I felt bad enough to die. No one knows what I've suffered."

"But you still look young and beautiful. Of course you do look tired now. But, Lucy, if my father had treated me like yours has you, I'm sure it would have killed me. Don't you hate him?"

"No, Norvena. I can honestly say I do not hate my father." She drew a long, deep breath. "In spite of everything he's done that I'll never be able to understand. I love him because he's my father, Norvena. I told him off the last time I saw him, then afterward I had a crying spell. I can't explain it. I know he must be badly mixed up inside, but every time I blame him or my home or Tom or anyone, I feel so miserable in my heart I—I can't even pray."

Norvena looked searchingly, wonderingly at Lucy without comment. Then she glanced out the window.

"By all means I must write to my father," remarked Lucy at length. "I told him I'd let him know where I was, but at Ashburys I never had time to sit down long enough to write and I didn't have paper or an envelope or stamps. I must get some tomorrow."

"Well, I'll give you paper and an envelope. We'll be going right past the post office on our way to town. I'm sure if my father had treated me the way yours has you—well, let me tell you, Lucy, I'd let him sweat and smolder and wonder for a good long while first. But here's paper. Take it. It's your life and you do as you like." Then after a long silence Norvena continued, "You know, there's something about you I admire. It's your spunk and pluck, or something you've got to go through all you have and come to this point without hate in your heart. I don't understand at all how you've done it. We're not all made alike, I guess."

"I couldn't have lived through it alone, Norvena," said Lucy with feeling. "Sometimes I thought I was falling apart. I thought I'd lose my mind. But what I learned at Sunny Creek Sunday school and at Black Bend from a preacher named Bustleton helped me a lot."

"What do you mean?"

"God, Norvena. God helped me."

"Yeh?"

"But I've fallen short of my ideal many times. Far too many." Lucy sighed from sheer exhaustion. "Maybe someday I can—" Was she going to faint? Lucy pressed one hand against her throat. "Norvena," she said, "could I have another cup of tea?"

"Of course. I'll get it for you."

Lucy thought bedtime would never come. Finally, at five o'clock, when she could scarcely hold her head up any longer, she said, "Norvena, I'd like to put my baby to bed for the night. I'm sure he's tired. And if you don't mind, I'd like to go too."

"Certainly. The room is all yours. Can't I give you something to eat? Toast perhaps with jelly on it or some cookies?"

"Just a glass of water. Thanks. Oh, that bed looks so inviting. And that beautiful soft warm blanket. Norvena, a bed never looked so good to me." She opened her flour sack to get out Eldon's nightgown. "Oh! Oh, no!"

"What's wrong, Lucy?"

"My Bible! Oh, my beautiful Bible!" Her face turned white. She flopped on the edge of the bed.

"What Bible?"

"The one Tom gave me," cried Lucy, "on our wedding day. I left it on the mantelshelf at Ashburys. Oh, how could I have forgotten to put it in my sack?"

"But can't you get it sometime?"

"I don't know when I'll get back there. And with seven children it might get torn or soiled. How could I have forgotten? Next to my baby I prize that Bible."

"But, Lucy," began Norvena, "I don't understand why you're so upset and look so forlorn because you forgot a Bible. If it had been your purse, I could easily see why you'd be excited. You're just tired, my dear. And nervous. You get a good long night's rest and in the morning write to Mrs. Ashbury and tell her to mail it to you right away. When Herman comes in, I'll tell him you're here and to be real quiet so you won't be disturbed."

"I know," said Lucy brightening a little, "maybe Mr. Ashbury could bring my Bible along to work and give it to your husband."

"No. No, Lucy. Not that." Norvena shook her head emphatically. "They don't see each other every day. And it might get lost. I wouldn't want to ask Herman to be responsible for something like that. You'd better tell Mrs. Ashbury to take care of it until you get back or send it. Now please don't fret. She'll send it."

"Do you have one I could borrow tomorrow?"

"No, Lucy, we don't have a Bible in the house. But I know someone who does. Gussie Jenkins. She's a sweet little old woman who cleans the shop for Mr. Flangenweiler downstairs. I give her things to eat now and then for sweeping down our steps. Not that I couldn't do it myself but I like to help her out. She lives back of us on the next street. Everybody likes Gussie and you will too. She goes to church every Sunday and I know she's got a Bible. And say, by the way, I wouldn't be surprised if Gussie could tell you where you might find a job. She knows some of the richest folks in town because she used to work for them. Now, good night, Lucy. Please don't worry about a thing. Will you promise?"

"Yes, Norvena, I promise."

O God, groaned Lucy pulling up the covers, *I'm sick. Do You know how sick I am? Please keep Your hand—and help—get my Bible back.*

She spent the night in fitful disconnected dreams, tossing and moaning. She was hovering over the hot cookstove back home and going blind like her mother, then her tongue and throat were parched and swollen but there was no water anywhere. She heard her father chopping at the plum tree while she was watching from her bedroom window and she called to him at the top of her voice to stop! stop! for Flossie's sake. But she could not make him hear. She screamed until her throat was paralyzed. Then she was running, running and stumbling all the way from Branton to Ashburys to get her Bible, but the road was uphill all the way and her feet were heavy with mud and she made almost no headway. Oh, what horrible dreams!

At daybreak Eldon squirmed and whimpered. Lucy sat up, forgetting for the moment where she was. She rubbed her burning, itching eyes. She remembered. Frantically she opened her gown with trembling hands and gave herself a going over. Oh, no! No! She stifled a groan. The thing she so much dreaded was unmistakably true. She knew she had measles!

CHAPTER 29

"**G**OOD MORNING, Miss Lucy."

When Lucy opened her inflamed, troubled eyes the brown face bending over her was a blur. Her parched lips refused to speak or smile.

"This is Gussie Jenkins," said Norvena. "I came in a while ago and got Eldon and pulled the blinds. You didn't know I came in, did you?"

Lucy shook her head. "I'm—so—ashamed," she managed to say, "to get—sick—like this here." Her voice was hoarse, thick, and tired.

"No, no, child," came a tender voice from Gussie, and Lucy felt a hand stroke her hair back from her hot forehead. "You needn't go complainin'. Mrs. Sellers ain't fretting 'cause you got sick here. She brought me to help you get well. You have nothing to be ashamed of, Miss Lucy. Worse things have happened to folks 'way from home. Mrs. Sellers told me how you happened to come here. I've done heaps of nursing sick folks in my day. I know every sickness a body can get and the cures for 'em all. I told her nobody needs fret 'cause I'll come twice a day or more if need be an' look after you an' your sweet boy baby. He's a fine one, only he cried when he first saw my old black face. But he'll make up with me. They all do." Here Gussie adjusted the blue scarf she had tied over her gray hair. "I'm going to make you some sage tea, Miss Lucy, an' we'll get you all warmed up inside."

She gently pulled the comforter up around Lucy's shoulder and patted her. "And we're going to make you some horehound drink too. Nothing better in the world for chasin' measles. And Mrs. Sellers told me you fret about your Bible. Well, you needn't. You can use mine till yours comes. But you mustn't read when you have the measles. You could ruin your eyes for life. You just stay in this good warm bed and rest up 'cause I hear how you been working too hard. You know, maybe the good Lord saw you need a good rest. We must keep these blinds pulled down. Light isn't good for measle eyes, you know. Are you real sick, honey?"

"I—feel—awful—sick," Lucy managed to say. "I hope my baby—won't—"

"Now, now," gently chided Gussie, stroking Lucy's forehead. "We'll do our best—our very best to take good care of your baby. I'm feeding your sweet baby some good hot porridge now. Now don't you fret. You'll get well faster if you just rest, Miss Lucy. Rest in the Lord. No matter what comes, He takes us through to the other side. He never allows trials unless He goes along beside us." Gussie drew her heavy dark sweater across her shoulders. "I go now and fix that sage tea."

"Tell Norvena—to come—to the door—after while, Gussie," Lucy whispered.

"My dear child, your voice sounds all woolly like I'd better grease you good and proper too."

"Here, Mrs. Sellers, let me get acquainted with this little baby. Miss Lucy wants you at the door. Come, baby dear. You needn't be scared of my black face. You're going to smile at me, aren't you? That's a sweet baby. Sure.

Come to Gussie." And Gussie chuckled over her early success as she took little Eldon in her arms. "So you're going to let me feed you too? More porridge? No? You just want to 'xamine me? Sure, you just look all you want. I'm just the way the good Lord made me 'cause He made my mama black an' your mama white. Sure. Smile at Gussie. That's a fine boy. We've got to team together to get your dear mama well."

"Norvena," whispered Lucy, "would you mail that—letter—I wrote my father and write to—Mrs. Ashbury for me?"

"Of course I will. Did you tell your father why you left Ashburys?"

"Yes."

"And that you were—feeling bad?"

"No. I—don't want—him to know."

For three days Lucy was too sick to talk more than absolutely necessary. Norvena was frightened. Mr. Sellers wanted to call a doctor but Lucy objected. Gussie Jenkins came three times every day and helped Norvena wrap Lucy in heated towels. Together they made poultices of steaming hot bread and chopped onions and put them on Lucy's chest to loosen a severe, deep-seated cough she developed.

Don't fret. How many times had Gussie, the kind little black woman, told her that? Those tender, soft-spoken words sounded so proper and tactful and should have had an unwavering tranquilizing effect on her. No one, not even Aunt Polly, could show more concern and genuine love for her and Eldon than Norvena and Gussie did. Yet when alone and with the door tightly closed, Lucy wrestled with the principle of her situation. Why didn't she go home when she feared she might get the measles? Peggy and Loretta would have been glad to take care of Eldon. Even though Norvena declared she wasn't a burden she knew full well she was, and an expensive burden. She'd never be able to live down the humiliation of it all. This was an imposition. Nothing less.

It seemed ages since she had been well and strong. Where had her energy gone? Every inch of her body ached and burned as though she had been scraped with steel wool inside and out. Even her earlobes hurt. Her fingernails ached. A horrible whirlpool of destruction was trying to suck her into eternal doom. What would become of John Eldon if she died? Oh, she dare not die. She had to live for him. Her deepest feelings and fears cried out in silent anguish. *God, I want to live, live to be, to do, to know, to grow, like the Bible says we should. If Gussie knows, then You do understand why I'm so sick and weak, don't You? And are You with me? O God, please.*

"Miss Lucy," began Gussie the fourth morning, "I think you should start to eat or you'll get thin as a stove poker. Your little son wants his mama to get well. I brought you some chicken broth and a pretty wing Mrs. Flangenweiler gave me for shaking her rugs. Here, taste it. Now, I know it's delicious, honey." Gussie propped Lucy up with two pillows.

"It is, Gussie. It's very good. Thanks."

"Now you'll get some strength in those legs and arms once you begin to eat, honey."

"You're too good to me, Gussie. How can I ever repay you and Norvena?"

"Repay?" exclaimed Gussie with mingled joy and consternation. "Who's mentioned pay? Not me. Don't you know what the good Book says about giving a cup of cold water?"

"What does it say, Gussie? Tell me."

"It says if we give it in the name of Jesus, we get a reward."

"Well, then, Gussie," smiled Lucy, "you'll get a big reward and Norvena too and Mr. Sellers. You've all been so kind to me. I can't understand it. I'm not even a relative and Norvena hadn't seen me for ten years."

"Miss Lucy," smiled Gussie clapping her hands, "this is the first time I've seen you smile so sweet. You begin to talk now and you eat and you get well and we'll all say glory hallelujah."

"Do you think my baby will get the measles?"

"I don't know, truly, but I ask the good Lord day by day to pass him by. My, he sure makes up to me. Bless him. And did you get your Bible yet?"

"Not yet. Mrs. Ashbury is very busy, but she'll most likely have her husband mail it."

"Are you a church lady, Miss Lucy? Or don't you feel like talking more now?"

A perplexed expression crossed Lucy's face. "Well, I never had a chance to go to a real church, Gussie. I often walked four miles to go to Sunny Creek Sunday school in a schoolhouse. I wanted to go until I earned a Bible but I didn't get to. But my husband got me a Bible for my birthday on our wedding day. That's the one I forgot and left at Ashburys."

"Mrs. Sellers told me how you got upset about forgetting it. I told her I'd loan you mine as soon's you dare read. I'd bring it and read a page to you, but I can't read good enough for others to listen. A lady I washed an' ironed for gave it to me. I believe every word in it. I know it's a good book, but there's lots I can't understand. I only got to go to school through fifth grade, so I can't read long, hard words. Our preacher told us we can be saved without knowing how to read 'cause a blind man had faith and was healed. So I know I have real saving faith and salvation 'cause I feel it in my soul an' it makes me love everybody."

Norvena in the kitchen heard the conversation and came to the bedroom door. "That's right, Lucy," she said. "Gussie's a Christian if there ever was one. I don't claim to be and I don't understand how you get to be one, but if there is such a place as heaven, I'm sure Gussie Jenkins will go there. She has a heart of gold."

"Isn't by good works you're saved," put in Gussie, looking very serious; "it's all by faith. So, Miss Lucy, don't you go thinking I come here to earn a ticket or chair in heaven. I do this all 'cause I get joy out of helping folks. I've been trying to tell Mrs. Sellers how the good Lord died on the cross for us all. Her Herman says it's good enough for old ladies like me but he doesn't want religion now. He wants a good time while he's young and he has powerful control over his wife. Now you best rest, honey." And she made Lucy comfortable.

What was this strange vacuum, this huge gnawing emptiness inside her? She should have read her Bible every night at Ashburys no matter how tired she was. That's why she forgot to put it in the sack. It was all her fault and it sifted down to self-pity. If God would forgive her, she'd do better once she was well. Would He really bring her out of this dreadful, weakening ordeal?

Father? How was he? And sweet Peggy and dear

Loretta? The boys; what were they doing? And Flossie and Clem? Oh, it couldn't be true they weren't getting along. Norvena. If she wasn't a Christian, what made her so kind? She and Herman both. They never argued or fussed, yet they never prayed. Never went to church. Didn't even have a Bible in the house. How was Norvena different from Gussie? Lucy was baffled. Her thoughts raced on and on.

The days made weeks and Lucy was able to be up. Her legs wobbled and she knew without thinking twice that she'd have to get a lot stronger before she'd be able to get out and hunt for work.

One day she carried Eldon to Gussie's house. She sank into the first chair she could reach. "Oh, I'm so weak, Gussie. I can't get over this. I'm as weak as a rag."

"Well, you were a very sick child. You don't know how close you came to having pneumonia. Measles are very tricky and mean on some."

"But I can't stay over there much longer. It's not fair. Tell me, if you can, why they've been so good to me and they don't care a thing about God or church. They never pray. I just can't figure them out."

"Well," remarked Gussie, reaching out and taking Eldon in her arms, "I worked for some very nice rich folks who never went to church except to weddings or funerals. But kind, my—and good—good to everybody, especially me. But God?" she shook her head. "No time for Him. Now the Bible says if we give our body to be burned without love, it's for no count. I'm no judge of nobody, Miss Lucy, but I fear Mrs. Sellers an' Herman miss the mark. I'm sorry, but it's the truth."

When she got back to the Sellers home, Norvena was

ready with a cup of hot tea.

"Lucy," said Norvena, "you got a letter from Mrs. Ashbury."

"Oh, good. I'll read it out loud."

Dear Lucy,

Just a line to let you know we're all sorry you got the measles. Yes, you left your Bible on the mantelshelf behind the stove. I hate to tell you what happened Tuesday night. Our chimney caught fire after we had all gone to bed and everything on the mantel got badly scorched. [Lucy's face turned white.] *We got the fire out before it spread, but the water and fire together ruined your Bible.* [Her hands shook.] *We all feel awful bad about it, Lucy. As soon as I get to town, I'll try to replace it. Kathleen has the measles now. She's number five. I've really had a time. We do miss you, Lucy. Write when you can. I'm getting stronger.*

With love,
Mrs. Ashbury

To Norvena's glad surprise Lucy did not burst into tears. She just stood there stunned, looking bleakly into space, then slowly folded the letter and stuck it back in the envelope.

CHAPTER 30

LUCY WAS not only disappointed and hurt, she was confused and smitten. If God had His hand over her, why would He allow her beautiful treasure to be burned? Did she love it too dearly? Was she too proud of it? Had she grieved the Lord, and was He punishing her in this way? Didn't He want her to have a Bible?

She was altogether confused, completely at a loss to know what to think or how to pray. The very foundation of her once established love—her promises on bended knees when Brother Bustleton baptized her, her devotion, her peace—was it crumbling completely from under her? The tapestry of her life was hanging in shreds before her now. She was rebuked, stunned, beaten. Her head and heart seemed completely severed. She wrestled with her dilemma long into the night. Finally falling on her knees beside the bed she buried her face in both hands.

O God, she breathed. *Are You there? Why did You let my Bible be destroyed? I thought it was a good book and You wanted me to have it. Did I only imagine it made me happy? I feel I've been betrayed or what is it that's wrong with me? I'm falling apart with fear and shame. And I don't know what to believe about myself or You or anyone. O God, if You hear me, help me out of this tangle I'm in before I die.*

The next afternoon while Eldon slept, Lucy walked over

to Gussie's house.

"Come in, Miss Lucy. How do you feel today? Come, take this rocker near the stove. You look like you've been fretting, child."

"I fear you're right, Gussie," admitted Lucy, sinking into the rocker. "I just can't understand this." And she read the letter to Gussie. "Why," she cried in exasperation, "did God let my Bible be burned?" Lucy's eyes were drawn with perplexity. "This is tearing me to shreds, Gussie."

"Why, honey," rebuked Gussie in a voice as soft as velvet, "you have no ground to be so upset and sour on the good Lord. It's not for us to know the whys of God. We shouldn't even ask why. Not for long. It's for us to trust, trust, trust, like your little Eldon trusts you, Miss Lucy. God makes no mistakes. Not one. He's good always. Can't you be glad the house didn't catch fire when you and little Eldon were sound asleep?"

Lucy sat back. Her arms relaxed. Slowly her frozen fears began to thaw. "I—I never thought of that, Gussie."

"I just thought you didn't," smiled Gussie radiantly. "Why, bless your soul, Miss Lucy. You mustn't blame the good Lord for any of your troubles. Could be the devil had your Bible burned so you couldn't read it anymore. You ought to just show him that won't burn your trust in God. There's plenty more Bibles just like the one that got burned. Why, Miss Lucy, the devil is trying to take over your trust in God because you're weak from your sickness. We gotta trust no matter what comes, and rejoice—be glad and rejoice and give Him thanks in all things. You know how the devil tried to ruin Job's trust in God? Huh? You know about Job?"

Lucy shook her head.

"It's in the Bible somewhere. Job said, 'I'll trust God if He kills me.'"

"Oh, Gussie," remarked Lucy shaking her head as if to sweep away all her doubtings and misgivings and answerless questionings, "I wish I had the faith you have. I'm so ashamed of myself."

"You must start goin' to church, honey." Gussie folded her hands across her breast. "No wonder you haven't learned faster the ways of God. You must get in with people who can help you. Now I'm not so sure Mrs. Sellers an' Herman are real, real happy. Wait till some trial comes by and see what happens. That's the test, child. How does the blacksmith know if the horseshoe or piece of iron is any good? He sticks it in the fire. Fiery trials make Christians stronger. Don't you see?"

"Yes," sighed Lucy, looking steadfastly at the pattern of the rug in front of her chair. She seemed to be reflecting on insurmountable mountain after mountain, doubt after doubt, sorrow after sorrow, until one by one each became trifles, dwarfed fears, groundless accusations.

"You're right, Gussie," she said at length, gathering her thoughts together. "I must go to church. You know, I've never been inside a church in my life. I'd have no idea where to go, a stranger in Branton; and Norvena probably wouldn't want to go with me. Would she?"

"I expect not. I wish white folks could come to our church. I doubt if Pastor Johnston would put a white person out, but I've never seen one there as yet."

"Gussie," mused Lucy thoughtfully, "you've helped me a lot. I'm glad I came over. I'm so ashamed I've let myself get so low in spirits. I beg God to forgive me. When I was only twelve I heard a Brother Bustleton preach in a schoolhouse. Only once and I knew he was a man of God by the expression on his face. I can see it now. From that day I wanted to know more about God. My father doesn't believe in anything. Only one relative, my Aunt Polly, is a Christian. God bless her. Gussie, if she saw how I've been acting, I know she'd be thoroughly disappointed in me. I'm ashamed and disappointed in myself. I feel as though I've been on a teeter-totter too much of my life."

"Well, now you've confessed it, Miss Lucy. And it isn't uncommon to be down. We all stumble sometimes or teeter as you say, but it's a sin to stay down when He's got all it takes to lift us up."

"Oh, Gussie." And Lucy threw her arms around Gussie's neck and planted a kiss on her cheek. "Maybe God let me get the measles here so I could learn to know you. How can I tell you how I appreciate the frank, honest way you talk to me so I can see myself the way I should and wouldn't without you."

"I'm not very learned, child," smiled Gussie, her dark eyes shining, her black face vivid with her inner peace. "But I know I've got something in my heart that's real, and I'm glad I can tell it to someone like sweet Miss Lucy." And at that Gussie kissed Lucy on the cheek.

Later that day Lucy was shaking a small rug from the upstairs window when she heard someone whistling a catchy tune. Where had she heard that before? It was strangely familiar. It was coming from the man approaching, swinging a lunch bucket. He looked up. Lucy held her breath. The rug slipped out of her hand.

"Clem Linsdale!"

"Lucy." He removed his hat. "What are you doing here in Branton?"

"What are you doing here in Branton?" mimicked Lucy.

"I've been working here for three months." He picked up the rug. "I'll bring it up to you. How do I get there?"

"Use the stairway beside the harness shop."

Lucy met him at the door. "Come in, Clem. You say you've been here for three months?"

"Yes." He handed her the rug.

"What are you doing?"

"I'm working in the stone quarry. But what are you doing here? Was I surprised, Lucy!"

"I came here to look for work. Then first thing I got down with the measles. I was dreadful sick and I'm just now getting on my feet again."

"You look like something's happened to you since the last time I saw you."

"I suppose. How's Flossie?"

"I don't know." Clem shifted nervously and cleared his throat.

"Don't know? Where is she?"

"I don't know, Lucy." Clem adjusted the buckle on his leather belt and looked at the rug in her hand.

"You don't know where she is?" gasped Lucy trying to redirect his glance. "What's happened?"

"Well," he began after a perplexing pause that left Lucy quivering, "we haven't been living together for over three months."

"Oh, no!"

"I'm sorry, Lucy, but she—she just refused to stay with me."

Sadly Lucy shook her head. "Mrs. Morehouse told me you were having troubles but I refused to believe it. I'm so sorry, Clem."

"I tried everything, everything under the sun, Lucy. I just couldn't please her. She was a perfect wildcat the last week we were together. Sorry to tell you this about your sister but it's the truth. She simply left."

"Oh, Clem," cried Lucy. "It seems impossible. I think this is terrible. I know Flossie always had a temper, but I thought surely she'd control it after she married you. Father liked you from the start. I supposed that would mean a lot to both of you. He never did like Tom."

"Your father doesn't blame me for this."

"You're sure?"

"I went over and had a long talk with him. He was convinced I did all I could to satisfy her. No man on earth could have tried harder, Lucy."

"Is she back home?"

"I don't know."

Lucy looked up at Clem, and when she spoke, her voice was warm with compassion. "Maybe I can persuade her to come back to you. If I can locate her."

Clem's hand was on the doorknob. "I'm glad we found each other," he remarked softly. "You'd better not go to work too soon. You've lost a lot of weight, haven't you?"

"Some. Step in the bedroom before you leave, Clem. Come, I want you to see my baby. He's asleep."

"Mighty nice," whispered Clem. "Looks like Tom."

"I've got to go to work for him," said Lucy following him to the door.

Norvena came in with a sackful of groceries.

"Meet Mr. Clemens Linsdale, Norvena. My brother-in-law."

"Good morning, Mr. Linsdale. Are you Flossie's husband?"

CHAPTER 31

BEFORE A week had passed Norvena answered a knock and Clem Linsdale stood there, tall, freshly shaved, and strikingly handsome.

"Is Lucy Hammon here?" he asked removing his hat.

"Not at the moment. She took her baby and said they were going to call on Gussie Jenkins, a neighbor."

"Then she is still here with you?"

"Yes, sir."

"She hasn't gone to work yet?"

"No, sir. To be honest, Mr. Linsdale, she's not strong enough yet. She keeps saying she's got to go out and hunt for a job but she was a very sick woman."

"That's what she told me. I hardly recognized her when she called to me from the window. I don't want to pry where I shouldn't, but would you tell me how it happened she came here to you?"

Briefly Norvena told the story. "Really, Mr. Linsdale, it's no wonder the measles were rough on her because she was run down when she left Ashburys. You should hear how hard she worked there. I don't know how she did it. I think it would have finished me."

"Well," began Clem scrutinizing Norvena intently, "since Lucy's not here, I'd like to talk over a matter with you." He hesitated momentarily, wetting his lips. "Ever since I saw how pale and frail she looked, I haven't been able to forget her. She told me because of her baby she's got to get a job. I appreciate her ambition and devotion to her child and I'm quite sure I understand how she feels. But where could she find a job with that baby?" Clem glanced down the steps.

"I don't know. But I know she won't take a job unless she can have him with her."

"Is she able to help you with your work?"

"She does some. Of course there's not a lot to do here. She's able to take care of little Eldon now."

"I suppose she feels she's a burden on you."

"I've tried not to give her that impression, Mr. Linsdale."

"I'm sure you have but this is what's on my mind. I would like to give you three-fifty a week for as long as it takes for her to get strong enough to work."

Norvena frowned. "Did she tell you she's a burden to us? We've tried our best to make her feel welcome. She frets too much."

"No, Mrs. Sellers, Lucy didn't say a word about being a burden, but she knows and so do you that you can't feed her for nothing. I'm drawing good wages at the stone quarry, and since she's my sister-in-law, I want to help her. I'd like to see her look and feel like herself before she goes out to find a job. You do have room for her here?"

"Oh, yes, we have an extra bedroom."

"Is she eating?"

"Very little."

"It could be," said Clem, thoughtfully weighing each word, "she's sensitive or embarrassed, don't you think, fearing she's running up your grocery bill? Lucy's a very conscientious person."

Norvena nodded.

"You know," continued Clem with fresh pursuit, "I room at the hotel. I eat breakfast and supper there and the cook packs my lunch for me. I'm terribly tired of that grub. I've been thinking, would you be interested in letting me eat suppers here? It would give Lucy something to do if she would help you with the meals and perhaps whet her appetite too. I'd pay you whatever you ask."

"You mean—"

"I mean I really want to do something to help Lucy and I can't think of any better way. I wouldn't want her to know I'm giving you three-fifty a week for her room and board, but I'd want her to know I'm paying for my meals. That is, if you agree. I realize I'm perhaps a little bold in proposing this. But I'm serious about it. You look quite surprised." And Clem laughed softly.

"I'll have to talk it over with my husband," said Norvena. "You stop by tomorrow evening and I'll give you our decision. You may be taking quite a chance, you know," she laughed. "You might not like our meals."

"Not worried in the least," answered Clem.

"But what will I say when Lucy keeps talking about going out to hunt for work? I'm sure she will."

"That's why I'd like to drop in every evening. If she goes to work too soon, she'll get down sick again."

"That's what I tell her. She's had a pretty sad life for one so young."

"Do you know how long she and Tom were married?"

"I think she said a little over two years."

"Well, I must be going. Tell Lucy I stopped to say hello to her, but please don't let her know I'm going to pay for her stay here."

"I won't."

The next morning Lucy got a letter from Aunt Polly.

Dear Lucy,

Tuesday Jake and I went to Black Bend. I over-heard a lady talking to the grocer and your name was mentioned; so I listened. When she was ready to leave, I introduced myself and she said she was Mrs. Ashbury. We talked for half an hour at least. She told me what a wonderful person you were and such a good worker. Then how you got the measles after you left. She gave me your address in Branton; so I hope you're still there. If not, I hope Mrs. Sellers will forward it to you.

Lucy, why don't you write to me? I've wondered about you so much I even drove over to your home one day and they hadn't heard from you either. The next day Floyd came over and said they did hear from you and he brought the letter along for me to read. But there wasn't a word about you having measles. When I stopped at your home, your father was very cold and distant to me. I believe he blames me because you didn't go home with him when you two left that morning. I supposed you would at least stop in a while. He said you got off at the corner.

How I'd love to see John Eldon. How is he? Does he still look like Tom? Please write and tell me what you're doing and all about Eldon. Mrs. Ashbury told me you left in such a hurry and forgot your Bible and how it got burned. I know that must have made you feel awful. I looked in Black Bend for one like it but I couldn't find any. If we ever get to Crawford, I'll look there. Do you remember the name of the store where Tom got it? I want to replace it for you. You can't be without a Bible, dear.

Isn't it sad about Flossie and Clem? Loretta told me Clem was over one day and told your father all about it. She ran off from him. He said he couldn't think of going back home even though his folks begged him to. They pity him so much. I think everybody does. Clem has always been a nice young man. He told your father he was going to Crawford to look for work. They never heard whether he found work or not or where he's staying. And no one knows where Flossie is. It makes me feel so sad. Your mother would be heartbroken. If I hear from you, Lucy, I'll feel much better. God bless you and keep His hand over you. I pray for you every day.

Your loving Aunt Polly

Lucy sat right down to answer the letter. But she must not tell Aunt Polly and Uncle Jake how weak she was or they'd come driving over to Branton and insist she go home with them to recuperate.

Dear Aunt Polly,

Your letter reached me here at Sellerses' and I was very glad for it. I'm feeling stronger every day and I hope to go to work soon. John Eldon is just fine and I'm so glad he didn't get the measles. We both had very good care. Eldon is growing and get-ting sweeter every day. If you ever hear anything about Flossie, please let me know. I feel just awful about what she's done to Clem. He's working here in Branton. I just found this out recently. I wish I could persuade Flossie to go back to him again. I think Clem looks sad and I'm sure he's very badly hurt. He thinks Eldon looks like Tom.

I felt real bad about my Bible and I intend to buy one after I go to work. It's very sweet of you to say you'll try to find one for me. I don't remember the name of the store. While I'm here, I have borrowed a Bible from a dear old lady who lives close.

I'm glad you pray for me and Eldon. I hardly know just how I stand with God, but I intend to hunt up a church here real soon. Give my love to Uncle Jake and please don't worry about us. We're both all right.

> *Sincere love,*
> *Lucy*

Norvena and Herman talked over Clem's proposition and decided to try it for several weeks. Mr. Linsdale could stop in for supper at twenty-five cents a meal.

"Listen to me, Norvena," said Herman, "I haven't met this Mr. Linsdale yet, but he seems to be especially interested in his sister-in-law."

"Sh. Don't talk so loud. She'll hear you."

"Then close the door. Three-fifty a week for her board and room. If there's five weeks in a month that's seventeen-fifty. And twenty-five cents a meal will be seven-fifty a month. So we'll get twenty-five dollars a month. I want you to keep books and keep track of expenses and see how we come out."

"Let's keep Lucy for as long as we can," whispered Norvena. "Every time she talks about leaving, tell her she looks too pale. Maybe by spring we can get a phonograph."

Herman chuckled softly.

Together Lucy and Norvena planned the first meal and Lucy prepared it while Norvena knitted on the muffler she had started for Herman. Pork chops, browned potatoes and gravy, buttered lima beans, cabbage slaw, baked apples, tea, and Lucy's freshly baked oatmeal cookies.

"This is the best meal I'd had for over a year, Mrs. Sellers," said Clem sliding his chair under the table.

"Tell that to Lucy," said Norvena. "She's the one who made it."

"It was indeed very good, Lucy," he smiled and nodded.

"Thank you, Clem. Before you go, I want to show you something. I wrote Flossie a letter today and I want you to read it. I don't want to say anything to make matters worse, but I do wish I could persuade her to come back to you."

Clem took the letter somewhat reluctantly and glanced at Lucy with an expression of half remonstrance.

Lucy watched his face as he read. She saw despair change to bitterness, then futility. He breathed heavily. "Lucy," he said handing her the letter, "I appreciate your interest, but I'm sure the letter would only make her angry. I didn't tell you that I heard from my mother Monday. Flossie's running around with Dick Galoway."

"No! Did she say where Flossie's staying?"

"She said she's working for the Galoways."

After Clem left, Lucy put the letter in the stove and watched it burn.

CHAPTER 32

"NORVENA," SAID Lucy one morning, "I believe I feel strong enough to walk to town today."

"Then let's go as soon as the dishes are done. The Christmas decorations will be up in the stores. And it's a beautiful morning. Not too cold."

When they returned, Lucy was wearing new slippers and in her paper bag was the prettiest cotton dress she had ever owned. She was more than pleased, for her hard-earned money went farther than she had anticipated. But she was so tired she could hardly climb the stairs. Norvena carried Eldon all the way home.

When Sunday morning came, Lucy put on her best clothes and combed her hair with extra pains.

"I'm going to church," she announced at the breakfast table.

"In the snow?" asked Norvena.

"Snow or no snow," answered Lucy. "Today I must go to church. Won't you go with me?"

"I'll keep Eldon," Norvena poured three cups of coffee. "You just go ahead and we'll keep Eldon inside where it's nice and warm. Sunday's the only day Herman and I have together. Which church are you going to?"

"I don't know. Where is the closest one?"

"There's a church on Center Street. That's four blocks north of Third Street. Then there's one on Vine, three blocks west of Center. I believe there's a church on the other side of town but I'm not sure where. You'll have no trouble finding one of those two. I've never been to any of them myself."

"There's Gussie's church," laughed Herman.

"Well," said Norvena sarcastically, "she wouldn't want to go there."

When Lucy reached the church on Center Street, to her surprise, she saw people coming out. An elderly man in a long flowing black robe was standing inside the door and as the people passed they nodded to him.

"Pardon me, lady," Lucy spoke to a kind-faced woman in a honey-brown fur cape, "the service is over already?"

"Yes, ma'am. Second mass. But if you have a special confession to make, you may speak to the Father." The woman had a distinguished elegance about her and she smelled of perfume, sweet and delicate as her voice. "Father Hallock is standing in the vestibule, dear. You needn't be shy. He's a very understanding person."

Lucy didn't answer the woman because she was at a loss to know what to say. Confession? Was she expected to make a confession whenever she went to church? Did all those who were coming out of the church make confessions? The sweet, elegant woman in the fur cape—did she confess something?

Lucy walked several blocks west. From the top of a small brown wooden structure a bell started ringing. Several persons were going in, so Lucy followed. What should she confess? Her heart began to thump as she entered the door.

"Wie gehts?" A balding, heavyset man with a stiffly bosomed shirt and stiff white collar held out his warm

plump hand and clasped Lucy's cold one. *"Schonen guten Morgen,"* he said smiling through his gold-rimmed spectacles.

Lucy looked bewildered in spite of her faint smile. Again she made no answer because she didn't know what to say.

"Nehmen sie Platz, bitte, irgendwo," and he pointed toward the benches.

Timidly Lucy walked halfway up the carpeted aisle and sat down. At once she felt like getting up and going home, but the man was still shaking hands with those coming in. If he would only move away from the door, she could slip out. Two women came in and sat down beside her. Both smiled and shook her hand and said something she didn't understand. She was sure she reddened with embarrassment. A lady in a dark green, velvet-trimmed dress and plumed hat made her way gracefully to the organ and began to play. The people all sang as a man directed them and repeated something in unison. Lucy feared she looked as blank as she felt.

Then the man who shook her hand at the door took his place behind the pulpit and read from a large stiff-backed Bible like the one at home no one was to touch. Lucy squirmed with unpleasant memories. After another song he preached. His manner was so sincere and gracious that although Lucy understood only the word God several times, it had a quieting, soothing effect on her. She noticed several elderly men in front of her nodding at intervals; so she concluded that what was being said was good.

Lucy had started out that morning with eager expectancy. She had planned to go back and tell Norvena and Herman what a wonderful message they missed by not going along. She had intended to renew her beliefs and get inspiration to rededicate her life and, as Gussie had reminded her, rejoice and thank God little Eldon was well and she was able to be out once more.

But Lucy walked home disappointed. Her first visit to a church was next to a complete failure. She couldn't read one word on the folded sheet the boy handed her at the door as she left. Had she been purposely gypped? Why didn't Norvena tell her what kind of churches those were on Center and Vine streets? Or didn't she really know? Lucy wasn't sure she'd try walking across town the following Sunday to try to find the third church Norvena mentioned.

"How did my Eldon behave while I was gone?" asked Lucy smiling as she removed her coat.

"He was as good as gold," answered Norvena. "And how did you enjoy church?"

Reluctantly Lucy related her experiences and, as she had feared, both Norvena and Herman laughed as if it had been a good joke. She was stabbed. But a steady, unseen hand grabbed the pointed weapon before it reached her heart. She would not succumb to their ridicule. After dinner she put Eldon to sleep and walked over to see Gussie Jenkins. After an hour Lucy returned with a firmer step and a stronger faith and a lighter heart. What would she do without Gussie?

Norvena hung a red paper bell in the center of the arch-way between the living and dining rooms. "How does it look there, Lucy?" she asked jumping off the chair.

"It looks fine. It's pretty."

"I wish I had some red and green crepe paper to twist

and drape at the windows like they do in the stores in town. What did you have to decorate with in your home at Christmastime."

"We never had any decorations," answered Lucy. "Christmas was just a holiday from school. In the evening we had popcorn."

"No gifts?"

"No."

"Nothing special for dinner?"

"Well, I remember a number of times we had baked chicken and once a goose. I think Father traded two fat hens with a neighbor for the goose."

"Well, Lucy my dear," said Norvena candidly as she placed her hands on her hips, "you've got an awful lot to live for and see and enjoy now that you're in the city. I'd think you'd feel like you've been let out of a cage. Didn't you think the stores were fixed up beautifully?"

"Indeed, I did. That store where I got my dress, remember that tree in the window with all those glistening snowflakes tied on the branches and yards and yards of popcorn hanging on it? I never saw anything like it. I know I've got a lot to see and learn. You don't need to remind me."

"All the well-to-do people in Branton buy trees and trim them like that one we saw, and some put candles in little clip-on holders that they light on Christmas Day. It's plenty dangerous with children around. There have been some pretty bad fires, I understand. If we had a tree, I'd skip the candles."

"Are you going to get a tree?"

"Herman wouldn't have time to go look for one. A lot of folks go out in the country and just take the trees. Even where it says no trespassing."

"Really? I wouldn't enjoy a tree if I got it that way."

Norvena laughed a dry, shallow laugh. "Well," she remarked walking to the couch where Eldon lay kicking and cooing, "it wouldn't bother me." She took hold of Eldon's little hands and raised him to a sitting position. "You have such a conscientious mother. Do you know that?" And she laughed again.

Clem arrived early.

"Merry Christmas, Lucy," he announced as he stepped inside the door. He removed his overcoat and warmed his hands by the stove.

"Is it cold outside?" Lucy noticed he had on a lovely dark blue suit. His shoes were polished until they shone.

"No, not really. But I want to warm my hands before I touch the baby." He drew an envelope from his inside coat pocket and handed it to Lucy. "It's a little Christmas gift for you and Eldon."

"Oh, Clem." She opened the envelope enough to see a crisp five-dollar bill. "I hardly know what to say. I—I wasn't expecting anything. Why did you do this?"

He saw her eyes sparkle. He saw color creep into her cheeks. He smiled with significant satisfaction. "Because I wanted to, Lucy."

"But I don't deserve it, Clem."

"You mean you're going to protest?" he suggested, chuckling softly, and he picked up Eldon and patted him lovingly. "No matter," he continued, "whether you think you deserve it or not. That's not to be considered. I want you to use it for something you need. I see you have on a pretty new dress. Or isn't it new?"

"I bought it since I'm here. I certainly can use this,

Clem. And I do thank you very, very much."

Clem stood close to her. "There's going to be a pageant at the Star tonight, Lucy. I want to take you to see it."

"What's the Star?"

"The Star Theater. It's a Christmas pageant."

"What's a pageant?"

"Well, to be honest, I've never seen one myself, Lucy. But let's go and find out. It's some kind of play, I guess. People act out a story, I think. This will be about the birth of Christ."

"Really, Clem?"

"I'm sure because I saw some of the pictures in front of the theater when I went past yesterday. I want to see it but I don't want to go alone. What do you say?"

Norvena, filling the water glasses on the table, overheard most of the conversation. "Why don't you go, Lucy?" she called. "I don't think it will be in Latin or German either," she laughed. "Maybe Herman and I will go too. Let's go together."

"I'll carry Eldon," Clem said with smiling contemplation. "See, he knows me and likes me, don't you, Eldon?"

"Just listen to that," exclaimed Norvena. "How many girls have a brother-in-law as nice as Clem Linsdale? Not many I dare say. So don't be stubborn, Lucy."

"No, Clem," she said looking up at him happily. "I don't want to be stubborn. If it'll make you happy, I'll go. I'll help Norvena put the supper on and we'll—"

"We'll let the men clear the table," said Norvena loud enough for Clem to hear. "Then we'll wash the dishes in a jiffy. I don't want to have dirty dishes staring me in the face when I get home. Here comes Herman now. Oh, Herman," she announced, "we're all going to the Star

Theater after supper."

"We are?"

"To see a Christmas pageant."

"Who said so?"

"I did. Clem and Lucy are going."

"And we're going along to chaperon? To see that they behave?"

"Oh, Herman! Of course not. What a thing for you to say! You should be ashamed of yourself. We're going to enjoy it. Clem said it's about the life of Christ."

"Well, don't I have something to say to this, Norvena?" scowled Herman with indignation. "You take for granted I'd enjoy something like that. Well, I'm very sure I'd rather stay at home by the fire and put on my house slippers and smoke that cigar my boss gave me."

"Oh, Herman," pouted Norvena, "I thought you'd like to go. You shouldn't act like an old man already and just sit by the fire."

"Well, I work hard, Norvena, and I like to relax when a holiday comes around. You should have consulted me. You can't get in the Star free, you know."

"I know," admitted Norvena peevishly. "You're right, Mr. Sellers. I should have consulted you. But Clem works hard too. Probably harder than you do."

"Let's drop the subject and eat. I'm starved." In the kitchen Herman whispered to Novena. "That pageant's for children. Why would we want to go to see the life of Christ? It'll be like a fairy tale."

"Lucy," Norvena handed her the freshly baked dinner rolls, "we'll keep the baby. We're not going this time."

Clem drew a quiet breath of relief.

Later, during the pageant, Lucy sat spellbound. The

birth of Christ was portrayed in fascinating realism. The characters performed beautifully, perfectly, and Lucy was thrilled.

"I've never seen anything like it," she whispered.

Clem watched her face grow radiant with wonder and delight. "You're glad we came, aren't you?"

"Oh, yes. It's wonderful. Absolutely wonderful."

At the door Clem took her hand and held it in both of his. "Seeing you enjoy the pageant has made me very happy, Lucy. I'm glad you weren't disappointed."

"I never had a Christmas like this one," she confided with sweet sincerity.

"And I've never seen you look better since you've been sick. Please take care of yourself," said Clem. "And don't work too hard, Lucy. I want to see you get real strong again."

"I'm sure I will. I feel stronger every day. Good night, Clem. I'm glad I could help make Christmas a little happier for you."

After Eldon was asleep and the light puffed out, the fingers of her thoughts started going through the file. The pageant had been so beautiful, so unbelievably real and splendid. She had never seen so many people in one place. Ladies in fine clothes. Such fancy dazzling bright gas lights. Clem was so thoughtful. So kind. So handsome. But — had she done the right thing to go with him? Flossie. How could she have treated him so heartlessly! Clem was wonderful! What if Flossie had been in the theater and seen them together? She shuddered. She buried her face in the pillow.

Oh, God, if I did wrong, forgive me. How could it be wrong when it made me so happy and helped me know the story of Your birth better? Clem. Poor dear lonely man. She had helped him forget his troubles for at least a little while. He was hiding his disappointment, his tragedy, just as she had been doing. Then they had something in common. That was what prompted him to take her to see the pageant.

And supposing Tom had run off and deserted her. Oh! She had never thought of that before. If Tom had run around with some other woman, how could she have endured it? How Clem must be suffering! If she could bring a few minutes of cheer into his life, how could it be wrong?

CHAPTER 33

DAY AFTER day Lucy declared she must make an effort to find a job. But Norvena insisted each time emphatically that she should give herself more time to regain her strength. "Lucy," she'd say, "you could do irreparable damage to yourself if you go to work too soon. You haven't gained all you lost and you should."

"But, Norvena," insisted Lucy, "it simply isn't right for me to stay here and live off your earnings."

"Have you heard me or Herman complain?"

"No."

"Well, you won't either. Herman's as concerned as I am you don't start out too soon. He has a real kind streak in him, Lucy, and it comes to the surface on folks he thinks a lot of. We'd rather do this for you than anyone we know."

One evening Clem asked Lucy to go with him to the theater again. "You stay in too much, Lucy. A walk would do you good."

"I go to see Gussie Jenkins often."

"But that's not like going to town, Lucy." Clem picked up Eldon and played with him until he laughed out loud. "He likes me," he beamed. "Tell your mother you like your Uncle Clem."

Lucy smiled. "What are they going to have at the theater?"

"I think it's a vaudeville."

"I know I'm ignorant, Clem, but what's that? Something like the pageant we saw?"

"Oh," he hesitated, casting a glance at Norvena in the kitchen. "It's more like gymnastics I'd say. Really now, I do think you should get out and take a nice walk. Norvena, you'll look after Eldon, won't you?"

"I'll be glad to, Clem. He's no bother at all."

"That's taken care of," he smiled and held Eldon high over his head and chuckled. "So we can go. Can't we, Eldon? He says yes, Lucy."

"Clem," began Lucy after they had walked about three blocks, "just how shall I go about it to find work here in Branton?"

"Work?" Clem looked down at her as if very much surprised.

"I've been at the Sellerses' over six weeks now. It just doesn't seem right or look right to stay any longer."

"Why doesn't it, Lucy? Who has given you such ideas?"

"Well, I know I ought to get a job and support myself and my child. Just think what a bill I'll owe them after I once start working. That worries me a great deal. I'll never feel right until I've paid them for all the bother and all the meals I've eaten there. Think of all the washings Norvena did for Eldon while I was sick. Gussie told me of three places where I might inquire. Really, I feel strong enough now, but Norvena keeps saying I'm not. Well, I know how I feel better than anyone else does."

"Norvena's not the only one who doesn't want you to go to work yet. Neither do I, Lucy." His voice, soft, deep, and rich, seemed to become a woven part of her coat.

"But why? I don't understand, Clem." They were walking under gas streetlights now. They would soon be at the theater. Vivid excitement was glinting bright in her eyes.

Clem noticed it. "Because—" He looked down into her face with growing tenderness. He took her by the arm. "Because you're plenty thin yet, Lucy."

"But I feel all right," she insisted, smiling at him.

"Even if you do, Lucy," he said with gentlest fervor, "I want you to wait a while. And you need worry no more about repaying the Sellerses. That's all been taken care of."

"What?" Lucy stood still. "What do you mean, Clem?" She touched the lapel of his coat.

"Just what I said, Lucy." His words were warm with feeling. "I didn't intend for you to find this out. But since you're so insistent about going to work, I guess I'll have to tell you. I've been giving Mrs. Sellers three-fifty a week for your board and room and Eldon's—"

"No! Oh, Clem! I'm—I'm almost—what shall I say—I can't understand this. Did Norvena ask you for pay?"

"No, she certainly did not, Lucy. Please believe me. I offered to do it for you."

"But why, Clem?"

"Why? Look at me, Lucy." He put his hand under her chin. "Because I love you. There couldn't possibly be any other reason." He took her one hand and pressed it between both of his.

"You—you mean—" Lucy took a deep, deep breath. "You mean in a sister-in-"

"Yes," laughed Clem softly. "I love you as a sister-in-law, to be sure. But," he added after a wordless pause, "I love you more than that. Come, dear, let's go inside."

To Lucy's surprise the performance was drastically different from the Christmas pageant. Comic pantomimes were accompanied with gay, light singing and scantily clad girls danced to hurdy-gurdy music. Clem watched Lucy's face again, but he was thoroughly disappointed. She wasn't enjoying the performance? Everyone else was laughing and clapping. Clem was perplexed. She wasn't pleased over his confession about paying Mrs. Sellers? She wasn't pleased with his confession of love? Clem looked troubled. Hadn't she guessed after all these weeks, when he ate at the same table with her, that he cared?

"Lucy," he began on the way home.

"Yes."

"Didn't you like it?"

"Like what?"

"The show."

"Well, it wasn't like the pageant." Her voice sounded strangely distant—strained.

"I'm sorry, Lucy. Do you want to tell me why you didn't like it?"

"Well, I never was at a vaudeville. I didn't know what to expect."

"I didn't either, Lucy. I thought it would be a place to go inside and relax. I thought you'd enjoy the walk."

"Oh, yes, I do. Very much."

"You didn't seem to enjoy the show." Clem remarked feebly. "You didn't even smile. Not even when the people all clapped."

"I know. It sorta—well—I felt sorta— Pardon me, Clem, I don't want to sound ungrateful, but it made me feel sorta wicked."

"Wicked?" exclaimed Clem. He promptly dropped his voice a step. "Is that why you're so quiet?" He took her arm as they crossed the street. "Aren't you happy tonight?" He searched her face.

"Yes. Yes, in a way, Clem."

"In a way? But, Lucy, can't you be altogether happy?"

"I don't see how, Clem. Oh, I wish I could."

"But why?" he begged.

"Because you—belong to Flossie." Her voice sounded sad and very tired. "Really, I have no right to love you even if I wanted to." She bit her lip. She felt a lump in her throat. She was trembling all over.

"But, Lucy," objected Clem earnestly, "how can I love your sister when she won't return my love? I tried it. I tried my best and she ran off three times before I gave up."

"Oh, Clem! I never knew that."

"I tell you the truth, Lucy. I did everything humanly possible to win that girl. If she would rather live with Dick Galoway, why should I waste my love or my hard-earned money on her?"

Lucy made no answer.

"I wish a thousand times now I had found you first." He walked close to her, so close he could feel her shaking. "We could have made each other very happy, I'm sure. You have such a different makeup from Floss."

They walked on in silence. They would soon be at the harness shop. "Don't you love me a little, Lucy?"

She made no answer. She was fighting tears.

"Can't you, Lucy dear?"

Still no answer.

"You don't want to love me?" His words held frantic disappointment.

"I'll think about it, Clem." Her voice was barely above a whisper. Quickly she brushed away a tear.

"Then you can't tell me tonight?"

Lucy pressed her one hand over her lips. Her brain was in a whirl. She must be alone to think.

Clem was hurt and Lucy could see it. After all his unsolicited kindness to her, how could she let him go back to the hotel feeling like this? She was heartless, cruel.

"Oh, Clem," she said touching his arm and looking up in the dark, searching his sad face, "I like you very, very much. You've been so good to me and Eldon. You've been the kindest brother-in-law a—"

He cut her off. "Forget I'm your brother-in-law. Forget I ever was your sister's husband. Forget everything that happened before that morning I saw you at the window. Please, Lucy. Just try."

"But I can't, Clem," she cried. "Flossie would hate me."

"I doubt that very much."

"She may change her mind and want you back. Oh, Clem, I've got to think this over. I can't be hasty this time."

"All right, my good sincere little lady," Clem said, trying to sound calm. "But promise me we'll be good friends."

"Yes, of course we will."

"The best of friends."

"Yes, to be sure, the best."

"And you won't be shy now when I come for supper?"

"I'll surely try not to be, Clem."

"And you'll let me take you places?"

"Yes, but not to any more vaudevilles, please."

"Whatever you say, Lucy. I'm sorry you didn't enjoy it. I really didn't either."

"Let's go to a church sometime."

"Where?"

"Norvena said there's a church over on the other side of town somewhere. I'd like to go visit there sometime."

"That's the Salvation Army, I believe. So you'd rather go to church with me?"

"I'd like to go there once to see what it's like."

"Anything your heart desires, Lucy dear, I'll do. I want to make you happy."

"Clem, if you were this kind to Flossie and I'm sure you were, I just can't understand why she left you."

They were going up the steps now. He took her by the arm. "Did the walk make you tired?"

"No, not really."

"I hope you'll sleep well."

"I hope you will too."

They were at the door. Lucy turned the knob. "Good night, Clem. I'll be seeing you."

"Wait a minute. You're sweet," he whispered. "You are the most beautiful girl I've ever seen. I just had to tell you this before I leave. You wouldn't run off and leave me, would you, Lucy?"

"Oh, Clem," she whispered, "if you don't quit talking to me like this, I'll be loving you even if I shouldn't."

CHAPTER 34

"IS THAT you, Gussie?" called Lucy from the bedroom.

"That's who it is, Miss Lucy."

"Come in here. I'm dressing Eldon. You're the very person I want to see this morning."

"And what might you be wanting of me this pretty morning?" Her dark face was radiant. "Hi, you sweet lamb. Where's Mrs. Sellers?"

"She's gone to town, Gussie; so we can talk. Take a chair. I have something on my mind."

"I see you do. So start out."

"You've seen Clem Linsdale and I want you to tell me what you think of him. Please, Gussie, be frank with me."

Gussie took Eldon in her arms and held his cheek against hers. "Well," she said rocking back and forth, "what I've seen he's a mighty fine man. But I don't know him. Why do you ask?"

"Because he told me," Lucy folded and unfolded her hands, "he loves me. He told me last night. Gussie, you're one person I can just uncover my heart to."

"Just what I expected, Miss Lucy."

Lucy sat on the edge of the bed and brushed her hand over the spread.

"Why, Gussie?"

"Because Mrs. Sellers has been telling me things. What

else's on your mind?"

"I don't know how to react."

"Why not?"

"I want to love him but I don't know if I should."

"Well, now, does his talk and action hang together? That's one way to know a man. Seems to me he thinks a heap of this boy baby too."

"I'm sure he does, Gussie, but you see he's married to my own sister, Flossie. That's my problem."

"Do tell. Where's she?"

"She left him. Ran away."

"What a shame, Miss Lucy."

"What do you mean?"

"That they couldn't pull together."

"I think it's terrible, Gussie. I never dreamed she'd do such a thing. Clem tried his best. I know he did. It's all Flossie's fault. She left him three times."

"Do tell. My, my, what a way to treat a nice man like Clem."

"Now what I want to ask you is this, Gussie. Is it right for me to love Clem?"

"Right, Miss Lucy? Well, what does your heart say? Do you love him or don't you? I didn't know it's something you can turn off or on."

"I'm asking you if I have a right to, Gussie. I'm so confused. Flossie might see her mistake and want to come back to Clem. She's a very jealous person. Oh, I wish I knew what is right."

"You're asking me a hard question, my dear lady. I don't know what to say."

"I thought you would, Gussie. You always had answers for everything else I've wondered about."

"There may be something in the good book, but I don't know where. Got no idea, Miss Lucy. I guess I could ask our pastor sometime if you want me to."

"Would you?"

"Has Clem got a divorce?"

"Not yet."

"Well, seems to me he has a right."

Two days later Lucy wrote Aunt Polly a short and hurried letter.

> *Dear Aunt Polly,*
>
> *Eldon took sick suddenly. I'm worried. He's very sick. Please have Uncle Jake come and get us at once. I want to be with you.*
>
> *Lucy*

Gussie was with Lucy most of the next two days and well into the night. Tenderly she did everything possible for little Eldon. Clem sent a doctor to the house and paid the fee. But Eldon could not keep the medicine down.

"Lucy," Clem stood close to her, speaking in his softest voice possible, "it hurts me to see you so sad. You're not going to eat any supper?"

"I'm not a bit hungry, Clem."

"I don't feel like eating if you don't."

"Oh, please go eat."

"It doesn't seem possible you're going to leave."

"It's the only thing to do, Clem. I hate to see you look so sad but I've been here long enough. Norvena and Gussie nursed me through my sickness and I just can't expect —" Her eyes filled with tears. "I've just got to go to Aunt Polly."

Clem looked at Lucy until the cords in his neck throbbed. He knew Uncle Jake would wade fire if need be to help Lucy. But there was a gnawing fear that something besides Eldon was making her anxious to leave.

"I brought you a little something," he said, "just a little something to remember me by while you're gone."

"I've never seen anything like it. Clem, it's beautiful." She had unwrapped a gold pin about two inches long and in the center was a miniature round picture of himself.

By noon the next day Uncle Jake arrived in a closed surrey he had borrowed from a neighbor. While Lucy gathered up all her belongings, Norvena and Gussie bundled up little Eldon.

"Is it cold outside, Uncle Jake?"

"Not very. I brought three warm blankets along."

"You'll be back, won't you, Lucy?" asked Norvena after she kissed Lucy.

"I can't promise anything now, Norvena. I'm so worried. But I'll write. And thanks a thousand times for all you've done for me. And you too, Gussie. You have been wonderful to know. I'll never, never forget you." Lucy couldn't control her emotions. She was crying when she waved good-bye.

Several days later Aunt Polly was holding John Eldon. His little arms were folded and a sweet delicate smile gave him an expression of perfect peace.

"Lucy," whispered Aunt Polly, "he's gone."

"What! Oh, Aunt Polly. I thought he was sleeping at last. O God! We've not been here two days. I—I can't understand this," she cried. "My Tom! My beautiful Bible! And now my baby! Oh, Aunt Polly, I've nothing left."

Uncle Jake was standing in the doorway. He heard. He

shook with sobs.

Gently Aunt Polly laid the lifeless body on the bed. "Don't cry so hard, Lucy," she begged tenderly. "He's better off than any of us, Lucy. It's hard, I know, but God makes no mistakes. Never. Never. We must trust Him at all times. God knows if he had lived, he may have met with great misfortune. Always think of it in that way, dear."

Aunt Polly opened her dresser drawer. "Look, Lucy. Jake found this in Crawford last week."

"A Bible?"

"It's for you, Lucy. It's only the New Testament and Psalms. He tried but he couldn't find one like you had."

"Oh, thanks, thanks. Do you suppose Uncle Jake will go tell Father about my baby? Oh, Aunt Polly," she sobbed out loud and dropped on her knees beside the bed and touched his hands and face.

"Of course I will, Lucy." Uncle Jake stepped into the room. "I'm—" he was crying— "I'm all broke up over this."

The next afternoon Uncle Jake, Aunt Polly, and Lucy drove through the mud in the covered surrey to Stony Point graveyard to bury John Eldon beside his father. The undertaker and his wife drove ahead with the little white casket. Lucy's father came in a spring wagon.

"Lucy," he stepped beside her at the grave and put one strong arm around her shoulder. A chill wind blew in her face and he stood in front of her to shield her.

How thin she looked. How tired she looked.

"Lucy," he repeated softly, "don't feel so bad."

"I—can't help it," she sobbed.

He held her so close she could feel his heart beating through his heavy lumber jacket. He held her until the grave was closed.

"Lucy," he whispered.

"Yes, Father," she did not look up.

"Won't you come home now?"

What could it mean the way he was holding her? Tom gone. Little Eldon, who looked like Tom, gone. Why not?

"I'll come," she said through her tears. "But I'll have to go back and get my things. I'll come home for a while." She heard him draw a deep breath.

"You will?"

"You may come and get me when it suits you."

Lucy had a long talk with Aunt Polly. She repeated what she had confided in Gussie Jenkins.

"Well, I tell you, Lucy," began Aunt Polly, "I don't believe in telling anyone who to love or not to love. All I have to say is, go slow. Clem seems like a very nice man but he's not a Christian. Or is he?"

"No. But he said he'd go to church with me sometime. I believe him. He's been so good to me. Look what he gave me before I left. Isn't it beautiful?"

"It certainly is. He must love you a great deal, Lucy, if he gave you his picture. I never did understand what the Bible says about divorce and remarriage. It just never comes up when people get along like we do."

"Uncle Jake isn't a Christian."

"I know, dear. But he doesn't oppose me either and we do get along very well. I believe he's doing some serious thinking about becoming a Christian."

Lucy sat in deep thought. "Do you suppose Flossie would want Clem back if she found out he loved me?"

"She might. She's unpredictable, that girl is."

"Oh, Aunt Polly, why do I have so many hard things to

face? Before I get over one thing, I'm plunged into another."

"Maybe God allows it to make you strong."

"Strong? I feel weak and—and, Aunt Polly, I'm going to be so lonely over home. I wonder if Father's sad about Flossie."

"Maybe that's why he was so attentive to you at the grave. He must have a soft spot in his heart after all." After a prolonged pause Aunt Polly said, "I read one time something like this—the greatest people are those who've gone through great adversity." Then she added, "You're lonely for love, aren't you, dear? I don't mean your father's love."

"Is it wrong for me to be?" cried Lucy in anguish.

CHAPTER 35

THE TRUTH, depressing, stinging, and at times almost brutal, pressed in on Lucy from every angle. It wasn't as easy to go back home as she had anticipated. Every place her eyes took her reminded her of buried loves. Corkie, Tom, Mom, and now her only one to live for, John Eldon. Memories sad and crushing wound in and out over the long heavy chain of years, days, and moments behind her. If she could only drop it, unshackle herself, and start a new life from now on. Now.

She read every night from the New Testament Uncle Jake had bought her in Crawford. How sweet of him. Especially since he wasn't a professing Christian himself. This could mean nothing else but his desire to see her spiritually helped. It did help. Especially when she read the Psalms. It was like brushing deep pile velvet the right way. Each morning when she woke, her tragedies glared at her anew, and memories' fingers brushed the velvet the wrong way. That hurt.

Both Loretta and Peggy were glad Lucy came home. So were Floyd and Kenneth. The four told her so. And Father. Everyone knew he was pleased without vocalizing on the subject. It wasn't John Winchester's habit to word his pleasures. But he observed and ate with a genuine gratification none of his children could ignore. But Lucy was home less than a week when she got a letter.

Dear Lucy,

You can't imagine how lonesome it is here with-out you. Norvena let me read your letter. Poor dear little Eldon. I'm so sorry. I loved him dearly because he was yours. When will you be coming back? I have a new job at the Federal Lead Works. I'm drawing better wages and the work isn't as hard as at the stone quarry. I work at the smelter. I'm rooming here at the Sellerses' until you come back. Please write to me real soon, Lucy. Tell me everything that's happened since you left. I'm inter-ested in everything you do, Lucy, because I truly love you from the depths of my heart.

With fondest wishes,
Clem

Lucy considered it from every viewpoint. She would take her father into her confidence as she had Gussie and Aunt Polly. She had deceived, shocked, angered, and grieved him once and she wouldn't do it again even though she was mature and a widow. If Father was still as fond of Clem as he had been before he and Flossie were married, she should have no fears.

After the others had retired for the night, Lucy pulled a chair next to her father, who was sitting in the rocker she had given to her mother.

"I'd like to talk to you, Father," she began.

"All right, Lucy. What about?" He looked at the letter in her hand.

"I didn't know Flossie and Clem weren't getting along until Mrs. Morehouse told me."

"You didn't?" He stopped rocking and bent forward,

wrinkling his brow. His hair was graying fast and age was making early lines on his face. He looked almost haggard. "Well," he said, breathing deeply as though unwinding his tightly wound feelings. "Flossie was downright mean to Clem. She did him dirty." He got to his feet to stretch, then sat down again. "Lucy, you must have worked too hard. You're thin."

"Yes," she admitted rubbing her arms, "I was pretty sick when I had the measles."

"You've got to drink more milk and eat cornmeal mush and get some of the color back in your cheeks."

"I will," Lucy replied. "You know, Father, when I was at Sellerses' in Branton, Clem walked by one morning when I was shaking a rug from an upstairs window. I had no idea he was in town. He was as surprised as I was. Well, he came up to see me and that was the first I knew Flossie had left him. He said she left him the third time. I thought it couldn't be possible."

"She was a rascal," John panted. "I don't understand her at all." He stamped the floor with one foot.

Lucy waited for him to calm down before she continued. "To hurry on about Clem; well, he and I saw each other every evening for weeks because he ate supper at the Sellerses. Then he took me to the theater twice."

John Winchester sat up very straight and his lips parted as he studied intently Lucy's face. "The second time he told me he loved me."

Silence.

"I'm going to read the letter I got from him today."

John Winchester sat as motionless as the cookstove, holding his breath.

Having finished the letter, Lucy looked up. "What do

you think of it?"

He drew in a long, long breath, then scratched his head. "Clem's a fine chap," he said. "I always did like him." He gripped the arms of the chair. "He deserves a good woman. There's nothing wrong with the letter that I can see."

Lucy could not hide her excitement. It seemed her soul had a dozen strings and each one was quivering. "Are you telling me you approve, Father?"

"I said I see nothing wrong with the letter, didn't I? Clem's a good all-round sensible young man, but I don't like to see you go back to Branton yet."

She saw his lip tremble. "Oh, I won't go for a while," she said with warmth. "I'll stay till I build up and gain what I lost. And I want to do some sewing for the girls and myself maybe. And I'll help Loretta with the spring cleaning. But I want to know if you'd object if Clem and I write to each other."

"Why would I care, Lucy?" he almost shouted. He rubbed his big strong hands, the one over the other.

"Not so loud, Father," smiled Lucy touching him on the arm. "Would it be fair to Flossie?"

"Fair?" he shouted. "There, I forgot myself already." He brought his voice down several steps. "Fair?" he repeated. "It's no more'n she deserves if Clem takes to lovin' you."

Lucy lay awake well into the quiet, strangely moody night. Life would be much easier if she and Clem exchanged letters.

One afternoon in February Lucy was sitting by the window patching a pair of Kenneth's overalls when a one-horse sleigh stopped at the gate. A young woman got out and hurried toward the house while the man stayed in the sleigh holding the reins.

The door opened. "Why, Lucy," exclaimed Flossie. "I didn't expect to see you here. When did you come home?"

"I've been here several weeks."

"Hi, Loretta. Lucy, what have you been doing? You're thin. And pale. Been sick or something?"

"I lost my baby."

"So I heard."

"I had the measles."

"Measles! Oh, horrors. Then I'm getting out of here. I just stopped in to let you all know I'm getting married to Dick Galoway one of these days as soon as I get my divorce. Well, don't look so shocked, Lucy. Clem and I haven't been living together for months. He's too tame for me. He'd suit you lots better." And Flossie pointed a finger at Lucy and laughed a hollow, unnatural laugh. "Well, anything new before I leave? I can't stay. Dick's waiting for me and I don't want to make him impatient."

"You needn't be afraid of me. I had the measles weeks ago."

Flossie opened the door. Lucy followed her to the steps. "Flossie," she ventured, "you wouldn't care if Clem loved me?"

Flossie's laugh was boisterous. "Care?" she said in an icy tone. "Me care? I wouldn't care that much," and she snapped her fingers, "if he married you. He's out of my life for good and I mean O-U-T, out."

"Where are you going to live?" asked Lucy. "You and Dick after you're married?"

"Oh, we don't know yet. We might land in Chicago. Or Buffalo. Dick's got big ideas. He's much more exciting and original than Clem ever was. No comparison."

"You'll write, won't you?" called Lucy as Flossie ran toward the gate. "We ought to keep in touch."

"Well, if I have time and think about it."

"Please do," called Lucy.

"Oh, Lucy," stormed Loretta. "She didn't even act concerned about John Eldon. She doesn't care about anybody but herself."

"Oh, well," returned Lucy trying to camouflage her own feelings. "Don't you ever act like that."

"Well, I hope I never do," came Loretta's immediate reply. "I can't imagine how she ever got like that. And I'm glad Peggy's not like that. She's sweet-natured like you, Lucy."

"Well, thank you, dear." And Lucy gave Loretta a hug. "But I fear you are just overlooking times when I wasn't very sweet."

"I wanted to go along with Father when your baby was buried, Lucy, but he said it was too cold."

That very night Lucy wrote Clem a letter. After it was stamped and sealed she opened her Testament and leafed through it. Loretta and Peggy were sound asleep. It was cold. She took the comforter off her bed and draped it around her shoulders and sat on the edge of the bed. The small oil lamp on the dresser made only a dim light to read by. She decided to start at the first page and read the book through. With great difficulty she plowed through the first eight verses of "begats."

Shaking her head she turned to the back and read the first psalm, then dropped on her knees. *Dear Lord,* she breathed silently, *I know You can hear my thoughts. This book is so hard to understand, yet I know it's right and good and I do want to believe it. Keep Your hand over me so that someday I can go to be with my little John Eldon. O God, he was so precious to me. It was so hard to give him up. Sometimes I feel so near to death since Corkie and Mom and Tom died, and my baby who looked just like him. Dear Lord, let it be all right for me to love Clem, for I know now for sure I do.*

Lucy's stay at home was next to unbearable until the night she had the talk with her father. And after Flossie dropped in, the plum tree episode and all the unpleasant experiences surrounding it before and after faded into insignificance. Her thoughts were in Branton much of the time. She found herself watching with eagerness for the mail carrier every Tuesday and Friday. Never once did he fail to leave a letter from Clem on those days. And Lucy answered every one. Why wouldn't she when Clem furnished her with stamps and stationery? She enjoyed writing to him all about what she was doing, sewing, cooking, baking, cleaning, reading, and gaining weight. It was wonderful to walk to the mailbox like a lady and hand the postman a letter addressed to Mr. Clem Linsdale in Branton. No sneaking down the road after dark to hide a note under a flat stone. No going to the hen house to get a letter delivered by Floyd. No clothes-closet secret readings; and Father knew and didn't object. Yet Lucy knew he was watching her with a strange uneasiness. Was it anxiety? He treated her with every kindness he could. He never asked her any questions about Clem or what he had to say. He only watched her. Day by day her cheeks got fuller, pinker, her eyes bluer, brighter, her blond hair more silky as it had been before all her sorrow and suffering. By the first of April, Lucy was the picture of health.

"Father," she announced one evening, "I think I'll be

going back to Branton very soon now. Clem wrote that Norvena has a job for me taking care of an elderly woman who is quite well-to-do and the work won't be hard. I can begin working right away; so Clem will be coming for me Sunday."

John Winchester looked at Lucy a full wordless minute. He ran both hands through his graying hair twice. He unbuttoned his shirt collar.

"Well," he managed to say at length, "we'll miss you, Lucy." He coughed. Slowly he walked to the stove, shook the coffee pot, poured what was in it into a cup, and took it with him to his bedroom.

Clem came in a handsome shiny new buggy he had rented for the trip. The usual Sunday card game was in progress and so tense was the interest that no one but her father heard Clem's gentle knock. He had told Lucy earlier in the day to slip out as quietly as possible. It would make it easier for her and for him as well if there were no good-byes.

There was still ice on the ground in spots. Clem tucked Lucy snugly inside a cowhide robe and away they went.

"I'm thrilled to see how well you look, Lucy."

"I drank lots of milk."

"You're absolutely beautiful, Lucy."

He showered her with love and endearing words all the way to Branton.

"You're as lovely as a princess," he exclaimed.

"But I'm just a poor girl, Clem. I've never known anything but hard work. Common work. I have only a fifth-grade education. Not that I didn't want to go to school longer, but I didn't get to."

"Don't talk like that, Lucy. And don't degrade yourself.

I love you for what you are, not for what you have or where you come from. You didn't choose your home, any more than I did mine. You couldn't help it your mother lost her eyesight and you had to quit school and stay at home. Listen to me, dear; look at me. I couldn't love you more if every hair on your head was strung with pure gold. You know enough to make a man happy and I want to be that happy man."

Lucy smiled sweetly.

Clem waited for her answer.

"What are you thinking about?" he asked after an extended silence.

"I was wondering," she said softly, and she looked him full in the face, "if you wouldn't like to be a Christian."

"A Christian?"

"Yes, Clem." Lucy touched his coat sleeve. Her voice was tender and sincere. "You are so kind and gentle, Clem. And thoughtful. And it just doesn't seem like it would be such a great step."

"Well, I'll think about it, my dear. I don't know the first thing about it, but it's all right. I'm sure." He winked at her and smiled. "My, won't Norvena be tickled to see you looking so good? We'll be there before we know it. You didn't get cold, did you, dear?"

"No."

"Look," he said pointing to a red brick house to the left. "That's the place. That's where Mrs. Ella Carrington lives."

"Who is Mrs. Carrington?"

"The lady who wants you to work for her."

"There! You mean I'm to work for someone who lives in a beautiful place like that!" Lucy caught her breath and held it. She leaned forward to look out. Her eyes opened wide. "Stop just a minute, Clem. Oh, look at those beautiful lace curtains. What must it be like inside! And that lawn, those lovely trees. I'm scared, Clem."

"Scared?"

"How can I ever fit into a place like that? A common country girl like me?"

"You'll fit in all right, my little princess. Mrs. Carrington will love you at first sight."

"How do you know?"

"How could she help but love you? And nothing could be too nice for you. Since you insisted you must work, I insisted Norvena find you a nice place and where you wouldn't have to work too hard. Shall we go on now?"

"Not yet."

"Promise me, Lucy dear, that you won't sign a contract to stay any certain length of time."

"Why?"

"Because I want you to come and live with me as soon as—"

Lucy looked up startled. "As soon as what?"

"As soon as the divorce is granted. I want you for my wife. You'll be the queen in our home."

CHAPTER 36

"CLEM," LUCY'S voice was a bit unsteady, "what if Dick Galoway isn't good to Flossie and she sees her mistake and wants you back after all?"

"Well," answered Clem tersely, "I wouldn't take that girl back if she got down on her knees. I could never trust her again. And what's more, I don't think now I ever really loved her."

"Why, Clem. Then why did you ask her to marry you?"

"Because I thought she was cute and pretty and stunning." Clem groaned. "Cute indeed," he snapped. "I was blind as a bat. I was infatuated. Yes, that's the word. You're the one who's more than pretty. You're beautiful, Lucy, and that evening you brought popcorn in for us I noticed it."

"I hope you don't want to marry me because you think I'm beautiful."

"That's only part of it, dearest." He took her one hand and squeezed it. "I love you for your beauty, yes, certainly, but also for everything you do and say. I love the you in you, darling. Can't you understand what I'm trying to tell you?"

Lucy was looking toward the brick house. The lace curtain at the big bay window moved. A white-haired lady looked out.

"Look, Clem. She's wondering why we're stopping here

so long. Do you suppose that was Mrs. Carrington?"

"Could be." Clem's voice was suddenly heavy with fresh fret.

"Why don't I go in and meet her? I might as well get off here. I'm anxious to begin working even if I'm excited and scared. Oh, Clem, I—I feel so—I don't know how."

"We'd better go on, Lucy." He held her by the arm. "Norvena's real anxious to see you, you know."

"But she lives only a few blocks from here, doesn't she? You can tell her I'll be over soon. I'll walk while you take the horse and buggy back. Won't that be all right, Clem?" And Lucy started crawling out of the cowhide robe.

"Just a minute, Lucy." Clem had a frustrated look on his face. "You haven't promised me yet." He looked at her with pleading eyes.

Lucy made no answer. She started gathering up her belongings.

"Don't get out here, dear," said Clem with extra tenderness. "I'll drive you around to the side entrance. You won't promise me?" he begged softly, breathing fast.

They were at the side entrance already. "Oh, Clem, you've been so very good to me. I love you dearly. You know I do, but I can't make any promises today. Let's see first how things work out."

"Oh, Lucy." He shook his head in disbelief and a withered expression crossed his face. He helped her down and carried her things to the door.

"Good evening." The white-haired lady opened the door before Lucy knocked.

"I'm Lucy Hammon."

"And I'm Mrs. Carrington. I've been looking for you. Come in." And she took Lucy by the hand and held it a moment.

"This is Mr. Linsdale, my brother-in-law, Mrs. Carrington."

"Mr. Linsdale, come in. We'll go into the living room and get acquainted." And she led the way to a spacious, thickly carpeted room where dancing flames were crackling in and out of two big logs in the fireplace. "Take off your coats and sit on the sofa by the fire. I'm so glad you came, Lucy. My son worries about me when I'm alone and he had to leave last Thursday; so I've been alone now for three days. I'm hardly able to take care of the house by myself and keep up the fires."

Clem cleared his throat and looked at Lucy. Mrs. Carrington had a son? What if Lucy smiled at him the way she did at this lovely lady, his mother? "Your son," inquired Clem, "is he gone a lot?"

"Yes," she answered pleasantly. "Oswald has a government job; so he must go where and when he's commissioned. The girl I had for seven years got married in March. Do you live here in Branton, Mr. Linsdale?"

"Yes. I live with Mr. and Mrs. Sellers."

"I see. And your wife was Lucy's sister?"

"Yes, ma'am."

"And how long have you been a widower, if I may ask? I'm sorry about that."

Clem was quite taken aback. The sides of his tongue felt warpy and he fidgeted with the flap on his coat pocket.

"My sister is in the east just now," put in Lucy, trying to select the right words to relieve her own and Clem's apparent embarrassment.

His eyes met Lucy's, but she wasn't sure whether he

was trying to thank or reprove her. She wanted to whisper in his ear and ask if she had hurt his feelings and if she did she was sorry. Her cheeks got pink.

"Why don't you hang your coat in the closet there, Miss Hammon?"

"Just call me Lucy, Mrs. Carrington," said Lucy in a cheery voice, opening the closet door. "And now you must tell me what to do next."

"But this is Sunday," said Mrs. Carrington taking her favorite rocking chair. "We don't do more than we have to on Sunday, you know. First of all, we want to get a little better acquainted, then we'll have tea before your brother-in-law leaves."

Clem got to his feet. "Thank you, Mrs. Carrington," he said courteously, "but I promised to have the horse and buggy back at the livery stable by five o'clock; so I must be leaving at once. It's been nice to meet you."

He picked up his hat. He thought he could not leave without talking alone with Lucy once more. His eyes scanned the richly carpeted rooms. Through a colonnade to the left he could see the beautifully furnished dining room. The snowy white tablecloth, the corner china closet, blooming potted plants in the low recessed windows, curtains tied back with heavy red cords that matched the thick carpet. The door to the right opened into another large room with handsomely upholstered furniture. And hand-painted lamps. So this would be where the girl he was madly in love with would be spending her days. Days, weeks—months—how many? Too good for her? Never. It couldn't be too good a place for Lucy. But how long would he have to wait? And Oswald? His heart started pounding.

"Good-bye, Lucy," he said taking several steps toward the side entrance. He never took his gaze from her.

"Good-bye, Clem," she answered, "and thank you so much for bringing me back to Branton. Tell Norvena I'll be over soon."

"Tonight?"

"Well, I'd better not leave Mrs. Carrington tonight."

Slowly, softly Clem closed the door.

"You know, Lucy," began Mrs. Carrington one morning at the breakfast table, "it seems as if you've been with me for years."

"Years?" Lucy put her coffee cup on the saucer. "In what way?"

"I'll tell you. Mildred was with me for seven years and I grew very fond of her. I told Oswald I'd never find another girl I'd like as well. I've always had a dread of breaking in a new girl. Now you've been with me three weeks and I'm so pleased with your work."

"Thank you, Mrs. Carrington. I want you to tell me if you're not."

"I will. But are you satisfied?"

"I like it here very much. Can't you tell I do?"

"I thought you did but I wanted to hear you say so."

Lucy took a bite of toast and gazed out the window. "The lawn is so pretty," she remarked, "and I noticed the peonies are up four or five inches. It must be beautiful around here when all your flowers and shrubs are in bloom."

"It used to be when Mr. Carrington was living. I hire a neighbor boy to mow the lawn. I wouldn't ask you to do that. Do you have any definite plans for the future?"

Lucy looked up with surprise. "Why, Mrs. Carrington?"

"Well, you see, I like you and if you like me and are satisfied here, I'll pay you three dollars a week starting the first of May if you'll promise to stay with me a year. I don't like this feeling of suspense that I've got a girl who might up and leave me. You understand how it is, don't you?"

"Well," answered Lucy thoughtfully, her one hand holding her coffee cup, "if—you're satisfied with me I see no reason at the moment why I couldn't stay a year, unless something would happen that I'd be called home."

"What a relief, Lucy," smiled Mrs. Carrington. "What a glad relief! I know Oswald will be happy too when I write and tell him I have a girl I like so well I've asked her to stay a year. Now, I'll feel free to write and invite my sister Nettie to come and stay several months. I'd be lost if she'd come and I would not have a girl I could depend on. She's a widow too, two years younger than I am. You'll like Nettie. She's a perfect dear. When she's here, you can feel free to get out and go places. Oswald will know I'm not alone. You've stayed here with me so faithfully these three weeks. I think your friend, Mrs. Sellers, feels you're tied down pretty close here, doesn't she?"

"Maybe so."

"And your brother-in-law does too, doesn't he?"

"I guess he does." Lucy sipped coffee.

"He and the Sellerses are big friends, aren't they?"

"Yes."

"He's a very good-looking young man."

"You mean Clem?"

"Yes. I think he's absolutely handsome. I can't imagine why your sister left him."

"I can't either," agreed Lucy.

"Does he have a divorce?"

"Yes."

"Well, he won't stay single long I dare say. I suppose plenty of young ladies have their eye on him."

Lucy blushed. She warmed all over. The biscuit in her throat wanted to stick there. She had never thought of such a possibility. Clem had been so devoted to her. The pin with his picture in the center was in her dresser drawer, but she hadn't worn it once in the past three weeks. Would Clem transfer his repeated declarations of love to another?

"Mrs. Carrington," ventured Lucy with some hesitancy, "do you think it's right for a man to remarry when he has a living wife?"

"Well, it seems to me that all depends on circumstances. The law grants it."

"I know that, but would you happen to know if the Bible says anything about it?"

"I presume if it says anything, it must not say it's a sin because the teacher of the men's Bible class in the largest church in Windom has his second wife. They say he's a marvelous teacher."

"And his first wife is living?"

"She is unless she died recently, and I haven't heard she did. She was a wild type, about as you describe your sister. I know the wife he has now and she's just the opposite. They get along perfectly. Why did you ask, Lucy? Do you think it would be wrong for your brother-in-law to marry again?"

Lucy looked out the window. "I hope it wouldn't be," she remarked trying to act modest. "I wasn't sure. But if that teacher of a Bible class did it, well—it must be all right."

"Is Mr. Linsdale thinking of taking another wife?"

Lucy's face flushed red. Her eyelashes swept her cheeks.

"Why are you blushing, Lucy?" asked Mrs. Carrington reaching over and touching Lucy's hand. "Perhaps it's you. Oh, Lucy, I'm sorry. I apologize. Don't be embarrassed. He's nice. Very nice. I thought to myself several times he was extremely attentive to you for a brother-in-law."

"But you know, Mrs. Carrington," said Lucy, "I keep wondering if my sister won't see her mistake and want him back. You see, it's such a difficult situation because we're sisters."

"Yes, but listen, Lucy. According to the law your sister has no more claim on him now than if she had never been his wife. That's the value of a divorce, don't you see?"

Lucy sipped coffee slowly as she sat in deep study. "If she just wasn't my sister. She's got such a jealous disposition. "

"You wouldn't both live in the same house, would you?"

"Oh, no."

"Or the same block?"

"No."

"Or the same town?"

"Probably not. No, I doubt that."

"He wouldn't take her back now if she wanted him, would he?"

"He says he wouldn't."

"Of course he wouldn't. That would be the height of foolishness. By the way, I noticed you had a New Testament on your dresser. Do you read it?"

"Yes, some every evening."

"What do you think of it?"

"I think it's a wonderful book even though I don't understand a lot of it. I like to read the Psalms. What do you think of the Bible?" Lucy's cheeks were still red and very warm.

"Well, I like to read the Beatitudes. And I say the Lord's Prayer every night and I like the Psalms too. As you said, there's so much I don't understand. I think only a few men have enough education to understand and interpret it to others, and they have to spend hours alone with God."

Lucy took in a deep breath and relaxed. Was Brother Bustleton one of those few men? He must be. Yet she remembered hearing him say, "I have not come to you with flowery language of a highly educated man but I come to give you the simple message of the Gospel. Jesus said if any man will do His will he shall know." But she did remember Brother Bustleton's honest, earnest, radiant face. She would never forget that.

"Mrs. Carrington, did you ever hear of a Brother Bustleton?"

"No, Lucy, never did. Who is he?"

"A preacher who held meetings in Black Bend Schoolhouse when I was a girl. He was a wonderful person. I don't think he had a college education, but I had the impression he could answer any question anyone would ask him. I was so impressed with his sincerity. He baptized me."

"I see. Where does he live?"

"I don't know."

"What denomination does he represent?"

"I don't know that either."

"Yet you would trust him to give you the right answer on any subject?"

"Oh, yes. I'd trust him to tell me the truth."

"Do you see that old gray stone house behind that hedge across the street?"

"Yes."

"Well, Reverend Utterback lives there with his daughter and husband, the Kansteiners. He's a retired minister. Someday when the tulips are in bloom, we'll go over there to see them. The Kansteiners have some of the prettiest tulips in Branton. Reverend Utterback is a grand old man, and any time you wonder about anything in the Bible, you ask him. He'll tell you the truth if anyone could."

That very evening Lucy met Clem at the door with a glowing smile. "Let's sit in the living room," she said and Clem followed.

Mrs. Carrington visited a few minutes, then excused herself and left the room.

"Lucy," exclaimed Clem, "I have a surprise for you. Guess what it is."

"I can't. What is it?"

"Try." His handsome face was radiant.

"Is it about—somebody—I—"

"No. No. It's something nice, Lucy. Not about people."

"Tell me. I can't guess."

"You really want to know?" He beamed on her and held both her hands to his lips.

"Of course. Tell me quickly."

"I bought a little house today."

"A house? Why?"

"Why? For us, Lucy. Who else would I be buying a

house for? I'm getting tired living with Herman and Norvena. I want you to do my cooking. I want to bring home the groceries for you, Lucy. I want to look after you," he smiled, "and do things to make you happy. I want to give you whatever you wish for. Let's be married in June, Lucy my love." He cupped her hands in both of his.

"In June?" gasped Lucy. "Oh, Clem. I—I promised Mrs. Carrington I'd stay here a year."

"A year!" choked Clem frantically dropping her hands. His face turned ashen. He wilted. "Oh, Lucy Winchester! How—how could you! You little witch!"

"Clem!" exclaimed Lucy.

"Oh, I—I don't know what I'm saying." He stood up, pale and shaken. He pulled her up in front of him. She could feel his hot breath on her forehead. He grabbed her by the shoulders and held her out at arm's length. "I don't know what to think of you, Lucy." His face was drawn with grief more poignant than bodily pain. His shoulders sagged and his hands trembled. "You've got me all tied up in knots."

CHAPTER 37

CLEM DROPPED like so much lead on the sofa and with one unsteady hand reached out and pulled Lucy down beside him. For some time he sat with his eyes fixed in shock and consuming bewilderment. "Lucy," he said as soon as he could collect himself, "do you think you're treating me fair?"

"I don't want to be unfair or unkind to you, Clem," she answered soberly. "That's the last thing I'd ever want to do."

"Has someone else stepped in between us?"

"What do you mean?"

"Has that son of Mrs. Carrington's come home?"

"No."

"Has some other man been making love to you? Tell me quickly, Lucy. This is tearing me apart."

"Please, Clem, believe me, I don't care for anyone in the whole world but you. How could I?"

Clem dropped Lucy's hand and a weak smile relaxed his face a trifle. "Would Mrs. Carrington care if we went for a walk? It won't be dark for at least an hour."

"I'll ask her."

Lucy was soon back. "She said we could."

They walked north toward the river. The air was fresh, sweet, invigorating. Waxy leaves were bursting out on most of the trees and every growing thing looked as if it wanted to be the first to announce spring was about to explode with new life.

"See that white boathouse down there?" Clem pointed to a clump of willow trees ahead.

"What a cute place!" exclaimed Lucy. "I wonder who lives there?"

"That's the house I bought. No one lives there now." Clem was watching Lucy's face as he spoke. "There's room for a garden and we can build a little porch on the front."

Lucy was gazing speechless.

"I got a raise Saturday, darling."

He waited.

Lucy was still gazing. Her face lit up.

Clem put his arm around her. "Don't you think we could be happy there, darling?"

"Yes."

"Do you like it?"

"Very much. Oh, yes."

"I'm glad. You don't know how happy I was to find it. I wanted to surprise you, Lucy."

"Oh, you did, Clem," Lucy answered. She bit the inside of her cheek. Who couldn't be happy in a little cottage like that, with a man like Clem? He was wonderful.

They had reached the willow trees.

"I'm sorry I called you a little witch, Lucy darling. I lost my head. I didn't mean it. Will you forgive me?" Clem looked down at her with a sort of reverent tenderness. "You really did hurt me."

"Of course, Clem. Don't think of it anymore. When I forgive, I mean to forget. I truly didn't want to hurt you. For that I ask forgiveness too."

"Did you really promise to stay at Carringtons' a year?"

"Oh, yes."

Clem let his arm drop heavily at his side. He looked out across the river, and when at last he spoke, his voice was dry and husky. "Then you mean I have to wait a year? And this little house will be empty waiting a year?"

"I honestly think it's best to wait a year, Clem," said Lucy with sweet but positive deliberation. "That will give us both time to learn to know each other better. We'll prove our love. I don't believe in hasty marriages since—well, you know how it went for you."

"But, Lucy," protested Clem almost shouting, "this is altogether different."

"How different?"

"Well, a lot different." He was almost panting. "It seems I've loved you all my life. You're the girl I've always dreamed of having for a wife."

"Something tells me it's best to wait and prove our love for each other, Clem dear."

"But a year's an awful long time," insisted Clem. "Why didn't you tell Mrs. Carrington you'd stay six months? Surely in that length of time she could find another girl. Why couldn't your sister next to you come and take over?"

"Loretta? I never thought of her."

"Can't you change it to six months? You didn't sign a contract yet, did you?"

"No. But I gave her my word. And I wouldn't break it and feel right. She's depending on me."

Clem tried desperately to hide his tremendous disappointment. "Let's go up and look in the windows."

"Do you have the key so we can go inside?"

"No. Not yet. Anyhow, if we're not going to live here for a year, I'd rather not go inside."

"We'd better start back so Mrs. Carrington won't be alone when it's dark."

On their return Clem had little to say. Finally when they were within sight of the house, he caught Lucy by the hand and said, "The next time you have an evening off, let's go call on Gussie Jenkins."

"Oh, Clem," answered Lucy in a pleased, excited voice, "I'd love that. Listen, after Mrs. Carrington's sister comes, I'll get many more free evenings. She told me so."

"Well, I hope you'll plan to spend most of them with me." He looked down at her with wondering, expectant eyes.

She answered him with a smile and a squeeze of her hand in his.

Nettie Godfrey arrived by train on the twenty-first day of June, evidently for an extended visit, for the liveryman brought two trunks, a suitcase, three valises, and a bulging handbag which contained her crocheting.

Lucy began spending two evenings a week with Clem. Sometimes they walked out along the river, rested a while on the quiet wooded bank, then returned by way of Branton Avenue, one of the prettiest avenues in town. Some evenings they walked to the park and sat on a bench munching popcorn or candy Clem had bought from a vendor at the park gate. Occasionally they called on Gussie, then spent the rest of the evening with Norvena and Herman.

After repeated refusals and much coaxing by Norvena and Herman, Lucy took hold of the cards Norvena placed in her hand. Clem slapped her on the shoulder with affection and smiling said, "That's my girl, Lucy. Come, sit here beside me and be a good sport."

With silent resignation Lucy allowed Clem to push her chair up to the card table. Something seemed to snap somewhere. She remembered with a shudder how it always distressed her mother when her father had those Sunday afternoon card games. She herself had formed a dislike for them. She had an impulse to get up and go back to Mrs. Carrington's. But something held her there with unrelenting force. Oh, for once she'd show them. She braced herself and started shuffling cards. To her own surprise and the surprise of the trio she proved to have almost immediate familiarity with the tricks of the game. They watched her wide-eyed and amazed. How they did play!

"You were marvelous tonight," remarked Clem as he walked Lucy back to the house. "And wasn't it fun?"

"Oh, I guess," she answered halfheartedly.

"And you don't feel so wicked, do you?"

"Well, she answered, "maybe a little."

"Oh, come on, Lucy. What's wrong with having fun playing cards?"

"Well," she replied with thoughtful deliberation, "I certainly don't ever intend to gamble. I'm sure I'd feel wicked if I ever did that."

"Then don't," mused Clem. "I don't want you to feel wicked. I want you to be your sweet natural self. But that doesn't mean you can't have fun."

After Lucy was ready for bed, she glanced through the sixth psalm and dropped on her knees. *Dear Lord, I hope I didn't displease You tonight. Was I wicked? I don't intend to be. I do want You to keep Your hand over me always. I've had so much sorrow in my life; was it awful of me to do what I did tonight? I wish I knew.*

When she got up from her knees, her prayer seemed so ridiculous and shallow she felt like recalling it entirely. Something odd was happening to her, some foggy inconsistency, a subtle elusive something she couldn't define.

Before she put out the light, she gazed at herself in the large dresser mirror. So Clem thought she was beautiful. She brushed her long blond hair. Brother Bustleton. His wife was a Lucy and had blond hair. Why did she have to think of him now? What would he think of her had he seen her playing cards? He surely wouldn't remember her after all these years. All these years weren't so many, come to count them—not quite four. Why did she always think of him? Was he praying for her? That was a new thought. She glanced in the mirror again. Was she really happy with herself? She turned down the lamp wick and crawled into bed. Sleep came late. She was caught in a revolving quandary.

The next day Lucy wrote two letters—one to Aunt Polly and the other to her sister.

Dear Loretta,

I wish you'd write and tell me how everyone at home is and what each of you is doing. Have you heard from Flossie? I wonder about her every day. You can't imagine what a beautiful place I have to work in. Mrs. Carrington is a lovely woman to work for. Do you think you'd like to take my place if and when I decide to quit? It's not hard work. She gives me three dollars a week. Does Aunt Polly come to see you? Do you have the garden planted? How's Father? Tell everyone I'm fine. Clem and I are good friends if you wonder. Mrs. Carrington's sister is here now; so we go for walks twice a week. There are some beautiful places in Branton and right now the lilacs are in full bloom, and the tulips. I wish you could have seen them. Well, I must go dust now. Please write. I'm sending you two stamps; so answer without delay.

Love,
Lucy

One morning when Lucy was dusting in the living room, Nettie Godfrey looked up from her crocheting and said softly, "Lucy, are you grieving about something?"

"Grieving? No. Why?"

"Oh," she remarked, taking a stitch, "I thought sometimes you looked a bit sad."

"Oh," Lucy smiled as bravely as she knew how, "I didn't know I looked sad. No, truly I'm not, Mrs. Godfrey. What would there be to make me sad?"

"Well, pardon me, Lucy. I shouldn't have asked. I just thought perhaps you had bad news from home or something."

"No. Not at all. They're getting along all right at home. I had a letter from my sister yesterday."

Lucy kept on dusting. "I tell you, Mrs. Godfrey," she remarked as an afterthought, "we would all feel better if we'd get word from my sister, Flossie. We don't even know where she is."

"Well, now, that would make a body anxious, wouldn't it? How long has she been away?"

"It'll soon be a year," answered Lucy. "She went off with the man she said she was going to marry and we've never heard whether she did or not. I wish I knew."

Lucy hurried to the next room. She must try harder to be happy in front of Mrs. Carrington and her observant sister, Nettie. She had no idea either of them would detect her anxiety about Flossie.

"Lucy," began Clem one evening when they returned from a stroll along the river, "it'll soon be a year now."

"Already?" remarked Lucy without looking up. She fumbled with a piece of paper in her coat pocket.

"Already?" Clem turned abruptly. He grabbed Lucy's one arm and held it with a tight grip. "How can you say it like that? This has been the longest year of my life. You almost make me fear that you might not marry me at all."

"Oh, I didn't intend it to sound like that, Clem."

"Haven't I been a faithful lover?"

"Yes, indeed, you have."

"Haven't I been telling you in a thousand ways how much I love you, Lucy?"

"Yes, you have, Clem. I never have doubted your love. And I love you. You surely know I do—but—"

"But what?" Clem's voice was terse, impatient, and resentful .

"I told Mrs. Carrington I'd stay until after Oswald gets married."

"What!" shouted Clem.

"Wait a minute," whispered Lucy, "those children playing there will think we're quarreling. Oswald came home yesterday and told his mother he's getting married and will be bringing his bride home in November."

"In November!" shouted Clem. "You mean to tell me I've got to wait six more months just because that Oswald took a notion to spoil our plans! Oh, Lucy!"

"Well, Clem," and Lucy looked up into his face and

smiled, "if I'm not worth waiting for another six months, I guess you can find someone else."

"Oh, Lucy!" and he stepped in front of her and placed a firm hand on each shoulder. He looked into her eyes as though trying to see the sun from the bottom of a deep well. "Lucy," he repeated and he shook her a little, "I just don't see how you can love me truly and treat me like this."

"But I do, Clem. Please, not so loud."

"I don't want to call you a witch again, but"—he squeezed out the words—"but I tell you—you have me so upset—I—I love you till I hate you."

"How can that be?" blinked Lucy.

"I—I don't know," he choked. "But you've got me so unstrung I'm all tied up in knots again. And let me tell you one thing," he added panting, half sobbing, "you're not going to get rid of me like this."

"Who said I was trying to get rid of you?"

"Well, it almost looks like it." His eyes glistened with sudden tears. "And that little house waiting for you. But I'm not going to be defeated," he tried to swallow the lump in his throat. "I'll show you I'll wait five—ten—yes, twenty-five, or—or what are you making me say, Lucy Winchester? I'll wait till I'm an old man if you make me, for you're the girl I love." His lip quivered helplessly. "You beautiful heartbreaker. Do you believe I love you?"

"Of course I do, Clem," answered Lucy in a warm, sincere voice. "I've never doubted you from the first time you told me."

CHAPTER 38

THE TWO walked on in silence until Clem turned to Lucy, "You evidently love Mrs. Carrington more than you do me." His injured voice was almost brash.

"I do love her, Clem," admitted Lucy, "but not more than I do you. That couldn't be, and please don't imagine it. I only promised to stay until her son and wife come home."

"Well, isn't her sister there?"

"She says now she's getting homesick and is leaving next week. And she's the one who likes to be waited on. She seldom ever comes to the kitchen. And Mrs. Carrington wants me there to cook and serve the meals when her son comes. Don't you see, Clem?"

"Why couldn't your sister come and do it?"

"That wouldn't be the time for Mrs. Carrington to break in a new girl."

"Oh, no," Clem groaned. "You have the awfullest way of tearing me to pieces, Lucy."

"Well, my dear man," she returned, "I'll do my best to put you back together again."

But every week thereafter he brought Lucy a gift: candy, pretty handkerchiefs, perfume, hand-painted plates, two blue bud vases, scented stationery, and other gifts he thought would please her. Three times he succeeded in persuading Lucy to go with him to the theater. The first time Lucy went to bed struggling with an uneasy feeling of having trespassed where her conscience said, *Do not enter.* But she soothed her uneasiness by reassuring herself she had opposed and hurt Clem more than enough and she went to please him. She knew her own motive and attitude and so did God. After the second and third trips the aftermath wasn't so disturbing. Nor were the card games. They became increasingly fascinating, challenging, and genuine fun.

Lucy's Bible became less and less interesting and her prayers shorter.

One night during a card game Lucy was certain the strange odor on Herman's breath was liquor. She was not only shocked; she was hurt and horrified.

"Clem," she said as soon as they reached the bottom of the stairs, "since when did Herman begin drinking?"

"So you noticed?"

"How could I help it?"

"He must have started recently. Tonight was the first time I ever saw his eyes bloodshot."

"I wonder what Norvena thinks of it. If she was embarrassed, she didn't show it. Clem."

"Yes, dear."

"Has Herman ever tried to get you to drink?"

"Oh, he offered me some one time."

"Once?"

"Maybe twice. No more than twice."

"But you didn't take any, did you?"

"No."

"Never once?"

"Never once."

"Not one drop?"

"Not one single teeny-weeny drop, Lucy."

"And you never will, will you?"

"Not if you tell me you don't want me to."

"Oh, Clem," Lucy's voice was threaded with terror. She grabbed his arm and put her head against it. If you take to drinking—if I ever find out you took one sip, I'll never marry you. Never."

He reached over with his right hand and patted her face. "Then, my love, I'll never do it."

"You mean it? It's a promise?"

"Do I mean it, Lucy?" he asked in a stabbed tone. "Don't you trust me, Lucy? Have I ever yet broken a promise to you?"

"No."

"All right then. Trust me. Nothing would hurt me more than to know you didn't trust me. You know very well, Lucy, I wouldn't do anything you wouldn't want me to. Let's walk around the block."

"Maybe you'd better not stay there at Herman's anymore," suggested Lucy thoughtfully.

"Then marry me so I have a good safe place to live." He looked down at her pleadingly. They took a few more steps. "I'm waiting for your answer, darling."

"I will," answered Lucy, "in November."

"Without fail?"

"In November I will, Clem, unless—"

He stopped abruptly and faced her. "Unless what now?" he demanded raising his voice.

"I want to ask someone a question to make sure about something."

"Your father?" Clem pushed his forefinger against her chest.

313

"No."

"Who then?"

"It's a retired minister, a Reverend Utterback who lives near Mrs. Carrington."

Clem drew a great breath of relief and dropped his hand. "You mean you want him to marry us?"

"No, not that," answered Lucy. "I just want to hear what he thinks about—"

"About me?" Clem's voice was sharp and fretted. Three furrows crossed his forehead.

"No, no, Clem. Please don't be upset. I've been wanting to go over and talk to him for months and I've just not done it yet."

"What on God's earth has he got to do about you marrying me in November or anytime? You have the awfullest way of putting my nerves on end. What are you going to ask him?"

Lucy stood mute.

"Tell me." He stood mystified. "Is it so secret you can't confide in me, your husband to be?" Clem's face was indignant.

"I want him to tell me what the Bible says about us getting married."

"The Bible?" Clem wilted with sudden pessimism. "As if our names would be in it."

"Come now, Clem," said Lucy in a gentle, sympathetic manner. "You know better. Don't be sarcastic. You know what I mean."

"I do? Sometimes I don't." He took her by the arm and they moved on slowly. "I'm sure the reverend will say it's all right by heaven and earth and God and all His angels. We've been true to each other, haven't we?"

"Yes," answered Lucy assuredly. "It's because of Floss—"

"No," interrupted Clem. "Impossible. No. You're making a mountain out of a molehill. Forget she ever existed, will you please, please?" His voice was taut with repugnance.

"It's not that easy, Clem," returned Lucy candidly. "I've wished a thousand times it was."

"Well, I think you're making yourself a slave of your own ideas," answered Clem dryly. "Come now, let's be happy and say sweet things to each other the way true lovers should."

They walked on in silence.

"Look." Lucy pointed to a group of people standing under a gas streetlight. "What's going on? Let's go over and find out."

Two young women and a man all in navy uniforms were singing and the one woman was strumming a guitar.

"It's some of those Salvation Army folks," whispered Clem. "Do you want to stop and listen?"

"Let's do." And Lucy pulled Clem with her to the very edge of the crowd.

For Jesus took my burden and left me with a song.

Lucy held her breath. The three voices blended beautifully.

> *Yes, Jesus took my burden*
> *I could no longer bear;*
> *Yes, Jesus took my burden*
> *In answer to my prayer.*
> *My anxious fears subsided,*
> *My spirit was made strong,*
> *For Jesus took my burden*
> *And left me with a song.*

Lucy watched with riveted eyes. She rolled her handkerchief into a tight ball.

"Let's go on," whispered Clem shifting uneasily.

If she heard, she made no response. Her feet were bolted to the ground.

> *When I was crushed with sorrow,*
> *I bowed in deep despair;*
> *My load of grief and heartache*
> *Seemed more than I could bear;*
> *'Twas then I heard a whisper,*
> *"You to the Lord belong."*
> *Then Jesus took my burden*
> *And left me with a song.*

Lucy felt Clem pulling her arm gently. She made no effort to move.

The man opened his Bible and began to read in a clear, strong voice that everyone in the growing crowd of listeners could hear:

"Let my cry come near before thee, O Lord; give me understanding according to thy word.

"Let my supplication come before thee; deliver me according to thy word.

"My lips shall utter praise, when thou hast taught me thy statutes.

"My tongue shall speak of thy word; for all thy commandments are righteousness.

"Let thine hand help me; for I have chosen thy precepts.

"I have longed for thy salvation, O Lord; and thy law is my delight.

"Let my soul live, and it shall praise thee; and let thy

judgments help me."

Two tears trickled down Lucy's cheeks. Quickly she brushed them away.

Clem feebly cleared his throat and looked around with a sidewise glance.

"I have gone astray like a lost sheep," the man read on. "Seek thy servant; for I do not forget thy commandments."

Lucy's heart was pounding. The lump in her throat grew all out of proportion and tears blinded her. The next instant she was sobbing in her handkerchief.

"Lucy," whispered Clem in a thick voice. "What's wrong?"

She made no answer.

He slipped his arm into hers and drew her close to him. "Let's go," he whispered. "People will think we've had a fuss and I've been mean to you. Come, Lucy."

But Lucy kept on crying.

"That man up there's watching you, Lucy," whispered Clem feebly, pulling on her arm. "He's wondering what's wrong."

"Please don't be ashamed of me, Clem," whispered Lucy wiping her eyes with her drenched handkerchief. "I just can't forget."

"Forget what, dear?" Clem's voice was subdued but perplexed.

"If there's any one of you," remarked the man in uniform, "who would like to be remembered in prayer, just raise your hand and make it known."

Lucy's hand went up.

Clem stood petrified and numb.

CHAPTER 39

"GOD BLESS you, young lady," Lucy heard the man say. "Also the gentleman who desires prayer. If you two will go with us to our hall where we worship, we'll have prayer with you. Let's go immediately." So saying he and his two lady colleagues started walking north.

"Are you ready to go home now?" Clem's voice was exceedingly kind. Very gently he put his strong arm around Lucy and turned her about-face.

"Yes," she answered.

They crossed the street and Clem took a long, deep breath, secretly glad she did not insist on following the trio.

"I hope you aren't ashamed of me for crying, Clem," remarked Lucy. "I just couldn't help it. That song and what the man read made me so homesick."

"Homesick?" he asked with astonishment. "Homesick for what?"

"You wouldn't understand if I tried to explain," choked Lucy.

"Try it anyway," begged Clem. "I want to know. I can't stand it when you keep things from me. I could wonder and imagine and speculate until I'd go mad. I don't intend to ever keep things from you and you shouldn't from me. It makes me feel just awful to see you crying like you did and especially out in public. I've got to think about my reputation, Lucy, and I don't want people to think I've mistreated you."

"Well, you see, Clem," began Lucy taking hold of herself, "I used to walk four miles every Sunday afternoon to Sunny Creek. Miss Basie was the teacher in the Sunday school. That song they sang brought it all back to me how I used to sing the songs I learned to little Corkie before he died."

Clem swallowed twice.

"And I—I sang—some of those songs to—little John Eldon."

Clem nodded, listening patiently.

Lucy continued, "'And once I—I had that peace.'"

"What?"

"That peace of God that takes our burdens away—and makes us feel like singing."

"What burdens are you talking about, Lucy?"

"Well, Clem, those terrible burdens they sang about. Heartaches when troubles come; and that guilty feeling when you're almost certain you've grieved the Lord."

Clem coughed unnecessarily.

"When I was a girl and going to Miss Basie's Sunday school, I really wanted to be good. I wanted so much to earn a Bible all my own. I wanted that more than anything else in the world. But Father made me stop going, and besides, when Corkie got so sick, I took care of him Sundays. Finally, Tom bought me a Bible. Next to little Eldon I loved it. You know, I told you I forgot and left it on the mantelshelf at Ash—"

"Yes, you told me once."

"Then Uncle Jake got me a Testament and the Psalms.

319

It's not the whole Bible."

"Yes," he agreed with a degree of uncertainty.

"Well, Clem—I used to read my Bible every night before I went to bed."

"You did?" He sniffed without necessity.

"Then I'd pray and ask God to keep His hand over me."

"Well, hasn't He?"

Lucy hesitated. She balled up the wet handkerchief in her coat pocket. "I hope so," she sighed. "But I just can't pray like I used to for some reason."

Wordless, Clem was baffled.

"It's me, Clem," exclaimed Lucy. "I ought to be very, very happy. Mrs. Carrington's so nice and kind to me. But something's wrong with me, and I know it now for sure."

"What is it?" ventured Clem, lacking enthusiasm.

"You all think I'm happy when we're playing cards."

Clem's Adam's apple went up and down. He ran one finger around the inside of his shirt collar.

"I even thought myself I was—but, Clem, honestly now, I'll tell you the truth. It's been bothering me. It cuts out God for some reason. It leaves me with such an uncertain, sad feeling when I'm all by myself. I've tried to cast it off but I can't really."

"Then that's another reason why we ought to get married soon," stated Clem with fresh persuasion in his carefully selected words. "I've been trying to convince you we need each other. Now I know it more than ever. I'm positive we could make each other happy."

Lucy lingered in deep meditation as they stepped together. Clem's arm encircled her. He drew her close. "Am I right, darling?"

"I'm longing for something, Clem," she said at length

looking toward a distant streetlight.

"I hope it's me. Tell me it is, Lucy dear."

"But it's something from God, Clem. I'm sure we would be happy together, but when I heard that man reading from the Bible, something inside of me broke loose. I felt as though I just couldn't go on living without it."

"Why, Lucy!" His voice was deep and husky.

"Let's go to the Salvation Army church some night."

"All right," echoed Clem in a subdued voice.

But Lucy was convinced Clem was not overly enthusiastic about the prospect. Maybe she had embarrassed him. Had she made a fool of herself? Clem hadn't ridiculed her. He hadn't scolded or laughed. Neither did he condemn her now. All in all, he had been extremely kind about her conduct.

Before he left her at the Carrington door, he took her face in both his hands and kissed her. "Lucy, dear," he said with tenderest compassion, "whatever it is you long for to make you completely happy I do hope you find it."

"Oh, Clem." And her tearstained face actually glowed with surprise. "You can't imagine how happy you make me, to hear you say that. Good night, Clem dear, my true love. O God in heaven, bless you, bless you."

The tulips and Nettie Godfrey had both come and gone before the trip was made to the gray stone house behind the hedge.

The elderly Reverend Utterback was resting in a big leather armchair in the sun parlor.

"My maid Lucy wishes to have a little private chat with you, Reverend, if you have time and feel able," said Mrs. Carrington.

"Yes, yes, of course," he answered, extending his hand

and half rising out of his chair.

Mrs. Kausteiner ushered Mrs. Carrington into the parlor and left Lucy alone with her father.

As briefly as possible she explained the reason for her inquiry. "Mrs. Carrington told me if anyone could answer my question you could."

"I see," said Reverend Utterback smiling and stroking his thin chin. "Well, you see, you're young and I'm old. You young folks must grapple with the problems facing you in the light of present-day circumstances. I've lived to see many changes in our churches and in society. When I was young, there were comparatively few divorces granted. It's fast becoming almost a popular thing according to statistics. Yet back in Christ's day there must have been couples with marital problems, for it led to much dispute among the Pharisees. Yes, our Lord Christ made provision for divorcements when a husband or wife proved to be untrue as you described your sister was. Now without question she committed a flagrant sin and the Scripture gives the husband in such a case the right to get a divorce."

"I see," nodded Lucy. "And now if I marry my brother-in-law, would I be doing wrong?" She bent forward, eager for the answer to her anxieties.

The aging minister stroked his chin again. "Well," he began, tapping his fingers on the ends of the armchair, "you know, one day I taught it was wrong if the one partner was living. But ministers today have spent many, many hours discussing and reviewing and reinterpreting this entire problem. They have to. It's a worldwide problem, you see. It's become a major issue of this century and will, by the consensus of the greatest church leaders of all faiths, require a satisfactory answer. There must be a way. Now I'm retired, you understand. I'm not performing any rites of the clergy anymore, but if I was, I could gladly and with a clear conscience marry you and your brother-in-law; that is, of course, you understand, if you were in full compatibility and truly loved each other and are free from all other engagements whatsoever."

Lucy sat spellbound.

"You would promise, of course, to love each other and remain true and faithful until death."

Lucy sat fascinated. She smiled and nodded.

The old man went on, seemingly enjoying his listener's fascination. "Too many young people do their serious thinking after the marriage. I take it you are not one such person or you wouldn't have come to me."

Lucy smiled under the mysterious influence of the old man's knowledge.

"I imagine you come from a godly home. You look so sweet and fresh and undefiled."

Lucy's cheeks grew hot. "No," she stated with chagrin. "To be honest, I'm the only one in our family who has been baptized. Or even tried to be a Christian."

"So?" He tilted his head in surprise.

"My father has nothing for religion. My mother asked for God—I mean, she did say she wanted to believe in my Jesus just before she died."

"My, my. Well, you and your husband want to start a Christian home, I'm sure."

"I do—yes."

"It won't always be smooth sailing, my dear," remarked the reverend in a fatherly manner, "but you'll promise to love each other and be true in times of sickness and adversity as well as in times of health and prosperity, and if you never let your love grow cold, you'll be able to wade together through thick and thin and come out on top. Then when you're both old and gray, should the good Lord let you live that long, you'll look back and recall and relive all those joys and sorrows, all those valley and mountain-top experiences you shared together, and you'll both say, 'Thank God, we stuck by each other when other marriages went on the rocks.' My dear, faithful wife and I enjoyed sixty-two years living together."

Lucy sat entranced. The ancient man of God, so thin and withered, had a powerful charm about him. His speech revealed that his mind and soul were not withered.

"It's been so nice of you to take an interest in me," smiled Lucy, moving to the edge of her chair. "I won't take any more of your time." She rose to leave.

"And have I answered your question sufficiently, Miss—"

"Lucy."

"Yes, Miss Lucy, have I?"

"Yes," she answered softly, "and I do thank you, Reverend Utterback."

"You're welcome. And call on me anytime you want to. And God bless you and the young man you're going to marry, and may the peace and light of God's love shine on you both always."

"Thank you."

Lucy was fairly trembling when she left the house.

"Did the old gentleman set your mind at ease?" asked Mrs. Carrington as the two crossed the street.

"I feel much better," answered Lucy.

"He's been a very prominent clergyman in his day. He's served on all kinds of church committees and boards and councils and has been held in high esteem as a pastor and Bible teacher and lecturer across the country. His daughter is very proud of him. I know it pleased her you called on him."

"You know," remarked Lucy, trying to sound casual, "I don't know why I expected him to look something like Brother Bustleton, but I did."

"You mean you were disappointed?"

"It's silly of me, I know," said Lucy, "but I had no right to be. Isn't it the strangest thing how childhood impressions stick with a person? Or am I just different from everyone else?" She forced a crippled laugh.

"I'd say you're one in ten thousand, Lucy," genially answered Mrs. Carrington. "But regardless of not resembling your childhood hero, isn't he quite brilliant for an old man his age?"

"Oh, yes," came Lucy's ready answer. "I liked to hear him talk. And he said a lot of good things I'll always remember. I pictured him opening his Bible and reading to me."

"And he didn't, did he?"

"No." Disappointment was in her voice.

"Well, he has memorized so many long passages that he's like a walking encyclopedia of the Word. He didn't need to open his Bible and read to you. He knows his Bible, Lucy; so you can depend on what Reverend Utterback says is right."

By evening Lucy's love for Clem had become more sure. She held her Testament in both her hands for some time before she turned to a short psalm. After reading the five verses in Psalm 43, she tucked it in the corner of the bottom dresser drawer and dropped on her knees. *Dear Lord, let me know that You're keeping Your hand over me all the time.*

Norvena got her long-wished-for phonograph. It was playing when Clem and Lucy entered. "Isn't it great?" she asked, dancing across the room. "Look what fun we can have now." And she swung herself into Herman's open arms and the two waltzed around the room twice. "You and Clem join us."

"I never danced in my life," said Lucy.

"It's nothing to learn," remarked Norvena. "Watch us a while and try it. We're all alone here; so there's no one to laugh if you trip each other a few times."

Clem took Lucy in his waiting arms. He had never seen her more beautiful. Her new raspberry red dress in soft cotton challis fit her with slenderizing perfection. "Shall we try it, darling? You're gorgeous tonight," he whispered. "This is all in private fun, you know."

The next thing she knew Clem was swinging her back and forth and around Norvena and Herman with astonishing ease. His strong arms and nimble feet all but swept her off the floor, and the record was such a gay, catchy tune. Lucy was soon intoxicated with a happiness she had never realized she could experience. The room fairly rang with her laughter. Clem was thrilled.

"Now wasn't that frolicking good fun?" asked Norvena, bringing in coffee and freshly baked raisin-filled cookies. "Let's sit down and rest and have refreshments. What say, Lucy? Your feet weren't so clumsy, now were they, for the first try?"

"She was great," said Clem, clapping his hands and

smiling broadly. "Absolutely great." And at that he reached over and tenderly pinched Lucy's flushed cheek. "I believe Lucy is capable of learning anything."

"Well," remarked Herman, "it sure didn't take her long to learn cards. How about a game before you leave?"

"Shall we, dear?" asked Clem.

Lucy looked down a second. "Whatever you say," she answered. She had never seen him happier. She had never seen him look more handsome.

Several days later Gussie Jenkins met Lucy in town.

"Well, if it isn't Miss Lucy." The two stopped in front of a variety store. "What are you troubling yourself about today?"

"Mrs. Carrington sent me to buy some curtain material. Her son Oswald is bringing his bride home next week."

"Well, so you have to pretty up her place, huh?"

"She wants everything to look just so, Gussie. She's real proud of that son of hers."

"Well, by the way, Miss Lucy, how're you coming with that fine-looking Clem? I see he brings you up to Mrs. Sellers' mighty often."

"You're right, Gussie."

"Are you certain now he's the one for you?"

"I'm very sure of it, Gussie. I know he loves me very much. And I love him."

"I expect you'll be married before long, not?"

"In November."

"That's real close then. An' that sister, I hope she won't drag up some trouble for you."

"I've never heard from her. Not once in all these months. I've put Clem off now for a year and a half and I see no reason why we shouldn't go ahead and be married.

He's bought the cutest little boathouse down by the river. You'll have to come see us sometime."

"Boathouse?" Gussie shivered. "Honey, you all must like water better'n I do."

"But it's fifty feet from the water," laughed Lucy. "There's no danger."

"Well, that Clem sure acts like a man of good common sense. I'm real happy for you, Miss Lucy, for I sure think heaps about you since the day you lay sick with the measles. Did you get a Bible yet to match the one that was burned up?"

"No, not one like it, Gussie, but my uncle got me a New Testament and Psalms."

"Good," said Gussie. "I asked my pastor one day about that marrying business and he says the long-ago folks were under law and we now-a-day folks are under grace and he said something about evil notions rolling off your mind like dew off a cabbage leaf. You know what he means?"

"Not exactly, Gussie," laughed Lucy. "I've got to hurry. Mrs. Carrington wants me to help her sew the curtains today."

"Sure, go on an' buy them. Remember, I'm your friend. God bless you all your life."

"Thanks, Gussie, and God bless you too. You've been the best friend I've ever had," and she pressed Gussie's beautiful black hand.

On the twelfth of November Lucy stood at Clem's side dressed in a simple, beautifully tailored blue dress he helped her select and the justice of the peace in Branton pronounced them husband and wife. Clem smiled proudly and kissed her tenderly. "At last," he whispered.

"At last," she repeated, "and we're going to stick together as long as we both live."

"That long," he answered. "We'll stick together."

One happy week followed another. The table was always set for two when Clem came home whistling, swinging his dinner bucket. On the stove Lucy had a tasty hot meal ready to be served as soon as he got washed and changed into clean clothes.

One Saturday evening as the two were hurrying home from town with their arms full of groceries, Lucy heard singing. She turned. Clem heard too and turned.

"Let's not stop tonight," he said.

"Just for a minute?"

"Let's not tonight, Lucy. It's getting late and we've got to get these groceries home. And it's getting cold. And anyhow, you're too tired."

Dear Lord, breathed Lucy as they hurried on, *Please keep Your hand over me. Oh, please don't forget me entirely—*

She never heard one measure of a sacred song or the mention of God or saw a Bible without feeling a tinge of guilt. She could not shake it off.

A year passed and they hadn't once gotten to the Salvation Army hall. Often on Sunday afternoons Herman and Norvena came, sometimes with their deck of cards.

Yes, a year passed and the only thing that kept Lucy from being completely happy was that silent, persistent voice within her. No matter how she worked, no matter where she went, at the most unexpected moments she would meet herself face to face with the eager Lucy at Sunny Creek, at Black Bend, or hovering over Grandmother Winchester's big stiff-backed Bible searching for those verses, *All we like sheep have gone astray—He was despised—He was wounded.* Every effort to push aside that voice failed.

Sometimes when Clem was sound asleep, she lay awake recalling, reliving, resuffering, but never, never quite relaxing. Not even after dear little Emmaleta was born. Clem was one happy, proud father.

"Lucy," said Clem one evening in February, tossing his cap on the nearest chair and grabbing Lucy in his arms, "guess what, my dear. I've landed a better job. Believe it or not, two hundred and fifty dollars a month at the American Steel Foundry in Duffield." He pulled off his overcoat.

"In Duffield?"

"Yes. And we're going by the first of March. They need a good pipe fitter and Norton sent in a recommendation for me. Think of it, Lucy, two hundred and fifty a month. Let's put this place up for sale tomorrow."

"What was that, Clem? I thought I heard a knock."

"Just the wind," answered Clem.

"Listen, Clem. It is a knock." Lucy opened the door. A young woman shivering in a brown plaid coat that hung on her shoulders like a sack on a stick stared at Lucy from the shadowy, cold wind. A knitted tam-o'-shanter was pulled down over her forehead and she held a bundle under one arm.

"Did I frighten you, Lucy?" she asked in a hoarse, throaty voice.

"What!" gasped Lucy, terrified. She grabbed the casing for support. Her lips turned white. "Is—that—you—Flossie?"

CHAPTER 40

"I—I DIDN'T mean to scare you that bad, Lucy." Flossie took a soiled handkerchief out of her coat pocket and blew her nose.

"Well!" Lucy took a step backward and looked at Clem who was standing immobile beside the kitchen stove. "Come in," she heard herself saying in a fearful whispered voice. Terror was stamped all over Lucy's face.

Clem stood fixed, paralyzed with awe.

Flossie stepped inside. She was trembling. Actually shaking. She sank on the nearest chair and dropped her bundle on the floor. "I—had," her voice was unsteady and her lips quivered, "quite a time finding you in the dark."

Lucy tried to speak but her tongue was thick and stiff. How old and worn! How wasted and haggard! Was it really Flossie?

"You act as if you hardly know me, Lucy," she remarked feebly.

An awkward pause followed before Lucy could collect her thoughts. "This is a big—surprise," she finally managed to say. She tried to swallow the uncomfortable lump in her throat. Her neck felt twisted. She groped frantically for a word or two to hide her emotions and found none.

Clem went into the bedroom.

"Hello, Clem," said Flossie, casting a despairing look at

him.

"Hi," came his dry, edgy answer. He gave her only a fleeting glance as edgy as his voice.

Flossie shivered. "You have a baby in that basket, Lucy?" she pointed.

"Our baby," answered Clem and he looked down in the basket at the foot of the bed with fatherly admiration. He stood there as if to protect the tiny infant from this intruder.

"What is it, Lucy?"

"A girl."

"What did you name her?"

"Emmaleta."

Spiritless and weary, Flossie dragged herself to the basket and peered into it for a moment. Clem drew back.

"Sweet," she remarked, dragging herself back to the chair. "How old?"

"Three weeks tomorrow," answered Lucy. Her mind was whirling, spinning, and her heart was pounding. She noticed now that Flossie's ankles were badly swollen. "Take off your coat and cap, Flossie." Lucy glanced at Clem still standing by the basket in the next room. She saw his mouth drop open. "You're thin." She laid the coat and cap on the bed. "Aren't you well, Flossie?"

"I haven't been well for a year. But I kept on working."

"Working? Where?"

"In Chicago. In a restaurant in a depot. I had to make enough," she coughed, "to pay my room and board," she sighed, "and save up to get back home."

"Home?" asked Lucy.

Flossie drew a long breath, then had a long coughing spell. "I'm this far now."

"But how did you know where we lived? We never heard from you."

"I wrote to Loretta. She told me you were in Branton and she gave me the Sellerses' address. I got there about four. This place wasn't easy to find in the dark. I'm going to write to Father," she coughed again, "and ask him to come and get me. Do you suppose he will?"

"But where's Dick?"

"Dick? Oh, I don't know."

"Don't know," exclaimed Lucy with wide-eyed fright. "Didn't you get married?"

"Yes. But we didn't live together long. He—he turned out to be a sour—well, I won't go into that." She cast a quick glance at Clem, and caught the hostile look in his eyes even from the dimly lighted bedroom. "I don't know where Dick Galoway is and I don't care to know." This time she covered her mouth with one hand and pressed the other against her chest and coughed severely.

Lucy went over and faced Flossie, looking her straight in the eyes. She was trembling from head to foot. "Then you're wanting Clem back?" Great tears welled up in Lucy's eyes and an unbearable pain slashed across her heart. She could hear Clem breathing heavily.

"Don't worry about that, Lucy," said Flossie smoothing back her disheveled hair. "I didn't come here—to make trouble. I'll say that so both of you—can hear it." She waved one hand toward the bedroom. "I told you—I didn't care if you married Clem. You make him a better wife than I ever could." She tried feebly to work the wrinkles out of her dress with both hands. "I want you two to go on—being happy. You have a cute place here."

An agonizing silence followed while each wrestled with

personal fears. Each wondered what the other was thinking but dared not say.

Lucy felt like a prisoner of her own tightly interwoven uncertainties, hopes, and conclusions. Was her life about to be suddenly torn up by the roots? Could she believe Flossie meant what she had just said? Her head felt woozy. She found a chair.

Flossie broke the silence. "Mrs. Sellers acted as though I shouldn't come here."

"Why?" asked Lucy.

Flossie twisted her handkerchief nervously. "I guess she thought I might make you both mad."

Clem stepped into the doorway. He was going to make sure he heard every word between the two. How clearly he remembered Lucy's fears and supposings and his year and a half of waiting until she was ready. And now! After fourteen months of married bliss and a beautiful brown-eyed baby and a new job in view; now this sudden attack on their happiness. Rebellion seized Clem. He ran his hands in his pockets and stood waiting breathlessly.

"If you didn't come to make trouble," Lucy said, "then I'm sure there won't be any from me. If Clem wants to take—"

"Lucy!" Clem's voice was sharp and anguished.

"Oh, I'm through with men," stated Flossie. "All men. I'm about done for. I'm going back home as soon as possible. If I—can just have a place for the night, Lucy, I'll be glad. I'm tired to death."

How strange it all sounded. Not at all like the frivolous, haughty, high-strung Flossie of less than three years ago. Lucy felt like crying. How forlorn—wretched and worn-out—Flossie looked with those dark rings under her eyes that had once been saucy and flashing. How could one change so in so short a time? What all had happened to her? That once pretty hazel-brown hair was unkempt, thin, and oily. Flossie, who had planned to show them all how to have fun and real class in living, sat there now like a sick, wilted flower draped in shabby clothes, her swollen feet squeezed into crooked slippers.

"We'll fix you a place to sleep," said Lucy. "I'll put the supper on. We were about ready to eat when you knocked. We'll go to bed early so you can rest."

As in a dream Lucy put on a third plate. Clem helped her dish up the food, speaking not one word. He ate almost nothing. He listened while the two exchanged bits of conversation, watching Lucy's every move. He saw her neck throb, heard her stifled sighs, noticed the sad expression on her face growing sadder every passing minute.

After supper Flossie wrote a letter to her father and told Lucy to be sure to remind Clem to mail it in the morning.

The next evening when Clem came home, Lucy took him into the bedroom and closed the door.

"Clem," she whispered, facing him and placing a hand on each arm, "will you do me a favor?"

"You know I will if it's in my power."

"I want you to take Flossie someplace after supper."

His knees sagged with his shoulders. "Where?"

"Oh, for a walk or anyplace."

"Lucy!" Clem stood horrified.

"I mean it."

"What on earth are you talking about?"

"I want to prove to her I love her and feel all right toward her."

"But you've already done that. You don't have to go overboard. That's crazy."

"I've been thinking about it all day, Clem. She's really suffered a lot. I want you to prove to her you feel all right toward her too."

"Lucy! Are you in your right mind?"

"Sh, Clem. She'll hear you."

"I don't have to prove anything to her. I don't care the snap of my finger what she thinks of me, and the sooner she gets out of here, the better."

"You mailed the letter?"

"Indeed I did. And I hope her father comes as soon as he gets it."

"But, Clem," went on Lucy, looking steadfastly into his troubled face, "if you'll only do this one thing for me, I'll feel better the rest of my life."

"But of all the unheard-of things, Lucy! This is the most absurd. Most wives would be furious if their husbands would do such a thing. And now you—you ask me to do this!"

"She's my sister, Clem."

"Have you gone completely insane?"

"I hope not."

His face darkened. "You—you don't love me anymore?"

"Yes, very much. "

"Aren't you one bit jealous of me?"

"Well—in a way. I really don't know."

"Don't know?" he demanded hoarsely. "Isn't she in the next room?"

"Yes."

"Is the door shut tight?"

"Yes."

Clem drew Lucy to the farthest corner of the room and put his face close to hers. "Now, you tell me Lucy, what this is all about. Did she ask for this?"

"No, Clem."

"Did she hint?"

"No."

"Does she know what you're in here for?"

"No."

"Is she here to make trouble between us?"

"I don't think so."

"Well, what pleasure would I have taking her out for a walk? A walk indeed! Where would we walk?"

"Anyplace."

"In this cold?"

"Is it so cold outside?"

"Not as cold as last night but cold, yes. And what would we talk about? I have nothing to say to her."

"Well," said Lucy, "she's my sister and I really pity her. After all she told me today."

"It's all her own fault," retorted Clem.

"I agree, Clem. But in her condition somehow," Lucy's eyes got misty with tears, "I just have a feeling she might not have long—unless she finds a good doctor. I keep thinking," a tear rolled down each cheek, "if—I had refused your love at the start—" Lucy leaned hard against him. "Oh, Clem, maybe she would be with you—"

"Lucy!" he pushed her back. "Stop it! I won't listen to such talk."

"The whole thing haunts me now."

"Now, Lucy," and Clem grabbed her with both hands and shook her, "you are absolutely a silly goose. What's come over you anyhow? We've been so happy. Now, listen to me, will you? I want you to stop this silly fretting. You've done entirely too much of it. You are going to make yourself go bats if you're not careful. Now take hold of yourself. Why let her come in here like a bolt of lightning and rip us up? There's a man coming soon to look at our place. And when he comes, I want you to be smiling and looking your happy best. Hear me? We'll soon be in Duffield and thank God for that."

"But, please," pleaded Lucy wiping her eyes, "just because you love me, Clem. Just take her for a little walk and let her know you're sorry."

"Sorry? Sorry for what? Sorry I married you? I haven't gone crazy if you have, Lucy. I won't tell her I'm sorry for anything if heaven falls on us."

"Then just take her someplace and show her one good time before she goes home. She's had so many disappointments, Clem. Life's been nothing but one broken bubble for her."

"I won't take her anyplace unless you go along."

"But the baby. It's too cold to take her out yet. Will you do it, Clem? Just this once do my crazy idea to make me feel better all the rest of my life?"

"Listen, Lucy," Clem put one hand on her head and looked her in the eyes intently, "will you promise me if I take her to the theater—I wouldn't know where else to go—if I do, you will immediately and ever after as long as you live drop this idea out of your mind that I ever loved her, that she has any claim whatsoever on me? Will you?"

"Yes. "

"You'll never again mention to me maybe you shouldn't have married me after all?"

"No."

"All right then. I'll take her to a show, much as I detest the idea, just to prove to you I love *you, you,* Lucy. You understand?"

"Yes."

"Well, I certainly don't understand you, Lucy Winchester Linsdale. And maybe I never will, but I'm crazy about you anyhow. You have the awfullest ways of getting me all knotted and twisted up. If you're not careful, I might snap."

Clem's eyes met Lucy's more than half a dozen times across the supper table. Once she read pathos, again anger, then revenge. Lucy returned each look with one of tender sorrow. Clem could read nothing else.

"Clem's going to take you to the theater after supper," began Lucy.

"Me?" Flossie dropped her fork. "Why me?"

"I asked him to," answered Lucy. "I want you to have one nice time before you go home."

"Well, Lucy," stammered Flossie. She looked stunned. "I—I always knew you were—a—a different sort of a Winchester—but I never thought you were quite this different." Her face flushed. "What gave you the idea we could have a nice time together?" She avoided looking at Clem when she spoke.

"Well, for my sake, try it."

Before supper was finished the man came and looked at the house and left without making a decision. "I'll bring my wife to see it perhaps tomorrow night."

Neither Clem nor Flossie looked a bit happy when they left Lucy.

For a long time she stood with her back against the closed door, her gaze fixed on nothing tangible.

CHAPTER 41

EMMALETA WOKE and brought Lucy out of her unrewarding daydreaming. She took her baby out of the basket and pulled the rocker closer to the stove. "I'll hold you a while, darling," she mused, "then Mother's got to do these dishes. If God lets me live and I find that quiet peace I had once and let slip, I'm going to teach it to you. You innocent little thing." She kissed her. "Your father's been good to both of us. He loves us very much, darling. But we must find a church in Duffield. You don't know a thing I'm saying, do you, dear? Of course not. So go back to sleep, my sweet baby."

Neither looked one bit happy when they returned. Clem's frown was shouting unspoken agitation and Flossie looked sick and exhausted.

"Lucy," began Clem after the bedroom door was closed, "this is the stupidest, most outlandish thing I hope I'll ever be asked to do for you. We both had a perfectly horrible time."

"Why?" Lucy twisted one hand over the other nervously.

"She was as embarrassed as I was." Clem flung both arms back and forth.

"What did you talk about?"

"We didn't." He jerked off his necktie and threw it on the dresser.

"Was the show any good?"

"I really don't know."

"You don't know?"

"I wasn't interested enough to watch it much. We sat close to the back. I just hope no one who knows me saw us."

"You poor dear," sighed Lucy putting her arms around him; then she kissed him and stroked his hair.

"So you pity me now?" He loosened himself and drew back.

"Yes, I do, Clem," she said emphatically. "And poor Flossie too."

"She could hardly make it back." He took off his shoes.

"Poor thing. But I hope I've proved to her I hold nothing against her."

"This was all uncalled for," said Clem irritably. "You didn't need to prove anything to her."

"Well, will you hold it against me?"

Clem read fear in her question. He looked at her searchingly. "Listen, Lucy," then he stepped over and took hold of her arm, holding it tight for a minute, "not if you keep your promise," he said with a tone of bitterness. "I want to forget the whole stupid thing. And I hope I can as soon as she's gone and we move to Duffield. Let's not talk any more about it."

It was late the next afternoon.

Lucy saw him coming and went out to meet him.

"Father," she said, "I see you found the place all right. Come in."

"I haven't long to stay," he said stiffly, jumping down from the wagon. "I'd like to get back before dark, but I fear we can't make it."

Lucy saw his hands tremble as he tied the horse to a tree. The hair below his cap was almost silver now and the lines of his face were deeper. She kissed him. Surprise and appreciation softened his tense expression.

"Where's Flossie?" he asked huskily.

"In the house."

"I can't understand that girl." He spoke close in Lucy's ear.

"Don't be angry with her, Father." Lucy touched his coat cuff. "When you see her, you'll pity her. She's a sick girl."

A few awkward sentences were exchanged. Both Flossie and her father acted self-conscious and embarrassed. He eyed her with cold elusiveness.

"We'd better head for home," he said grimly.

"Take a chair, Father," said Lucy.

While Flossie gathered up her belongings, Lucy inquired about each one at home, Aunt Polly and Uncle Jake.

"Come into the bedroom, Father, and see our baby. We have a little girl, Emmaleta."

"Very nice," he said. He looked at Lucy more than he did the baby. What was it about her that made it hard for him to control his emotions? Was he getting old and lax? He turned the collar of his coat up around his neck and put on his leather gloves. He must get out of her presence. She made him think of the night she came to him and begged him to chop down the plum tree.

"Can't you come home sometime?" He was at the door, his gloved hand on the knob. He cleared his throat impulsively.

"I don't know when, Father. We're moving to Duffield in

a week or two."

"Duffield?" He shifted his cap. He swallowed.

"Clem's got a job there in the steel foundry."

"That's awful far away, isn't it, Lucy?" Every word held disappointment.

"I know. But he'll make two hundred and fifty a month."

"Whew! What doin'?" John Winchester's mouth dropped open.

"He'll be a pipe fitter. Maybe I can come sometime on the train. We'll see."

"We gotta be goin'," he said abruptly.

"Just a minute, Father. Here's a fresh coffee cake"—Lucy quickly wrapped it in a piece of brown paper—"to eat on your way home."

She stood at the window and watched until the wagon was out of sight, and wondered what they'd talk about or whether they would ride eight miles in silence. She shook her head. Why had she asked Clem to take Flossie out? It probably was absurd and uncalled for. Oh, poor dear faithful Clem. Lucy shook her head, plagued with burning misgivings.

The young couple who bought the boathouse purchased the furniture, the curtains, most of the bedding, the garden tools, even the dishes and pots and pans. Clem was well satisfied with the transaction.

"We'll get furnished rooms until we find a place that suits us," he told Lucy. "We don't want to bother to take anything on the train but our clothes and the baby's things."

"I'll have my first train ride. I'm so excited, Clem, I'm almost ashamed of myself."

"Ashamed?" he laughed. "Well, I'm excited too and I'm older than you. Won't it be fun to live in a big city?"

"I don't know," answered Lucy, shrugging her shoulders. "I guess we'll soon find out."

"Well, remember, Duffield's a lot bigger than Branton. Ten times bigger. Maybe twenty for all I know."

The train ride to Duffield was exciting, but exhausting too.

Opposite a large grocery store on a busy street on the west side they rented a modern five-room house after living in furnished rooms one week. Clem had to carry his lunch and leave home in time to catch the first streetcar running south. It was after six when he got home. The only time they could go shopping together was on Saturday nights. Since everything from a paring knife to a stove had to be purchased, it required repeated and tiring Saturday night trips going through one huge store after the other. Weeks rolled around and still there were things they needed. The cost far exceeded what Clem had anticipated.

"Remember, we can't buy much more," he remarked on their fifth trip home.

"We should get some stamps."

"The post office isn't open this time of night, Lucy."

"But I must write and tell my folks where we live. I ought to write to Norvena too and Aunt Polly and Mrs. Carrington sometime."

"Then we'll have to stop at the corner drugstore and get some out of the slot machine. We'll get six tonight so you can write to my folks too."

One evening when Clem came home, he found Lucy on her knees beside the bed crying.

"What's wrong, Lucy?" He came close and put a hand on her shoulder. "Is Emmaleta sick?"

She shook her head. Then he noticed a letter on the bed. He picked it up and read:

Dear Lucy,

Flossie died on the second of April and she was buried on Wednesday. We couldn't let you know until we heard from you. We looked for a letter every day for weeks. She was awful sick and looked bad. The doctor came out once but he said he couldn't do a thing for her. Aunt Polly came over and stayed three days. I don't know what we would have done without her. She had Bright's disease and went almost blind before she died. It was awful sad, Lucy. I wish you could have come but we didn't know how to locate you. She was buried beside Mom and Corkie. Father still doesn't want me to leave home to work. Peggy doesn't either.

Love,
Loretta

"Don't cry, Lucy," said Clem tenderly. "Just be glad she was at home. Come, dear, let's have supper."

"Oh, Clem." And Lucy got up and threw her arms around his neck. "I'm glad now—"

"Don't say it. You promised. Remember?" He put his finger on her lips.

"But I could see she hadn't long—"

"Don't say it, Lucy. I know what you're thinking. Come, come. We have each other."

"Well, Clem, anyhow, everything will be different now."

"All right," he said candidly, "then let's both be happy. I'll wash up and hold Emmaleta while you fix the supper. I'm hungry."

"Come and sit in the kitchen. I want you both near me. I was so lonesome all day. I should have written to them sooner. Oh, I should have."

"But we couldn't have afforded to let you go home anyhow, Lucy."

"I know. I know."

Life in the city was a new experience for both Clem and Lucy. It reminded Lucy of two constantly moving belts, one running north, the other south, carrying with it people of every description and nationality, streetcars, hucksters, carts, hacks, fire wagons, bread wagons, bicycles, hearses, umbrella vendors, workmen, children, women, dogs, and policemen. It kept moving all day and most of the night. Trains a block away sped and screeched and roared by, shaking the house on its foundation.

At first Lucy thought everything was about to smash in upon her. But in a couple of months the newness of it all wore off and she became accustomed to the constant traffic and constant noises. The shrill train whistle didn't annoy her anymore. She could lock the door and feel safe and secure and let the world rush by with all its commotion.

But Lucy heard it above all the clanging noise and din. She felt it. It never left her. That still small voice, more delicate than breath. It whispered to her when she washed dishes, shook rugs, went to town, bathed Emmaleta. No matter where she was or what she was doing, she heard it. If she woke during the night, it whispered to her. It lived with her, breathed with her.

One afternoon while Emmaleta slept, Lucy opened her Testament. "How long wilt thou forget me, O Lord? forever? how long wilt thou hide thy face from me?"

O God, she cried with alarm, *please don't hide Your face from me.* She checked the door to make sure it was locked and dropped onto her knees beside a chair. *O God, how can You be patient with me much longer? If there's a church in this city where I can get help, please, please, help us find it.*

She approached him while straightening the bedspread. "Let's go to church this morning, Clem." It was early October. "The weather is perfect."

"Church? Which one?"

"I don't know. By the sound of all the bells there must be several in this end of town."

"I wouldn't be surprised there's forty in the city. But Sunday's the only day I have to rest. I work hard all week."

"I know, dear. But remember, we didn't go one time to the Salvation Army hall in Branton. We just talked about going. We've put this off too long now. Please?"

He stepped into his house slippers.

"Don't you remember what you told me at Mrs. Carrington's door one night?"

Clem cleared his throat. He started combing his hair. "What?" He didn't look at her.

"You said you hoped I'd find what it takes to make me happy."

"You're not happy?"

"You know what I mean, Clem. I want that peace in my heart again that comes from being close to God."

"But I thought you said God is everywhere."

"He is."

"Then why must you go to some church to get close to God?"

"Don't you understand, Clem? It's necessary to be with other Christians. God's with me, yes. I know it's true because He speaks to me every day."

"He does?" Clem gave Lucy a quick, disconcerted glance.

"Not out loud," she said, "but a quiet voice in my heart and conscience. But I need to be with people of God whose faith is stronger than mine. I've got to have help from some minister like Brother Bustleton who can explain what I need to know. Don't you understand?"

Clem made no answer.

"You told me so sweetly that night. Remember when you took my face in both your hands and you said you hoped—"

"Yes, yes. I remember," interrupted Clem in a yeasty voice, "but I don't think I promised to go with you, did I? Did I, Lucy?" he repeated wrinkling his forehead.

"I guess not," she answered, sad-faced, "but I wish you would have. Oh, I was so thrilled that night."

"Can't you go with one of your neighbors? You say you've made friends with two of them."

"I hardly know. Mrs. Taylor's a nice lady, but there's a lot of things in the Bible she says she doesn't believe at all. I don't know where she goes to church, but if that's what her pastor teaches, it wouldn't suit me. When I become a Christian, I want to be a real one."

"Well, good for you, Lucy," remarked Clem, buckling his belt. "That's the only kind I'd want you to be. You go ahead and find the Lord the way you want to and I won't try to stop you. And then you can tell me all about it."

"You mean then you'll be a Christian too?" asked Lucy excitedly. "You mean we'll have a real Christian home like I've always dreamed of having and we'll—"

Clem walked toward the kitchen. He talked over his shoulder as she followed. "If there is a God and a heaven and a hell and all that sort of stuff you believe in—well, I hope to find it out before I die." He made a dry, abbreviated laugh. "Of course," he added, "I don't figure on dying for a while yet. What say I'll set the table while you get the breakfast?"

"All right." And Lucy took her apron from the hook beside the stove. "You know," she said, measuring the coffee, "none of us figures on dying."

"Well," Clem laid the knives and forks, "I'm satisfied just as I am; so don't try to get me all shook up. If you want more religion, you go ahead and I won't interfere. We have a pretty nice comfortable home here, I have a good job, we have plenty to eat, a nice baby girl, and I'm going to start saving all I can to buy a car. I think I'm doing pretty good."

"Then we could ride to church," smiled Lucy with a ray of hope.

"As far as I know—" The table was set and Clem took his place. "If the coffee's ready, pour me a cup, will you?"

"What were you going to say? It's not quite ready yet."

"As far as I know the only man in our division at the plant who goes for religion is an old man the guys all call deacon."

"You too?"

"No, I never have. I think they carry it too far. I couldn't take all the jeering he gets. It would burn me up."

"But Brother Bustleton said he was often ridiculed and it only made him a stronger Christian."

"Well, that Brother Bustleton must have impressed you as being one marvelous person the way you're always bragging about him," said Clem. "You certainly have him on a pedestal."

Lucy put two sizzling eggs on Clem's plate. "Maybe I do," she admitted, "but I'm sure he knew God because I never think of the one without the other. And how could I talk about anyone else? He's the only preacher I ever knew."

While Lucy washed the dishes, Clem lay on the living room floor and played games with happy Emmaleta. *He's a wonderful father,* she mused, watching the two out of the corner of her eye. *If only we were both Christians.* And while church bells rang somewhere in the distance, Lucy dreamed about trying to find where their two-toned invitation was coming from. The clock struck ten and she was still wondering which step to take and when and where.

Spring came and Lucy was still dreaming.

"Let's go somewhere to church this morning, Clem," she suggested, eyeing him intently.

"I told you I wouldn't stand in your way." If Clem said it once, he had said it a dozen times.

"But I haven't the courage to go alone, Clem, and I don't know where to go." If Lucy said it once, she had repeated it a dozen times. "After that experience in Branton, I'm too shy."

In May, Philip was born, but he lived only three days.

"God is cruel," stormed Clem, looking very bitter.

"Don't say that," begged Lucy. "I know you wanted a

son and I know how disappointed you are, but if he had lived, maybe he would have grown up to miss heaven. We can be sure he's with God in some happy place."

"How can you be so sure of all that?"

"Because he never sinned. He's pure and innocent. If he grew up and turned out bad—"

"Bad like who?" asked Clem with a tinge of resentment.

"I didn't say who, Clem," Lucy cried softly in her handkerchief. "Clem," she said, "when John Eldon, died I was so hurt and Aunt Polly told me perhaps if he had lived, he'd grown up to suffer. I try to think of that now. It helps me take it, don't you see?"

CHAPTER 42

LUCY HAD supper ready and waiting. It was August and a summer thunderstorm was brewing. Seven, and still Clem hadn't come. She stood by the front door anxiously watching each streetcar. At seven-thirty he got off. She saw him stop on the walk and wipe his mouth with the palm of his hand. He staggered up the steps. Lucy opened the door and caught him by the arm.

"Are you sick, Clem?"

He stumbled past her and dropped like lead on a chair. His dinner bucket clanked to the floor.

"No, I'm not sick." He put one shaking hand on his head and held it.

"You look sick, Clem." Lucy came close to him. "Does your head hurt? Oh!" Fear gripped her. She was almost too horrified to ask the next question. She put her arm around his shoulder. "Isn't something wrong?" she ventured feebly. She had a moment of dizziness. She held her breath.

"I—I just got into the wrong bunch tonight, Lucy," he managed to say.

"You mean—Oh, Clem!" Lucy tried to keep her voice down. "Have you been drinking?" she gasped.

"Just a little, Lucy," he measured how much with one unsteady hand. "Just a little," he repeated. "Don't scold me, please. I—I'll never do it again—never as long as I live."

"Oh, Clem!" cried Lucy, falling on her knees beside him. She looked up into his face pleadingly. "You promised me, darling. Don't you remember you promised?" Tears started trickling down her pale face.

Clem stroked her hair. He touched her face. "I know it, Lucy. I know it. I was bad tonight. I didn't mean—to do it." He took a deep breath. "Please forgive me—just this one time—an' I'll never take another drop."

"Oh, Clem, darling." Lucy got up and kissed him on the forehead. "Come. Get washed. I've had supper ready since six o'clock. When you didn't come I got so worried about you." She helped him off the chair and led him to the kitchen.

"You're a good sweet girl, Lucy," he said in an unfamiliar thick voice. "I promise not one more drop."

Lucy lay awake most of that night. What possessed Clem to do such a thing? Had she failed in some way to help him keep his promise? If so, where had she failed? Clem had been very good to her. For over three years he had proved his love and faithfulness in countless ways. He slept in unbroken soundness while she groped for answers to each baffling question. The one decision she made was to make no mention of the incident in the morning or anytime. Of course she'd forgive him even though she was heartbroken. She'd treat him with the greatest kindness as though it never had happened. He said he was sorry—got into the wrong bunch and would never take another drop, and she believed him.

Every evening Lucy had on the stove something Clem was especially fond of: chicken with dumplings, pork chops and browned potatoes, raisin pie. She had his house slippers at the door so that he could take off his clumsy work shoes and slip into them and relax. Emmaleta was in a clean dress, a ribbon bow in her hair, waiting to be picked up and kissed.

Eight weeks passed and not once had Lucy altered her decision. She was confident Clem was going to keep his promise and she would do everything to help him keep it.

A chill autumn rain loaded the streetcars with people who were caught unprepared. That was probably why Clem didn't get off the six o'clock number-thirty car. Lucy watched three more cars stop at fifteen-minute intervals. No Clem. Anxiety changed to dread.

"Daddy come?" asked Emmaleta.

"Not yet, dear. He's late tonight." Lucy was biting the inside of her cheek when she saw him stagger from the group of passengers that got off the fourth car. It was well past seven.

"Lucy," began Clem as she opened the door, "I know you'll be mad at me—but please—please," he put one arm around her shoulder. "You—you," she led him to a chair. He looked up at her with bleary eyes. "You see, honey—"

Lucy stood petrified and speechless. Little Emmaleta clung to her mother's dress. "You see," he went on with difficulty, "that gang got me again. I—hones', Lucy, I didn't want to break my promise." He rubbed both hands over his face, then looked up at her with a pathetic expression. "You just don't understand," he half cried.

"Understand what, Clem?"

"How it is—with a man in such a place. I can't stand to be called a cream puff all the time. I took it for two months to keep my promise to you. I just had to go along with them this once, Lucy."

"Why, Clem?" she could scarcely keep from crying.

"Just to show them I'm a he-man, no cream puff. Help me to the bed, Lucy, honey."

She helped him; took off his shoes and damp coat. She got a washcloth and washed his face tenderly. Then she pulled a chair beside the bed and sat in silence. She covered her face with both hands. Had she failed? Was this her fault? What could she do? Emmaleta crawled up on her lap, wide-eyed and frightened.

"What's the matter with Daddy, Mama?"

"Oh, he's not feeling well, honey. Don't be scared."

"Lucy."

"Yes, Clem."

"You there?"

"Right here, Clem."

"Are you going to stay here with me?"

"Why, certainly, if you want me to."

"I'll take a little nap then."

"Supper's ready." She waited. She shook him. "Supper's ready, Clem."

"I'll eat pretty soon. Let me rest a bit."

But Clem slept on. Lucy and Emmaleta finally ate alone. But Lucy only tasted the supper she had so lovingly prepared. Each additional bite was harder to swallow. She felt like crying, but for Emmaleta's sake she dared not. Inside she was grieving deeply.

"Won't Daddy eat?"

"He's tired, honey. He'd rather sleep."

"I go tell him to come eat."

"No, honey. Don't bother him."

Again Lucy made no mention of the incident. Clem's attitude the next morning convinced her he was ashamed and sorry and would try harder than ever before to renew his promise. What good would it do to scold or shame or condemn? He kissed her with extra affection when he left for work. She followed him to the door and patted him on the shoulder. His face spoke volumes as he turned around and looked at her. It was more than she could read. She simply smiled.

One evening at the supper table Clem said, "Mike Easley got fired today. He worked at the plant close to five years."

"Why was he fired?" asked Lucy.

"He came to work drunk."

"Drunk? Well, doesn't any man know he can't hold a job and drink?"

"Well, there's few men who don't carry a little in their dinner buckets to drink at noon," Clem said.

"No!"

"Sure thing."

"But you wouldn't, Clem?"

"I never have yet."

"Yet?"

"I said I never have."

"And you never will, will you?"

Clem helped himself to more beans. He made no answer.

"Men who drink have a very bad habit," Lucy remarked with tender seriousness as she looked at him across the table.

Clem said nothing.

"Don't you agree?"

"Oh, I don't know," he answered rather abstractedly. "They all have high-salaried jobs. Seems not to affect them as I can see."

"But it finally got Mike Easley down, didn't it?"

"Well, he likely had trouble at home or he wouldn't have taken it in the morning."

"Maybe he had too much the night before."

"Mama?" Emmaleta touched her mother's arm.

"Yes, dear?"

"Too much what?"

"Oh, it's bad stuff some men like to drink, dear. Now eat your supper."

Then turning to Clem she said, "I want you to despise it. I thought you did. You see what it did to Mike. The poor man."

"But he lost control of himself. Any man ought to know he can't fit pipes without steady hands and nerves."

"Well, I hope and pray you never even look at the stuff again."

"OK," answered Clem. "By the way, our foreman is giving a party for our division tomorrow night at the Grand Hotel. I want my suit brushed and ready so I can get dressed as soon as I get home. I don't want to be late."

"Will it last long?"

"It might. I don't know."

Lucy sobered. "Will they serve drinks?"

"How would I know?"

"Oh, Clem, I hope not."

"Business is picking up. We'll be working through Saturday afternoons from now on, which means more pay."

Emmaleta crawled over to her father's lap and looked up into his face. She pinched his cheek and smiled. He hugged her. "What say, my little lady, suppose we all go for a walk since I'll be gone tomorrow night."

"Mama too?"

"Oh, to be sure, Mama'll go along."

Clem helped Lucy with the dishes, then they walked out toward the edge of town to the end of the car lines.

Emmaleta walked, skipped, and ran on ahead until she was tired; then Clem carried her.

"We can take the streetcar back," he said. "Are you getting tired, Lucy?"

"A little. Look, what's going on over there?"

A group of people were clustered around a man in Indian costume standing on a small wooden platform. He was shouting at the top of his voice. In his uplifted hands he was holding a live snake.

"Let's go see what it is," said Clem. "It's a medicine show," he remarked as they got closer. "Look, Lucy, that's a rattlesnake he's got there."

"Oh, dear," shivered Lucy.

"He knows how to handle it. Don't worry."

Children screamed. Women shuddered, but everyone watched as the snake writhed and sent out his poisonous fangs.

"Hi, Lindy."

"Hi," answered Clem in surprise.

A short, stocky man in blue overalls pulled on Clem's coat sleeve. "That your kid?" he asked.

"Yes," answered Clem, "and this—is my—wife—Lucy." He said it with noticeable hesitation He took Lucy by the arm and tried to move her close into the crowd.

"Good stuff, wasn't it?" The man followed.

"Huh?" grunted Clem scowling.

"You know," grinned the man, showing his half-decayed teeth, "at the Blue Moon."

Clem shook his head.

"Saturday night. Don't forget. No sissy cream puff. Remember?"

"Shut up," whispered Clem, casting the man a meaningful glance.

But Lucy had heard every word. Her eyes widened with horror. Her thoughts went on a rampage.

"I'm glad you'll be getting your check Friday," she began on the way to the streetcar. She made special effort to sound calm.

"Why?" asked Clem.

"So we can go to town Saturday night. You need socks and Emmaleta needs shoes. Look, those are getting too tight for her. And look how they're worn through at the toes."

"Whatever you say," answered Clem with gaiety. Lucy was deep in thought all the way home.

Saturday evening Lucy set the table early and supper was ready: vegetable soup, fresh pan rolls, and butterscotch pie, one of Clem's favorite desserts. She and Emmaleta were dressed and ready to go to town.

This time Lucy did not see him coming because a tramp had knocked at the back door and she was in the act of giving him a handout when Clem walked in.

"What's all this about?" he demanded in a gruff voice.

The surprised tramp dropped his spoon and stared at Lucy with gaping mouth.

"Feeding men on the sly?" Clem seized Lucy by the arm and shoved her into the corner of the kitchen.

"But, Clem," cried Lucy, "he's only a tramp."

"How many times has he been here and you fed him?" The heavy lids over his bleary eyes dropped.

"I never saw the man before," she insisted, "believe me, Clem."

"I'll bet," he snarled.

"Thanks, lady. Here's your dish," and the tramp tipped his hat and left.

"Come, Clem," begged Lucy, taking him by the hand. "I have supper all ready. Let me help you get washed. You're not feeling a bit good." She was trembling and so was her voice.

"What's to eat?" Clem staggered to the table, looked it over, sniffed, then took hold of one corner and tipped it over. Dishes, spoons, hot soup, crackers, and pie went on the floor in one loud crash.

Lucy and Emmaleta both screamed. Clem kicked the table.

Lucy shook from head to foot. She grabbed Emmaleta in her arms, for she was crying convulsively and screaming, "Daddy! Daddy! Daddy! No!"

"Be still," whispered Lucy holding the frightened child tightly. She carried her to the living room and put her on a chair. "You stay right here. You'll be all right. I must help Daddy."

"Come, Clem," Lucy said softly, taking him by one arm. "Come and lie down. You're not yourself at all. Oh, Clem."

He made no effort to disregard her. Like an obedient child he followed her into the bedroom and lay down. She took off his shoes. "Now, I'm going to bring you a cup of good hot coffee," she said stroking his forehead, "and when you come to yourself, we're going to talk this whole thing over."

CHAPTER 43

I T WAS nearly noon when Clem woke out of his heavy
sleep. Church bells were ringing. He sat up, rubbed
his eyes, and stretched.

"Lucy."

"Yes."

"Is breakfast ready?"

"Any time you are. Emmaleta and I had ours."

He dressed, stepped into his house slippers, and walked
to the kitchen. He stopped abruptly. He gasped.

"What on earth, Lucy?" He pointed to the overturned
table and broken dishes scattered in every direction.
"What happened?"

"You mean you don't remember?" She broke an egg into
the hot skillet and poured a cup of coffee.

"Remember what?" Clem looked dumbfounded.

"Why, Clem, you did that last evening. You mean you
don't remember?"

"When did I do a thing like that?" He walked around
the sticky food and broken dishes in unbelief.

Lucy turned the egg. "You don't remember you came
home drunk?"

Clem looked shocked, then completely baffled. His face
got red. He scratched his head and took a deep breath. "If
I came home drunk, I was overpowered." He gulped.
"That's all there is to it." He shook his head and groaned,

still looking at the floor.

"You did it, Daddy," said Emmaleta half crying. "The pie," she pointed to the ruined, upside-down pie.

"Honest, honey?" he picked her up in his arms and held her a moment. Then he kissed her and put her on a chair.

"Lucy," he said, "I simply cannot understand this. How on earth could I have done such a thing? Are you sure I— I—? This must have been an accident. That's all, Lucy."

"Accident?" she asked. "Well, I decided to leave everything as it was so you could see for yourself." Her voice had no harshness in it. "Yes, you certainly did do it, Clem. You were angry and even swore."

"No! Not at you, Lucy?"

"Come," she said, "help me set the table so you can eat. Your egg is ready."

"Oh, Lucy, this just about ruins my appetite." He shook his head repeatedly as if mystified.

"Come, Clem. Sit down and eat what I've fixed for you. Then I'll help you clean it up. Emmaleta, you go on in the other room and play with your dolls."

Clem took a few bites. His face was still very red. "I guess Tuffie overpowered me," he remarked at length. He sipped coffee. "I can't believe this."

"But, you do remember drinking?"

After a long pause he said, "I didn't want to. Believe me, I didn't, Lucy. I declared I wouldn't ever get drunk. But that last one—"

"Then you do remember having more than one?"

Clem finished the egg and toast. "Yes," he said after a long pause. "Guess I did."

"I was feeding a tramp when you came home. Don't you remember?"

He shook his head. He frowned. "No. Not a thing. A tramp?"

"You accused me of feeding men on the sly."

"No, no. I couldn't have." He hit the table with his fist.

"But you did, Clem." Lucy kept her voice subdued. "I'm so sorry Emmaleta has to know about this." Her lips quivered. She fought tears. "You talked mean to me too." She sank on a chair opposite him.

Clem reached across the table and took Lucy's hand in his. "Why would I ever talk mean to you, of all persons on earth? I love you with all my heart."

"Clem," cried Lucy, "I had supper on the table—vegetable soup and butterscotch pie. We were all ready to go to town to buy Emmaleta new shoes. You looked at the table, then took hold of one corner and tipped it over."

"Terrible," panted Clem. "Just terrible. Here," he got up and pulled out his leather billfold, "I'll make this right. You go to town and replace everything that got broken, and you get the prettiest dishes you can find. Why!—Why!—" he gasped.

"What's wrong, Clem?"

"Where's my money? Did you take it?"

"No, of course not. I never touched your billfold."

"Then who did?" Clem exclaimed in shock. "Oh, Lucy! I had over sixty dollars. I know I did. Here's only two ones."

"Oh, Clem," cried Lucy.

"I've been robbed," he shouted. His breath came in gasps. His face became ashen.

"Do you suppose that fellow you call Tuffie took it?" asked Lucy, horrified.

Perspiration broke out on Clem's forehead like small beads. He muttered something under his breath and reached for the broom. "I've been a plain fool, Lucy," and tears started streaming down his face, now drawn with shame and defeat.

Lucy had never seen Clem so broken.

"You won't kick me out, will you?" he sobbed.

Lucy didn't answer. She just looked at him with sad, misty eyes.

He leaned on the broom and cried outright. She had never in her life heard a man cry like that. Suddenly she was crying too.

"If you'll only forgive me, Lucy," he choked, "I'll never be guilty of such a thing again as long as I live. Promise me you won't kick me out."

Emmaleta couldn't help hearing. She tiptoed to the kitchen door whimpering with fright.

"Don't cry, honey," said Clem, "I was a bad daddy last night. Tell Mama to love me anyway, won't you, sweetheart?"

Emmaleta stood fixed.

"Love you?" cried Lucy stepping close to Clem. "You know I love you. You know I won't kick you out. I promised to stick by you and I have no intention of breaking my promise."

"You won' t pick up and go back home when I'm gone?"

"I hadn't thought of that, Clem."

"You won't, will you?" He shook with sobs.

"I hope I'll never need to, Clem," answered Lucy brokenly. "You said we'd have fun in the city, but this certainly isn't fun for any of us."

"It'll be the last time. I promise." Clem wiped his face, then started sweeping together the broken bits of soiled dishes. "I just can't imagine why I'd do a thing like this."

"Drink makes men do very foolish things, Clem," said Lucy.

CHAPTER 44

IN THE next three years Clem and Lucy buried two more infants. Lucy was beginning to feel she was destined for a life of sorrow and disappointment. Little Edward appeared to be a normal healthy baby in every way, but he lived only two weeks. Eighteen months later frail Lottie died ten days after birth. Lucy was smitten. But for Clem's sake she knew she had to suppress her grief when he was at home since he insisted God was cruel and evidently got some satisfaction out of snatching their little ones away from them.

"This makes three," complained Clem with smoldering animosity. "I don't see how you can take it so calmly, Lucy."

"If you knew how it hurts me inside, Clem, you wouldn't say I'm taking it so calmly. But what good will fretting and crying do? I've asked God every day to keep His hand over me and you and our little ones."

"So this is how He's doing it!" There was teeming sarcasm in Clem's voice. "He likes to abuse us. That's the way it looks to me."

Lucy was very thoughtful.

"And so you stop at the saloon to try to drown your bitterness," she remarked sadly. "You just can't come straight home anymore, it seems. Every Sunday for three years, that's over one hundred and fifty times, Clem, you've promised me you wouldn't take another drink. I thought you were going to lay up money to get a car."

"I know it," Clem wilted like a rag. "I—can't deny it. I still want to get a car but—"

"Well," said Lucy drearily, "the way you squander your money on drink, how could we feed and clothe four children, had our three babies lived? It's nip and tuck with one child. Am I right?"

"Oh, Lucy, I just get lured in by those men in our division. They all stop for a drink on their way home. It's not just me. They say it's part of living."

"Let's go back to Branton and get away from those men who are dragging you down."

"Dragging me down?" exclaimed Clem as if stabbed. "Don't talk like that, Lucy. That sounds awful."

"But, Clem, it's the truth. Unless you break away from that gang soon, you'll become a drunkard."

"Don't talk like that," he shouted. "Don't you know I need a wife to stand by me? Can't you put some confidence in me?"

"Confidence?" cried Lucy brokenly. "Why, Clem, that's what I've been doing ever since you took the first drink. How many times have I forgiven you and believed you were going to keep your promise? But you don't seem to have the power to say no. Listen"—Lucy got close enough to touch him—"let's both start going to church somewhere. Let's get ready and start today." She took him gently by the arm. "I know the Lord could give you the power to say no, and quit this drinking."

He brushed her hand off his arm. "The church roof would fall in if I stepped inside."

Lucy shuddered. "I've heard that same remark before,

Clem. What church would fall in?"

"Any church." He walked across the room twice. "Now listen, Lucy, give me time to get hold of myself a little better. Then we'll go. I mean it."

"I hope you do, Clem."

"I do mean it. Just believe in me, please. I need someone to believe in me."

"All right, darling. Right now I'm sure you mean what you've just said. I decided years ago not to hound you all the time about your drinking, but once in a while I get so blue and discouraged I can't keep still."

"I know," answered Clem meekly. "You've been real, real good."

Lucy waited. The long hot summer, then fall and winter, and through another spring, she waited. In spite of her prayers, her many expressions of affection and occasional pleadings, Clem could not break away from the gang who made nightly stops at the saloon before boarding a streetcar.

"Clem," she began one Sunday (it was nearly noon again when he roused from a deep sleep), "you know it's nearly two years since you said when you got hold of yourself a little better, we'd start going to church." She was standing in the doorway of the bedroom.

Clem was sitting on the edge of the bed. He stared at her in agony. His body was motionless. The prolonged silence was frightening, almost deafening. Lucy stood trembling.

"Remember?" she asked feebly at length.

Silence.

Lucy shuddered. She had never seen Clem with such an expression on his face. She could not interpret it and she thought she knew him well. Fear mingled with bewilderment and pity made her weak in her legs. With troubled eyes downcast she turned to walk away.

"You're not trying to start an argument, I hope," Clem stated disdainfully.

"No," answered Lucy sadly. "I never liked arguments. But I would so like to start going to church before our next baby comes."

"The town and all the churches in it are yours," stated Clem waving his hand. "You can go to any one of them."

"But I don't feel like going alone," remarked Lucy heavily. "I'm just not up to it."

"And I don' t feel like going at all," added Clem with finality. "Now, please, don't tangle up my nerves. Sunday's my day of rest and I can't stand anyone trying to mess it up for me."

Lucy went to the kitchen to cry. She could not hold back the tears.

Marvin was a beautiful child from the start, bright-eyed and lovable. Clem was more than pleased. With every passing month he looked more like his mother and Clem proudly told Lucy so repeatedly.

With Emmaleta's devoted attention, Marvin was walking at eleven months and in eight more was forming sentences and could carry a little tune.

"You precious little boy." And Lucy showered him with kisses many times a day. "Your daddy's so proud of you."

"I'm Daddy's pet."

"He calls you that, doesn't he? Well, you show him how nice you can sing when he comes home. Let's sing them once more." She taught him parts of two songs she had often sung to Corkie.

And with all her heart Lucy hoped every night that Clem would come home sober. Saturday was the night she dreaded most.

Everything Marvin did simply thrilled Clem, his cute way of talking, his funny little pranks, his rippling laughter, and even the tunes Lucy had taught him. Of course Clem purposely disregarded the words. "Jesus loves me" made him nearly flinch the first time he heard his boy sing it.

"You're the greatest son a dad ever had." And Clem would take Marvin on his knee and play with him for an hour or more.

At four he ran to meet his father when Lucy saw Clem was coming home walking straight.

But one day Marvin started coughing. He cried and fretted. He was soon running a high fever. Lucy called a doctor. Two weeks passed and little Marvin showed no improvement. Clem and Lucy were nearly frantic.

"You must take him to the hospital," the doctor said. Marvin lay in the hospital for two weeks and, with all the medication, was no better. One day while the nurse was bathing him he had a coughing spell and something shot out of his mouth. She picked it up.

"A tack!" she exclaimed.

She called the doctor immediately and showed it to him.

Marvin died during the operation.

"I'm sorry," said the doctor, "but we found out what was wrong with your boy too late. His one lung was badly infected. He hadn't a chance to live. You had no idea the child had swallowed this tack? The nurse was with him when he coughed it up." He showed it to them.

"No," sobbed Lucy, shaking her head. "I have no idea when it could have happened."

"I just can't take this." Clem's whole body shook with sobs. "This is too much."

Lucy and Clem agreed to tell the undertaker to bring the body to the house in the white casket they had selected. They both wanted Marvin with them as long as possible, but the sight of his beautiful lifeless body was a crushing experience. This time Lucy could not hide her sorrow for Clem's sake. She cried until she thought her heart would break into a thousand pieces.

"Clem," she said between sobs, "don't you think maybe God is trying to speak to us?"

"What?" He looked at her as though she had thrust a dagger through him. "This would be a very strange way to speak. All it tells me is that it's mean and cruel and unjust. Philip, Edward, Lottie, three babies in a row. Tiny infants—but—Marvin? Oh! No! He lived long enough to give us hope."

"I know this is different, Clem." Lucy put her arm around him. "After we all got so attached to him. Oh, it's so hard to give him up. It's so hard to understand. He was such a sweet, lovable child. He reminded me often of my baby brother, Corkie. He was so sweet and dear."

"You still say God is everywhere?" Clem's words were brittle.

Lucy nodded.

"And you still think He has His hand over you and our children? How can you?"

"Well, I—I hope so," sobbed Lucy.

"Why didn't He see to it that our boy didn't swallow that tack?" Clem wept his bitterness.

"I don't know," cried Lucy. "I just don't know. Sometimes I wonder about a lot of things." She put her face on the casket and sobbed out loud.

Lucy told the undertaker to get some minister, any minister, to come to the house and offer a prayer before their little boy was taken to the cemetery. But she was so grief-stricken she scarcely heard a word the minister prayed. He shook hands with her and with Clem and said, "God bless you and comfort you," and was gone. Lucy expected him to come back someday and pay her a visit, but he never came. She was deeply disappointed. She didn't even remember if he had told her his name. Who cared they mourned? If this minister showed no interest in them, what was the use in trying to find a church? Lucy's doubts grew steadily.

Clem drank more than ever. Several times he came home so drunk Emmaleta was frightened and stayed out of his sight. He accused Lucy of all kinds of things with abusive words. The next day if she told him about it, he begged forgiveness and declared he was ashamed and would never do it again. One Saturday night he broke a kitchen chair in a drunken rage.

"I don' t know why I did it, Lucy," he cried the next day. "You've stood by me like a good, faithful wife. Don't kick me out or leave me," he begged. "I love you. I love you with all my heart."

"No, you don't, Clem. You love that old whiskey more than you love me."

"That's not true, Lucy. You're the only girl on earth I ever loved or will love and I hate the old whiskey."

"Then stay away from it."

"I can't."

"Then you love it."

"No, I don't. I hate it."

"Then you're a slave to it. Look what it's doing to you, Clem. Look what it's doing to me and to Emmaleta. Now we've got to move to a cheaper house because you owe the landlord rent. We need groceries and coal. And look at my shoes. Two hundred and seventy-five dollars a month you're getting now and what have we got to show for it? Nothing but bills piling up. The saloonkeeper gets what we need. Emmaleta needs a coat and dresses. Your own daughter, Clem. You must treat the whole gang every night. It's not fair to us or yourself, Clem. You'll lose your job if you're not careful. Your hands aren't steady anymore. I guess I'll have to go out and find a job." Lucy sank into a chair completely exhausted.

"No, you won't," shouted Clem. "My wife's not working out. I'll try to break away from the gang. Try me just once more."

"Once more?"

"Yes, once more, I said."

"How much of your last check did the saloonkeeper get?"

Clem made no answer.

"I'd better come out there to the foundry every night when you get off work and bring you straight home. I know I could help you go past the saloon."

Clem bristled. "Don't you ever try that." He paced back and forth nervously across the kitchen. "Don't you ever think of it," he repeated shuddering.

Three weeks after they moved to a smaller, cheaper house on the south side of Duffield, Lucy walked with Emmaleta to the nearest school where she was enrolled for the next school year.

"I hope you can get more education than I did," she remarked on their way home. "I only wish when you get to the fifth grade and higher I could help you with your lessons but I fear I won't be able to."

"Why not, Mama?"

"I had to quit school because my mother went blind."

"Oh. I hope you never go blind."

"I hope so too, dear."

"Look, Mama, the mailman left something in our box."

"Sure enough. A letter from home."

It was stamped in small purple letters, *Held for better address.*

She opened it with eagerness before she went in the house.

Dear Lucy,

Floyd found Father lying on the bed dead—[Lucy caught her breath] *last night about six o'clock. He had his shoes and all his clothes on so he couldn't have been in there long. None of us knew when it happened. Come home at once if you possibly can.*

Peggy

"Come home at once," gasped Lucy. "Why, why this was mailed two weeks ago."

Dazed, she unlocked the door and dropped on a chair submerged in fresh grief.

"Mama," exclaimed Emmaleta pulling on her arm, "what's wrong?"

373

CHAPTER 45

FOR ALMOST an hour Lucy sat with her handkerchief over her face. The sheet of paper on the kitchen table in front of her was still wordless. Twice she picked up the pencil and dropped it.

"What's the matter, Mama?" asked Emmaleta, hanging over the back of the chair and looking very distressed.

"I can't tell you, honey."

"Why not?"

"You wouldn't understand."

"Who would? Would Daddy?"

"No, dear, I'm afraid not."

"Who would then?"

Lucy wiped her eyes; unspeakable misery and loneliness and grief held her. Who would understand her turmoil of emotions, her mountain of whys, and this ordeal of repeated grief that seemed to govern her very existence? Life. It seemed so brief, so uncertain, so transient, while death seemed sure, so shockingly sudden, so crushingly real. Who would understand? God? Did He really realize the sum of all her shattered dreams? True, she had some bitterness in her heart because Marvin was taken. She had harbored doubts about His love and caring, but would He still keep His hand over her? She knew she still believed in God. Yes, surely He alone understood her feelings. Father. She had never been able to understand him.

Now he was gone forever. Sobs shook her body. Even though he had been unreasonable with her too often, even though he hated Tom, she loved him. But he had no use for God. She wanted to scream. He had no possibility of avoiding punishment if what Brother Bustleton preached was true. She covered her face and wept hot, uncontrolled tears.

Emmaleta pulled her mother's hand away from her face.

"Why do you cry like that, Mama?" she whimpered.

Lucy put her arm around her child and drew her close. "I'm sorry, dear, you have to see me cry like this but the letter makes me very sad. You have your daddy but mine is gone now."

"Gone where?"

"I don't know, Emmaleta."

"Well, where is he?"

"In the ground."

"Where in the ground?"

"Back home."

"Where is back home?"

"At Black Bend where I used to live when I was a girl."

"I never knew you had a daddy."

"Yes, dear, I had a daddy. Of course I did."

"Is he like my daddy?"

Lucy shook her head. "He died, honey."

"How?"

"He just lay down on the bed and died, I guess. Oh, Emmaleta dear," cried Lucy, "I must find God or I can't stand all this. I wish now I could have gone home with you on the train so Father could have seen you again. He saw you only once when you were a tiny baby."

"How tiny?"

"Real tiny, dear. In a basket. Oh, if your daddy doesn't stop drinking, I'll never get home. How I wish we could go tomorrow. Now, go play with your doll, Emmaleta. Mama must write a letter to Peggy."

Reluctantly Emmaleta went into the next room. She held her doll against her face and whispered strange soothing words she hardly understood herself.

Dear Peggy,

We moved three weeks ago. I just got your letter today. I am heartbroken. I didn't get it in time to come home but maybe it's just as good I didn't because I couldn't have come anyhow. Someday when I feel better I'll write you a big letter. I'm too sad to write any more now. I can't imagine what you children will all do but I guess you are pretty grown up now. It's been a long time since I heard from any of you at home. Please write again soon now that you have our address.

Much love,
Lucy

She went through every dresser drawer twice.

"What are you looking for?" asked Emmaleta.

"My Testament. I can't find it anywhere. I haven't seen it," Lucy was seized with dismay, "since we moved. Oh, dear me, what next?"

Two months later Lucy was scrubbing the kitchen floor when she heard a knock at the front door.

"Hello," came a voice.

Through the screen she saw a young hunchback, a

stranger—yet there was something familiar about his face.

"Don't you know me, Lucy?"

"Floyd," exclaimed Lucy. "Come in. Why, Floyd," Lucy's hand went to her mouth to smother a scream. "What's wrong with your back?"

"Didn't Loretta or Peggy write and tell you?"

"No! Floyd, what happened? Take a chair."

"Well, I was on a load of wood Father was taking to town. I don't remember how it happened but I fell off and the wagon went over my shoulders."

"No! Oh, Floyd! Father knew you were hurt, didn't he?"

"Yes, Father knew it. I screamed."

"And—he never took you to a doctor?"

Sadly Floyd shook his head.

"Oh, Floyd! I can hardly get over this. Why didn't he?"

"You know how Father was, Lucy. He never took Mom to the eye doctor, did he? He never did anything for Corkie till it was too late."

"How long ago did this happen?"

"It's been well over a year."

"Oh, what a shame! But you really surprised me! You came on the train?"

"Yes. Then I got a taxi to bring me here when I found out how far it would be to walk."

"Tell me about everyone quickly."

"Well, Peggy went to live with Aunt Polly."

"She did? That's fine. Aunt Polly is a dear. I wonder why she never writes to me."

"She had a stroke. She can't write."

"Oh, poor Aunt Polly."

"Kenneth is going to take over the home and get married soon."

"Really? Who to?"

"Mary Davis. Don't you remember her?"

"A little perhaps."

"Loretta got married last week."

"She did? Who to?"

"Arthur Spencer."

"I don't know who he is."

"He's a nice fellow. He's been working for Charlie Morehouse."

"I hope he'll turn out to be a good provider," sighed Lucy, "and never start drinking."

"Why?" asked Floyd. "Does Clem drink? I noticed you made such a big sigh. Maybe I shouldn't have asked."

"I'm terribly sorry to say he does, Floyd. He may come home full tonight but if he does, don't say anything. Don't have any words with him. He's always ashamed the next day."

"I never thought Clem would drink."

"I never did either, Floyd. Oh, it's a terrible life to live."

"I came here to try to find work. I hesitate to ask you, Lucy, but do you suppose I could stay here till I get lined up?"

"Why, certainly you can. If you'll be satisfied with what I can give you."

"I will. But I'll pay you room and board. I wouldn't think of sponging off you. I'll have to find work that's not too hard for me, you know. I'm not too strong since I was hurt."

"Well, whatever you do, don't apply for a job at the steel foundry."

"Why not?"

"I've wished a thousand times we'd stayed in Branton, Floyd. It must be an awful rough bunch of men who work there. You know, Clem makes two hundred and seventy-five dollars a month, but entirely too much of that goes to the saloonkeeper."

"That's a shame," said Floyd. "Well, I tell you, Lucy, if I find a job, you'll never be in want if I can help it. And I don't intend to let any saloonkeeper get any of my money."

"Oh, Floyd," cried Lucy in tears, "you just break my heart. You're such a nice-looking young man, but that awful lump on your back. You told me so many things already I'll have to sit and think about it all. Aunt Polly—Loretta—Kenneth—and you coming in to surprise me."

Floyd was not long in locating a job as a mechanic in a garage. He was promised fifteen dollars for the first week and if his work was satisfactory, he would get twenty.

To Lucy's glad surprise Clem came home sober and treated Floyd like a perfect gentleman. In fact, three weeks passed quietly and Floyd was about to conclude that Clem wasn't a drinking man after all. Lucy took fresh courage. Maybe Floyd's presence was helping Clem say no. Floyd was such a pleasant person to have around. From the start Emmaleta loved her uncle, who often played with her.

One evening the door opened suddenly and Clem was holding something shiny in his right hand. His eyes were bloodshot and he was breathing heavily.

"Lucy," he called.

"Yes, Clem. I'm here." She held her breath.

"You see," he stammered, swaying from side to side. "You see."

"See what, Clem?"

"Did you see—a man come from that house?"

"What house?"

"Right down there."

"What house are you talking about?"

"That brown house, you silly. Can't you see?"

"Clem," cried Lucy, "I don't know what you're talking about."

"Yes, you do." He staggered toward her and almost fell. He braced himself on the kitchen table. "Didn't you see a man come out of Gene Lockavino's house?"

"No."

"Yes, you did. Say you did."

"But I didn't, Clem. How can I say I did when I didn't?"

"Well, hurry up and say yes. Say it, Lucy."

"Why should I lie?"

"Gene'll give me five dollars if you say you did. See?"

"But, Clem," answered Lucy, "I won't tell a lie for you or anyone else for any amount of money. Why should I?" There was fear, horror, and pathos in her voice, but she held her head up and looked straight into Clem's angry, bloodshot eyes.

He lifted his right hand and pointed the shiny revolver at Lucy's face.

Something unseen but real made Lucy stand up very straight and sent courage into every fiber of her body. She looked Clem straight in the eyes and said in a clear, steady voice, "I've done many things for you, Clem Linsdale, but there's one thing I will not do. I will not lie for you. You can shoot me if you want to, but you cannot make me do wrong."

Frenzied, Clem groaned. He snarled, then dropped his

arm like a whipped dog. He was wet with angry sweat as he staggered, reeled, and almost fell out of the house and down the steps. Gene Lockavino was waiting on the sidewalk. He snatched the revolver out of Clem's hand.

"No luck?"

"Nah."

"She wouldn't say it?" he bellowed.

"Nah."

Together the two men swayed and zigzagged down the street, bumping into each other as they went.

"Emmaleta," said Lucy, gathering her child into her arms, "listen, darling, whatever you do, don't ever tell a lie for anybody. It's a sin. It's wicked. The Bible says so and liars go to hell. The Bible says so."

"What's that, Mama?"

"Oh, if I could only find that Testament Aunt Polly gave me," said Lucy. "What on earth happened to it? But I'm going to try to tell you about it someday, my child. Soon. What I know. See if I don't. Oh, thank God I know now He has His hand over me. He hasn't forgotten me after all. What else could it have been, Emmaleta, but God who took away my fear at that horrible moment? I'm shaking now but, oh, thank You, Lord Jesus."

Emmaleta looked at her mother in silent awe.

CHAPTER 46

L UCY CUDDLED Emmaleta and then sat beside her humming softly until she was sound asleep.

"Are you going to bed now, Lucy?" asked Floyd.

"I'll wait until he comes home."

"Aren't you afraid?"

"No."

"You're sure you don't want me to wait up with you?"

"No, Floyd. You try to relax and get your rest. Oh, I'm so sorry and ashamed you had to get in on this. You see what unbelievable things drink will make a man do?"

"I never would have believed it of Clem if I hadn't seen it. How can he face you when he comes in?"

"That might be him coming now. You'd better not be here. I'll be all right. Go on to bed."

But the footsteps she heard passed on by. Lucy waited and prayed until midnight but Clem did not return. Finally she went to bed, but dawn was about to break when sleep came to her overtired body. The alarm woke her with a start, and she realized at once that Clem hadn't come yet.

"I don't know what to think, Floyd," Lucy said at the breakfast table. "He never stayed away like this before."

In the meantime not far away Clem sat up and rubbed his eyes. Where was he? He got to his feet and looked around. Was he dreaming?

Footsteps. "Lindy?"

"Yeh."

"You'd better gather yourself together or we'll both be late to work," said Lockavino, handing Clem a cup of hot coffee. "Here take this; I snitched it when the missus wasn't lookin'."

"What am I doing here in your basement?"

"I put you on that cot last night. Guess we both had a little too much, but you were really tight, man. Go ahead and drink it. We've got to be goin'. You may be kicked out of your house when you get home for what you did to your old lady last night."

Perplexed, Clem knit his brows. "What do you mean by that?"

"You had my revolver."

"How did I get it?"

"I suppose I gave it to you. Come on before the missus upstairs uses a broom on both of us."

Clem looked horrified. "You—you don't mean," he gasped in terror, "I hurt my Lucy?"

"Nah," answered Lindy, "you jes' scared her."

"You're telling me the truth, Lockavino?" exclaimed Clem as the two men started down the street. "I can't believe what you're telling me."

"I don't remember everything either, but late last night the missus went over and walked past your house to make sure and your old lady was sittin' there an' she wasn't hurt none. But you'd better be ready for a row. I'm almost certain you put the revolver to her."

"But, why?" panted Clem in a frantic voice. "And I don't want you calling my wife the old lady. She's a lady, yes, and a good one and we get along. I—I— No!" he shouted in sheer madness. "I couldn't shoot my Lucy! You mean I didn't go home all night?"

"If you did, why were you in my basement when you woke up, you fool?"

Clem tried all day to wade out of the night's fog. He had been a fool. The biggest fool who ever lived. Harm Lucy? Use a borrowed revolver on Lucy? Never! Never in a million years. He'd go to the electric chair and rightly so for such a deed. Was he losing his mind altogether? Was Lockavino telling him the truth? It was Lockavino who was beside himself with wife problems. Lockavino was the instigator of this whole dirty mess. He'd prove to Lucy he didn't know a thing he had done. Floyd? Did he know about the incident if what Lockavino said was true? Or half true? Oh, he sincerely hoped not. Floyd was a real nice fellow. A likable fellow to have around and Emmaleta liked him. Oh, he'd prove—he'd prove a lot of things he wanted to. And Floyd. He'd be smart not to start drinking this crazy, damnable, powerful stuff his body craved—craved like wild.

Clem came home sober and as pleasant and courteous as Lucy had ever seen him. His affection and kind words nearly stunned her. Emmaleta had never seen her daddy so sweet to Mama. She eyed him with silent fascination. As the supper progressed, Lucy relived those first months of their happy married life in the cozy little boathouse in Branton.

Floyd joined in the pleasant conversation, amazed at Clem's transformation.

"I saw a pretty stove downtown," said Clem reaching over and touching Lucy's arm. "I'd like to get it for you. A good cook like you deserves a new stove." He smiled at her lovingly. "It's a delicious supper, wouldn't you say, Floyd?"

"Sure thing," answered Floyd looking at Lucy.

She made no answer. Instead, she gave Clem a long, pleading look. A stove? No, it wasn't a stove she wanted. It wasn't anything money could buy that her soul was crying for. She'd gladly put up with the stove she had— she'd gladly cook on a tin can if Clem would only stop drinking. Poor dear trapped Clem. He was fast becoming a drunkard. Couldn't he see it? Couldn't he see his doom? Couldn't he tell he wasn't succeeding in this special effort to erase his conduct of the night before? Did he know what he had done? Did he remember any part of it? Why was he trying so hard to tell her he was sorry and ashamed? Where was he all night? She was glad it wasn't winter. Oh, poor dear wonderful Clem. She'd never ask him. How long could they go on living together in two separate worlds? She was drowning in a deep well of despair.

Floyd was given one advancement after another at the garage. What he paid Lucy for his board and room helped her put the delicious suppers on the table and pack Clem's lunch bucket. She reminded Clem of this more than once.

The day came when Floyd was ready to start a business of his own. He had a sign made, "Winchester Car Repair."

"I'm so glad for you," said Lucy. "Now you see what a young man even in your condition can do when he lets drink alone and saves his money."

"I've seen enough since I came here," he answered. "I intend never to start drinking. I wonder what Clem's folks would say if they knew how he squanders his money."

"I've wondered the same thing lots of time, Floyd."

"You've never written and told them?"

"No," answered Lucy, looking at the floor. "I've always kept hoping tomorrow will be different."

One evening Floyd put on a new suit he brought home from town. He shaved, polished his shoes, and dusted his hat.

"I'm going out for a while, Lucy."

"You are?"

"I got acquainted with a real nice young lady who lives on Terrace Avenue."

"Oh?"

"She was with her father several times when he brought his car to my garage." His face lit up with a contagious smile Lucy caught and returned. "She said I could call on her tonight. I wouldn't go out and not let you know where I am."

"That's real sweet of you, Floyd."

"You know," he remarked, walking to the door, "if she'll love me—bump and all—well—"

"You'll be a happy man then, won't you?"

"You said it." He waved and was off.

Charles, a pretty dark-eyed baby, came that year. Anxiously, tenderly, Lucy watched over him. Would he live? A year later Freddie was born—born to die! To die? Why couldn't her babies live? What was wrong? For the fifth time she and Clem watched someone carry a small white-covered box out of their house. Once again Lucy wept softly, for she was burying part of herself in the cold dark earth. She hugged Charles with increased affection.

"Clem," whispered Lucy.

"Yes."

"Now, don' t you think perhaps God is trying to speak to us?"

"I'm too stumped to think." Clem's voice was dry and brittle. "If He is, He'll have to speak to me in plainer, louder words before I understand what it's all about. Another burial bill. I can't hear God's voice in that."

Lucy shuddered.

Summer and winter passed. Lucy had to stretch and skimp and deny herself as never before to feed and clothe growing Emmaleta and little Charles. Clem continued to promise he wouldn't take another drink inside or outside the saloon, but each promise sincerely made was helplessly broken.

"I know your patience is running out, Lucy," he cried one Sunday. "I'm sorry."

"You're an alcoholic, Clem," said Lucy with a look of deepest despair. "It's a disease. You need help or you'll kill yourself."

"Don't talk like that," he sobbed. "Love me. I need love."

"I do love you, Clem. I have never for one single instant stopped loving you."

"Even when I'm as drunk as you say I am?"

"I have never stopped loving you, Clem. I'm not that kind of person. You've disappointed me, to be sure."

Clem covered his face.

"I've tried to understand why you can't keep your promises. Clem," she said, putting her hand on his chest, "look at me. Lift your head. You need the best doctor in the world."

"I couldn't afford it and you know it."

"You need God, Clem. He makes no charge. I doubt if

any other doctor could help you at any price."

Clem slumped. He dropped his head.

The twins came. Willard and Wilson. Two neighbor ladies came in to see them.

"Aren't you proud, Mr. Linsdale?" one asked.

"You bet I am. And excited. They're not identical but they're both beautiful, I think. I'm so proud I don't know how to act."

Both ladies laughed.

"Clem," said Lucy after the two had gone, "you've got something new to live for now. We'll need your wages for these two little ones."

"I know—I know," answered Clem. "I'm going to be careful."

One evening when the twins were six weeks old, a large black car stopped in front of the house and a man in uniform knocked.

"Is your name Linsdale?" He removed his cap.

"Yes, sir."

"Is your husband Clem Linsdale?"

"Yes, sir."

"Does he work at the steel foundry?"

Lucy's legs trembled. "Yes, sir."

"He's in St. Mary's Hospital, ma'am."

"What?"

"He was hit by a train a while ago at the Lashner Avenue crossing."

"Why," gasped Lucy, "I don't understand why he was there! He doesn't come home that way."

"Well, lady, he probably was lost because he was drunk; so the men who saw it happen said."

Lucy turned white. She swayed with sickness of body

and soul. The world was spinning. Emmaleta grabbed her around the waist and tried to hold her up. "Mama," she cried.

"Shall I call a cab for you, Mrs. Linsdale?"

Oh, God! Clem hit by a train! Where was St. Mary's Hospital? Lucy tried to think. "I—I haven't any money."

"I see," said the officer. "I'll call one of your neighbors to come over. Do you feel faint? Better sit down."

"Mama," cried Emmaleta.

"Take your mother to a chair, little girl. I'll go for help."

Everything got black. Was she going blind? The floor was smashing to her face.

A neighbor came. Two came. Two women. They put cold cloths on Lucy's face and arms. They helped her into another dress as soon as she could stand on her feet. A third neighbor came and offered to stay with little Charles and the twins.

"I'll have to walk," sighed Lucy. "I have no money for a taxi."

"We'll go with you then. It's not far."

The two women supported her all the way, one on each side. Emmaleta followed, frightened and half crying.

Dazed, Lucy followed the nurse into the room. Yes, that was Clem. But, oh, how white! How still! There was a nurse on both sides of the bed. One was holding his wrist, the other watching his closed eyes. She lifted one lid and closed it.

"Is he hurt—awful bad?" whispered Lucy.

Both nurses nodded.

"Will he—" Lucy could not form the word.

"We can't tell yet."

Uncle Floyd came. He put his arm around Lucy and let

her cry on his shoulder. "Take Emmaleta home with you. She can't stay here."

"But I want to stay if you do, Mama."

"You can't, dear. The nurses won't allow children here overnight."

"Will you be here all night, Mama?"

"I may be, dear. I don't know yet."

"Come with me, Emmaleta," said Floyd. "It's best. You'll want to go to school in the morning, won't you?"

"I don't know," she sobbed. "Oh, Mama!"

"Don't cry, dear. I'll come home as soon as I think I can leave Daddy. You must not come back until you've had special permission. It's the rule. The nurse said."

The nurse begged Lucy to take a chair by the window. "If he rouses, we'll call you."

"How bad is he?" choked Lucy.

"Very bad, Mrs. Linsdale. Critical."

Midnight, and Clem hadn't responded.

Morning and still no reaction.

When the night nurse went off duty at seven in the morning, she said, "Mrs. Linsdale, you'd better go home and try to get some rest. It may be hours before he makes a change."

"Must I leave?

"No, I wouldn't say you have to, but for your own health you ought to get some rest. This may be a long tiring ordeal, you know. Aren't you awfully tired?"

"Yes, but I'd rather stay. The neighbors will take care of my babies."

"You have babies?' '

"Three. Twins and a small boy. Maybe I'd better run home. No. I'll stay a while."

It seemed like weeks before Clem opened his eyes.

"Lucy." His voice was scarcely audible.

She bent over him. "Yes, Clem."

"I want Lucy."

"This is Lucy. Clem. This is Lucy."

His eyes closed and she waited breathlessly. It was almost an hour before he roused again.

"It's Lucy, Clem. Do you know me?"

He opened his eyes. He answered with a moan.

"You're very sick, aren't you?"

He moaned.

"Try hard to get well, Clem."

His eyes closed.

"Clem."

Oh, was he sinking! "Try hard to get well, Clem. Oh, please try. I'm here with you, dear."

Lucy shook with fear. The statement he made when Freddie died seemed to hover over his bed. Would God take Clem now? Is he awake enough to hear God's voice?

Clem coughed.

Lucy froze.

Salty, thick, dark blood ran out of his mouth. Lucy wiped his mouth with a paper cleaner. She touched the pale face that yesterday was ruddy and windblown. He tried to speak. He moved two fingers.

"I—must be—"

"What is it, Clem?"

"Lucy."

"Yes, dear."

"I'm—dead."

"No, you're not, Clem. You're talking to me."

Two nurses came in swiftly just then. A doctor followed.

"You're this man's wife?"

"Yes."

"We must take him upstairs at once."

"Up where?" asked Lucy.

"To the operating room. We didn't do much for him last night, thinking he hadn't a chance. But now since he roused, we'll try. We'll do our best. He has broken ribs, a severe back injury, and possible internal injuries. Please step aside, Mrs. Linsdale. The cart is coming. Please step to the office and sign the paper."

Lucy watched Clem disappear in the elevator. *My God, my God,* she cried, *please keep Your—* She staggered, then crumpled into a wheelchair in the corner of the hall.

CHAPTER 47

"COME, MRS. Linsdale."

Lucy felt a hand on her shoulder. She lifted her throbbing head. A prim, uniformed woman was saying something. She tried to raise her tired, swollen eyelids.

"Let me help you to the waiting room." With all the effort she could muster, Lucy got out of the wheelchair and walked beside the woman. "How about sitting here by the open window, Mrs. Linsdale? You must try to brace up, dear."

Brace up? That's what she had been doing for years and years. Brace up? Had she ever known anything else since she was a girl in braids?

"I'll bring the paper over to you."

"What paper?" asked Lucy blankly.

"Your husband is in surgery, Mrs. Linsdale. Since he wasn't able to sign, you need to. I'll be right back. Will you be all right?"

Lucy nodded absently. Her careworn eyes saw everything in confused outlines. The hands of the clock on the wall looked warped and too tired to move.

It seemed hours later that the elevator doors opened. Breathless, she watched. The doctor was whispering to the two nurses. Yes, it was Clem on the cart. They wheeled him down the hall in the opposite direction from where he had been. Almost numb, Lucy followed. The doctor met her outside the door. He twisted his gold watch chain and said, "We have put your husband in a private room. He's a very sick man. I suppose you want to know the truth about his condition."

"Of course," Lucy heard herself say.

"Well, Mrs. Linsdale, there's nothing we can do for him."

"Oh."

Lucy leaned hard against the wall. She grasped her throat in dread and dismay.

"You see," continued the doctor, "he was hit in the chest and thrown over twenty feet, so the officer reported. He has seven fractured ribs and one has punctured his left lung. If there were nothing else, that alone is very serious. He hasn't a chance to pull through—especially," he hesitated, "since he's been a heavy drinker I understand."

"Oh." Lucy was too stunned and weak to say more.

"We're very sorry," she heard him add.

Her eyes followed the doctor vanishing down the hall but all she saw was Clem—Clem standing beside her looking abused and dejected at the five baby corpses. *He'll have to speak to me in plainer words,* and four little faces, Emmaleta, Charles, and the six-week-old twins, Willard and Wilson, fatherless, hungry, cold, naked, forlorn baby faces looking up into her tearstained one crying, Why! Why!

For a moment rebellion surged through her that verged on insanity. Why was she chosen by the hand of fate to travel such a steep, hard road? Wasn't she capable of handling happiness? Just a reasonable amount of happiness? Tom was killed in a tavern—a tavern where men gather to drink and lose their senses and do things they can't account for. And now Clem got killed because of that abominable saloon, that abominable drink, that made him lose his sense of direction. Why was he on Lashner Avenue? Oh! She wanted to scream until every star in the sky trembled. If she had gone to meet him, he wouldn't have stopped at the saloon. They would both be at home with their babies. Oh, what an abominable death to die! The wall was closing in on her.

As she stood there, Lucy came to the despicable realization that her lot was as hard as her dear mother's had been. Harder. Nearly everything in her life was a twisted, punishing struggle. Insurmountable! With this realization came despair like a great stone hanging around her neck. It would get heavier as long as she lived. It had been hard with Clem, but without him it would be increasingly harder. Long, bleak, lonely days stretched out in front of her, pulling her heart out by the roots.

A doctor entered the room where her dear Clem lay dying. He hurried out again.

Lucy gathered together the broken pieces of herself and stepped into the room. Clem was muttering incoherent sounds and a nurse was wiping blood that kept seeping out of his mouth.

"Is he worse?" whispered Lucy fearfully. She stepped close enough to touch the bed.

The nurse shook her head. "Same."

"No better?" shivered Lucy.

The nurse shook her head.

Lucy watched Clem for long painful minutes, then stepped close to the nurse and whispered, "I'll go home and see how the children are. I'll be back. Will you stay here with him?"

"Someone will be with him all the time. Here comes Miss White. Miss White, can you stay while I go and get Mrs. Linsdale her husband's clothes?"

"Certainly."

She returned with two bundles wrapped in newspaper. "These are his shoes, Mrs. Linsdale. Be careful when you unwrap this other bundle—there's broken glass. "

"Glass?"

"There was a broken bottle in his pocket."

Lucy would have fallen, but she caught hold of the end of the bed. Oh, the disgrace! The humiliation! Then everybody knew why Clem was hit by a train. It would be in the paper. Clem Linsdale hit—because— Oh, she wanted to drop out of sight. The Linsdales were a highly respected family in and around Black Bend. Any girl would have been proud to be called Mrs. Clemens Linsdale, wife of that handsome, sensible, promising young man. John Winchester's daughter Floss—a maddening remembrance engulfed her— Oh, no, it couldn't be the reason he started drinking. He had promised her— John Winchester's oldest daughter—that he would never drink. He'd do anything in his power to make her, Lucy, happy—anything, anything but go to church. Now all the roofs were falling, falling, burying both of them in bloody, muddy, glassy, debris.

What was happening to her? One night an unseen strength had given her courage to face the unexpected when Clem pointed a revolver in her face. Afterward she knew without a doubt that God had His hand over her and she thanked Him again and again—and now facing this, the unexpected, she had no courage or strength at all. She cringed with rebellion. Her blood surged with resentment. For the first time in her life she was tempted to stamp the floor and curse. She shuddered. No curse word had ever come from her lips. Was Satan tempting her? *Oh, God!*

"Lucy."

She jumped. The nurse stepped back and Lucy bent over him. Her face was close to his.

"Lucy, dear." His open eyes looked straight into hers.

"Yes, Clem." Tears blinded her. "I'm here." She trembled like a leaf.

"Be—a—brave—girl—darling." His eyes closed. He winced in pain.

Clem knew her! He called her dear and darling! He knew what he was saying! Her broken heart started beating fast, faster, faster. The resentment and rebellion, the temptation to stamp and curse was being transformed into something unexplainable. She felt it again. That sudden invisible supporting Something that gave her courage at this crucial moment. He was not dying? Or was he? *Be a brave girl, darling.* Would he say that knowing he was going to leave her? Her face burned with a secret sense of guilt for entertaining those hateful rebellious thoughts. *Oh, God! Oh, God! Forgive.*

Lucy put the bundles on the floor and took Clem's one limp hand in both of hers and held it tenderly. The hand that pointed the revolver in her face. The hand didn't want to hurt her. No. It had never struck her. Clem's hands were both kind and hardworking. She held it, caressed it. The hand did what the abominable drink told it to do. *Oh, Clem, where have you gone? Are you sinking?* She kissed his hand, his forehead.

"Darling," she whispered, "I'll try to be brave. Oh, I'll try so hard. God help me. God help you too, my dear. Oh, we need you so. Please try to get well. Do you hear me? If you do, open your eyes again, Clem."

His eyes did not open.

Lucy sobbed softly.

Clem lingered.

Day after day Lucy trudged to the hospital expecting it to be her last trip. Neighbor women took turns staying with the babies.

One evening she overheard two men talking as they followed her in the hospital hall.

"They've got him in Number 24. That's the death room."

"Sure enough."

Clem's eyes were open, head slightly propped up. The men hesitated at the door.

"Doesn't look natural, does he?"

"He's a sick man. Oh, God, is he ever."

Lucy stood at the foot of the bed.

"We all hate this, Lindy," said the one man.

Clem made no answer.

"We brought you something from the gang at the foundry. We thought maybe your youngsters might need something as it'll be a while before you can get back on the job."

"Never." Clem moaned and closed his eyes.

"Don't say never, Lindy. Pluck'll pull you through."

Clem didn't reach for the envelope. The man handed it to Lucy. "We won't stay, Mrs. Linsdale. The lady at the desk told us to step in and step out. I hope we haven't tired or excited him too much. He seemed to know us."

"I think he does. And we both thank you for this. It's

very kind of you."

Lucy opened the envelope and took out a bunch of bills. "It's sixty dollars, Clem. Look. Wasn't that nice of them to think of our children? Clem," she whispered bending over him, "don't you think God has His hand over us?"

"You—not—me," he groaned.

Stunned, Lucy looked into Clem's thin, pallid face getting thinner every day. Would God have His hand over her and pass Clem by? Would He love her more than Clem who needed love so desperately? Oh, she wanted God to love Clem every bit as much as He did her. How she loved him. How she wished she could ease his pain! Her dear husband, once handsome, straight, and strong, now so crushed and helpless and spiritless.

"Clem," said Lucy in a soft voice, "look at me."

He obeyed.

"If you'll only ask God—and mean it with all your heart, He'll keep His hand over you."

"I'm—not—fit." He had to labor with every word.

Lucy placed a chair close to the bed and sat watching him. His eyelids fluttered. He tried to touch her but couldn't.

"What is it, Clem?"

"That you?"

"Yes, dear."

"I—mean—flesh—and blood, you?"

"Yes, Clem. I'm real. I'm here right beside you. Were you dreaming?"

"I don't—know. Were you?"

"Perhaps. I dream a lot, dear, when I'm here with you." She stroked his hand. "Dream of you coming home. Dream about many things, Clem. You can't imagine what all. You ought to see the twins. Oh, they are sweet."

Clem tried to smile. He failed.

Two weeks later Clem still lingered. It seemed he could neither live nor die. "I never had a case like it," the doctor told Lucy one day. "I don't know what it is that keeps him alive, but as long as there's life, there's hope. So we'll keep on hoping."

Six days more of uncertainty followed. The night nurse was making her rounds; she entered Room 24. She stopped short. A big silver moon shone through the window making an eerie light on the patient's face. She couldn't hear him breathing. Stepping to the bed she lowered her face close to his. She felt his pulse, then hurried to the nurse at the desk.

"Linsdale's made a definite change."

"Dying?"

"No. I mean he's better. Come and see."

Chapter 48

*D*EAR LUCY,
  Floyd's two letters made us all feel so sad and anxious. Aunt Polly and I both had to cry for you and your children. Uncle Jake is worried too. It sounds as though Clem might not pull through. Oh, Lucy, I wish I could come and help you but Aunt Polly is bedfast and I can't leave her unless they find another girl. What will you ever do? I can't get you off my mind day or night. I suppose you are so broken up you can't write. We are heartbroken to learn Clem had been drinking. [Lucy almost dropped the letter. So Floyd wrote— the truth—the hideous truth.] *Floyd wrote he's vowed never to touch the stuff. I hope he never does. Father wasn't always easy to live with, but if he drank we never found it out. Aunt Polly says to tell you she's praying for you and asking God to keep His hand over you. Also that Clem will live. I'm glad for one thing; the stroke didn't damage her mind for very long. Write when you can. We wonder and wonder about all of you.*

                              Lots of love,
                              Peggy

The doctor stood at Clem's bedside, making him the

object of study before he felt his pulse. He listened to his heart, tapped his abdomen, looked at his fingernails, then asked him to wiggle his toes.

"Mr. Linsdale," he said at length, "you've kept us guessing long enough. You missed an awful good chance to die." He smiled and touched Clem's hand. "I believe you're going to live." He put his stethoscope in his pocket and turned to the nurse. "Bring the tape. Plenty of it—that three-inch. We're going to move you over to Room 10 with another patient. And I want your chart to show you're beginning to eat a little. You've been on intravenous long enough."

Clem's brother walked in unannounced one day.

"Frederick," said Clem in surprise.

"I just had to come," he said. "Your accident just about did Mother up."

"How is she?" asked Clem.

"She and Dad are both pretty tottery. From the letter we got from Lucy you've been through a pretty tough ordeal."

"Yes," answered Clem, "I've been pretty sick."

"You're doing better now?"

"Yes. "

"The report came to us you'd been drinking when this happened, but none of us could believe it unless you or Lucy said it was true."

Clem squirmed. He got hot all over. It was difficult to look at Frederick. "Have you seen Lucy?" he asked trying to hide his anxiety.

"No. I'd like to if I have time. I came in on the ten-fifty and I want to catch the twelve-twenty-two for Mikulla. I'm told they need men at the cement plant there and I'm going up to find out. If I get a good-paying job, I'm going to move the family and take the folks along. Dad's not able to do much on the farm anymore, and we want to get the children away from Black Bend before it grows up in weeds. If I find good schools in Mikulla, we're going to put the farm up for sale."

Clem's thoughts went wild. Couldn't Frederick get a job at the foundry—the vacancy he made? No. Oh, no. He wouldn't want his brother to get in with that gang and start—Clem shifted his glance and cleared his throat.

"So you're getting stronger?" asked Frederick.

"I think so."

"Are you able to eat?"

"Some."

"Do you get good care?"

"Yes."

"Does Lucy come to see you every day?"

"She did until this week. It's been pretty hard on her and she got so behind in her work. There's the twins, you know."

"I'd sure like to go see them." Frederick looked at his watch. "It's quite a tramp to the depot. If I don't stop to see them now, I will on my way back. That will be Saturday. I suppose Emmaleta's quite a girl by this time."

"Yes." Clem's effort to smile failed.

"Well, Clem, I'll say good-bye." Frederick took Clem's hand and held it in a firm grip. "I'll tell the folks that was a false report. It just beats all, doesn't it? I don't understand how such tales get started."

Clem wished a nurse would come in and interrupt the conversation. Nervous perspiration chilled him. "What report?" As soon as he uttered the two words, he wished sincerely he hadn't. He pulled at the sheet.

"That you were hit while drunk."

"Well—I don't know." Clem's eyes were riveted at the foot of his bed.

"Don't know?" Frederick's eyebrows raised.

"I can't remember a thing." Clem avoided his brother's eyes.

"Well," remarked Frederick, "you surely know whether or not you had been drinking."

His tone cut Clem. He wanted to pull the sheet up over his face. "I'm sorry," he uttered with difficulty. "When—I came to Duffield—I—I—never imagined I'd—land here in this condition."

Frederick looked at his watch again and stepped toward the door. "I've got to be on my way, Clem. Hurry up and get well. You've got a good wife to live for if she's still what she was when I first met her."

"She is," Clem said feebly.

When he first met her. Yes, Lucy was as good as when he first met her. She had kept every promise she'd made. He hadn't. How often had he promised he'd never drink again? He winced with self-reproach. He wasn't worthy of Lucy's faithfulness and affection. He should have died. But—but no, he wasn't ready if—if there was a place of eternal punishment called hell. He flinched. Was there actually such a place? Maybe it was all bunk. Lucy, sincere, tenderhearted; how young and beautiful she was when he had taken her to the Christmas pageant. How he loved her. How he wooed and waited and bought gifts to please her. How long had it been since he surprised her with a gift? And yet she loved him, forgave him for all his drunken acts. Did he really put a revolver to her face?

Lockavino said so. Lucy had never accused him. How could she be so patient and kind to him now? She knew he had been drinking when he got hurt. Did she write and tell the folks? He moaned. It was Tuffie and Lockavino's fault he took that last drink, or was it three? No wonder they both looked guilty when they came in to see him.

Failure—broken promises, whiskey, profanity, whiskey, babies dying, whiskey, Emmaleta crying, promises, whiskey, Lucy's pleadings to go to church with her— whiskey, more whiskey—everything—whirling, swirling, twisting, and he was caught in the angry chaos and it pushed him in front of the mad roaring train. Picked up for dead. What a horrible mess he'd made of his life! What sweet, patient, faithful Lucy had suffered because of that first drink! It tasted awful. It bit. It stank. It made his head ache. What a crazy fool he'd been to try it again.

Lucy started to pray regularly. Her prayers were not long, but every night she knelt beside her bed and asked God to keep His hand over her and spare Clem's life if possible. She searched again but could not find her Testament.

One evening when Lucy was getting the twins ready for bed, she heard a knock. A well-dressed middle-aged man tipped his hat. A uniformed chauffeur was waiting in a black limousine at the curb.

"Are you Mrs. Linsdale?"

"Yes, sir."

"My name is Birdell, the mayor. May I chat with you for a few minutes?"

"Come in," said Lucy. "Take a chair."

"Thank you." The man smiled at Emmaleta and Charles. "I understand it was your husband who was hit by a train some weeks ago."

"Yes, sir. He's in the hospital."

"I received a petition from a group of men at the American Steel Foundry requesting I make an investigation about your financial circumstances and render some substantial help if necessary. I understand your husband was drawing reasonably good wages, but since he wasn't hurt while working at the plant, the company is not under obligation to give compensation. Neither will the railroad company since your husband had been drinking and had some in his possession at the time. You could, I suppose, find a lawyer who would he glad to fight the case, but I'm sure you wouldn't care to go to that expense."

Lucy's heart burned as she listened. Then the entire town, even the mayor, knew Clem was drunk. She picked shamefaced and crimson at the rickrack on her apron.

"I cannot ignore this petition, Mrs. Linsdale." He glanced at the children. "Would you mind telling me your circumstances?"

"Oh," began Lucy, "I—I hate to tell you the truth," her lip quivered, "but right now I have only one dollar in the house." Her eyes filled with tears. She tried desperately to fight them back. "My brother is staying here and he's been helping me, but he's getting married soon."

Mayor Birdell got up and shook hands with Emmaleta and little Charles, then he crossed the room and patted the twins on their cheeks. "Well, Mrs. Linsdale, we'll see what the city can do for you until your husband is able to work again. I can't promise a great deal, but I'm sure it will be at least a dollar a day and I hope more. Good evening."

"Good evening, Mr. Birdell. Thank you for coming."

A dollar a day? Rent—coal—groceries, milk, clothing, and no garden? There was more than one reason why Lucy's eyes were brimming in tears when she tucked the twins into their bed.

The day finally came when Clem was released from the hospital. Lucy hurried out to the taxi and with the help of the driver they got him up the steps. He panted and groaned. How thin he was! How pale and haggard! His black hair was streaked with gray.

CHAPTER 49

"EMMALETA," SAID Lucy, "push the rocking chair over here closer to the door for Daddy." Exhausted, Clem slumped into it. His shoulders drooped.

"My," he gasped as though he had been running a mile, "it's good—to—be home."

"This is the day we've all been praying and waiting for," replied Lucy planting a kiss on his lips.

"Come—Emmaleta," Clem said holding out one shaky hand, "kiss your—daddy. My—how—tall you've grown." He put one arm around her and she kissed his cheek. He smiled. "You look—like a brown-eyed Susan. Charles— come to—Daddy. No? You—don't know me?" His words held disappointment. "I've—been—gone too long, haven't I? My, my, how—you've grown."

"He can say a long list of words now, Daddy," said Emmaleta eyeing her father with an expression of bewilderment. His sunken eyes and pale cheeks almost scared her even though Mama had told her repeatedly he would come home looking thin.

Clem smiled and held out one hand, but the child would not go near him.

"Mama," said Emmaleta, "can I bring out the twins to show Daddy?"

"As soon as they wake from their naps. You'll be surprised, Clem," she said. "They walk around chairs now and hold their own bottles."

"And they play so cute with each other, Daddy," added Emmaleta. "They roll all over each other on the floor and pull each other's hair and act like two little bear cubs. You ought to see it."

"I—can hardly—wait."

And when they woke and Lucy brought out Willard and Emmaleta brought Wilson, Clem was delighted. His eyes filled with tears and one hand pressed his chest. "My," he exclaimed at length, "I've just got to—get—back on the job with these four beautiful children—to feed." His lip quivered and he shook his head despairingly.

One evening Clem was standing close to the kitchen stove watching Lucy stirring the corn bread batter. "Lucy," he said, limping to the nearest chair, "were you ever very sick?"

"When I had the measles at Sellerses' I was the sickest I've ever been. Why?"

"Well, it seems to me," he said with gloom, "I'm an awful long time getting over this, I haven't any energy at all. I doubt if I could mix that batter the way you do."

"Try not to get discouraged, Clem."

"Get discouraged? But I am and there's no use trying to deny it."

"But, Clem," said Lucy, "we're just thankful we've got you with us. Have you forgotten how near you were to death? It's nothing but a miracle you're alive." Only Lucy herself knew how hard she had been trying to keep from showing her own low spirits. Clem wasn't gaining strength or weight as anticipated, that was evident. And the financial help they were getting from the city was not enough to meet their needs, no matter how carefully Lucy figured. For days she had postponed mentioning the fact to Clem but she could postpone it no longer.

"Clem," she began. She hesitated. His once strong, straight shoulders were stooped and his shirt collar was two sizes too big for his thin neck. "I hate to say this—but since Floyd's married, we can't expect help from him. I don't see how we can keep on giving these three little ones milk. We're going to have to put them on some cheaper canned milk. I'm going to use water on my oatmeal."

"Then I will too."

"No, you won't, Clem. You've got to have milk to give you strength. I'll eat only one meal a day so you can have what you need."

"Oh, Lucy," groaned Clem. "You're getting thin. I've been noticing you eat almost nothing anymore. Even when the neighbors bring something in you insist the children and I have it."

"That's all right, Clem."

"No, it's not. This is half killing me. You're—you're—oh, Lucy," sobbed Clem pitifully, "you're beginning to look haggard—and—old. I can't stand it." Tears streamed down his hollow cheeks. "I—I don't know what's come over me that I act like this."

"It's your nerves, Clem." Lucy put the corn bread in the oven and went over and put one arm around his shoulder. "I wish we had some good nerve pills to give you. Now please don't fret about me."

Soon after Lucy started the twins on a cheaper brand of milk Wilson, the larger, plumper of the twins, got sick. Willard thrived on the new formula and soon outweighed his twin. Lucy was baffled.

"I don't understand this," she fretted. "Just look how fair and plump Willard is, but Wilson—look, Clem, he's thinner every morning. There's something drastically wrong. What shall I do? He's beginning to look strange out of his eyes. I tried the other milk, but he won't take it."

"His crying is getting on my nerves," said Clem. "Take him to the doctor and find out what's wrong. I can't stand this any longer."

"The doctor?" said Lucy. "How will we pay him? Or buy medicine?"

"I don't know how," Clem answered with despair, "but that baby's got to have help if he doesn't snap out of this soon. He's going backwards."

The next day little Wilson was too weak to hold his head up. "I'm going to take this baby to a doctor if I have to sell these shoes on my feet."

"They wouldn't bring much, Lucy," mumbled Clem glancing at her shabby oxfords.

The doctor who examined Wilson next day shook his head. "I might have been able to help your baby if you'd brought him in two weeks ago, but I fear it's too late now. The inflammation is extensive and serious. I'm sorry."

Oh, no. Lucy was stabbed to the quick. Must they go through another crushing experience? One of the twins? The healthiest of the two, until she had changed their milk? How could she go home and face Clem with such a devastating report? Their darling playful twins. The joy of his life since he had come home! Lucy felt a weakness seep over her that was nauseating.

"You might try Doctor Shoeman," the doctor said. "He's the best baby specialist in the city."

She tried to hold back her tears. "How much do I owe

you?" she asked wearily.

"That's all right, Mrs. Linsdale. There's no charge this time."

"Thank you." A tear fell on the baby's blanket. "Could you tell me how much Doctor Shoeman would charge?"

"Not exactly. But you'd have to make an appointment. It might be several days before he could see you. He's a very busy doctor."

Somehow Lucy found her way through her blinding tears down the steps and out to the street. All the way home it seemed she was carrying her own heavy heart in her tired arms. Her whole body ached. Poor Clem. He would be waiting with high hopes. She saw a whole row of little open graves ready to swallow up their beautiful sweet children. Hot, defeating, unbearable tears overcame her as she entered the house.

"Lucy," cried Clem in panic. "Is he that bad? Tell me!" He wrung his hands.

"It's true," sobbed Lucy, sinking into a chair. "He said I came too late."

"No," cried Clem in anguish. "I can't believe it." He opened the blanket and looked at the wasted little body that only several weeks before had been the picture of rosy health. "He's just got to live, Lucy. I can't give him up. Try the other milk again."

Once more Lucy knew she had to brace up for Clem's sake. It wasn't the first time she had found solace by calling on God. Nor was it the first time she experienced superhuman strength, physically and emotionally, at the hour of extreme anguish.

The death angel came for little Wilson the next day. Several kind neighbors brought in food and did what they could to ease their sorrow, but for three days Clem lost all desire to live. He stayed in the bedroom and refused to talk to anyone. Lucy took his meals to him and insisted he eat. Weeks passed and he was still weak and tottery. One day a neighbor brought in a beef roast.

"This is wonderful," exclaimed Lucy. "How can we ever thank you enough?"

"I just want to see that husband of yours get well. We're all getting worried about him."

It was two more months before Clem felt able to think about looking for employment. He began scanning the want ads in borrowed newspapers. He answered one, helping a paperhanger. "I can spread paste, sir, and cut borders," he told the man. "I'm not very strong yet, but anything is better than sitting at home fretting when I watch other men hopping the streetcars with their dinner buckets."

"I'll give you a try," answered the man.

In three weeks Clem was able to help hang paper on the walls. The boss did the ceilings.

"Well, Lucy," he said one evening in April, "I'll never make hanging paper what I did at the foundry, but at least we can have something besides beans and flaked hominy once in a while. Look at this," and he handed Lucy a savory smoked jowl.

"Oh, Clem," she exclaimed in delight, "it smells delicious. Emmaleta, wash your little brother's hands and we'll soon be eating something wonderful your daddy brought home."

When baby Jerry came in September, Clem was as thrilled and proud as he was when Emmaleta was born. "Lucy," he whispered with affection, "I don't know how you do it, but you have the sweetest babies."

"I imagine all fathers feel the same way, Clem. You're just prejudiced."

"All right, my love," he kissed her. "Maybe I am, but you can't argue with me that we have beautiful children even though we're poor and live in a very humble home."

Lucy answered Clem with a warm and sincere smile. She watched him take Willard on his knee and laugh and talk to him. How dear, how charming Clem was when he was himself. She didn't want to complain or rub it in because their home was humble, but if he would have left drink alone, it wouldn't have been necessary to change the twins' milk, Clem wouldn't be hanging wallpaper, he would be strong—he would be—they would have—would have—would have— Her mind ran on madly, indulging in imaginary possessions. Did he ever think about it, her precious, broken, growing-old-too-soon Clem?

Much as she hated to, she did it out of necessity. Lucy wrote a letter to the welfare agency. The worker who called to make the investigation was soon convinced the Linsdales were worthy of further aid and assured Lucy her request would get immediate attention.

Spring brought with it more paperhanging and interior painting. But Clem was always tired. He stayed in bed every Sunday until noon, but the children robbed him of the extra sleep he needed and, much as he adored them, that frayed his nerves.

"I just don't know why I can't get over feeling so worn-out all the time," Clem complained one Sunday afternoon. "I thought surely by this time I could go back to the foundry."

"I'd take in washings, but I haven't space here to dry

our own."

"Forget it, Lucy. It's out of the question. You have your hands full as it is."

"I'd bake bread to sell, but the oven is too small and I haven't enough pans."

"Forget that too," mumbled Clem. "It makes me tired to even talk about it."

Another winter and there were seven with wee Victor. Paperhanging jobs slumped drastically. Clem saw an ad, "Men Wanted to Deliver Coal." He knew without trying he couldn't handle such a job when it hurt his back to clean the snow off their walk. He did, however, take a night job cleaning and restocking shelves in a large grocery store. Lucy did her utmost to keep the little ones quiet during the day so that he could sleep, but in such a small house it was an utter impossibility.

"I just can't stand this much longer," he told Lucy at the end of one week. "I can't work all night and lie awake all day."

"I'm sorry, Clem, but I—"

"I'm not blaming you," he said. "I know you do your best, but ever since I got hurt, I can't drop off and sleep as I used to."

Lucy caught her breath and held it, remembering with stark vividness how soundly he slept before the accident. Oh, what could she do to keep the babies from crying and laughing and squealing? If they only had a large house with a private upstairs room, thickly carpeted, where Clem could go and close the door and get the sleep he so much needed. He wouldn't resort to drinking, would he? The thought of it drove her to fervent incessant prayer.

Dear Clem,

How are you by this time? The last you wrote, you weren't able to go back to the foundry. We like it very much here in Mikulla and I have a good job at the cement plant. I'm not drawing yet what you were getting at the foundry, but it's enough to support the family. [Clem squirmed.] *Why don't you pack up and join us here in Mikulla? I'm quite positive you could find work here, and I'll help you out until you get settled. I'm not kidding. I mean this, Clem. I saw an empty house on my way home from work last night, and if you'll write and say the word, I'll look up the landlord and ask him to hold it for you. It's a rather small house, but I'm sure you could make out. I'll even pay the first month's rent and try to get you a job if you'll say so. Let me know your answer at once.*

Frederick

Clem didn't laugh. Neither did he toss the letter in the stove. He stood in mute unbelief, then handed the letter to Lucy. "What do you say to that?" he asked at length.

"Whatever you say." Her entire body tingled. "Maybe now this is God's hand over us."

Clem's mouth fell open. He stared at her in silence bordering on wonder.

"Well, you don't know, Clem," she said, "how many hundreds of times I've asked the good Lord to keep His hand over me."

"Over you," remarked Clem. "Yes, maybe He has His hand over you, but I can't say I feel it over me."

"But have you ever asked Him?"

"No, I haven't. I don't feel like bothering or begging Him for anything."

"But, Clem, when you were so near death, I begged Him to keep His hand over you. And He did, didn't He?"

Clem cleared his throat uneasily.

"Didn't the doctor say you barely missed death or words like that?"

Clem made no answer. He picked up little Jerry and found a chair. He did not look at Lucy but slowly stroked his little boy's head. He knew his hand was trembling and it embarrassed him greatly. He felt Lucy's penetrating eyes.

"I'm sure you don't realize, Clem," began Lucy with fresh persuasion.

"Realize what?" he looked up momentarily.

"Realize how glad and happy and pleased God would be if you'd only ask Him yourself to keep His hand over you. It would tell Him you believe in His love and protecting care. He wants us to believe in Him, Clem."

"Well"—he got up and inched his way close to Lucy, so close she could feel his breath on her cheek—"if that's the way you understand the ways of God—well, you just keep on asking for the whole family. I want only the best for you and these sweet children we've got."

CHAPTER 50

CLEM ANSWERED Frederick's letter that evening and Lucy mailed it the next morning. As soon as the last piece of furniture was sold, they called on Floyd and his wife, who had a delicious supper ready.

"You have such a nice cozy home," remarked Lucy at the table. "We're so glad for you both. Aren't we, Clem?"

"Yes, indeed," added Clem. "And, Floyd, we think you did real well in selecting a wife too."

"Christine, you're an excellent cook," remarked Lucy.

"Well," said Floyd, "Christine and I have been very happy. We both hope your moving to Mikulla will be the wisest move you've ever made. We wish you the best of everything."

"We hate to leave so soon," stated Clem looking at his watch, "but we'll have to start for the depot."

"I'm going to drive you over," said Floyd. "So let the children finish their dessert. Christine, you're going along? We'll do the dishes when we get back."

At the depot Floyd slipped a tightly folded bill into Lucy's hand. He kissed her. "Write to us," he said. "And don't wait too long to do it."

"Please do," added Christine. "We care about you very much."

"I will," promised Lucy. "Oh, Floyd," she choked, "you've been so good to me."

"He says you've taught him a lot," whispered Christine in Lucy's ear. "He thinks you're a wonderful sister."

Frederick was waiting at the depot in his secondhand car. Dawn was wrapping up the night shadows and the seven-mile ride along the deep, silvery river gave each of them a hearty appetite.

"That's it," pointed Frederick, "the cement plant. I got you a job. You can start tomorrow if you want to."

Clem drew a deep breath. "I hope I can handle it."

"I told Mr. Bradshaw you couldn't do quarry work; so he said he'd give you a job at the scales. And here we are, folks. Vada will have breakfast ready for us."

It was a quaint little house with a white picket fence around a spacious yard. Magnificent evergreens stood tall and stately on either side of the stone walk.

What excitement when the nine cousins met for the first time! What handshakings! What questionings and laughter and gaiety!

"Mother and Dad," said Clem. "They're not up yet?"

"I forgot to tell you," answered Frederick. "They've gone to be with Elizabeth for several months. Not because you came. They had plans made before we knew you were coming. They'll be back."

What a delicious breakfast Aunt Vada served! Lucy watched her children eat eggs and toast and drink fresh cow's milk to their happy stomach's fill. She saw Clem's face brighten with an expression of new hope.

"I told my boss I might be a little late on the job this morning," said Frederick, "but what say we go now?" He reached over and felt Clem's flabby arm. "Hey, what's wrong, brother? You've got to put on some weight. You probably can sit down part of the time on your job at the scales. There'll be quite a lot of writing down figures but you can do that all right. Your wages won't be the best to begin with but you'll stand a pretty good chance of advancement. Vada, fix a lunch for Clem in case he stays on. Do you feel up to it?"

"I'm anxious to try it," answered Clem, "even if I do feel a little nervous."

Mr. Bradshaw, the hiring clerk, asked Clem a list of questions, had him sign a paper, then introduced him to a foreman he called Butch. Clem was positive it was liquor he smelled on the breath of the jolly, loud-mouthed Butch. It made him run his tongue over his lips with an awful craving. He was glad and relieved when Butch finished his instructions and left.

In a few days the Linsdales were settled in their four-room house Frederick had graciously rented for them. It was furnished with not-too-good, yet not-too-bad second-hand furniture Lucy considered most essential. Emmaleta went to school with her cousin Louisa and came home with happy reports.

"I love Louisa, Mama, and I love school and I love my teacher."

"Then you're a happy girl," beamed Lucy. "And this makes me happy."

"Daddy too?"

"Yes, of course. He's very proud of you."

Clem started coughing. Lucy noticed it with increasing concern.

"You've been coughing for weeks, Clem. I'm getting anxious."

"I guess it's the cement dust." He washed for supper. "I don't know how much longer I can take it."

"Oh, Clem."

"I have a pain in my chest."

"Oh, dear. Since when?"

"Don't look so frightened, Lucy. If it gets worse, I'll have to find another job. I hear there's openings at the wheel foundry."

"Wheel foundry? Wouldn't that be hard work? Too hard for you?"

"It might be harder, but I wouldn't have to breathe dust all the time."

"But isn't the wheel foundry way over on the other side of Mikulla?"

"Yes. I know you wouldn't like the idea of moving and I hate to think of pulling Emmaleta out of school when she's doing so well but—well—"

"Regardless," said Lucy, "we've got to do what's best for you. We'll move a dozen times rather than have you work where it's harmful to your health. I'm sure if you went to a doctor with that cough, he'd say get away from that dust."

"I'll start wearing a mask. That may help a lot."

"I hope so."

The following week while Clem was washing, Lucy stood close watching him. "Does the mask help?"

"I'm not sure yet."

"You're still coughing pretty much at night. It worries me, Clem."

"Seems worse when I lie down."

Lucy shook her head. "I got a letter today from Peggy." She took it out of her apron pocket. "Sit down and I'll read it to you. You'll get the shock of your life."

Dear Lucy,

So you're living in Mikulla. I hope you like it there and Clem does well in his new job. I think it's wonderful what Frederick did for you. I'm still here with Aunt Polly, but I won't be much longer. I'm getting married in June to Raymond McLeod. We've been going together for almost two years; so we know each other pretty well, wouldn't you say?

Aunt Polly is very feeble but as sweet as ever. A Cliffton girl will take my place as soon as I leave. Maybe I can persuade Raymond to come to see you on our wedding trip. We're going somewhere and I'd so love to come and see you. I can't imagine what your children look like.

Uncle Jake gets the Branton newspaper, and I read something yesterday that will interest you. Your friend Norvena Sellers died. Isn't her husband's name Herman? Well, he was taken to the Dorsey State Hospital. ["What?" Clem looked up sharply.]

He must have gone crazy. Raymond knows him. He told me one day when it was storming and the lightning cracked, Herman looked up to the sky and cursed God. Wasn't that terrible? Raymond also said he drank a lot too. [Clem drew a deep breath as he shifted on his chair.] *I'm thankful for one thing, Lucy, I know Raymond doesn't drink. Aunt Polly and Uncle Jake told me to tell you hello for them, and they wish you all everything that's good. They would be thrilled if you could come to see them. Write before too long while I'm still here.*

Love,
Peggy

P.S. *I forgot to tell you your old friend Gussie Jenkins died too. It was in the paper some time ago. I was going to cut it out and send it to you and I forgot to. Now the paper's been used. No one knew how old she was, but some thought she was past ninety-five.*

Clem sat motionless.

"Isn't that awful about Herman?"

"Bad enough," he answered.

"I'd be afraid to mock God during a storm or anytime for that matter."

Clem seemed to be in deep thought.

"Did you suppose he'd ever do such a thing, Clem?"

"Well," answered Clem after a prolonged hesitation, "I'm not too surprised. I heard him make some pretty terrible statements I never repeated to you and I won't do it now."

Two more months at the cement plant and Clem told the foreman he couldn't take the dust any longer.

"I know some can't," said Butch, "and when you know you can't, the best thing to do is get away from it. You're not the first one to tell me this. It happens all the time. Sorry to lose you, though. Your work has been good."

Clem's speech convinced the superintendent of the wheel foundry that he was a man of experience and he was hired without delay. "We'll put you on one of the rollers, Mr. Linsdale. I hope you're stronger than you look."

"I hope so too," answered Clem.

"Be here at seven in the morning. We'll start you at four dollars a day."

"Back already?" asked Lucy.

"And think of this," exclaimed Clem when he walked in. "Yes, I hopped a ride all the way with a man who went on to Baxter and I found a house close to the wheel foundry so I can come home for dinner. Just think, no more fixing my dinner bucket, Lucy. Start packing. Emmaleta, help Mama put the skillets and things in the the the washtub. I hired a man to come out with his truck this afternoon."

"Why, Clem," gasped Lucy, "things are happening so fast. I—I don't know what to think."

"Let's eat first, then get busy. I'm going to start working at seven in the morning."

"You're really excited, aren't you?"

"I am. Why not?"

There was a knock. The door opened and Louisa was out of breath.

"Daddy—got hurt at the plant."

"When?" asked Clem.

"This afternoon."

"What happened?"

"A rock fell off one of those cars and hit his leg."

"Broken?"

"I guess not. He can walk but it hurts pretty bad. He drove home. He has to limp. Mama sent me over to get the arnica she loaned you when Charles stubbed his toe. If there's any left she wants it."

"I'll see," said Lucy. "Here it is. There's not much left. I'm sorry, Louisa. Did your mother say I should come over, or Clem?"

"No. Daddy's not crying or anything like that. He just makes bad faces and says it hurts."

"I know a bruise can be very painful," said Lucy. "I hope

424

he feels a lot better by morning. We're getting ready to move."

"Move? Where?"

"Over by the wheel foundry."

"Oh!" cried Louisa in disappointment. "Why over there?"

"Your Uncle Clem had to get out of that dusty plant, honey. We'll miss you like everything. We've been so happy here—but—"

Emmaleta threw her arms around Louisa and both cried out loud.

"I gotta go," and Louisa ran sobbing all the way home.

CHAPTER 51

FREDERICK BROUGHT the family along when he broke the news to Clem. "Mother died suddenly last night."

"At Elizabeth's?"

"Yes. They phoned the telegram out to Vada this afternoon. The funeral will be there. Will you be going?"

Clem ran both hands back over his graying hair. He looked at Lucy. "I—I just don't see how we can afford it."

"I thought of driving and taking you along, but I'm not sure my old car would run that far and back. And we'd have to drive straight through. I suppose Dad and Elizabeth will be terribly disappointed if neither of us come. They haven't seen you since you left Branton, have they?"

"No." Clem walked to the door and gazed at nothing but his own distressing thoughts. He'd stood by six of his own little graves, but this would be different, much different. His own mother's. The one who had loved him, fed him, raised him, praised him, had put implicit confidence in him, and refused to believe the report that he drank unless he himself or Lucy admitted it. How could he stand by her casket—look at her still face, look into her open grave? His whole being shrank from it. He'd rather send a card of sympathy and work at the hot roller. "I—I don't think I should ask off work," he said, still facing the street. "We need every cent I can earn."

"Are you going to go anyhow?" asked Lucy.

"I'd like to," answered Frederick, "but I can't decide for sure. I think I'll go to the telephone office and try to call Elizabeth and find out how she feels and ask about Dad. We've been real close and I surely don't want to hurt anyone's feelings. But I'm rather short on money right now too."

Less than an hour later Frederick returned and said he was leaving on the eleven o'clock train, that Dad would be coming back with him and offered to pay for his return ticket.

"I'm glad you're going," said Clem with relief.

In the seventeen years of his married life Clem hadn't realized a greater sense of joy than he did the day Emilee Sue was born. He held the tiny baby in his arms and caressed her with genuine pride.

"Are you glad it's a girl?"

"Glad, Lucy? I'm simply thrilled. Come here, Victor. Look at your baby sister. Isn't she sweet?"

"Yes. But how can her fingers be so tiny?"

"They are tiny, aren't they?" smiled Clem. "You must be nice to her. She's tiny all over. Run along now and play. Someday she'll be big enough to play with you."

Seven years passed and Clem was still working at the wheel foundry and those seven years had aged him rapidly. His hair was gray and his coffee cup shook when he lifted it to his lips.

One noon Lucy smelled something on Clem's breath that sent a terrified expression over her face Clem didn't miss seeing.

"Don't worry now, Lucy," he said. "I'll never come home

drunk like I used to. I promise you that. I've been doing pretty good, don't you think?"

"Yes, you have, Clem, and I surely do appreciate it. But once you start drinking again, it's going to be the same story all over. Oh, please stay away from it." She caught hold of his arm and clung to it.

"But I got so hot today, Lucy," he said pulling away from her. "And I got so tired. You just don' know how a nice cold beer can quench a man's thirst and give him a little pep."

"Oh, Clem," Lucy could scarcely keep back her tears. "I don't want little Emilee Sue to ever see her father do the things Emma—"

"Sh, Lucy," Clem held up one hand. "Don't worry, I said. I don't want her to either. Please don't bring up that horrid past. If I didn't have to walk right past Biscay's place twice a day—but when the other fellows stop in for a drink—well—and when it's so beastly hot, I just can't help it. I've simply got to now and then or quit that hot job."

"Then this isn't the first time you've stopped there?" Lucy's eyes opened wide with sudden shock.

"See, you never knew the difference," remarked Clem blinking. "So there. I guess I didn't take enough to hurt anyone."

Lucy caught Clem now by both arms and looked him full in the face. "Please, please don't ever come home drunk."

"I won't. Didn't I say it with a promise? Now believe in me."

He held Lucy out at arm's length, then crossed the room and picked up Emilee Sue and held her face against his cheek. "You sweet little thing," he said. "You're my pet, yes, you are, little one."

During Clem's seventh year at the foundry, he and Lucy had the joy of seeing tall, slender Emmaleta become a bride. Lucy relived more than one of her own romantic evenings with Clem when she watched her daughter leave the house with David Cole. She liked the young man, and it gave her a real sense of satisfaction that Emmaleta had never been a lazy girl but was eager to learn to cook and bake and sew. She was young but sensible. And capable of keeping house. This Lucy knew well.

"We'll miss you," said Clem after the ceremony. He kissed Emmaleta. "And the best to you, David," he added.

Lucy tried to swallow the lump in her throat. "I intend to be a good mother-in-law to you, David," she said, pressing his hand. "Come home often. I think it would be a wonderful thing," she looked at both of them, "if you two would find a church where you'd both feel at home and begin a Christian home from the start. Emmaleta, you know that's the one mistake we made. So profit by what you've seen, and consider seriously my advice."

Emmaleta kissed her mother and patted her on the shoulder. "I know you're right," she whispered.

Frederick and his wife walked in one Sunday afternoon. "Well, Clem," he said, "how are you doing at the foundry by now?"

"I feel pretty tuckered out till the day is over," admitted Clem. "It's hard work. It's about all I can take. Seven years of it now."

"Well, I guess my days at the cement plant are over."

"What's gone wrong with you? I noticed you were limping when you came in."

"You know way back there when that rock fell on my leg?"

"Yes, the day we moved in here."

"It's been getting worse right along."

"What do you mean?"

"It pains me so it keeps me awake at night. I had to go see a doctor yesterday. He ordered me to bed; so I thought we'd drive over to see you first."

Vada wiped silent tears.

"The doctor said it's TB of the bone now. He might put it in a cast."

"I thought you just got a bruise and it cleared up years ago."

"Well, I thought so too at first, but this is what it's turned into. The doctor would go all over me if he knew I drove in here, but I just had to before I went to bed."

Vada blew her nose and wiped her eyes.

"You know, Clem," a serious expression crossed Frederick's face, "when I saw you in the hospital in Duffield, I thought to myself when I left, if I had been in your shoes and got banged up like you did, I'd wished I was right with God. I know you were pretty close to death, weren't you?"

Silence except for the clock ticking.

Clem stared at Frederick's leg.

"I tell you, Clem," went on Frederick, "I believe there's a God and I believe there's a heaven and a hell. Maybe you don't, but I do. I know our parents never took us to church, but I believe there's an Almighty God and each one of us is going to have to answer to Him someday. Something tells me once I take my bed, I'll never get up again. I've suffered more with this leg than anyone can imagine. Even Vada. I came right out and asked the doctor what to expect. He wasn't going to tell me, but I insisted. I'm one of those that wants to know; so he told me this leg might have to come off. I wanted to see the X ray, but he didn't want to show it to me."

Frederick stopped to draw a deep breath. Vada wiped more silent tears.

"You know, I've seen several real wicked men get crushed to death there at the plant—I mean without a moment's warning, and it's an awful thing to see. But when Hank Sunderlick got his one leg cut off and the other mangled, I had to help carry him out. I heard that man many a time curse God, but when he was being carried in that condition, he called on God to have mercy on his soul. I heard him beg God to forgive him for his evil ways, his drinking and cursing and lying and everything. I can't forget it. He was in dead earnest. So there must be a God if Hank Sunderlick thought so."

"Did he—die?" asked Clem in a throaty voice.

"Right there with his head on my hand. He prayed till he drew his last breath. I never heard anything like it. I can't erase it from my mind. I know there's a lot of suffering ahead for me with this bad leg. And I don't want to wait till the end to make my peace with Almighty God. I never drank and I'm not the cursing kind either, but I'm not right with God and I know it. I just wish I knew what to do. Let's go, Vada. I'm miserable; my leg pains me so." Frederick wiped his forehead with his handkerchief.

"I wish Brother Bustleton was somewhere around here," said Lucy. "I know he could help you. I'd gladly walk miles to tell him about you, but I have no idea where he lives. But I know what I can do, Frederick."

"What's that, Lucy?"

"I can ask God to keep His hand over you and give you a chance to find that peace before your time comes."

"Any way you can help me, Lucy, I'll appreciate. I'm in dead earnest."

"How's Dad?" asked Clem.

"He's taking this plenty hard. I asked him to come along, but he didn't want to. He's failing fast."

"Clem," began Lucy after the two were gone, "don't you think it was the hand of God that allowed Frederick to only get his leg hurt?"

Clem made no answer. His mind was in a turmoil.

"I mean that he wasn't killed outright without a chance to get right with God?"

"Maybe so," and Clem sat as in deep thought until Lucy had supper ready.

A week after Clem quit his job at the wheel foundry, he found employment at a button factory. The work was much lighter than at the foundry, but the wages were likewise less.

"I want to tell you boys something," said Lucy one evening when Charles, Jerry, and Willard came home from school. "We're all going to have to help Daddy. I'm sure you've noticed how bad he looks most of the time. You know, he's never been strong since the day he was hurt. Willard, you were a baby then; so you never knew your daddy when he was strong. And, Jerry, you weren't born, but your daddy once was strong. He couldn't stand the work at the cement plant because of the dust. He worked at the wheel foundry too long. It was very hard on him. Now he's got this easy job at the button factory, but he's getting only twenty-five dollars a week. We can't live on that and rent this house. I found out today we can rent a piece of ground outside the city limits for a dollar a month."

"Where?" asked Charles.

"They call the place Cotton Wood Valley."

"That's where Willie Watson lives," spoke Jerry with excitement.

"Who's Willie Watson?"

"A boy in my room in school. I like him. He told it in school one day how his father shot a coyote in Cotton Wood Valley."

"I don't know about that, Jerry; it may be true but listen, if we can rent a piece of ground for a dollar a month and if we could find some secondhand lumber, would you boys help Daddy build us a house?"

"Sure we would," all three answered in unison.

"Well, bless your hearts, boys. I'm real proud of you. And we could have a garden. Would you all help me make one and help me take care of it?"

"Sure we would," again they answered in unison.

"Well, it's like this," went on Lucy, "we're going to all pull together and make it as easy as we can for Daddy. You make me real happy and proud of you. After supper let's all walk out there an see what Cotton Wood Valley looks like."

"Maybe I can find some kind of job and help out," suggested Charles standing up very straight.

"That's the spirit," smiled Lucy. "You're a real Linsdale. We'll make it somehow. But right now you have to go to school."

Lucy's suggestion became a reality. A plot of ground in Cotton Wood Valley was rented and Lucy and the boys helped Clem build a house. It wasn't a magnificent structure with hardwood floors and built-in cupboards, but it was a place they called home and everyone had a sense of involvement and achievement.

Running a button cutter wasn't hard work, but it was monotonous. White buttons, pink buttons, gray, blue, brown, or whatever color the mussel shells happened to be. Monotonous or not, Clem was glad for the job. It kept them from starving. But when the river was high, shells were scarce. In February the river rose higher than it had for years. Only enough shells were gathered to keep one machine busy. Seven men were laid off and Clem Linsdale was one of them.

Lucy knew something was wrong the minute he opened the door. "I'm a man without a job. No shells no buttons, no buttons no work, no work no pay, no pay no nothing." Clem sank on a chair inside the door and covered his face with his hands."

CHAPTER 52

O
N A vacant lot adjoining the one the Linsdales rented stood a tree on a gentle slope beyond a shallow ditch. Its naked branches hung over the ditch like the skeleton of an umbrella. It was a hackberry tree about two feet in diameter and in season bore a small reddish fruit.

The people who owned the plot of ground on which the hackberry tree stood, as well as additional ground in Cotton Wood Valley, lived some twenty miles from Mikulla. Jim Unkenholtz, a local man, was appointed overseer of the ground. He gave Clem and his boys permission to pick up all the dead wood they found on the ground he had supervision over.

"I appreciate this very much," Clem told him, "for since the river's up, I'm out of work at the button factory. It makes it pretty tough with a family of eight."

"I can imagine. Well, you help yourself to all the dry wood you want, Mr. Linsdale. If you find more than you need, you can sell it."

"Thanks. We can use the wood. It's unusually mild for February, but one of these days we'll be needing lots of wood. I'll have my boys help when they get home from school."

"By the way, Mr. Linsdale, I've noticed for several weeks now that someone has been chopping away at the base of that hackberry tree over there. The landlady sure wouldn't like it if she knew it. Someday that lot may be sold and it would make a nice shade tree. I have an idea who's doing the sneaky thing, and if I catch him at it, he'll have to make it right."

"Well, I'm sure my boys haven't done it, Mr. Unkenholtz."

"I know that, Mr. Linsdale, because it's been hacked on before you folks moved in the Valley. You see, if it's who I think it is—well, you keep your eyes open. They think I won't notice it down in the grass, and I see they've even put brush and leaves up around the base to hide the chips. Then when a good wind comes along, over will go the tree. Then it's considered dead wood and can be worked up and sold. See what I mean?"

"Well, my wife always tells the children it never pays to be dishonest. That's one thing I must say for Lucy. She drills them to tell the truth. One time our little Victor picked up an apple off the top of a basket down there at Swainey's market. Lucy never noticed it till they got home, and she marched that boy right back and made him put that apple back where he got it and apologize to Mr. Swainey. I'll never forget it and neither will Victor. I sorta pitied him at the time because I don't think he meant to steal, but that's Lucy for you."

"Well, if there'd be more mothers that conscientious, we wouldn't need so many reform schools and penitentiaries. I hate a racket, but I've been appointed to oversee this ground and I'm getting paid to inspect and take care of it and rent it, and if I find out who's ruining that hackberry tree, I don't know what's going to happen."

"Who owns the ground?"

436

"Mrs. Hodgkin in Draden. She's very particular. That's why I'm uneasy. Woe on me when she finds out about her prized hackberry tree. I'm afraid it's been hacked on enough to kill it."

Charles and Jerry helped their father gather dead wood after school. Clem told Lucy about his conversation with Jim Unkenholtz, but they agreed it would be unwise to tell the boys.

"If I told them," explained Clem, "it would only be natural for them to go over and investigate, then someone might accuse them of working on it."

Clem hadn't fallen asleep yet when he heard the crash. He grabbed Lucy's arm. "Did you hear that?"

"Hear what?"

"That hackberry tree fell. I'm sure that's what it was."

"Don't worry about that tree, Clem," whispered Lucy. "It's nothing to you. Weren't you asleep?"

"No."

"You must be nervous. Try to relax."

"I'm going to tell Mr. Unkenholtz the hour I heard it fall and that our boys were all in bed. And listen—there's no wind blowing."

"Calm yourself, Clem," begged Lucy, "and stop worrying about that tree."

"But I know someone helped that tree to fall. That is all there is to it."

"Well, the truth always comes to light in due time and a crook usually squeals on himself. You wait and see. Now try to relax."

Several evenings later Charles and Jerry were busy gathering and stacking wood outside the house. Charles went in to get a drink. "Mama," he said, "the wind must have blown over the hackberry tree. That would make dandy wood for us."

"But, Charles," began Lucy, "that tree isn't on our ground. Let it alone."

"But Mr. Unkenholtz told us we could have all the dead wood we found on these two lots. It's dead, isn't it?"

"I know, Charles, but you'd better not start on that tree unless you ask Mr. Unkenholtz first."

"Why?"

"It would be best, Charles. Anyhow, it's not dry yet."

"Can't I run over and ask him?"

"You let your father do the asking, Charles. Please. He knows Mr. Unkenholtz better than you do. Just go on and gather the dry wood and forget about that tree for now."

Jim Unkenholtz decided to do what he was being paid for; so he walked out over the grounds.

"Well, I'll be," he muttered when he saw the hackberry tree on the ground. He removed his cap and scratched his head. Then he spotted the boys on the other side of the ditch. "Hey there," he called, "when did this happen?"

"We don't know," answered Jerry. "It was down like that when we came out here after we got home from school."

"Do you boys know anything about this tree?"

"What do you mean?" asked Charles.

"Did either of you ever see anybody monkeying around this tree with an ax or hatchet?"

"No, sir," both answered.

"Well, look here, you boys, I'm going to give you the right to work up this tree. You understand? It's not on your land—I mean it wasn't while it was standing. But now since it's down, the top branches are on your lot." Mr.

Unkenholtz kept casting restless side glances toward a small brown house on the front of the slope. He raised his voice. "The party who got this tree to fall isn't going to get to work it up and cart it off if I have any say to it, and I do. So you boys just start to work on it right now if you want to. And you start carrying it home. It's all yours." And Jim Unkenholtz walked away muttering.

Clem stepped in the front door and tossed his cap on the bed. At that moment Charles opened the back door and said, "Mr. Unkenholtz told us we could have that tree, Mama."

"Are you sure?"

"Yes, he did, Mama. He was right out there a while ago and told us we could start working it up."

"If that's the case," said Clem putting on his cap, "I'm going out and help the boys."

In a short time Charles had chopped an armful of the smaller branches and stacked them in Jerry's arms. Clem also had an armful ready to take to the house.

"What's going on here?" an angry voice cracked in Clem's ear.

He turned in surprise. Behind him stood his neighbor, Mack Shelton, shaking and gritting his teeth.

"Well," answered Clem, "I guess it looks like we're working up a fallen tree."

"It's not your tree," snapped Mack.

"Well, Jim Unkenholtz said we could work it up. He told me he has oversight of these lots. I didn't ask for the tree. He said we could have it."

"I don't believe a word of it," snapped Mack. "That tree's not on your ground."

"Well, it's not on yours either," answered Clem, stepping back.

"But I've got first right to it. I've done asked for it a long time ago. Jim told me if it ever fell, I could have it or any other fallen trees on this ground." He waved both arms frantically and gave Clem and the boys a contemptuous look. "Drop that wood this minute," he demanded. "You too, boy. You're not getting any of that tree." He took a step toward Clem and shook his fist at Jerry.

Frightened, Jerry dropped his armful of wood and stepped close to his father.

"Drop it, you—" and Mack towered in front of Clem, giving him a brutal grin; then he knocked the wood out of his arms.

"Very well, Mack," said Clem. His voice was a bit unsteady. "Come, boys," he said, "let's go home."

The three walked toward the house. Mack followed close behind, muttering curses with every step. The boys went in the back door and Clem walked around to the front.

"Now, look here, Clem, or Lindy or whatever you wish to be called," growled Mack, standing about three feet away. He fumbled in his hip pocket and pulled his cap down over one eye. "I'll take nothin' smart off you or your boys. You leave your hands off that there tree once and forever or there's bound to be a fight on."

"It takes two to make a fight," answered Clem.

"Well, there's two of us right here."

"Yes, but I'm not fighting." Clem stood with his arms folded.

Lucy was in the kitchen preparing supper. Breathlessly the boys told her what Mack Shelton had said and done.

"Where's Daddy now?" she asked, wide-eyed and fearful.

"He went around to the front of the house and Mack followed him."

Lucy hurried to the door and just as she opened it, she heard Clem say, "I'm not fighting."

"That's right, Daddy," she whispered. "Don't fight." Charles and Jerry stood beside her, watching in silent fear.

Lucy saw fire in Mack's dark eyes and it seemed to further anger him to see her standing there. Just then the door of the little brown house opened and a woman in a red dress stepped out.

"Sock him one, Mack," she yelled in a shrill voice that sent a chill over Lucy.

"I'm not fighting," repeated Clem. "You can have your tree."

"Smack him, Mack," shouted the woman louder. "Don't stand there like a silly boob. Show him you mean business or he'll be back there at that tree as soon as you turn your back."

Clem stood with his arms folded.

"Don't fight," whispered Lucy.

The next thing she knew the man had Clem clenched in his arms and was dragging him out toward the road.

"I'm not fighting," she heard Clem repeat.

Mack slammed Clem to the ground, face forward. He lifted his right hand in the air and brought it down with a mighty blow on Clem's spine, between his shoulders. Clem felt bones crunch and instantly was limp as a rag.

"Mack," Clem groaned, "you've—you've hurt me."

Lucy screamed. She saw something whiz through the air and land somewhere in the thicket on the opposite side of the road.

Mack gasped for breath. Two men came running. One with a whiskery face and a younger man. Charles and Jerry both ran to their father.

"What'd you do, Mack?" demanded the older man.

Mack pranced nervously. "He—he fell on a boulder."

"No, he didn't fall on a boulder," shouted Charles, half sobbing. He bent over his father. "You struck him with that—thing you threw in the weeds. Daddy!" he cried hysterically.

Clem groaned.

"Call the law," shouted the older man to the younger.

Mack turned Clem over. He tried to pick him up but Clem was limp and heavy. Mack whistled through his broken teeth. "Help me," he panted. "You guys get ahold there."

Charles grabbed one leg and Jerry the other. Mack and the man with the whiskery face took hold of Clem's shoulders. He moaned. Slowly, awkwardly they carried him through the door.

Lucy was crying and wringing her hands. "Put him on the bed."

"I'm sorry," Mack said in a hoarse, guttural voice. "I never meant to hurt you, Mr. Linsdale." Large drops of sweat fell from his forehead onto Clem's flannel shirt. Carefully they laid him on the bed Lucy pointed to. "Can't you move?" asked Mack in a breathy voice. Nervously he eyed Lucy, then the boys, then the door.

"I'm hurt," whispered Clem. "I—can't—move. Lucy—don't cry—like that."

"I can't help it," she sobbed, "but I'm glad you wouldn't fight. I saw it all. And so did my boys. Mack, you hurt him."

442

Mack Shelton stood terrified. His chest rose and fell.

Someone pulled on Lucy's dress. She turned. Jerry pointed. Three men in blue uniforms with revolvers at their sides and each carrying a club on a strap were nearing the house. They stepped inside without knocking.

"Come on out here," demanded one.

"Who?" asked Mack grabbing the foot of the iron bed.

"You." The officer pointed his club at Mack's face.

"Me?" asked Mack, squinting and trying to act surprised. "What for?"

"Come on out with us. You know what for." The officer pointed to the door. "Take him out, you two."

"Are you hurt, mister?" The officer stepped to the bed and touched Clem on the arm.

"He—hurt me, sir."

"He's out of his head," cut in Mack over his shoulder. "He fell on a boulder out there on the road. I saw it happen. No one can blame me for this."

"You try to tell God that," cried Lucy through her tears.

"Officer," said Clem, "don't—be—too hard on him."

CHAPTER 53

T HE OFFICER took Mack by the arm and marched him out. Cursing, he stumbled down the steps. "If that woman up there would-a kept her big mouth shut—"

"Lucy."

"Yes, dear." She bent over Clem.

"Can't you—pray—for—me?" His eyes searched her face. "I'm—in—terrible pain." He had to labor for every breath.

"Oh, Clem!" Lucy dropped on her knees and put one trembling hand on his forehead. "I'll do the best I can. Jerry or Charles, one of you run and tell Mrs. DeLashmar to come over. Maybe she knows how to pray. Oh, Clem, are you—hurt awful bad?" She stroked his hair.

"Awful—bad. I—can't move—a toe or—a finger." He moaned.

"Oh, Clem!" she gasped, stabbed with penetrating dread. "Oh, you poor dear!" Her lips quivered and huge tears flooded her eyes.

"Thank God—I can talk. Pray—Lucy," he begged. "Surely—you know God—that—well, don't you?" Clem's lips tightened over his teeth in pain. "This is—my—last," he moaned. "I know it. Frederick was—right. Now— here—I am—not ready—but if God—gives me—breath— I'll confess—everything. Oh, Lucy," he moaned, "keep your hand—on my head—till I tell you—before I die—you've been a good wife. I didn't—deserve you."

"Yes, you did, Clem." A tear fell on his face. Gently she wiped it with the corner of her apron. *O God*, sobbed Lucy, *please keep Your hand over Clem and give him a chance to confess everything he wants to. O God, please save him if You can, please.* And she shook with sobs.

"Lucy—let me talk. It's all—I can do—now. Thank God—I can think and talk yet."

"Does it hurt to talk?"

Victor and Emilee Sue were standing wide-eyed and motionless in the corner of the room.

"Yes—but—I'm going to—talk—anyway. Forgive me—Lucy. I've been mean to you—sometimes." A tear trickled down his temple to the pillow.

"Oh, Clem, don't."

"Let me—say—it quick—before I die. I want—God—in heaven—to forgive me—and save my soul—if He can."

"He can, Clem. I'm sure—if you mean it—surely He will."

"I do. If I had it—to do over—I'd go to church—with you. You begged me so many times. If I had it—to do over—I'd never take—that first sip. I wish I—would have—been the kind of a husband—I aimed to be—when we got married. I've known for a long time, Lucy—it's not possible to live—right without God."

Lucy wiped her tears on her apron and kissed Clem.

"Lucy."

"Yes, darling." Her face was close to his.

"Don't feel bitter toward—Mack if you—can help it I guess—I got—what I deserved."

"No. No," cried Lucy. "Don't say that."

445

"But—it's true—I fear. You—get paid back in—your own coin. Remember—the night—I came home drunk—and pointed a revolver at you?"

"Yes, but you didn't know what you were doing, Clem. I never threw it up to you, did I?"

"No, darling. But—it's been—eating my heart out—ever since. Oh, I've often thought—what if—I would—have killed you that night?"

"Oh, don't, Clem." She wiped away the tears. "God didn't let you. His hand was truly over me that night."

"I was drunk. Lockavino told me—what I did. I stayed—in his—basement—all night. God knows—I've always—loved you. I've always—been crazy—about you, Lucy."

"I've always loved you too, Clem."

"That's—what—I—can't understand. I should have—made your—life easy instead of hard. But—you stuck—by me."

"Yes, Clem—because I loved you."

"I'm glad—I wasn't drunk tonight. Mack will probably try to say—I was. I didn't take a drop all week."

"Clem, we all know you weren't drunk. Oh, I'm so glad for that."

"He'll say I started—the fight, but you know—I didn't."

"Of course we do, Clem. And God knows it too."

"Let him—say—what he will. God—will—give him—what he—deserves. Oh, Lucy—my neck is killing me."

"You poor dear," sobbed Lucy.

"Please—teach the boys—to let drink alone. Oh, if I could only—live my life all—over and be a real father." Clem started coughing.

"Oh, Clem!" cried Lucy. Fear overwhelmed her. Was he

choking to death!

My God, she cried, *if You possibly can, keep Clem alive until someone gets here who knows how to pray better than I do. O God, I should have gone to church alone even though I felt I couldn't. Please forgive me and forgive Clem before he—O God.*

Jerry and Charles burst in, out of breath. Mrs DeLashmar followed.

"Oh, my, Mrs. Linsdale, what happened?"

"Please pray for Clem. He's hurt awful bad."

"Oh, I wish I could, Mrs. Linsdale, but I'm not on praying terms with God today. Thad and I had a terrible round yesterday and I'm all off. I'm truly sorry. Your boys said Mack Shelton knocked him down. I'll go get Brother Hayes. He knows how to pray."

"Please," choked Clem.

"Haven't you called a doctor?"

"No," answered Lucy, wringing her hands. "What's the matter with me? Why, I've lost my head. Won't you please stop someplace where there's a phone and call a doctor for me?"

"What doctor shall I call?"

"Any doctor who will come out here." The full realization of Clem's condition came down over Lucy like an avalanche.

"But—it's a preacher—I need—Lucy," said Clem laboring for his breath. "All—the doctors in town can't help—me—now. I—won't—be—here long."

"I'll hurry," said Mrs. DeLashmar. "I see he's a very sick man, Mrs. Linsdale."

"O God," cried Clem, "forgive all my—my—sins. I've been—so wicked. I'm sorry—for every wrong—thing I've done."

With teary eyes Charles and Jerry stood frightened and speechless. What was Daddy talking about? He must be out of his head. They had never heard him call on God.

"Boys," said Clem, "come close so I—can see you. I can't—turn—my head. Be good—to your—mother; mind—what she—tells you. Stay out—of bad—company. And never—never start drinking. Lucy—bring Emilee Sue so I can see—her—once more."

Victor started crying and clung to his mother's dress. Lucy lifted her little one up.

"Kiss Daddy," Clem whispered. "Be—good, little—pet. Don't—cry like that—Lucy. Remember—boys—you—get paid—back—someday what you give. Oh, God—my back." Clem closed his eyes.

"Charles," said Lucy, "get that paper over there and fan your daddy. Oh, I wish that preacher would get here. And a doctor. Oh, God! Oh, God! Clem! Clem!" she cried. "Don't go yet."

"I'm here, Lucy. But—such pain. Oh, Lucy—such pain."

"I'm so sorry, dear. I wish I could help you. It hurts me to see you suffer like this."

"Pray for me—Lucy."

She dropped on her knees again. *O God, how I wish now I knew You the way I once did. These twenty years of longing and waiting have been too long. Dear God, hear me if You ever did, and keep Your hand over Clem until he finds the peace he wants. Help that preacher to get here soon.*

"Maybe—I lost—my job—so I couldn't—have—Oh, my God! I'm glad Mack—didn't knock—me—out. Lucy—I'm glad—he didn't do this—while I was drunk."

"Yes, dear, I'm glad too. Remember, I loved you always, even when you were drunk."

"I didn't—deserve—that—kind of love."

"But you were good when you were sober. We've had some happy times and some hard times but—"

"But—you—stuck by me. You—had reasons to leave me."

"No, Clem."

"God—bless you—Lucy dear. You've been—so good to me. Oh, God, I'm in such—misery."

Willard had gone with a neighbor after school to help collect scrap iron. As soon as the truck turned in the Valley, a man waved them to stop and reported the incident. Willard jumped out of the truck and ran home, past a group of neighbors clustered outside the house. When he stepped in and saw his father, he was nearly overcome with grief.

"If I would have been here, this wouldn't have happened to you, Daddy."

"I—don't know, son."

"Willard," whispered Lucy, "I wish you'd help take care of Emilee and Victor. I had supper ready. Won't you go eat and feed the little ones?"

"I'm too upset to eat, Mama."

"Well, help the children then. I wish you'd go tell Emmaleta."

It was long past dark when Mrs. DeLashmar returned with the minister. His wife and another couple came along. He could scarcely see Clem's face in the dim light of the oil lamp on the table in the far corner of the room. He spoke a few words to Clem, then the four knelt around the bed and prayed for some time earnestly. The group outside heard and talked to each other in undertones.

Mrs. DeLashmar touched Lucy's arm. "I had quite a time locating a doctor. They're all in a medical meeting at the hotel. But I finally got Doctor Wilcox to promise to come out but he's tied up until nine o' clock."

"Nine o'clock!" Lucy could hardly keep from screaming.

Jerry saw him coming and opened the door. "This man needs all the air he can get," frowned the doctor when he saw the four kneeling around the bed. "You people must get out," he said with stern professional authority. "This man isn't to be excited."

The doctor felt Clem's pulse, stuck a pin in his leg and arm, then drew Lucy aside and asked her many questions.

"Mrs. Linsdale, your husband is in bad shape. That is all there is to it. He must have been given a blow with something harder than a man's fist."

"Is he really—near death?"

"I can't promise you anything at the moment. If he lives till morning, we'd better get him to the hospital where we can give him the care he needs. You can't possibly handle him here."

"Can't you give him something for pain?"

"I'll give him a shot, but I'm not sure it will help much."

In an hour Emmaleta came with Willard. He had tried to prepare her for what to expect, but to hear her father calling on God for mercy was a completely overwhelming experience. She put her arm around her mother and cried with her.

"Daddy," she whispered, "God hears you "

"Where's—David?"

"He's working the night shift now. He'll be terribly hurt

when he finds this out."

"I—hope—you're going to—church."

"We've been going some. Please don't worry about us, Daddy."

"I set—a—poor—example—Emma," he winced in pain. "God—forgive me."

"What do you want me to do, Mother? Stay here all night or take Emilee and Victor home with me? I'll do whatever makes it easiest for you."

"Well, I suppose it would be best for the children if you'd take them to your house."

Clem prayed during the night when he had the strength and the breath. Lucy sat on a chair beside him, scarcely taking her gaze from his face. She relived every day, every joy, every fear, every sorrow from the moment he looked up at her when she was shaking the rug at the window in Branton. As the hours wore on, every past disappointment and crushing sorrow faded into insignificance. To hear Clem pray—her own beloved, wayward, penitent Clem call on God in such reverence—made her feel almost as though she were standing on sacred ground. It was the strangest blending of happiness and sadness she had ever experienced.

Morning came. Clem was still living. The ambulance arrived at eight-thirty. Three boys with sorrowful faces watched their mother follow the stretcher and climb up into the long, gray automobile.

"He'll never come back," sobbed Jerry.

CHAPTER 54

THE AMBULANCE driver sensed the seriousness of Clem's injuries and drove slowly and as carefully as possible, but every vibration hurt Clem's head and neck with excruciating pain.

"Lucy."

"Yes, Clem," she bent over him so that he could look into her face.

"I—want to—tell you—"

"Yes, dear."

"If—God—heard—my prayers—"

"Yes."

She waited.

"It's getting harder for you to talk, isn't it?" She brushed his hair. She stroked his forehead. She kissed him.

He drew a painful breath that had a deep rattle. His eyes closed. Lucy held his wrist. She could feel his pulse.

"I'm—glad—you—kept on—believing. You—convinced me."

"It makes me happy to hear you say this, Clem, but I feel wicked for not going to church regardless of how I felt about going alone."

"All—my—fault. If—I—make—heaven, will I see Wilson?"

"Of course, dear. And little Philip and Edward and

Lottie and Freddie."

"I'm afraid—"

"Afraid of what, Clem?"

"God—may shut me—out."

"I sincerely hope not, dear. As far as I'm concerned you're forgiven a thousand times. I want you to"—a tear fell onto his shoulder—"go without a single heartache or fear. The Bible says He was wounded for our transgressions. I wish I knew the rest of it. I was disappointed last night the minister didn't come sooner and talk more to you. But just believe God can and wants to save you."

"I do," his whispered answer faded.

Lucy followed the cart into the elevator and down the long hospital hall. She recalled with vividness dozens of weary trips to the hospital in Duffield, the humiliations, the painful heartaches, the long days that ran into long weeks of anguish, hoping, praying, waiting, wondering.

But Lucy felt no humiliation now as she followed her husband and watched him being laid on the bed. No doctor would remind her he had been drinking.

The clock in the hall clicked the hours—one—two—three. Poor Clem! How he had to struggle to get his breath! The trip from the house to the hospital had been almost more than he could endure.

Charles tiptoed into the room, followed by Jerry and Victor. They all stood around the bed in silent helplessness, longing to do something. Emmaleta came.

"I left Emilee Sue with Mrs. Watson, Mother," she whispered.

"Did she cry?"

"A little. Is Daddy worse?"

"He's too weak to talk."

"Oh, Mother," and Emmaleta put her arm around her mother's shoulder, "I just don't understand why this had to happen. You've had so many hard things to bear."

"But if he's ready to meet God," Lucy cried softly, "I won't complain. Oh, you children will never know how I've loved him and prayed God would give him a chance to see his mistakes before his time to go."

Lucy stepped close and touched Clem's forehead. "Darling, do you hear me?"

Clem moaned.

"I'll hurry home and see how Emilee Sue is. She's with Mrs. Watson. Jerry will stay here with you. I'll be right back. I'll hurry, darling," she kissed him. Charles and Victor followed her out of the room.

"Daddy," whispered Emmaleta, "I'll run home and fix supper for David and I'll be right back. Did you hear what I said?"

Clem moaned.

"Mother loves you dearly, Daddy," she whispered. "We all love you. We're all heartbroken this happened to you." She kissed his forehead.

Jerry watched his father, sad-faced and teary-eyed. It was all he could do to keep from crying out loud. Oh, the unfairness of it all! Mack was cruel. He was a savage and a beast.

Four o'clock. The door opened and in slipped a nurse.

The nurse watched Clem closely for a moment. Then she turned to Jerry and whispered, "You step out in the hall until I change this spread." She touched him lightly on the shoulder. "Close the door when you go out."

Jerry stood in the hall and gazed out the window. A man was unloading coal, transferring large shovelfuls from the truck to a chute. He couldn't help comparing the strength of the man with the smashed, paralyzed body of his father. His eyes glared through his tears and he ground his teeth. "All because of that mean, selfish Mack," he muttered under his breath, "he can't even move a finger, my daddy can't."

The door opened slowly. The nurse slipped an arm across Jerry's shoulder.

"Your father has passed away," she said with strange tenderness.

"What?" Jerry looked up sharply, his eyes swimming in tears.

"Does your mother have a phone?"

In utter dismay he shook his head.

"Then you'd better go tell her right away. We won't do anything until she gets here."

Jerry tried to speak. He couldn't.

"I'm going off duty now, but listen," she tightened her arm across Jerry's shoulder, "you tell your mother—your father"—she hesitated; she cleared her throat—"prayed the best prayer I ever heard before he went."

She hurried down the hall without looking back.

At that same time Mack Shelton was sitting on the hard cot in his cell, his hands over his face. Voices. Men talking. Footsteps. Keys rattling.

"Shelton."

"Yes, sir."

The chief faced him. "You say you can give bond?"

"Yes, sir." Mack lit his pipe and tried to act undisturbed.

The door that held him prisoner for forty-eight hours was unlocked. "Come with me to my office."

In ten minutes Mack Shelton was walking the streets of Mikulla. His head ached. His legs shook. His heart pounded violently. He walked directly to the nearest newsstand and bought two papers. Leaning against an empty building around the corner he read the bold headlines: *Clemens Linsdale 48 Critically Wounded. Mack Shelton 50 Being Held.* He bit his pipe and held his breath, then he half ran to the lawyer's office on Second Street and entered, papers in hand.

"I was about ready to lock up. Is it something urgent?"

Mack unfolded the papers. "I'm Mack Shelton." He pointed to the headlines.

"I see. Sit down, Mr. Shelton. The paper reports Mr. Linsdale's condition critical. Looks like he's not going to make it."

Mack's face paled. His hands trembled.

"I can't be detained long but just what happened?" asked the lawyer.

"Well," began Mack, drawing a long breath, "that Clem Linsdale was drunk. Clear beside himself. And he an' his two boys were stealin' my wood. I jes' told him nice like to leave my wood alone. I needed it. But he got mad an' tried to strike me with a pair of iron pincers. Well," Mack shifted uneasily in his chair and rubbed one hand over his unshaven face, "you see, I grabbed the pincers out of his hand before he could strike me an' I threw 'em over in the thicket," he stopped to get his breath, "an' he slipped an' fell when he lunged toward me, fell backwards an' hit a big boulder. An' I'm bein' accused of tryin' to kill the man But I didn't."

"Well," remarked the lawyer calmly, "we'll get things straightened out. You go on home and try to relax and rest. You let me do the worrying. You'd say this Mr. Linsdale's a drinking man?"

"Is he ever. Was drinkin' all week. Why, someone told me," he coughed, "when they lived in Duffleld he was walkin' the tracks drunk and got hit by a train. I'll have your money, whatever it takes, to get me out of this dirty mess of lies."

CHAPTER 55

LUCY HEARD a gentle knock. In the semidarkness stood Mack Shelton. "Boys," she said in undertones, "stay in the kitchen until he leaves."

Mack cleared his throat nervously. "I—I—" He hesitated. He shifted from one foot to the other as he rubbed his hands. "I'm sure sorry fer what happened. I never meant to do Mr. Linsdale no harm whatever an' I never dreamed he was hurt bad 'nuf to die. Didn't his heart go bad on him?"

"Well, Mr. Shelton," answered Lucy with a steady but sad voice, "I'm sorry too for what happened. But I'm very thankful Clem hadn't been drinking. No one can accuse him of that. He used to drink quite a bit when he lived in Duffield, but I know for a fact he hadn't taken a drop all week. And I know too he did not want to fight with you. My boys and I heard him say so more than once."

Mack seemed to sway for an instant. He swallowed an unpleasant obstruction in his throat.

"You know Clem lived until four o'clock."

"So I heard." Mack avoided Lucy's face and looked at her feet. "Sure do feel bad about it. I—I liked Mr. Linsdale ever since you all moved in the Valley. I—I tell you," he looked away, "if that Cindy would-a kept her mouth shut—nothin' would-a happened."

"Well," answered Lucy, "Clem wasn't a Christian, but I

know he had been doing some serious thinking since his brother got down sick—but I'm sure if you could have heard him pray after you left and all through the long night while he was suffering such terrible pain, you would have to believe there's a God in heaven who sees and knows everything. I believe God heard Clem's prayers and I believe he died in peace."

Mack fumbled nervously with the buttons on his jacket. He glanced toward the road several times and backed away from the door.

"If Clem was in the wrong," continued Lucy, "I know God forgave him before he died. My boys told me never to speak to you again, but Clem told me not to hold this against you."

Mack looked up in surprise.

"If you are not telling the truth, Mr. Shelton, God knows it and you'll have to answer before Him, not me. Are you out for good?"

Mack didn't answer. He was looking intently toward the thicket.

"Are you out for good?" repeated Lucy.

"Well, I had to give bond. There'll be a trial later. I—I do hope to God—" Mack never finished his sentence. He seemed to be swallowed up by the darkness he backed into.

Emmaleta sent Floyd a telegram and he came the next day by train. His concern and affection for Lucy brought great comfort to her. She asked Brother Hayes to have charge of the funeral at the Simmon's Funeral Home. Clem's aged father was there and Frederick, thin, hollow-eyed, and hobbling on crutches. Vada had to help him. Lucy had cried so much for days that at the funeral she was almost numb, but the tumult of her tearless grief surged through her when voices from somewhere in the balcony sang, "Sometime We'll Understand" and "Nearer, My God, to Thee." All during the service her one thought was that she must find God if He was to be found in Mikulla and make Him the Master of her life.

At the grave Brother Hayes clasped Lucy's hand and said, "May the God of all comfort comfort you, Mrs. Linsdale. And I want to give you a warm invitation to visit our church on Bastille Avenue."

"Thank you," answered Lucy. "I may do that."

That evening after Floyd and the last of the neighbors had gone home, Lucy took Emilee Sue on her lap and said, "Now, boys, we'll have to work and pull together as never before. Charles, since you're the oldest, I'll look to you first."

"Of course," he said. "I'd expect you to."

"I was thinking, if you'd go down to the city barn and tell them who you are, maybe they'd give you a job for Saturdays and after school. Will you do that?"

"Sure."

"I want to help in some way too, Mama," said Jerry.

"Thank you, dear, but you and Victor can help me around the house after school. By another year perhaps you can find some kind of paying job. I might make paper flowers to sell."

"No," objected Willard getting to his feet.

"No," added Jerry. "We won't have our mother walking the streets selling paper flowers. I'll quit school and get a job so you won't need to."

"I'll quit school too," said Victor with brave loyalty.

Lucy shook her head. "Don't think of it. I want my children to get more schooling than I had. I had to quit school when I was ready to pass to the sixth grade because my mother was blind. Thank God, I'm not blind. But listen, boys, I hate to tell you this but it's true. I have nothing but a nickel in my purse and hardly a thing in the house to eat. I'm not hungry, but I know you children are. I don't like to beg, but listen, Jerry, will you go over to Watsons' back door and ask Mrs. Watson if she has some potato peelings she would let us have?"

"Potato peelings?"

"Yes. Please don't ask for potatoes. I'm sure they need what they have, but if she would give you the peelings if she has any, I could wash them well and fry them with an onion. I have one. I haven't enough flour to make two biscuits. But listen, children, I believe in God and I don't think He'll ever let us starve."

"Jeff Sims told me how I could make sixty cents quick," said Willard.

"How?"

"If I'd go steal something for him."

"Oh, Willard!" exclaimed Lucy. "Whatever you do, don't steal. Not even a rotten apple. It's wrong. If you steal a nickel, you'll lose a quarter. I'd rather die of starvation than die a thief. Don't ever let Jeff Sims or anyone talk you into doing such a thing."

"I won't, Mama. Don't worry."

After Mrs. Watson gave Jerry the few potato peelings she was about to throw away, she turned to her husband and said, "Dan, if I don't give that family more than potato peelings, I won't be able to eat a bite of this supper I've fixed."

"Call him back," said Dan.

Mrs. Watson ran to her front door in time to see the boy darting across the road. "Jerry," she called. "Come back. Listen," she said, "I have something else I want to give you." In a sack she put a dozen potatoes, a large can of beans, and a small sack of flour. "There you are, my boy, and you're not to return any of it. Tell your mother what I said."

"Thanks, Mrs. Watson. My mother will be real glad and I am too. Thanks a lot."

Sometime after Lucy had gone to bed, she thought she heard a noise outside. She went to the door and looked out. In the light of the moon she could see something on the steps.

"Willard."

"Yes. What's wrong?"

"Come here. Look out there on our steps."

"Who brought it? Why Mama, it's two bushel baskets! Full of groceries."

"Full and running over," cried Lucy. "Bring them in."

"Where did they come from?"

"Willard, I have no idea. Oh, this is wonderful—only God knows."

"Light the lamp, Mama."

"Look, Willard." They started putting the things on the table. Potatoes, lard, flour, milk, crackers, beans, salmon, bacon, cookies, sugar, cereal, noodles, jelly. "And no name. We have no idea who to thank but God. Willard, you see, if you would have let that Jeff persuade you into stealing, the good Lord wouldn't have sent us all this. And you would have a guilty heart besides. Now, go back to bed and sleep and just think about how good God's been to us. Won't Jerry and Victor be surprised in the morning?

Think of it! We'll have cereal and biscuits. We may see some hard times, but I'm going to keep on believing God has His hand over us."

Lucy slept very little that night. She was too sad one minute and too happy the next.

When Mack Shelton appeared in court the following week, his lawyer presented his case in such forceful words that the judge concluded it wasn't a case for contest, the accused must be innocent, and Mack was acquitted without one witness called to testify against him.

"It's not right!" stormed Willard, pacing the floor. "It's not fair."

"There are a lot of things in this life that don't seem fair," remarked Lucy. "But your father in his grave is far better off than Mack Shelton walking the streets. He may have paid the lawyer well to fool the judge, but he's not fooling God."

"I'll never speak to him as long as I live," shouted Jerry, pounding his fist on the table. "Just because we don't live in a nice big house like those on Chehalem Avenue and have a fine car and expensive clothes, Daddy didn't get a fair trial. I'm mad! It makes me boil! Why didn't they call us down there to tell what we saw? Why didn't they ask Mr. Unkenholtz to tell what he knew and that he said we could have that tree? Mack lied and got by with it. It's not right. I'm so mad I see blood."

"Well, Jerry," said Lucy with feeling, "we all agree it's not fair. But try not to hold ill will toward Mack. Just as sure as you're living, he's a miserable, unhappy man. Listen now, Mrs. DeLashmar was here to see me today and she said Mack told her husband that every night since he's been out of jail, your dear father lies on his doorstep and moans all night and keeps him awake."

"Mama," gasped Victor, wide-eyed, "does he really?"

"Of course not. It's Mack's guilty conscience bothering him. I told you, boys, that God will deal with him the way He wants to. We don't need to. I wouldn't want to either. And Mack told Mr. DeLashmar if it doesn't stop, he's going to move out of Cotton Wood Valley."

Before many days passed, a man with a horse and wagon drove into the Valley and out, loaded with Mack Shelton's household goods. Lucy stood at the door and would have waved, but Mack looked in the opposite direction and so did Cindy Gibson seated beside him.

CHAPTER 56

"MRS. LINSDALE," said Brother Hayes one Sunday evening as she and Emilee Sue were about to leave the church, "I'd like to talk with you a little. You've been worshiping with us occasionally now for several months, I believe."

"I think I've been here about seven times," answered Lucy.

"How about it? Wouldn't you like to join our fellowship?"

"Well, Brother Hayes," answered Lucy thoughtfully, "I'll have to think it over." She was holding Emilee's hand and unconsciously squeezed it. "I really do want to join a church someday if I can feel—" She hesitated trying to find the right words.

"Feel at home?" suggested Brother Hayes patting Emilee Sue on the head.

"Yes, feel at home, but I was going to say, feel led of God. I don't know much about the Bible but I'm anxious to learn all I can. You know," she added, smiling, "when I was a young woman, I attended revival meetings in a country schoolhouse. The evangelist's name was Bustleton. You wouldn't happen to know him, would you?"

"No, I never heard of him."

"Well, anyway, he had such a convincing way of

explaining the Scriptures, it seemed to me he just lived and walked with God, and I—"

Brother Hayes frowned. "You mean," he said, "I don't explain the Scriptures the way he did?"

Lucy blushed. "I beg your pardon, Brother Hayes," she said. "I do hope I didn't offend you. I wouldn't want to do that. I have no right to compare you with any man. Every minister has his own way of preaching. But for some reason he made a lasting impression on me."

"Well, God bless you, Mrs. Linsdale," said Brother Hayes with evident dismay. "I hope you keep coming. I sincerely trust you will feel at home with us. I'm sure you'll find out we're the friendliest church in town. We are a small group and we need you to help boost our membership. So think it over, won't you?"

"I will," answered Lucy.

In the month following, Lucy visited two other churches with Mrs. Watson. Each time she went home and spent much time in meditation. The minister of the one church was a very likable, friendly man. But what was it her soul longed for? Something deeper than she had yet found. If she only had a Bible. Someday she'd buy one. But when? She was going without supper so that her boys would have enough.

Charles did not get a job at the city barn. The hiring agent looked him over and said, "Perhaps in several months we'll have something for you, son."

It wasn't easy for him to go home and tell his mother what the man had said.

"In that case, then," said Lucy, "I'll just have to make paper flowers. You boys said you didn't want me to go out on the street to sell them; so will you do it for me? You've got to eat."

"I'll try," said Jerry, "after school and Saturdays."

"I'll help," added Charles.

"All right, then, tomorrow I'll go to the variety store and buy what paper I can and get to work."

One evening as they were finishing their simple supper of biscuits and beans, Mrs. DeLashmar knocked.

"Have you heard the latest?"

"What now?" asked Lucy.

"Mack Shelton saw my husband in town this evening and he said Mr. Linsdale lies outside his door or at his window every night way over there on the other side of town just as he did here in the Valley, and he moans and begs him not to strike. And Mack said it's about driving him crazy. He thought he could get away from it by moving out of the Valley, but Clem haunts him just as sure as he goes to bed. But that's not all," went on Mrs. DeLashmar, "he's blaming that Cindy Gibson for it now."

"Why her?"

"Well, I don't really know. Mack's wife died up there in that little brown house about a year ago. That Cindy came to live with him right away. No one knows where she came from or who she is. That might not be her real name. Mack says now she's the one who ought to be haunted because she put him up to it. Anyhow, he told Cindy to get out and he's leaving tonight by train for someplace—he's not saying where. He said he hates this town and this state and he's never coming back."

"He will," said Lucy. "He'll come right back here in Cotton Wood Valley every night as long as he lives. He can cross the ocean, but his conscience will follow him. Poor Mack, why didn't he just come out and confess what

467

he did? Boys, I hope this will be a lesson to you, you'll never forget."

Spring came and Lucy had visited several more churches. The more she hunted for the peace she wanted, the more confused she became. She wanted to buy a Bible, but it took every cent Charles made at the city barn to buy the barest necessities. *Dear God,* she prayed one night, *I can't imagine what happened to my Testament. Perhaps I was too careless about reading it; so this is my punishment. I want peace, but where can I find it? Or am I searching for something impossible? O God, have I sinned away my chance by putting it off those years waiting on Clem?*

Fear took hold of Lucy, a terrible consuming fear that she was doomed to be lost. Oh, God! Miss meeting Clem? And John Eldon and their babies? What was the use in trying anymore? What was the use in praying? Or caring? Everything in the future looked so black. And hopeless. What was there to live for if peace wasn't to be found?

And yet in the midst of her darkest broodings Lucy's inmost soul longed, cried out, groped for God's nearness and the assurance of His hand over her.

"Brother Hayes left town," Mrs. Watson told Lucy one morning.

"Why?"

"For his health, I heard."

"What about his church?"

"I heard it's closed, just folded up."

"Closed?" asked Lucy. "Then I'm glad I didn't decide to join."

"Let's visit some other church Sunday."

Lucy shook her head.

"What's wrong? Don't you feel well?"

"Mrs. Watson," said Lucy, "I've lost interest, if you want to know what's wrong. Maybe I'm queer but I'm looking for something I haven't found."

"You won't find it staying home. My husband tells me the churches are full of hypocrites. He's right, I know, but I'm going to visit around anyhow."

"Sometime," sighed Lucy, "somewhere I hope I find what I'm looking for, but right now I've lost interest."

Her children wondered why she stopped going to church.

"My leg hurts," was her only answer. She didn't want them to guess her deep despair. Her defeated hopes and expectations were a tangled mystery she could not unravel. She had helped Clem to peace at his dying hour. She had helped her own mother on her deathbed. She had promised God before Clem died she'd go out in search of her own renewed peace and had not found it. What was wrong? It must be herself. Her courage was gone and she was unable to recover it. Melancholy played havoc by degrees.

Then came a letter from Vada.

Frederick is very bad. The bone in his leg has fallen apart. He suffers something terrible. Lucy, haven't you found a preacher yet who will come out and talk to him? He has accepted Christ in his heart, but he would like to be baptized. He was definitely worse after going to Clem's funeral, but he would have it no other way if he dropped dead. His father is very feeble and is getting quite childish. How are you getting along? We think of you every day. Frederick is so happy that Clem made his peace with God before he died. We know it's because of your faithfulness. That should give you constant satisfaction. Please pray for Frederick, Lucy, and please send out a man of God.

Love, Vada

Lucy was smitten. Shame and condemnation sent her to her knees. *My God, my God,* she cried, *I am a wretched failure, unworthy to even call on You, but, dear Lord, if I ever needed help, it's now. If I ever needed forgiveness, it's now. O God, if You can hear the earnest cry of a poor, needy soul, help me find You somehow soon—real soon. And help poor dear Frederick. Somewhere in the world there must be a man of God who can help him before he dies. I'm so terribly unhappy with myself and ashamed for being so discouraged.*

"Mama," Emilee pulled on her mother's arm, "what's the matter? Why are you crying like that?"

"My child," Lucy got up from her knees and wiped her face, "I must write a letter to your sick Uncle Frederick. And I don't know what to tell him. I've got to go to the store and get some paper and a stamp if I don't eat all week."

"Are you going now?"

"After supper, dear."

"Can I go along?"

"Yes, dear, you can go with me."

CHAPTER 57

LUCY HAD made her important but meager purchase and she and Emilee Sue were on their slow walk home. The misery of her troubled heart was noticeably engraved on her face.

Write she must. But what could she tell Vada and Frederick but the grievous, heartbreaking truth, that she hadn't contacted a minister she could ask to call on them. Why? There must be an answer. Had she forgotten how to pray? Had God closed both ears to her years of calling? Wasn't it His will that Frederick have the spiritual help he so desperately needed? Or had she drifted, carelessly, from His presence, misplacing the blame for her regrettable plight? Frightening impulses and tormenting voices of self-condemnation left her bodily fatigued and emotionally melancholy.

Lucy stopped short. She heard singing. It was coming from the two-story brick building across the street. Wasn't that Huck's Barber Shop? Then she saw the printed sign, *Revival Meetings—Come Tonight.* It stood out in bold letters above the double door.

"What is it, Mama?" asked Emilee pulling on her mother's hand.

"Let's cross over and find out."

Lucy looked in. Several dozen people were seated on straight-backed chairs and four young men standing in front of a homemade pulpit were singing, their faces radiant and expressive.

To wealth and fame I would not climb,
But I would know God's peace sublime.

Lucy stood motionless; her feet seemed glued to the sidewalk.

And everywhere and all the time
I want my life to tell for Jesus.

She felt goose pimples come out on both arms. The singers closed their books and sat down, and a large, tall, gray-haired man stood up.

"Now, let's all turn to page 79 and sing together this blessed song I love so much, 'I Need Jesus.'" He looked up from his blue songbook. His eyes met Lucy's in the open doorway.

She caught her breath and held it. Could it be? Was he Brother Bustleton? No, it couldn't be. Brother Bustleton wasn't that tall. Or had she forgotten?

"Come on in, lady, and take a seat." The man smiled, held out one hand, and beckoned, then pointed to several empty chairs to his left.

Lucy could feel color creeping into her cheeks. Was he speaking to her? To her? She hesitated. Then he asked one of the singers to go to the door to help them find chairs. Before she could collect her thoughts, Lucy was being ushered to a seat close to the side door. She took the songbook the young man offered her and sat down; Emilee Sue, wide-eyed and wondering, curled up on the chair beside her.

"Mama," she whispered, "over there. Look."

Lucy glanced across the aisle. There sat Mrs. Watson trying to find page 79.

472

"Now, let's sing it, folks," said the tall man, and the building fairly vibrated as the people sang.

I need Jesus, my need I now confess.
No friend like Him in times of deep distress.
I need Jesus, the need I gladly own.
Thou some may bear their load alone,
Yet I need Jesus.

Lucy had never heard the song; so she didn't even try to help sing. Instead, she kept her eyes riveted on the man's face. Could he possibly be Brother Bustleton's brother? There was something so strikingly similar, especially when he smiled; and he had that same glow of joy and confidence on his face and he sang with the same sincerity. Lucy sat spellbound.

He read the next stanza in a deep, rich voice. Lucy listened in rapt amazement.

I need Jesus, I need a friend like Him;
A friend to guide when paths of life are dim.
I need Jesus when foes my soul assail.
Alone I know I can but fail,
So I need Jesus.

"Now, let's all sing it," he said. Lucy's heart beat faster and faster. The man looked directly at her. Amazement turned to bewilderment, then awe. "How many of you here tonight have been trying to make it alone?" he asked. "I wonder. I tried it for several years and I was a first-class failure. Oh, how I needed Him to put me back on the right path! I needed this Friend Jesus to guide me and I still need Him, every minute of every hour of every day. Jesus is the answer to my every need and yours. Now the last verse. If you believe it, sing it with all your heart."

I need Jesus. I need Him to the end.

No one like Him. He is the sinner's Friend.
I need Jesus, no other friend will do;
So constant, kind, so strong and true,
Yes, I need Jesus.

He closed his book and sang alone, holding one hand high, his face beaming. "I *have* Jesus. I *have* Him to the end."

"Friends," he said, "some take Jesus for a while, then think they can make it alone. But they cannot. I need Him to the end. So do you. Let us pray."

Lucy sat motionless. She hadn't heard such a prayer since she sat in the Black Bend Schoolhouse. Was this really the unforgettable Brother Bustleton and she hadn't remembered exactly what he looked like? After all, over the years he may have changed as much as she had. His face, honest and radiant, sent a strange warmth over her starved and shriveled heart.

"And now, Father," he concluded, "speak to every soul in this building tonight and use me, dear Lord, to make Your eternal Word speak."

The man took his Bible and read in a voice so much like Brother Bustleton's that Lucy was almost convinced it must be he. She scarcely moved a muscle. " 'Behold, the Lord's hand is not shortened, that it cannot save; neither his ear heavy, that it cannot hear.' Friends, in my experience conducting evangelistic meetings throughout the country I always meet some who say, 'Yes, I believe God can and does save others but not me. No, I've gone too far, or I've tried it several times and couldn't hold out, or I've waited so long I'm afraid I've sinned away my day of grace. No, salvation's not for me.'

"Well, let me tell you, if any such fears or excuses have

been keeping any of you here tonight from enjoying peace, God reaches out His hand of love to you, for the Bible says the Son of God came to seek and to save *all* who are lost. His arm reaches around the entire world. His hand reaches down to the deepest pit to lift men and women out of the mire of failure, sin, and despair.

"To any who are sad, or lonely; to any discouraged, despondent, or bewildered, fearing they've lost every hope of ever finding peace and joy, I have good news for you. Jesus came to give life everlasting and full of glory and a peace that passeth all understanding. His love goes out with His nail-pierced hands to reach those who have had one bitter disappointment after the other. And believe me, dear people, I've had some bitter disappointments in my life; so I speak out of personal experience. Do you realize God is seeking you [he pointed to his right, to his left] and you and you? [Lucy winced.] Don't try to dodge Him or run away and hide.

"If any of you have ever been lost in a cave or in a dense woods, you were mighty glad to learn someone was out trying to find you. God sent His Son, Jesus Christ, to earth to live as a man, that He might understand every man and each of his temptations and needs and bring him to God. And when God finds a man or a woman, a boy or a girl, He never says, I remember all the wicked things you've done. I remember all your failures and every mean or selfish thought you ever had in your head. No. He says the moment you receive My Son, Jesus Christ, as your own personal Saviour, believing He died on the cross for your sins and rose again, I'll forgive, blot out, and forget your sins. I'll cast them into the bottom of the sea and never bring them up again. God sent Christ to seek, to save, and to reconcile lost, sinful man to Himself. This glorious ministry of reconciliation has been given to me as a servant of God and I'm here to invite you to accept Christ's gift of everlasting life.

"This does not mean you'll have an easy life or a bed of roses. Never. The Bible says all that live godly in Christ Jesus shall suffer persecution. And again I read here in Hebrews 5:8, 'Though he were a Son, yet learned he obedience by the things which he suffered.' If Christ suffered, why should we expect to live in ease? But listen to this, 'Come unto me, all ye that labour and are heavy laden, and I will give you rest.' Rest from carrying that burdened heart alone. The Christian in spite of suffering can have a peace that passeth all understanding. A peace the world cannot give and cannot take away. [Lucy drew a long, deep breath.]

"I hope this week some of you will step out and take God at His word and receive this abundant life. This Holy Book I hold in my hand is the eternal Word of God and God cannot lie. You can stake your life on what it says. Every promise in this book He will keep, and every promise is for every living person. There's no questioning, no guessing, no wishful thinking, no speculating about the Bible. This Word is God's and His Son says, 'I am the way, the truth, and the life: no man cometh unto the Father, but by me.' "

The magnetic reality of everything the minister was saying held Lucy's undivided attention. For twenty more minutes he preached, frequently reading from the Bible. To Lucy it was like watching a basket of long-wilted flowers being revived one by one. Shyly, secretly, she drank in the sweet fragrance of each flower.

"And now," said the minister, "although I'm reluctant to, I must bring this service to a close." He put his closed Bible on the homemade stand and stepped close to his audience. "Everyone bow your heads, please. Now, let me ask, Is there anyone here who wants to be remembered in prayer? Yes, I see your hand and yours and yours. God bless you."

Very slowly Lucy raised a trembling hand.

"God bless you. Another hand was raised. And now who wants to go a step farther and stand or come forward and take my hand and by so doing testify to God and all these people you're ready to accept Christ as your Saviour, turn your back on the world, and let Him be your Guide, your Friend, your Master from now on? Who'll do it right now?"

Two teenage girls, a man, and two women stood.

"God be praised," said the minister. "One soul is worth more to God than all the world; so there's great rejoicing in heaven tonight. Those of you who responded, please come forward after the benediction and the pastor and these four young men who have dedicated themselves to God will talk to you and pray with you while I shake hands with the rest of you. Then I too want to speak to each of you who stood. Let us pray."

Lucy waited until most of the people had gone. She tried her utmost to steady her trembling hands.

"Your name, please?" asked the minister.

"Linsdale."

"And this is your little girl?"

"Yes. My youngest, Emilee Sue."

"Let me shake hands with you too, little sister. I hope you come back."

He turned to Lucy. "Did you enjoy the service, Mrs.

Linsdale?"

"Yes. Very much."

"Are you a Christian?"

"Well," began Lucy with nervous hesitancy, "I made a decision years ago in a schoolhouse in another state. I was baptized," she looked down at nothing in particular, "and for a time I was sure I had the real—" She fumbled with the small package in her hand.

"It didn't last?" he suggested.

She shook her head. She bit her lip. "To make a long story short," she began again, "I lost my Bible. I got careless and discouraged. Hard times came, and well—" She fought tears.

"I know what you mean, Mrs. Linsdale."

"You do?" she looked up in surprise.

"Of course I do." His voice was kind and sympathetic. "You raised your hand indicating you want to be remembered in prayer?"

"Yes," came Lucy's feeble answer.

"I take it then you want to get back into close fellowship with God."

"Yes," she said. "Yes, I do, if at all possible."

"Well, it's possible, Mrs. Linsdale," smiled the minister. "You wouldn't want to tonight?"

Lucy saw Mrs. Watson waiting outside. "I'll try to come back," she said, "but I didn't learn what your name is."

"Molenhaur."

"Molenhaur?" repeated Lucy. "Would you happen to know Brother Bustleton?"

"Bustleton? What's his first name?"

"I don' t know."

"Why do you ask?"

"He was the evangelist when I made my stand. He baptized me. I—I thought perhaps you were brothers when I—I mean your voice and manner made me think of him." Lucy felt her face and neck get warm.

"I have in my possession several fine tracts written by a J. T. Bustleton, but I never met the man. Do you have one of our invitation cards?"

"No, sir."

"Here are several. Give them to your neighbors and friends. And here's a list of my favorite promises." He handed her another card. "And I hope you'll come back."

"I want to," answered Lucy. "I loved the singing and I enjoyed your sermon. Before I leave, I'd like to ask if you ever go into people's homes and pray for the sick."

"Certainly."

"Oh." Lucy's face brightened. "Would you, please? I have a brother-in-law who lives about five miles from here, down past the cement plant, and he's going to die before long, I'm sure. He has TB of the bone. He suffers a great deal."

"I tell you what you do, Mrs. Linsdale. Here, write his name and address on the back of this card and I'll have the pastor take me to see him tomorrow."

"Tomorrow!" exclaimed Lucy. "Oh, you can't imagine how thankful I'll be if you'll do that. He'll be so glad to see you. And do you ever baptize anyone who is bedfast? You know, he can't stand or kneel."

"To be sure, Mrs. Linsdale, if the person is sincere and requests it."

"I know he's sincere, Brother—"

"Molenhaur."

"Yes, Brother Molenhaur," she repeated, "he's already

accepted Christ in his heart."

Mrs. Watson walked home with Lucy and Emilee Sue.

"Sounds to me like real salvation preaching," commented Mrs. Watson. "I'm sure going to try to go every night."

"I wish it wasn't quite so far to walk," began Lucy. "My leg will probably be worse tomorrow, but I am so glad I stopped in. He's going to go see Clem's brother, Frederick, tomorrow."

"Is he worse?"

"Yes. He's very bad. I walked all the way to the post office to buy a stamped envelope. Oh, how I do hate to beg, but I did it. I asked the lady clerk if she could spare me a piece of paper."

"You could have asked me, Lucy."

"Yes? Well, bless her heart. She looked at me astonished and gave me two sheets. I was about to go home and write to Frederick and his wife the saddest and hardest letter of my life. Then, thank God, I heard singing when we crossed Benton Street."

"And we went over to see who it was," put in Emilee Sue. "Me and Mama did."

"I went past the place yesterday on my way to the grocery store," said Mrs. Watson, "and a man handed me a card. That's how I knew about it."

"Why didn't you tell me you were going?"

"Why?" asked Mrs. Watson. "Well, I didn't want to be turned down again. You told me you had lost interest in going to church."

Lucy's smitten heart burned as they walked on in silence.

CHAPTER 58

S HE WAS reading through the list of precious promises for the third time when Mrs. Watson knocked.

"Do you want to go with me tonight, Lucy?" she asked, opening the door.

"I want to very much," answered Lucy. "Come on in and take a chair. As you can see, I'm nursing my bad leg." She had it propped up on a wooden box.

"It does look bad, Lucy. You should have one of those elastic bandages."

"I know it would help. More than one doctor has told me to get one. But they cost—"

"Money. Yes, I know," nodded Mrs. Watson sympathetically. "If we only had a little more of the filthy stuff," she laughed, "we could both hire a taxi to take us to and from church."

"When my boys saw me binding up my leg this morning, they said what's the difference walking from door to door selling paper flowers or walking way up there to Huck's Barber Shop to a meeting? Well, I had no answer."

"They think you shouldn't go then?"

"They don't object to my going to church, but they don't like to see my leg get worse. They worry about it more than I do."

"I guess we ought to get a tandem bicycle," chuckled

Mrs. Watson, patting Emilee Sue on the head. "One with a basket on the front or a seat on the back for this little miss. Well," she added, going to the door, "I must run along and start supper. Shall I stop by for you or not?"

"Well," answered Lucy, frowning and looking at her leg, "whistle or call as you get close, and if I feel I can and ought to, I'll go along. I'd like so much to go. That preacher surely impressed me as being a real man of God. And I'm anxious to hear what he has to say about Frederick."

Lucy got ready. She waited. But Mrs. Watson neither called nor whistled. "Emilee Sue," she said, glancing at the clock on the shelf, "stand at the door and watch for Mrs. Watson. I wonder what's keeping her. We're going to be late. Neither of us can walk as fast as she can. We're going to miss that beautiful singing I fear."

Five minutes passed and Mrs. Watson did not come by.

"Mama," whispered Emilee, "a car stopped. Here comes a man."

"Are you Mrs. Linsdale?"

"Yes."

"I'm from the church where Brother Molenhaur is conducting revival meetings. My name is Schmidt. I'm one of the four men who sing every evening."

"I remember your face," said Lucy. "I was there last evening."

"That's what Mrs. Watson said. She's your neighbor, I believe?"

"Yes."

"Well, she came early and told Brother Molenhaur you wanted to come but it was hard for you to walk that far. He told me to come for you."

"Oh, my!" Lucy could not hide her surprise.

"We'd better go if you're ready, Mrs. Linsdale."

"This is too much," said Lucy, getting in the backseat.

"Not at all," answered the young man. "There're many ways to help in the work of the Lord. Someone will take you home after the service."

"I have no words to thank you enough, Mr. Schmidt. You'll never know what this means to me."

"Someone will be after you every evening unless you send us word not to come."

"This is too good to be true." Lucy smiled and brushed away an unbidden tear.

She sat spellbound night after night. Only in her dreams had she heard music as beautiful and as stirring as the selections sung by the four young men.

Could it be that at last God was to be found? That peace could be hers after all her shattered dreams and years of disappointments and heartaches? Intently Lucy listened as Brother Molenhaur explained in dramatic simplicity the profound truths of the Word. With his open Bible he preached, often reading from its thumb-worn pages. Each sermon seemed to be directed to her. In the course of a week he had answered many questions that Lucy had asked herself scores of times and had found no answers for. Slowly the tangled strands started to unravel. Secretly she reached out to take God at His word, without doubtings. She was surprised at her new interest in the Scriptures. Brother Molenhaur made everything so plain. Yet his simple explanations were spoken with dignity and strong conviction, in sincerity and deep emotion that Lucy could not question. He proved everything he said by the Word of God. He read from his Bible with a knowing, personal faith and with genuine, earnest reverence.

"Now this is the last night I'll be with you in this revival effort." Brother Molenhaur placed his Bible on the stand and again stepped closer to the audience. The place was packed. "We've seen souls step out for God every evening. Over thirty decisions have been made. Most of them for the first time. This has been a rich and a blessed experience in my ministry. It doesn't take a big fine church to have a revival. Souls have knelt on this bare floor in this onetime barber shop and found personal, satisfying peace, that priceless gift of God many a millionaire would be glad to buy but cannot. Some of you here tonight have been putting it off night after night. You're under conviction. I can see it on your faces. Why do you wait? There is no case too hard for God. He has peace for the troubled heart, pardon for the penitent soul, and eternal life for the lost. If you've tried and failed, try once more. Would you believe that one of these fine young men in this quartet told me he tried seven times before he had the victory? But God didn't say to him, 'Go away. I'm sure you don't mean it; you've tried it too often and I can't believe you're sincere this time.' Never. So come tonight while we sing. Who's ready?" He held up both arms.

Lucy bent forward in her seat. She trembled from head to foot. She held to the chair in front of her. A boy three rows ahead got to his feet.

"God bless you, son."

Then Mrs. Watson stood.

"God bless you, lady. Is there someone else before we close?"

Lucy stood.

"God bless you, my friend. We've all been praying for you."

She sat down. She drew a long, deep breath of relief. A strange sweet restfulness swept over her entire body.

"After the benediction I want to talk to the three who made their decision. Will you please come forward and take these seats? Thank you. Now let us pray."

The evangelist talked to the young man, then to Mrs. Watson. "And the pastor here will help you further."

"And now, Mrs. Linsdale," he said, turning to Lucy and shaking her hand, "would you like to tell me just why you stood tonight?"

"Yes, sir," answered Lucy. "I stood because I need God and I couldn't put it off any longer. I've been wanting to know the way and the truth for years and years. I've been frustrated, bewildered, and discouraged so many times I actually feared my case was hopeless until I heard your sermons."

"And you don't feel like that anymore?"

"I sincerely hope I never will again. It's a terrible situation to be in."

"Thank God you won't need to, Mrs. Linsdale. The Word enlightens. It brings joy to the sad of heart. It changes doubts to hope, discouragements to faith. Remember, His hand is not shortened that it cannot save you, Mrs. Linsdale, neither is His ear heavy that it cannot hear you. Are you ready to believe God, take Him at His word, and live for Him and Him only as long as you live?"

Tears streamed down Lucy's cheeks. "Yes," she said, "I am."

"And you're ready to hand over to God your last key?"

"Yes, sir, if you tell me what that means."

"It means simply this, that you are ready to say an unqualified yes to all the will of God. It means you'll let

485

Him lead you and you'll follow because you love Him. It means your entire life is now His, not your own. He holds the keys in His hands. He decides everything for you and you will not resist or complain. He may take you through more trials and sufferings, Mrs. Linsdale, but you'll bear it all patiently, remembering it is all a part of His plan for your life. He holds all the keys. Not one thing do you hold in reserve. Your life, your body, your children, your possessions are all His. You will not doubt or fear because you trust Him. You will believe in Him, act as if you believe, tonight, tomorrow, and every day on into the future, no matter what comes, remembering God's almighty hand is over you in love. He holds the keys. You see?"

Lucy's famished soul drank in every word.

"Are you ready to get down on your knees and ask forgiveness and promise you'll live for Him the rest of your life, Mrs. Linsdale?"

Without hesitancy Lucy answered, "Yes." She got on her knees and in a clear voice, free from all pretense, poured her heart out to God. Then Brother Molenhaur prayed for her and Mrs. Watson and the young man. When they all stood once more, Lucy's eyes were shimmering in tears but her face was radiant.

"And now," concluded Brother Molenhaur, tucking his worn Bible under his arm, "is there anything you'd like to ask me?"

"I would like to ask you a question, Brother Molenhaur," answered Lucy rather timidly.

"Be free to ask."

"Would you marry a woman to a man who had another living wife?" asked Lucy, looking up at him.

"I could not do it, sister," he answered. "Here, let me show you." Brother Molenhaur thumbed through his Bible. "In Luke 16:18 we read, 'Whosoever putteth away his wife, and marrieth another, committeth adultery: and whosoever marrrieth her that is put away from her husband committeth adultery.' And Paul wrote in Romans Chapter 7, verse 2." (Brother Molenhaur paused until he found the passage), " 'For the woman which hath an husband is bound by the law to her husband so long as he liveth; but if the husband be dead, she is loosed from the law of her husband.' " Brother Molenhaur looked kindly at Lucy. "Some ministers today remarry those who are divorced. But Lucy, the Bible is clear. Remarriage while one's former partner is still living is sin."

Lucy breathed a big sigh. It sounded like a sigh of relief rather than despair.

"I'm so glad someone finally showed me from the Bible," she answered, blushing slightly. "I always thought something wasn't right about remarriage, but I wanted to know for sure. I want to ask the Lord to forgive me for having lived in adultery."

"God bless each one of you," said Brother Molenhaur, "and be sure to read your Bible every day. It's of greatest importance."

"I have no Bible," said Lucy.

"No Bible? Then the pastor will see that you get one. You'll do that, won't you, Brother Walker?"

"Yes, sir." He stepped behind the partition and returned with a Bible. "Here you are, Mrs. Linsdale."

"Not to keep?"

"Of course. It's yours to keep."

"Really? I can't believe it," exclaimed Lucy in tears.

"I've been wanting a Bible for years. Oh, this has been the happiest week of my life," she cried. "So many prayers have been answered for me it nearly takes my breath away. And I'm so glad you went to see my brother-in-law. I'll thank you for that as long as I live."

"It was our pleasure, Mrs. Linsdale. We believe he's ready to meet God in peace. And now good-bye, son; good-bye, Mrs. Watson; good-bye, Mrs. Linsdale. When I come back to Mikulla, I expect to find you victorious, faithful Christians and I'm sure Brother Walker would be glad to have you become members of the church too."

Lucy smiled. "By God's help," she said, "I mean to be just that. I want to serve God with my whole heart as long as I live. I don't want to be a lukewarm Christian. Never. I know now He kept His hand over me all these years even when I was careless and strayed away. Brother Molenhaur, you helped me find Him again, the way I always wanted to."

An expression, tender, peaceful, joyous, and satisfying, which the Master Himself had painted on the face of His servant, was beautifully reflected on Lucy's face.

The End

POSTSCRIPT

Lucy was one in the group of twenty-seven that was received into church fellowship following Brother Molenhaur's meetings. She was very faithful in church attendance and participation.

One evening after a midweek prayer service she asked if she could be anointed with oil. There were five open sores on her one leg and nothing she had tried had helped and she had been to a number of doctors. Her request was granted. The pastor invited only those who truly believed in the New Testament teaching of anointing and knew they were spiritually ready to help pray for Lucy to remain. A handful remained.

Lucy's own prayer was so simply worded it was childlike. Yet everyone in the circle experienced the very presence and power of God while she prayed. There was no crying, no begging, no insistence, no complaining, just a simple, "I know You can; I believe You want to. I know You will and I'll thank You as long as I live."

Lucy's leg healed overnight and remained healed all her life.

From that eventful evening Lucy was considered the mother of the church. Whenever anyone was sick, or discouraged, or in trouble of any kind, Lucy was called to help pray. It was because of her healing incident and her constant, positive witness that I approached her several years later about writing her life story.

In the summer of 1960 Lucy went to be with the Lord after being hospitalized eleven days. I was at her bedside only hours before she passed away. She told me she was at peace with God and ready to go.

"Lucy," I said, "you've lived to realize that one wish you made. I received word that a woman attending a mountain mission church in the East gave her heart to God after she read your story. She said, 'If Lucy could step out and trust the Lord Jesus after all she went through, I can too.' Lucy," I said, "now you know you didn't live your life in vain."

Her smile lit up her entire face and soon she fell into a peaceful sleep.

✳ ✳ ✳ ✳ ✳ ✳ ✳

Christian Light Publications, Inc., is a nonprofit, conservative Mennonite publishing company providing Christ-centered, Biblical literature including books, Gospel tracts, Sunday school materials, summer Bible school materials, and a full curriculum for Christian day schools and homeschools.

For more information about the ministry of CLP or its publications, or for spiritual help, please contact us at:

Christian Light Publications, Inc.
P. O. Box 1212
Harrisonburg, VA 22803-1212

Telephone—540-434-0768
Fax—540-433-8896
E-mail—info@clp.org